Prepared to Answer

A Step-by-Step Guide to Bring the Power of Christian Evidences to Your Life

Rob van de Weghe

CLASSIC DAY
PUBLISHING

Seattle, Washington
Portland, Oregon
Denver, Colorado
Vancouver, B.C.
Scottsdale, Arizona
Minneapolis, Minnesota

Thank You, Lord, for showing me the truth and giving me the privilege to share this with others.

I hope and pray that this book will be beneficial for each reader and that it will help him or her to better understand, appreciate, and accept the unshakable foundations for our faith in God the Father, our reverence for His revelation through the Bible, and our salvation through Jesus Christ.

For skeptics: please let this information equip you better to decide your beliefs and remove any intellectual roadblocks between you and your Creator.

For believers: please let this information help you grow mature in your faith and equip you with better tools to share it with others.

Windmill Ministries

*"As the windmill can do nothing without the wind,
so men can do nothing without God."*

The objectives of Windmill Ministries are threefold:

1) To equip Christians with factual evidence to strengthen their faith and enable them to defend their beliefs as well as share them with others.
2) To help non-believers to overcome intellectual stumbling blocks that keep them from turning to God and accepting Jesus Christ as their Savior.
3) To show the world that Christianity is not only for "the gullible" and children, but that it is based on solid historical and factual evidence.

Many people reject Christianity not for intellectual reasons, but for moral considerations. That is, their WILL does not want to submit to God; therefore their MIND explains and defends this rejection. For this reason we want to equip Christians and non-Christians with information that empowers them to identify and reject these intellectual objections by defending and explaining the Christian faith with objective and factual evidence.

Windmill Ministries
www.WindmillMinistries.org
e-mail: info@windmillministries.org

In memory of Cor and An van de Weghe

"I believe in God the Father Almighty, and in Jesus Christ his only Son, our Lord. And in the Holy Spirit, the holy church, the resurrection of the flesh."
STATEMENT OF FAITH FROM THE EARLY CHRISTIAN CHURCH, END OF THE FIRST CENTURY.

Table of Contents

Preface

Thank you for your desire to better understand the foundations on which the Christian faith rests. In this book we will discuss extensive evidence from a wide range of scientific and historical sources and disciplines. Through these, God has provided help for us to better comprehend and appreciate the basis of Christian belief.

Before I became a Christian myself, I was at best indifferent to religion. Although raised in a Roman Catholic family, later in school and college I was taught "the fact" of evolution. The more educated I became, the more I believed God and Jesus Christ were mere myths, nothing more than invented stories. Modern science – evolution – explained our existence, so, any need for God? If the Bible began with a fairy-tale creation and its "Garden of Eden," the rest of the book could hardly be any different. After all, it told of a world-wide flood and people more than 900 years old, of one man parting an entire sea with only a word and prophets performing astounding miracles, of a sav-ior born of a virgin and dying on a cross only to return from the dead.

No, I was "smarter" than that and church was for the gullible, you know, uneducated people. My ambition was to start a successful business and to make money, lots of money. I was no atheist, because in the back of my mind I still believed in God. Religion itself became unimportant, and I was indifferent.

In 1999 – when I was 40 years old – I was ready to retire. Life had been good to me. Riding the crest of peak success, the company I had joined 15 years earlier had grown from a local Dutch organization with 300 employees to a worldwide consulting business, in 30 countries with 20,000 employees. This growth spawned numerous opportunities. One of these brought my family to settle in the United States in the mid 1990s.

Around the time of my retirement, my wife started to attend a church close by. As a good husband, I had to go – at least occasionally – with her on Sunday. To my surprise, people there were quite nice, and they engaged in thought-pro-voking discussions. Before long, I began to become interested. I wondered, What if this is true? It seemed most unlikely, as I recalled the stories from my childhood, but still, suppose it was. I had to know for sure, so I decided to launch my own personal investigation into the facts behind the Christian claims.

From the start I researched whatever I could find; some tried to prove, others tried to disprove Christianity. I thought I would need to read only a few books, but my project quickly turned into a full-time study, stretching over six months and taking me through hundreds of books and articles. As I struggled with the evidence, a mountain of facts emerged, coming from many disciplines, each objectively pointing to the truth of Christianity. I was taken aback by both the quantity and quality of this evidence. Especially amazing to me was how modern day science reveals more and more about God. In time, my position became clear; I had no choice but to face the facts, and once cornered by the evidence, I obeyed the gospel of Jesus Christ.

I noticed during my research that church-going Christians seemed to have little knowledge of the proofs for their belief. I had asked myself questions such as, Why should I believe in God? Was there really a flood? How do we know Moses wrote Genesis? What does archaeology say about the Bible? Were the gospels written by Jesus' disciples or by others? Are the accounts of the miracles of Jesus exaggerated, or could such really happen? How can we know for certain that the resurrection is a historical event? I found very good answers to these questions, but to my surprise I had to find these answers in books. Most people could not give me any answers. Some claimed their personal experience with God needed no answers. Others, believers all their lives, simply had not thought about it. Still others never had the time to look for answers, and most of them were not even sure what to believe. Before long, men and women were telling me that they wanted to know these answers too, and they asked to share with them my findings.

Much that was published about these evidences seemed to focus on single issues such as the uniqueness of the earth, or archaeological evidences for the Bible, or the prophecies that were fulfilled by Jesus. However, I did not find in one book, a comprehensive source, which would give an overview of all the evidences.

This triggered me to share a summary of my findings, all of them. Over the last several years I've shared this information in seminars and churches, in schools and home groups. Now this material is ready for a book.

The information here comes from hundreds of sources. No, I make no claim to be an expert on the topics, but I have done lots and lots of legwork, sifting through huge amounts of available material about the multi-faceted evidence for our faith. And I have tried to structure this information logically so that it will be more accessible for those interested. The vast amount of information compelled me to trade in-depth detail for comprehensive overview, so I have been able to spend hardly more than a few pages of text on various topics. However I have supplied numerous sources for additional information for the interested and energetic reader.

This book is more than just a book for me. It is the path of my personal search for the truth. I am compelled to share this information, with the hope and prayer that it will help anyone willing to read this material to make a more informed and more committed decision about his or her personal commitment to God and Jesus Christ.

Structure of this Book

"Therefore everyone who hears these words of mine and puts them into practice is like a wise man who built his house on the rock. The rain came down, the streams rose, and the winds blew and beat against that house; yet it did not fall, because it had its foundation on the rock. But everyone who hears these words of mine and does not put them into practice is like a foolish man who built his house on sand. The rain came down, the streams rose, and the winds blew and beat against that house, and it fell with a great crash."

JESUS, IN THE SERMON ON THE MOUNT, MATTHEW 7:24-27

QUESTIONS, SECTIONS, AND EXHIBITS

This book of evidence is intended to be a comprehensive study of science and history. Its logic moves the reader toward the undeniable and verifiable conclusion that Christianity is based on facts. We follow five main questions. Answers to the first three eliminate the various worldviews, logically concluding that Christianity is the only worldview consistent with and supported by modern day science as well as history with its manuscript studies, archaeological digs, and scholarly analysis. Answers to the remaining questions provide valuable additional information, which solidifies the unique truth of the Christian worldview.

Each question is addressed in one complete section of this book. The first chapter of each section introduces the question, provides additional background, and explains the logical analysis that follows. Later chapters present observations, facts, and evidences – I call them *"exhibits"* – and these are examined, analyzed, and explained.

Exhibits are numbered in each section and identified by the symbol ☼. At the end of each section, the exhibits are summarized and a conclusion is presented.

THE FIVE QUESTIONS

The following questions form the foundation of this book:

Section I: Does God Exist? Is there conclusive evidence for the existence of a Creator? Do modern day scientific observations prove – or disprove – the presence of such a Creator? If proof proves positive, we can eliminate all worldviews that reject a Creator, such as atheism (which insists there is no God), and pantheism (the belief that the universe has always existed and that the universe itself is God).

Section II: Is the Bible True? Should a Creator God exist, it would only be logical that He would communicate with His creation. The Christian Bible claims to be that communication, but is this claim valid? We will examine the Bible to see if it is historically accurate, trustworthy, and reliable. If we can prove that to be true, all other worldviews are eliminated that do not accept the Bible and/or base their claims on other revelation, such as Islam (that claims that the Bible was corrupted by the Jews and Christians and argues that a "higher quality" revelation has been preserved by the prophet Mohammed in the Qur'an). And this conclusion will strike down views such as polytheism (there are multiple gods) and deism (God exists and created the universe, but is no longer interested/involved in his creation).

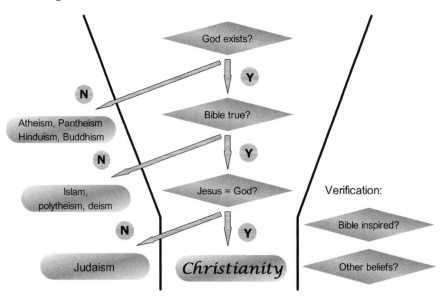

The Structure and Relationship of the Five Questions

Section III: Is Jesus God's Son? If God exists and the Bible is historically accurate and reliable, the great question to answer is, if Jesus is indeed God's unique Son, or, is Jesus God in a human form? If not, Judaism is the complete and accurate religion. If Jesus is indeed divine, then Christianity is true.

A positive answer to these three questions leads logically to the conclusion that Christianity is true. To verify the consistency and correctness of our reasoning, two more questions are discussed.

Section IV: Is the Bible Inspired by God? Does evidence prove the Bible is not only textually and historically reliable, but actually the divinely inspired Word of God? Can we find in the texts of the Bible evidences that strengthen the claim that these sacred writings were inspired by God and not written by ordinary men?

Section V: What do others believe? If Christianity is true, other worldviews must be false. Examining other prevalent worldviews on the same basis of objective evidences as we test Christianity, we can verify that indeed only Christianity is based on truth as a genuine divine revelation.

GUIDE ON HOW TO USE THIS BOOK

The book follows a logical line of reasoning and discovery. Each chapter builds on information proved in the previous chapters. Therefore, I advise you to read this material from cover to cover. If you would like to skip the detailed discussion on some of the questions and exhibits, you can jump to the summaries presented at the end of each of the five sections.

This information will also be a helpful reference for studies of particular subjects. Both the table of contents as well as the index will be useful tools for such an approach.

CHAPTER 1

Christian Apologetics and Truth

"Always be prepared to give an answer to everyone who asks you to give the reason for the hope that you have."
1 PETER 3:15

CHRISTIANITY IS A FACT-BASED RELIGION

Christianity is grounded in facts, both historical and scientific. Its claims about God, God's creation, God's plan of redemption, the Bible, the ministry, miracles, and above all – the resurrection of Jesus can be objectively verified by studying astronomy, physics, molecular biology and genetics, archaeology, history, the Bible, and ancient non-Biblical documents. These claims are not merely imposed as "truth" by one person through some revelation. Therefore, Christianity (and Judaism) stands on a foundation completely different from other religions. In comparison, Islam, Buddhism, Hinduism, and all the other religions of the world largely rely upon a revelation to one "prophet." This prophet subsequently writes a book of his revelations, which becomes the "bible" on which the faith of his followers rests.

Jesus, however, never wrote a book, perhaps not even a letter. How did Jesus actually conduct his "three-year campaign," and how would it compare to the ways people nowadays try to get their message across? *When we consider the basic facts about His life, the vast impact He has had is nothing short of incredible.*

Jesus taught his apostles, who after His resurrection took the gospel message throughout the world. That message is still spread by Christians today. Unlike the approach of most other religions, non-believers are invited to hear the Word, assess the message themselves, and by exercising their free will, choose to become (and remain) a believer. Unlike Islam, Christianity does not try to insulate its believers against the influence of other religions; rather it trains its followers to distinguish between true and false teachings. To do this the Christian believer must research and challenge, then verify and assess these first principles, the basic truths of the faith. One needs to make up one's own mind about this. Do not accept something as true just because someone tells you so. Accept only those truths that YOU, after *careful* consideration, believe to be TRUTH. Only then you can know these truths and honestly accept them as such, grow stronger in your faith, and *"Stand firm then, with the belt of truth buckled around your waist"* (Ephesians 6:14).

The study of the evidences for the Christian faith is called apologetics. This word comes from the Greek απολογια ("apologia," which means a verbal defense, answer, or reply). Therefore, Christian apologetics deals with all critics who oppose or question the revelation of God in Christ and the Bible. It includes complex subjects such as Biblical manuscript transmission, philosophy, biology, mathematics, evolution, and logic, but it can also consist of simple answers to questions about Jesus or a Bible passage.

It is important to approach these questions and issues with an open mind. Try to be objective and judge the information in such a manner. Seek to avoid the bias of preconceived ideas. Presume innocence until guilt is proved. Position yourself to be the jury in a trial and insist upon objective evidence. Remember that the faith of Christianity is not afraid of open, honest inquiry; no truth fears investigation.

THE GREAT MEN OF HISTORY

Ask anybody: "Who are the great men in human history?" Likely you will hear names such as Alexander the Great, Julius Caesar, Napoleon, George Washington, Abraham Lincoln, Theodore Roosevelt, John F. Kennedy, or perhaps even Ronald Reagan. What do these men have in common? What made them great? They were successful because they were powerful, and with this power they changed the course of history by their heroic actions, or by ruling countries or even whole continents.

How different these "great men" are when compared to the person of Jesus of Nazareth!

Jesus had little of what made these great men of history great: certainly no political clout, no military machine, no war chest. Most of us know the basic facts about Jesus' life and ministry, but still, read the following summary of the powerful impact of His message, His death and His resurrection:

"Jesus was born in an obscure village, the child of a peasant woman. He grew up in another village where He worked in a carpenter shop until He was thirty. For three years He was a traveling preacher. He never wrote a book. He never held an office. He fathered no family; he owned no home. He didn't go to college. He never visited a big city. He never traveled more than two hundred miles from the place where He was born. He did none of the things that usually accompany greatness. He had no credentials but himself. He was only thirty-three when the tide of public opinion turned against Him. His friends ran away. One of them denied Him. He was

*turned over to His enemies and went through the mockery of a trial. He
was nailed to a cross between two thieves. While He was dying, His executioners gambled for His garments, the only property. He had on earth.
When He was dead, He was laid in a borrowed grave through the pity of
a friend. Twenty centuries have come and gone, and today He is the central figure of the human race. All the armies that ever marched, all the
navies that ever sailed, all the parliaments that ever sat, all the kings that
ever reigned, put together, have not affected the life of man on this earth,
as much as that one solitary life."* [1]

How different is Jesus compared to the great world leaders. Alexander the
Great and Napoleon were fabled warriors – Jesus never held a sword or led an
army. George Washington liberated his people from foreign occupation – Jesus
never raised even His voice against the Roman occupiers of His country.
Abraham Lincoln, Theodore Roosevelt, John F. Kennedy, and Ronald Reagan
were all elected to head powerful governments – Jesus never ran for office. He
never marshaled the power of government to enforce social changes. Most
renowned leaders have been wealthy – Jesus owned little and lived with the
poor. And lastly, all great world leaders were famous during their lifetime, but
are dead now – Jesus died as a criminal and was executed by crucifixion, but
His death was the birth of Christianity.

Jesus of Nazareth is by far the greatest person in history. He did not pur-
sue the agendas which made others great, still He towers above them all. He
turned the world upside down as no one had done before or has done after
Him. Now one-third of the world population calls themselves His followers,
Christians, and even those who do not follow Him still experience the impact
He had, has had, and will have on the world. This observation alone sets Him
aside from all others.

Truth and Absolute Truth

Christianity is based on facts and evidences, and its claims demand nothing less than *truth*. Throughout the Bible, God's word is claimed to be *true*, as
Jesus himself said in John 14:6: *"I am the way and the truth and the life. No one
comes to the Father except through me."*

Jesus was arrested by the Jews and tried by the Romans. Interrogated by
the governor, *"Jesus answered, 'You are right in saying I am a king. In fact, for
this reason I was born, and for this I came into the world, to testify to the truth.
Everyone on the side of truth listens to me'"* (John 18:37).

Take special note of Pilate's reply, asked whimsically: *"'What is truth?'
Pilate asked"* (John 18:38).

Today truth is a very sensitive subject. Many say truth is whatever you declare it to be, and no absolute truth exists. Any argument for absolute truth is considered a political blunder, a self-incriminating mark of judgmental intolerance.

Absolute truth does exist, logically proved by the statement: "There exists an absolute truth." Suppose we claim this to be false, that is, that there is no such thing as absolute truth. By making that assertion, we claim that the sentence "There exists no absolute truth" is absolutely true. That statement is self-contradictory, so its negation is true: "There exists an absolute truth."

The same concept applies to Christian truths. Objective proof that Christianity is based on valid facts implies other religions and/or beliefs cannot be true at the same time. Modern society calls that intolerant, but it is the logical consequence of absolute truth.

The discussion of truth and absolute truth has filled many books and has fueled long arguments. For our purpose here, it is important to realize that truth and even absolute truth does exist, and it is essential to recognize some characteristics of truth are not always well accepted in our society:

Truth is intolerant: This is a necessary implication. Two plus two adds up to four, and the answer cannot be three or five. Hence the correct answer is only four, and that truth is absolute. It is not open to various "interpretations," nor can it be changed to better fit our "politically correct" culture. This also applies to Christianity. If claims of Christianity are true, then conflicting claims cannot be true. Therefore, it is logically impossible to consider the option that "all religions are the same, and it does not matter which one you believe" as many people think. Each religion makes claims that conflict with those of other religions, and such cannot all be true.

Truth does not have to be liked or to be popular to be true: Many people reject God or Christianity because:
- They do not like a God who allows evil and suffering to exist.
- They do not like God's commands.
- They do not like a God who ordered innocent children killed and commanded whole nations be destroyed.
- They do not like a God who allows only believers in Christ's sacrifice for our sin to go to heaven.
- They think the church is full of hypocrites.
- And so on.

Disliking the truth does not make it less true! I might not like the speed limit on the highway or taxes to be paid, but these are still the rules, and I must obey them. If I decide not to do so, these laws are still valid; if I speed, I can get a ticket, and if I do not pay my taxes, I will suffer the consequences.

Truth does not have to be the majority opinion: Truth does not require a majority consensus. For instance, for a very long time most folks thought the world was flat, but we long since discovered the fallacy of that belief. Fifty years ago the scientific community preached modern man had been around for more that 1 million years. Now the scientific majority opinion has shifted to less than 100,000 years, and many believe mankind has been around even less than 50,000 years.[2] The truth has not changed, only the majority opinion. So we must be careful as we search for truth to be certain our conclusion is backed by solid evidence and genuine facts, and that it is not just what the majority wants it to be.

The famous writer G.K. Chesterton summarizes our tendency to dislike the truth:[3]

"Truth, of course, must of necessity be stranger than fiction, for we have made fiction to suit ourselves."

Ultimately there are only three reasons why people do not accept and follow truth:

Ignorance: They just do not know about the truth because either they never had an opportunity to hear about it (like people who live in remote places where the gospel has not yet been heard) or they were wrongly informed.

Rebellion: They have heard the truth but decided not to accept it. Many people in our society today for self-centered reasons simply like the way they live and do not want to change their behavior.

Apathy: They just do not care for it. It is simply not interesting to them. They are indifferent. In our times, this might be the largest (and fastest growing) group of non-believers as people are more and more occupied with themselves. Day-to-day affairs of the world distract them so thoroughly that even thinking about truth is not relevant. Such concerns do not make it on their radar screen, so to speak.

Agnostic-turned-Christian apologist and historian C.S. Lewis summarized the current tendency towards apathy in the following quote:[4]

"The safest road to Hell is the gradual one – the gentle slope, soft underfoot, without sudden turnings, without milestones, without signposts."

Finding truth requires one to be open-minded, objective, and honest. Only when one is willing to consider all the facts and evidences without a preconceived conclusion can one find truth. This sounds simple and obvious, but in practice it is always much harder to apply.

TWO MAIN ARGUMENTS AGAINST CHRISTIANITY

Non-believers present numerous vigorous objections against Christianity. Of these, two arguments are likely the most popular and seem to be the strongest:

- **The problem of evil:** How can a good, all-powerful God allow for evil to exist? There is no easy answer to this. In a way it is not relevant, as God does not need our agreement or consent for the world He created. Good explanations can be found by understanding that:
  - Evil comes from man, not from God. It is generally the result of wrong choices by man.
  - Evil is not created by God, but it can be considered the absence of good, as dark is the absence of light.
  - Without evil our world would be meaningless and boring. Evil allows us to understand what "good" is and allows us to choose between both.
- **Science has replaced religion:** Science explains much of what once was considered supernatural, and it seems often to conflict the teaching of the Bible. Yes, we have now more knowledge than ever before, but the facts of modern science do not contradict the existence of God or the inspiration of the Bible. Actually it reveals more about the unimaginable design and amazing detail both of the universe and living organisms, which all point to the work of a Creator much superior and more powerful than previously assumed. We will see many examples of this in the next chapters.

LIFE'S BIG QUESTIONS

As far as I can tell, every human being at some point in life struggles with some variation of these four basic questions:

1. Who am I?
2. Where did I come from?
3. Where am I going?
4. To whom am I accountable?

Throughout human history, people have tried to answer these questions. Science and philosophy are silent on these questions. Only religion, along with its associated worldview, is able to show purpose and provide meaningful answers.

Early, more primitive civilizations associated the supernatural with natural phenomena, such as the sun, moon, and stars. World religions[5] today center upon three views of God:

- Eastern religions (Hinduism, Buddhism) believe God is in everything around them – this is *Pantheism* ("pan" means all) – and they seek the answer to these questions in each individual.
- Judaism, Christianity, and Islam recognize the existence of one God – generally called *Monotheism*.
- And *Atheism* believes the world and mankind are the result of combination of random processes, chance, and a lot of time, and therefore rejects the existence of a divine power/Creator altogether.

This leads to the following (simplified) overview of the possible answers to "life's big questions":

	Pantheism	Monotheism	Atheism
Who am I?	*Part of God*	*God's creation*	*An "accident"*
Where did I come from?	*You always existed*	*You were created by God*	*You are a product of chance and time*
Where am I going?	*Endless cycles of reincarnation*	*Heaven or hell*	*Nowhere, you will cease to exist*
To whom am I accountable?	*To oneself, as you are part of God*	*God*	*Nobody, you can do whatever you want*

Table 1-1: The Various Worldviews

Clearly these answers vary widely dependent on one's view of God. Therefore, it is only logical to start our quest for truth with an in-depth analysis to decide if we can find conclusive evidence for the existence of God. This will be the topic of our first discussion in the next chapters.

Section I
Does God Exist?

CHAPTER 2

How Can We Prove That God Exists?

*"I am the Lord your God, who brought you out of Egypt,
out of the land of slavery."*
EXODUS 20:2

WHERE DID I COME FROM?

How can we know that God really exists? Would it not be great if He would show Himself every morning, say around seven a.m., and greet us from the clouds with a "Good morning, America"? That would certainly tell us that God really exists. Too bad He does not do that. Well, even if He would appear on this cloud, still many would explain this as only a freak natural phenomenon, or mass hypnosis, or the result of drug abuse.

During my research I asked many Christian believers: "Why do you believe that God exists? What is, for you, the evidence for His existence?" After a few moments of thinking, I usually would get one of the following answers:

- I just know it.
- I feel it in my heart.
- I have seen Him at work in my life.
- God has answered prayers.
- Because the Bible reveals Him.

These are all good answers, and after I myself became a Christian, I also experienced God "at work" in my life. As a skeptic, however, looking for hard evidence, these answers are not sufficient. They are all purely subjective. As such, they relate to personal experiences and convictions, but none is based on hard and objective evidence.

And that's just exactly what I needed, objective evidence. In order to commit and submit my life to God, I required solid, hard, undeniable, objective evidence. I also believed that, if God is for real, and He indeed created us, He *must* have made sure to reveal Himself to us in some manner; if not in person, then at least through His creation – the world around us. It would be logically inconsistent to me that God would exist and not communicate to His creation.

As many others before me, – I realized that I could turn to science to find evidence for His existence by researching the origins of our existence.

Studying our origins has, over the centuries, always attracted much attention. Only three serious alternatives have ever been proposed:

1. We've always existed and will always exist – a *steady state* universe.
2. We are created by a Creator.
3. We are the product of natural processes solely influenced by chance and time.

It is interesting to realize how these three views of origins are reflected in the three main views of the world religions: Pantheism believes we've always existed; Monotheistic religions such as Judaism, Christianity, and Islam believe we are created by a Creator God. And finally Atheism rejects the existence of any intelligent force (Creator) in the universe.

How can modern science help us find clues to our origins?

Let's start by eliminating the first alternative view – that we have always existed. Through astronomy we know as a virtually undisputed fact that the universe, our solar system, and our planet have not always existed and also that our sun and earth at some point in the future will cease to exist. We can also prove that the universe is expanding, showing that there was some central point of beginning. Also through paleontology (studying early life on earth) and archaeology we know that mankind has not always existed on earth but has only been around for a relative short period of time. So, no serious scientist believes anymore in a steady state universe, and we can focus our research on studying:

How did we come into existence?

Evolved or Created?

Before mankind became "enlightened," there was never a question if God existed. However, over time, man has grown more impressed with himself at the center of the universe. In 1859 Charles Darwin published *The Origin of Species*[6] presenting an alternative theory to explain our existence. Darwin's theory became the basis for a belief system independent from God.

It has been said that Darwin has done more harm to the Christian faith than any persecution in history. The evolutionary model, largely due to its posture as the "scientific" explanation for the origins of life, caused many believers to doubt the existence of God and the truthfulness of the Bible. It planted a serious seed of doubt as to the credibility of the Bible: *"If the first chapter of the Bible is not true, then likely the rest of the Bible is questionable as well!"*

We need to emphasize upfront that – despite many claims – evolution is NOT a fact. Neither evolution nor creation is a natural law or a scientific fact, but each is merely a model. What does this mean? The process of evolution, just as the act of creation, cannot be observed or repeated, so both models remain unproved by science. Therefore neither can be called a *natural law* (such as the law of gravity or the laws of thermodynamics, which describe well-proved and observed behavior subject to laws of nature) nor a *scientific theory* (which requires the possibility and evidence of repeated observations). So evolution – just like creation – is only a model used to explain the observations in the world as we know it. It is not a fact, not a natural law, not even a scientific theory, but just a model!

I would also like to emphasize that there are only two possible models for the origins of life: evolution or creation. There is no alternative, and these two are mutually exclusive. Either our space/time-based universe needed a Creator, or it did not. This has an important implication: If we can prove that evolution is NOT a viable model/explanation, then we have indirectly found evidence that God exists! Therefore in studying the evidences, we will focus both on evidence to show that evolution is a faulty model as well as evidence pointing to the existence of a Creator.

WHAT IS EVOLUTION?

In the *evolution model*, the entire universe is considered to have evolved by natural processes and random selection into its present state of high organization and complexity. In this model the universe began in a state of pure randomness. Gradually it has – by "survival of the fittest" – become more ordered and complex. In order for the complex structure of the universe to have been produced by present natural processes, a vast amount of time was required.

As taught in our public schools today, the *Organic Theory of Evolution* account for the origin of mankind goes something as follows:

"Life on this planet originated several billion years ago, when electrical disturbances caused reactions in the chemicals of the primeval ocean. These reactions produced amino acids, which organized themselves into living cells. In time, the descendants of these one-celled organisms at random began to mutate, developing into various multi-celled plants and animals. As each new organism appeared, a natural selection would occur. Each life form was either better or less suited to its environment, and accordingly it would flourish or disappear. Those species of plants and animals more adaptable to their environments developed; those that could not adapt simply died. Man is the highest product of this development. He descended from the same ancestors as did the apes; more remotely, from the same ancestors as all mammals. He is himself still developing; that process is stalled by our present lifestyle, but biologically ongoing evolution is inevitable."

The concept of evolution is associated with Charles Darwin, who set forth evolution in *The Origin of Species* and further developed his ideas in the later *The Descent of Man*. These concepts have been applied to many scientific disciplines, and the theory has been revised along the way. More recently its tenets have been upgraded with more recent scientific discoveries especially in the areas of genetics/DNA (usually called *Neo-Darwinism*).

The basic elements of the evolutionary model remain:

- **Change over long periods of time:** entities/organisms change over time. These changes are random and are only based on pure chance.
- **Natural Selection:** positive changes strengthen the organism and increase its chances for survival. Therefore (random) positive changes will be preserved and even favored over the original organism.
- **The only forces at work are random change (chance) and (long periods of) time**: evolution is completely controlled by natural processes and the natural environment. There is no controlling power or other influence.

Simplified, evolution's equation for mankind becomes this:
Chance + *Time* ➜ *Mankind*

Many education systems have spoon-fed and brainwashed us with these concepts. These ideas sound so reasonable and have been taught by many highly educated people; therefore, many believe it is the truth. However, is it actually true? In the following chapters we will examine the concept to find if scientific observation does support this model.

We like to believe in chance!

Have you noticed how many people tend to think that if there's a chance something can happen, it actually will occur? The statistical probability might be very small, and all odds are against it, yet many still are willing to wager. That's the idea behind gambling. The odds are against us – we all know that – but we might be lucky. So many folks are willing to bet their money on it. Casinos and lotteries capitalize on this tendency of many to think that if they only try, and keep trying, they have a good chance at winning.

Evolution is an identical concept. This idea is that, even if its chances are tiny, it *could* happen, and if you just try enough times it *will* happen; that's exactly the idea behind evolution. That's probably why it appeals so strongly to so many.

WHAT IS THE CREATOR MODEL?

The *Creator model*, on the other hand, postulates a Creator or Intelligent Designer. Random chance and lots of time simply cannot combine to create life. Intelligent intervention is required. This occurs either by a comprehensive act of creation, bringing basic systems of nature into existence at once, fully functioning at the start, or by a process directed over time by the Creator towards completion.

Among Christians there are different models on HOW God created our world. These differences largely relate to timing; that is, did God directly and immediately create the world, or did He only design and guide the natural processes? To simplify, we identify two main views:

• **Creationism** (also called *Scientific Creationism, Young Earth Creationism,* and *Six Day Creationism*). This view believes God created everything in six literal 24-hour days. Everything was created by the direct act of God. The creative sequence is described precisely in Genesis, chapter 1, and occurred 6,000-10,000 years ago. Proponents base this view on the literal reading of the Bible and support this interpretation by data from natural sciences explained to show a young age of planet earth. Well known creationist organizations are the *Institute for Creation Research,*[7] *Answers in Genesis,*[8] and the *Creation Research Society,*[9] which present programs to demonstrate the evidences for a young world, limits to the original created species, the uniqueness of human life, and a global flood about 5,000 years ago.

• **Intelligent Design** (also called *Theistic Evolution, Old Earth Creationism,* or *Progressive Creationism*). This view accepts the majority view of scientists that the universe is old, several billions of years old, in fact. Proponents agree with evolutionists that species of organisms formed over extraordinarily long periods of time, but dispute and deny that this happened only by random chance. Divine interven-

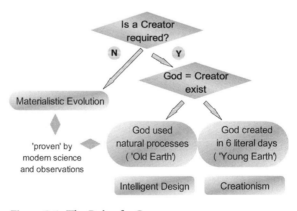

Figure 2-1: The Role of a Creator

tions and/or guidance over the course of time have brought about present life forms. There are a number of different approaches within this view.

- The *Intelligent Design* movement argues that certain features of the universe and living organisms can be explained logically only by an intelligent cause and certainly not by undirected natural forces. A well-known organization in this movement is the *Discovery Institute*.[10]
- Proponents of the *Gap Theory* believe in direct creation by God, but also in an old earth, explaining the age of the earth by postulating a large time gap between Genesis 1:1 and Genesis 1:2.
- *The Day-Age Theory* is probably the most popular view among Old Earth believers. To explain the age of the universe and earth, adherents translate the Hebrew word *"yowm"* as *period* or *age* rather than *day*. Thus God created the earth as described in Genesis; however, each creation "day" lasted an entire age. Various Christian organizations are proponents of this view. *Reasons To Believe*[11] is likely the most well known.

So there are multiple views on how God created human life. These views differ mostly on how to reconcile Biblical creation with scientific observations. According to surveys over the last twenty years, Christians are evenly divided between the Young Earth and Old Earth views.

In our approach to creation, the question of "how God did it" will not be further debated as it is irrelevant to evidence for God's existence. We will explore the proofs that support the existence of a Creator/Intelligent Designer, not how the process worked.

Note that all views of creation share these points in common:
- The concepts of time and three-dimensional space are designed by the Creator God.
- God, the Creator, designed all natural laws to support His creation.
- Life forms are too complex to come into existence just by natural laws. The Creator was involved in their development/formation.
- Mankind is created in the image of God and not just a more advanced animal.

A FRAMEWORK FOR DISCUSSION: THE BIG BANG

As we prepare to examine the evolution model in more detail, we need to understand its claims about human origins. As this is the model taught in schools and universities and is widely accepted by non-believers, it provides an excellent framework for discussions with honest seekers of truth. For this reason we will use from here on the Big Bang model and the associated time line as a reference for our discussions.

Do not allow *time* to become the focus of discussion!

Unfortunately many discussions about the existence of God end up being discussions over a young earth versus an old earth.

The non-believer argues the earth is much older than the Bible claims; therefore, the Bible is not true, and its God does not exist. Often the believer starts to defend the Bible, and the discussion quickly centers upon arguments about "time."

A famous illustration of this is the 1925 *"Scopes Monkey Trial."* Lawyers William Jennings Bryan and Clarence Darrow (the latter representing teacher John T. Scopes) tested a state law that barred the teaching, in any state-funded educational establishment in Tennessee, of *"any theory that denies the story of the Divine creation of man as taught in the Bible, and to teach instead that man has descended from a lower order of animals."*[12] This is often interpreted as meaning that the law forbade the teaching of any aspect of the theory of evolution. The state won, but the defense was made to look ridiculous defending – by only using scripture – the young age of the earth. On a side note, the Scopes trial was presented in a very distorted and biased movie titled *Inherit the Wind* that portrayed Christians supporting the creation view as scientifically ignorant and closed-minded.

The age of the earth is not relevant to the discussion of God's existence. The evidence that the evolution model is not adequate to explain our existence is supported by scientific observations. As we will see, these scientific data are also consistent with the claims of the Creator model.

Lastly, always keep in mind that God created time; therefore, He has total control over it, and it can never limit Him in anyway. *"But do not forget this one thing, dear friends: With the Lord a day is like a thousand years, and a thousand years are like a day"* (2 Peter 3:8).

According to many in the scientific community, a significant amount of data suggests the universe came into existence via the so called *Big Bang* event. This is said to have occurred perhaps 15-20 billion years ago, when the universe began to expand outward from one infinite small point in space. Through nuclear fusion processes, hydrogen (the first element) was converted to helium, followed by other heavier elements. Through the force of the initial "explosion" – the Big Bang – these elements pushed outward. Even as stars and planets are formed from dust, the universe is still expanding. Observations of the so-called red shift have led scientists to postulate that stars at the edge of the universe are moving outward at velocities approaching the speed of light (186,000 miles per second). This expansion has left various traces (*cosmic background radiation*) that have been measured[13] and seems to confirm the theory of the Big Bang event. Currently this model is generally accepted by the vast majority of cosmologists and astronomers.[14]

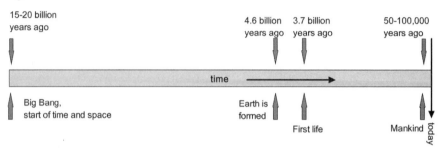

Figure 2-2: A "Scientific" Timeline

Through analysis of our solar system and the earth's geology, the consensus opinion among scientists is that earth was formed 4.6 billion years ago. The first microscopic life forms (bacteria) are said to have appeared 3.7 billion years ago. There is a wide range of views on how long humankind has been around, but recently most estimates are in the 50,000 – 100,000 years range.

This framework identifies four major events that each allows us to study what science can teach us about how these events came about:

1. The Big Bang
2. Formation of planet earth
3. First life on earth
4. Appearance of human beings

Each of these events on the evolutionary timeline will be the main subject of one of the next chapters. We will enter the realm of cosmology and astronomy and use a telescope to find out how "random" the Big Bang and how "common" our planet really are. Later we will use a microscope to study molecular biology and genetics to discover what these disciplines can teach us about the complexity of even the simplest life forms and genetic mutations.

CHAPTER 3

Studying the Big Bang

"In the beginning God created the heavens and the earth."
GENESIS 1:1

During the last decade cosmology/astronomy has become increasingly friendly to the Creator model. Discoveries about the origin of the Big Bang as well as the requirements for life on a planet like earth reveal more and more the hand of a Creator and make it less and less likely this could all have happened by mere chance. This chapter will investigate the possible cause of the Big Bang and the fine tuning of the universe towards life.

☼ EXHIBIT #1: HOW COULD THE BIG BANG HAPPEN?

The scientific community has made a lot of claims that 15-20 billion years ago some hard-to-define event, the Big Bang started time, gave us spatial dimensions (length, width, height), and initiated the universe. Over time this model has been refined to explain how subsequently stars and galaxies; our own galaxy, the Milky Way; our solar system; and our home planet earth were formed.

However, it intrigues me how little attention is given to the question: why did this Big Bang happen? How could it happen? Before the Big Bang there was nothing; no time/space, no universe, no energy, no matter. Then boom, suddenly all the energy and matter required to develop into our universe "pops" into existence. How can that be?

Assuming this would happen independently of an outside force such as a Creator directly violates one of the best proved and observed natural laws of science: the law of preservation of energy (or matter), technically known as the *First Law of Thermodynamics*. This principle states:

"Within a closed system, during any transformation the net energy increase or decrease is zero."

This means energy (or matter) cannot be created or destroyed, and the net effect of any transformation is zero. Simply stated, without energy from the outside, no reaction or transformation alone can generate additional energy, nor will energy merely disappear.

For instance when you operate a car, all energy put into powering the car (by the combustion engine) will be transformed into mechanical energy (moving the car) and heat (exhaust). But the sum of the mechanical energy and the heat/exhaust produced will be *exactly* equal to the energy produced by the burning of the gas/oxygen. No net energy is created or lost.

This also relates to the Big Bang. The explosion cannot have just happened by itself, as the energy released then (and even today drives the expansion of the universe) must have come from somewhere – the ONLY source possible would be a creating force, i.e., *a Creator*. Evolution has no explanation for this initial energy, a dilemma also described as the *cause-and-effect problem*. There simply is no explanation other than just to pronounce dogmatically all matter eternal!

Dr. William Lane Craig summarizes this cause-and-effect principle in what is called the *Kalam cosmological argument*[15]. The Kalam argument is as follows:

1. Whatever begins to exist has a cause.
2. The universe began to exist.
3. Therefore the universe has a cause (being a Creator).

Atheists are eager to claim that this argument is invalid, because even the Creator would need a cause (something must have created the Creator). However, the Kalam argument does not claim that everything that exists needs a cause, but only whatever BEGINS to exist. As God, the Creator, always has existed, He does not need a cause. He is the *"uncaused cause."* As can be proved by the concept of time and by the expansion of the universe, the universe started to exist. Thus the universe had to be caused by a Creator.

This principle (law) applies to all things in our cosmos. There is no dispute about this law in the scientific community. The only exception would be the Big Bang, but how can something come from nothing?

Science has no explanation for this; even its greatest minds are at a loss. Honest scientists are forced to admit that the Big Bang is strong evidence for the existence of a Creator. Steven Hawking, perhaps the most famous scientist alive, made this startling admission during the 1997 PBS program, *Universe:*

> *"In this century* [twentieth century], *science has come to understand how the universe began from a tiny point, fifteen billion years ago. No matter how incredible it sounds, it seems that the church's ideas of a moment of creation were right from the beginning."*

☼ EXHIBIT #2: STRUCTURE AND ORDER

The universe is controlled by fundamental laws of nature and constants of physics, also known as natural laws. These laws control gravity (how objects attract each other), electromagnetic forces (the attraction between positive charged protons and negative charged electrons, magnetic fields, electricity, radio waves, etc.) and the weak and strong nuclear forces (the forces that control the stability in atoms between the protons and neutrons in the nucleus). These laws control how stars are formed, how chemical reactions take place, how and at what temperature water freezes and boils, how a match ignites, even how sugar and cream mix in our coffee. These laws control everything in our universe and how nature works around us.

In the 1950s scientists started to study these laws and their relationship in depth. Many have become increasingly impressed, even amazed, by the extraordinary balance between the factors and parameters that control these laws. Since the 1980s much research has been published about what scientists now describe as how the universe appears to be *fine-tuned for life.*

For example, a gravitational force just a tiny bit stronger would crush human life on the earth's surface. A tiny bit weaker, and everyone would float into space.

These forces and constants are exactly right to make the Big Bang model work. To use the illustration of gravity once more: if gravity were slightly weaker, the expansion after the Big Bang would disperse matter too rapidly, preventing the formation of galaxies, stars and planets. If slightly stronger, the universe would have collapsed in on itself. Either way, we would not be here today![16]

According to Dr. Robin Collins in *Case for a Creator,*[17] gravity is fine-tuned to one part in a hundred million billion billion billion billion billion (1 in 10^{53}). In his interview with Lee Strobel, Collins also explains the delicate balance between the masses of neutrons and protons and the perfect relationship between the electromagnetic force and the strong nuclear force.

Astronomer Dr. Hugh Ross[18] has summarized work done by him and others analyzing this phenomena. He has produced a list of 35 characteristics that must be "set" to the exact value in order to support a sustainable universe. These factors include many of the constants that we recognize from formulas in our science class: the gravitational force constant, electromagnetic force constant, the charge of electrons, velocity of light, etc.

Research by Dr. Michael Denton[19] shows the unique characteristics of water and carbon to precisely support the requirements for living organisms. For example, carbon has an unusual ability to combine chemically not only with itself, but with many other elements, making possible the vast number of complex compounds needed by living cells. Several other elements – notably hydrogen, oxygen, nitrogen, and phosphorus – are unusually well suited to combine with carbon to form biologically active molecules (including the essential building blocks of life: amino acids, proteins, and DNA). Hydrogen and oxygen also combine to form water. Most of the chemical reactions for life take place only in liquid water. Water's ability to absorb and retain heat also buffers living things from sudden temperature changes. In Denton's words:

"Water is uniquely and ideally adapted to serve as the fluid medium for life on earth in not just one, or many, but in every single one of its known physical and chemical characteristics." [20]

Assuming that this just happened by random chance is not realistic. How can there be laws without a lawmaker? Why is the universe so regular and predictable? It all shows the hands of an Intelligent Designer and Creator. Evidence of design surrounds us. As physicist, astro-biologist, and author Paul Davies describes it:

"It is hard to resist the impression that the present structure of the universe, apparently so sensitive to minor alterations in numbers, has been rather carefully thought out... The seemingly miraculous concurrence of these numerical values must remain the most compelling evidence for cosmic design." [21]

And in the words of Steven Hawking:

"It would be very difficult to explain why the universe should have begun in just this way, except as the act of a God who intended to create beings like us." [22]

CHAPTER 4

Earth, No Ordinary Rock

"The heavens declare the glory of God;
The skies proclaim the work of his hands;
Day after day they pour forth speech;
Night after night they display knowledge.
There is no speech or language where their voice is not heard;
Their voice goes out into all the earth;
Their words to the ends of the world."
PSALM 19:1-4

Do you believe in aliens? Do you believe in UFOs? Do you believe life exists on other planets? Many surveys indicate perhaps as many as 60% of Americans believe in life on other planets. Why? Well, it could be due to a constant diet of science fiction in the movies and on TV, such as *Star Wars*, *War of the Worlds* and *Star Trek*, but, also because of the strong popular belief of the 1990s that the universe had to be full of alien life.

JUST AN ORDINARY ROCK?

Cosmologist, scientist, and author Dr. Carl Sagan, himself an atheist, was a strong believer in extraterrestrial life. He played a leading role in NASA's Mariner, Viking, Voyager, and Galileo spacecraft expeditions in the 1970-1990 period. He also introduced the universe to the public via his mega-hit television series *Cosmos* as well as through his many popular science publications.

One of Sagan's best known statements is about our planet earth. Contemplating a Voyager picture taken in 1990 of earth at a distance of four billion miles (the well known *Pale Blue Dot* picture) he wrote:

"There is nothing unusual about earth. It is an average, unassuming rock that's spinning mindlessly around an unremarkable star in a run-of-the-mill galaxy – a lonely speck in the great enveloping cosmic dark." [23]

On the surface his point makes logical sense. Why would it be unique? If earth formed 4.6 billion years ago, as scientists claim, what makes it unique? The universe is full of planets, many the same size and composition as earth, so if we are just a rock on which life happened to evolve, there must be, oh, so many other planets like us where too life chanced to evolve.

A few numbers make this case even stronger. Earth is part of our solar system, one of the nine (or is it eight, now that we're uncertain about Pluto) planets that orbit the sun. Our sun is part of a large collection of stars in our galaxy, which we call the Milky Way galaxy. In the Milky Way alone, there are an estimated one hundred billion (100,000,000,000) stars. That is about 15 stars for each person on earth. And just like the sun, many of these stars have planets in orbit. If there are so many planets, just in our galaxy alone, chances seem very good for finding life!

Go beyond the Milky Way, and the numbers soar even further beyond the limits of our imagination. In the total universe the number of stars is estimated to be in the order of ten billion trillion – 10 with a whopping 22 zeroes! So it is safe to say there are at least that many planets (10^{22}), or about one trillion planets for every person who has ever lived on earth. How can we be so arrogant to think the earth could be unique? Some scientists estimate as many as ten trillion (10^{13}) advanced civilizations. Sagan set this number at one million for our Milky Way galaxy alone! [24]

In the last decade our knowledge of the universe has grown exponentially. Observations via satellite telescopes, our advancing knowledge of forces at work in space, growing insights into the complexity of living cells, and a better understanding of the required conditions for life to exist has lead to a new branch of science called *astrobiology*. This discipline studies the possibility of life in the universe by combining insights from astronomy, biology, and geology. Application of this recent knowledge to our planet earth has given us a fresh look at how unique our home planet really is.

WHAT WOULD E.T. LOOK LIKE?

What would alien life look like? To scientifically explore the likelihood of life on other planets we must define criteria for this life. What properties would alien life exhibit?

If we would believe Hollywood, then "everything goes." Aliens could dramatically differ from earth life in many, many ways. Some might have acid in their veins, breathe toxic gasses, require extreme hot or cold temperatures; life can be very different from ours. Wait. Is that realistic?

We need to realize that all the laws of nature on earth are the same throughout the universe. The same is true of chemistry and biology, the table of elements and characteristics of solids, liquids and gasses such as water and oxygen.

Therefore life elsewhere would be subject to the same "rules" as life on earth. Given these *laws of nature* we know our kind of life is the only type of life possible. Any life anywhere in the universe would require the same building blocks and demand the same conditions that make life possible on our planet.

Simply said, if E.T. exists and there is life on other planets, it will be quite similar to life as we know it: carbon based (complex organic molecules built from combinations of carbon, oxygen, hydrogen, and nitrogen) with specific restrictions on gravity, presence of water, atmosphere, temperature, size, etc. In other words, any planet that supports life would have to be similar to earth, very similar. And E.T. would not be that different from us!

☼ EXHIBIT #3: EARTH, A TRULY PRIVILEGED PLANET

Popular science often assumes the presence of liquid water for a long enough time on any given planet is the most important criteria for life to exist. Recently NASA engineers were interviewed about the discovery by the 2004 Mars Landers. They were excited at indications that liquid water might have been present. This, they insisted, suggested discovery of life on Mars was only a matter of time. However, water is only one of the many prerequisites (or *factors*) required for life to exist.

FACTORS FOR LIFE ON A PLANET

Let's look closer at some of these essentials:

- **Distance from the sun**: Life will exist only where temperatures range between the freezing and boiling points of water. Earth's temperature is determined by the distance to its heat (and light) source: the sun. Only planets in a consistently temperate region around a sun (star) where liquid water could exist on the surface for an extended time (this is called the *Circumstellar Habitable Zone* or CHZ) would be potential candidates for life. In our solar system, earth is the only viable candidate. Venus, next closer to the sun is too close and thus too hot (about 475 degree Celsius); Mars is our closest outward neighbor and averages a surface temperature below zero degrees Celsius, the freezing point of water. With these temperatures none of our neighbors can reasonably support/sustain life.
- **The right sun**: Not any sun will do. First of all only planets that orbit in a single star system would qualify; zero or two-plus star systems fail. Next, the star must be a specific mass. A star more massive than ours will burn too quickly and too erratically to sustain consistent temperatures. Smaller stars with more frequent and violent flares would require a planet to be so close that the distance would cause tidal effects and restrict proper rotation of the planet. And the star must also be the right age to be at a stable burning phase without devastating temperature variations.
- **The right planet**: To sustain life, many factors have to be just right for the planet. These include the age of the planet (stability, surface temperature, rotating speed), mass of the planet (gravity), presence of vital ele-

ments such as carbon and water (human life requires the presence of 26 essential elements), atmosphere (of the right composition), magnetic field around the planet, volcanic activity, plate tectonics, axial tilt, rotation period, oceans to continent ratio, quantity of water, shape of the orbit, ozone levels in the atmosphere, and atmospheric pressure.

- **Presence of a moon**: Earth's moon is relatively large. It causes lunar tides, it stabilizes the tilt of the earth's axis, and it slows the earth's rate of rotation. Without the right size moon, complex life forms are not possible.

Our unique moon[25]

Having a relatively large moon, as earth does, is very uncommon. Most moons are formed as the planet they orbit is formed, and are quite small compared to the planet. Other moons are objects captured out of space that once circled the outer planets of a solar system.

Earth's moon is very different. It is too large to have formed at the same time earth did, and analysis of moon rocks indicates it is 350 million years younger than earth. The position of earth so close to the sun means the moon cannot be a captured object. This has long puzzled astronomers, many of whom now conclude the moon formed after a collision of a Mars-size object with earth 4.25 billion years ago.

This collision was essential for creating life-supporting conditions on earth: it ejected earth's heavy, life-suffocating atmosphere into space (replacing it with our current breathable and transparent air), it slowed down earth's rotation (from an 8-hour day to a 24-hour day, avoiding sustained surface winds of 500+ mph), and it established earth's current axial tilt of 23.5° (that allows us to experience our four seasons).

- **Protection from comets and asteroids**: A planet that supports life needs to be in a solar system with at least one much larger planet. In our solar system this planet is Jupiter, it is two and a half times more massive that all other planets combined. Jupiter's gravity attracts and captures incoming comets and comet debris thus preventing numerous collisions that would be destructive to the earth.
- **Location in the galaxy**: There is a so called *Galactic Habitable Zone* (GHZ) – the area in a galaxy where habitable places can be found. As we learn from studying the Milky Way, the GHZ is an extremely small section of a galaxy, since the inner (most heavily populated) regions are too

dense with too many collisions and interference. The limited number of planets in the outer regions do not provide enough heavy elements to form terrestrial planets like earth. Galaxies outside the Milky Way appear even less inviting to life, as they are less luminous and therefore – in general – lack the heavier elements needed for planets and life.

- **Age of the universe:** The concept of *Cosmic Habitable Age* (CHA) further limits possibilities of life other than on earth. Only planets in galaxies formed at the right age of the universe will be worth considering. Life-essential elements heavier than helium weren't present in the universe until they were made in the first stars and then ejected from their interiors; that excludes all the older galaxies. Galaxies/stars/planets formed in later ages of the universe not only have too many heavy elements, but also lack vital radioisotopes essential to support geological activities on these planets.

This list of factors is not complete but merely a subset of the currently identified requirements as mentioned in the following three books:

- *The Creator and the Cosmos* (1993) by Hugh Ross was one of the first publications to use scientific data to show the uniqueness of planet earth. Ross is an atheist-turned-Christian as a result of his research.
- *Rare Earth* (2000) by Peter Ward and Donald Brownlee. In *Rare Earth* the authors (both professors at the University of Washington in Seattle) conclude from an evolutionary perspective that, based on evidences from a wide range of disciplines, earth is a rare place indeed and that complex life must be extraordinarily rare in the universe.
- *The Privileged Planet* (2004) by Guillermo Gonzalez and Jay Richards builds a strong case for a Creator, based on the evidence from unique factors that allow life on earth as well as earth's unique location for observation of the universe.

These factors show that earth is not just an ordinary rock, but that many things had to go "just right" when earth formed in terms of time, location, and subsequent events. Earth is surely considerably more "rare" and "privileged" than realized in the days of Carl Sagan.

How Rare is our Rare Earth?

You've probably heard about of SETI[26] (*Search For Extraterrestrial Intelligence*), an institute that searches for intelligent life in the universe using huge radio-telescopes. These are designed to listen and zoom into any radio signal that might come from a particular area in space. If that signal is more than random noise, that would show that the signal must have originated from an advanced extraterrestrial civilization (as occurred in the movie *Contact*). Obviously nothing has been detected, and millions upon millions of dollars have been spent. This sparked a former senator to say: "*The millions spent on the search for intelligent life in the universe are better spent on the search for intelligent life here in Washington DC.*" [27]

The founder of SETI, Radio Astronomer Dr. Frank Drake, devised an equation in 1961 to calculate the number of advanced civilizations in the Milky Way galaxy able to communicate with radio signals. This well known equation – the Drake Equation – is still used to get an educated estimate for the number of civilizations in the universe:

$$N = N_0 \ x \ f_p \ x \ n_e \ x \ f_i \ x \ f_i \ x \ f_c \ x \ f_L$$

In this formula, the multiplication of N_0 (the total number of stars) by various fractions, gives the total number of civilizations. The fractions in the original Drake Equation are:

f_p = fraction of stars with planetary systems

n_e = number of planets in a star's habitable zone

f_i = fraction of habitable planets where life does arise

f_i = fraction of those planets on which intelligent beings also evolve

f_c = fraction of those planets on which sufficient communication technology arises

f_L = fraction of the average planetary lifetime when there is an advanced civilization

All fractions are between 0 and 1 and obviously estimated close to 0; therefore the resulting number of civilizations, N, is much smaller than the original number of stars, N_0.

We have already mentioned that in the days of Drake and Sagan (1960-1990), calculations made by applying the Drake equation were in the order of magnitude of one million advanced civilizations (N) in the Milky Way alone. Advancing knowledge of factors required for life has forced the Drake equations to be modified to incorporate the new data. And the results are now very different.

In *Rare Earth*[28] Ward and Brownlee add a number of fractions to their own version of the Drake Equation, which they call the *Rare Earth Equation*. The fractions added include: fraction of metal-rich planets, fraction of stars in a galactic habitable zone, fraction of planets with a large moon, fraction of solar systems with Jupiter-sized planets, and a fraction of planets with a critically low number of mass extinction events. They do not attempt to exactly calculate N but conclude that: "*To us, the signal is so strong that even at this time, it appears that earth indeed may be extraordinarily rare.*"

In *The Privileged Planet*[29] Gonzalez and Richards take the Drake Equation to the next level and formulate the *Revised Drake Equation*. They enhance the equation to include a total of 20 different fractions, allowing for critical factors like: enough oxygen and low carbon dioxide concentrations in a planet's atmosphere, right mass range, proper concentration of sulfur in the planet core, presence of the right-sized moon and right planetary rotation, right amount of water in the planet crust, steady plate tectonic cycling, low number of large impacts, and more. Discussing and estimating some of these, the authors conclude the discovery of even a single new civilization in the Milky Way galaxy is extremely unlikely.

Fermi's Paradox[30]

In 1950, Nobel laureate and physicist Enrico Fermi (1901-1954) asked his colleagues:

"If there are extraterrestrials, where are they?"

He reasoned that if there were indeed many other intelligent civilizations in our galaxy, some surely would be further developed than we are. These advanced civilizations would also explore or even colonize the universe. In time, say perhaps a million years, the blink of an eye on galactic timescales, they would have reached the rest of the galaxy or sent self-replicating robots. They would surely target habitable planets such as earth.

In our galaxy, that could be 12 billion years old, there is no trace of such colonization, either now or in the past. The conclusion: They are not here because they do not exist.

In *The Creator and the Cosmos*[31] Hugh Ross advances the concept of the Drake Equation to include a total of 128 identified factors. He also has calculated a probability estimate for each particular factor to be within an acceptable range to support life. Combining all probabilities (and compensating for dependencies) Ross calculates a probability for occurrence of all 128 factors to be a chance of 1 in 10^{166}. So even with a total number of planets in the range of 10^{22}, the chance is less than 1 in 10^{144} (one in one thousand trillion trillion trillion trillion trillion trillion trillion trillion trillion trillion trillion) that any such planet in the entire universe exists! This chance is so small, it is beyond the comprehension of a human mind! In any other context results such as these would imply an absolute impossibility.

How Big is Small?

Numbers like 10^{22} planets and chances of 1 in 10^{144} are beyond our comprehension. We can write the numbers and count the zeroes, but they do not mean much. And as always with chances, it is so easy to say: "*There's still a chance – so give it enough time and it will happen.*"

Therefore we need an illustration to understand these chances better:

- Imagine the total land surface of the USA, including Hawaii and Alaska, a total of three and a half million square miles.
- Also imagine one silver dollar. A silver dollar is about the size of a square inch.
- Now cover all the land surface of the USA with silver dollars.
- And start adding new layers of silver dollars to cover the surface again and again until a height is reached of 10 miles everywhere.
- Now all the land surface of the USA is covered with silver dollars 10 miles high everywhere.
- Next, imagine a single silver dollar marked with an X placed at random in this mass.
- Finally, blindfold a volunteer, drop him anywhere, send him to wander about until he chooses a point to dig into the 10-mile high pile, and grab only one coin.
- The chance of that person picking the silver dollar with the X is about 1 in 10^{25}!
- Therefore, a change of 1 in 10^{144} is like repeating this experiment six times in a row, and each time selecting the X marked silver dollar – a virtual impossibility.

☼ EXHIBIT #4: DESIGNED FOR DISCOVERY

Have you ever gazed at the skies on a clear summer evening? Is it not amazing to see all these thousands and thousands of stars as well as our moon and some of our neighboring planets? Does it not give a feeling of awe and at the same time make you realize how small and insignificant you are?

Have you ever thought about how amazing it is that we can actually see all these stars? If our atmosphere was just a little thicker, the sky would look like a bank of mist or fog. If earth had been located anywhere else in the Milky Way, the view would have been very different too. In a more "crowded" part of the galaxy we would see only a few nearby stars, which would have given so much light, that the weaker stars would not be visible. In a more remote area of the galaxy, few stars would be close enough to be visible at all.

In *The Privileged Planet*[32] Gonzales and Richards set forth a number of intriguing examples of how uniquely earth is positioned to observe the universe. They also show that the circumstances required to allow optimum observations are the *same* requirements essential to allow life to exist on our planet. Let's examine a few of these examples.

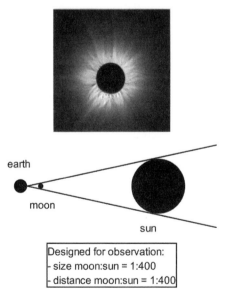

earth

moon

sun

Designed for observation:
- size moon:sun = 1:400
- distance moon:sun = 1:400

Figure 4-1: A Perfect Solar Eclipse

A TOTAL SOLAR ECLIPSE

Once every few years a total *solar eclipse* is visible from a limited area on earth. During a perfect or total solar eclipse, the light of the sun is totally blocked by the moon, which is in a position exactly between the location on earth where the eclipse occurs and the sun. What makes the event "total" is that from the point of the observer, the moon exactly blocks the sun. Over history, total solar eclipses have not only been amazing to observe but also have resulted in important scientific discoveries not possible without a total eclipse.

In our solar system with 9 planets and more than 63 moons, earth is the best place where observers can witness a total solar eclipse. This is because of the remarkable "coincidence" of the relationship between the size of the sun compared to that of the moon and the distances between the sun, moon, and earth. The sun is 400 times larger than the moon, and the sun is also 400 times as far away from earth as the moon. If this relationship would have been any different, the eclipse would only be partial or the moon would also cover the sun's corona making it a much less impressive and scientifically revealing observation.

Just coincidence? Or design?

THE CLARITY OF EARTH'S ATMOSPHERE

For complex organisms that breathe oxygen, the atmosphere of a planet requires 10 to 20% oxygen (earth's atmosphere is roughly 21% oxygen, 78% nitrogen, and trace amounts of other gases). The atmospheric balance is crucial not only to breathe oxygen but also to protect from ultraviolet solar radiation and to reduce temperature extremes between day and night.

This delicate composition of the atmosphere also "happens" to render it completely transparent. More carbon-based gases, like carbon-dioxide – breathed by plant life (less than 0.04% of our atmosphere) or more water vapor (typically less than 1%, however much higher on a rainy, misty, foggy day in the Pacific Northwest) would not only reduce the transparency dramatically, but would also cause greenhouse effects.

Visible light is radiation of a certain wavelength. To the human eye only wavelengths from ultraviolet to red light (the well known rainbow) are visible light, and these wavelengths range from about 4,000 Angstroms to 7,000 Angstroms (1 Angstrom is 10^{-10} meter). "Coincidentally" earth's atmosphere is only transparent for radiation (light) coming in from space in the range from 3,100 to 9,500 Angstrom (and radio waves). So the range of visible light to the human eyes is right in the middle of the range of light for which the atmosphere is transparent. This is also the range in which about 40% of the sun's energy is emitted.

In the words of Richards and Gonzales:[33] *"As it happens, our atmosphere strikes a nearly perfect balance, transmitting most of the radiation that is useful for life while blocking most of the lethal energy."*

Evolutionists will now probably jump out of their chair eager to say: *"Yeah, right, of course, we evolved on this earth with these circumstances, so, obviously, the human eye evolved – by natural selection – to function exactly in this spectrum of light in our atmosphere."* But that is dead wrong. The process of photosynthesis can only happen at wavelengths (light) that fall roughly in the visible light range. At other wavelengths it just does not happen; molecules do not absorb radiation of wavelengths outside visible light.

As German astronomer Hans Blumenberg stated in 1975:
"The combined circumstance that we live on earth and are able to see stars – that the conditions necessary for life do not exclude those necessary for

vision, and vice versa – is a remarkably improbable one. This is because the medium in which we live is, on the one hand, just thick enough to enable us to breathe and to prevent us from being burned up by cosmic rays while, on the other hand, it is not so opaque as to absorb entirely the light of the stars and block any view of the universe. What a fragile balance between the indispensable and the sublime.” [34]

Earth's Location in the Milky Way Galaxy

One more striking illustration of how perfectly the conditions for life match with optimum conditions for observation is the location of earth in the Milky Way galaxy.

The Milky Way – like other galaxies – is crowded. It contains more than 100 billion stars (some estimate as many as 400 billion). It is dish-shaped with branching arms (called *spiral arms*, therefore the Milky Way is called a *spiral galaxy*) when viewed from the top. Most stars are concentrated in the center, the rest scattered along the spiral arms. These arms are mostly in a flat plane, and this makes the Milky Way resemble a flat disk when seen from the side (see the pictures in figure 4-2).

The Milky Way – like any other galaxy – is also a hostile place.[35] Life at the galactic center is impossible because the density of stars leads to almost continuous collisions (like rush-hour traffic at a busy intersection). Plus there is the presence of many lethal stars (stars going super nova or emitting deadly radiation). The same problems are present in the spiral arms too. As a result, habitable planets in the Milky Way can only exist in-between the spiral arms. On the other hand, to have access to heavier elements, such a planet cannot be at the outer edge of the galaxy either. Earth is located roughly between two spiral arms, halfway between the galactic center and the outer edge – right in that relatively tiny area of the Milky Way in what astrobiologists call the Galactic Habitable Zone.

Figure 4-2: The Milky Way. The left picture[36] (artist impression) looks down on the Milky Way from a position outside of the galaxy. The right picture[37] (an actual picture taken by the COBE spacecraft) shows a side of the flat plane.

This also happens to be the best place for observations. Being in the flat plane of the galaxy provides us with great views of the closer stars in the spiral arms around us. In the vertical plane we can observe other galaxies far away from us without being hindered by the light of the other stars from our galaxy. In a differently shaped galaxy, this would not be possible. If we were in a spiral arm itself, or even in the galactic center, the density of light from close by stars would blind us just like the bright beams of an approaching car, and we would not be able to see dimmer stars at greater distances.

Once again, the place in the universe best suited for observation is also the only place in the universe where observers could actually live. The universe is not only designed to support life, but also to be discovered. As King David wrote long ago:

> *"The heavens declare the glory of God"*
> PSALM 19:1

CHAPTER 5

Simple Life Forms: an Oxymoron

"Then God said, 'Let the land produce vegetation: seed-bearing plants and trees on the land that bear fruit with seed in it, according to their various kinds. And it was so.'"
GENESIS 1:11

Our universe is remarkably fine-tuned for the existence of life. Also, we have seen that our earth is a rare planet, against all odds, providing the perfect characteristics and critical conditions required to support life. All this is necessary for any life to exist, but it does not mean that if all these conditions are present, life just starts. What does it take for a living organism to come into existence? Is a "simple" life form indeed very simple? Or is even the "simplest" life form more complex than anything we as humans can even imagine?

LIFE IN A SOUP – FIRST LIFE ON EARTH

How did *first life* start on earth? According to the Big Bang model, when earth was formed about 4.6 billion years ago it was a lifeless, very hostile place. But the fossil record teaches us that more than 3.7 billion years ago somehow in a period of less than a billion years the first life forms came into existence. These were micro-organisms, the simplest life forms imaginable, one-cell bacteria and organisms that resembled blue-green algae. Very "simple" life, but still living cells. These organisms were able, using information stored in their cells, to absorb and process energy from their environment to grow and replicate.

How this giant leap from *no-life* to *first life* (also called *abiogenesis*) happened is one of the most intriguing mysteries in science. Especially our generation has learned a lot about how living organisms actually work. We are able to study and analyze all the different components in a cell and observe their role and behavior. We can watch as genetic information is unraveled and is used to build new molecules, and we're all baffled by its perfection and complexity. But all today's life on earth came from previous life. As a child needs a mother to be born, likewise, all known living organisms come from parent organisms (this is referred to as *biogenesis*). Can this chicken and egg cycle be broken? How did the first living organism come into existence?

Charles Darwin himself never spent much time researching first life. He assumed simple life was so simple that it would just "start to exist." In a letter of Darwin to Joseph Dalton Hooker of February 1, 1871, he made the suggestion that life may have begun in a *"warm little pond, with all sorts of ammonia and phosphoric salts, lights, heat, electricity, etc. present, [so] that a protein compound was chemically formed ready to undergo still more complex changes."* He went on to explain that *"at the present day such matter would be instantly devoured or absorbed, which would not have been the case before living creatures were formed."* In other words, the presence of life itself prevents the spontaneous generation of simple organic compounds today – a circumstance that confines the search for first life to a controlled environment in a laboratory.

Of course evolutionists have diligently searched for answers. You might recall the narrative of the *prebiotic* or *primordial soup* as the construction site for life from your school days. The following typical *"recipe for life"*[38] is found in evolutionary textbooks:

"To find out if there is life in the Universe, it's useful to look at how it began here on earth. Follow our step-by-step recipe to see how life started:

1) *Mix ingredients. For life to evolve, simple molecules have to combine to form more complex ones. This mixing would have happened in the seas of the early earth, often called the primordial soup.*

2) *Add energy. Next you need energy. This may have come from lightning storms or hot underwater springs. This injection of energy sparked chemical reactions. These simple molecules began joining to form larger, more complex ones, called "amino acids". In a classic experiment in 1953, Stanley Miller and Harold Urey recreated the primordial soup in the laboratory. By passing electricity through a mixture of simple molecules, they were able to make amino acids.*

3) *Form complex molecules. Amino acids then joined together end-to-end to form long, chain-like molecules, known as proteins. Proteins are essential for building a living creature. They are involved in the formation of just about everything in your body, from the color of your skin to the layout of neurons in your brain.*

4) *Wait for life to reproduce. Another complex molecule that was formed during these reactions was DNA. DNA has an amazing characteristic that makes it essential for life – it can reproduce itself. It also carries all the code to make a living creature."*

However – does this make sense? Is this what modern evolutionary scientists really believe? Before we can answer these questions, we need to better understand what a simple life form really is.

☼ Exhibit #5: Life Cannot Have Started by Chance.

Have you ever heard of an *oxymoron*? An oxymoron is a figure of speech that combines two conflicting terms. Famous oxymorons are "jumbo shrimp," "big details," "larger half," "civil war," or terms more politically loaded like "military intelligence," "Microsoft Works" and "civil libertarian," or even a term like "Christian fiction."

All above examples are good illustrations, but I personally have come to believe that one of the best oxymorons is the term "*simple living cell.*" That term just does not "compute." Even the most elementary one-cell living organism is orders of magnitude more complicated than anything mankind has ever built or even imagined.

The simple one-cell organism at the beginning of the evolutionary chain does not appear to be such a simple organism after all. As an illustration, a single-cell organism could well be described as *"a high-tech factory, complete with artificial language and decoding systems; central memory banks that store and retrieve impressive amounts of information; precision control systems that regulate the automatic assembly of components; proofreading and quality control mechanisms that safeguard against errors; assembly lines that use principles of prefabrication and modular construction; and a complete replication system that allows the organism to duplicate itself at bewildering speeds."* [39]

Or perhaps this is an even more illustrative description: "*a living cell is like a robot factory, completely run by robots, that builds new robots who will build new robot factories.*"

The simplest one-cell organism is far more complex than anything that man has ever been able to put together. In other words <u>there is no such thing as a simple one-celled organism</u> – the simplest cell ever known is <u>extremely</u> complex!

One of the most complex machines built by man is a modern airplane, like the Boeing 787 *Dreamliner*. It contains an estimated four to five million different parts. By ingeniously assembling all these four to five million non-flying parts together, the engineers at Boeing are able to build a machine that can fly. Look how that compares to a cell: A living cell consists of multiple billions of non-living parts (atoms and molecules). So a living cell is in the order of magnitude of one thousand times more complex than a modern airplane.

Molecular biology teaches us that the three basic components of every living cell are *proteins*, *DNA*, and *molecular machines*.

Building Proteins

Proteins are the molecules of structure and function. They are like the structural framing members (concrete, studs, sheetrock, joists, and rafters) of a house. For instance, hair is mostly protein, skin cells are packed full of protein, and the enzymes that break down food are mostly proteins. Even the simplest living cell in our body or a single-cell living organism contains about 200 protein molecules.

Proteins themselves are built from *amino acids*. A protein molecule is actually a long chain of linked amino acids. Amino acids are molecules build around (a number of) carbon atoms. One carbon molecule can bond four other (chains of) elements/molecules, each of these consists of other carbon links, or combinations of oxygen, hydrogen, and nitrogen. In nature there are 80 types of amino acids; however, only 20 of these are found in living organisms. If any of the other 60 amino acids would be in the chain, it would actually make the protein not viable for use in a living organism. It takes about 100 or so correctly "selected" amino acids to assemble one protein molecule.

To make things more complex: amino acids come in equal amounts of so called *right- and left-handed orientation* (this has to do with how the other elements are bonded to the central carbon atom). So, any primordial soup would not only contain a random distribution of the 80 different amino acids, but also each amino acid would be present in a random distribution of right- and left-handed orientations. For some, not yet scientifically understood reason, proteins found in viable living organisms only contain left-handed amino acids.

Can a protein form by chance? A calculation for the chance of one functional protein molecule forming randomly would be:

1/80 (select the right amino acid, one out of 80 possible choices) multiplied by 1/2 (only left-handed amino acids are usable) = 1 in 160. This is the probability of selecting the correct first amino acid for the protein. This needs to be repeated 100 times, since there are about 100 amino acids required to assemble one protein molecule. This chance is: 1/160 times 1/160 times 1/160 times… 1/160 (one hundred times) = 1/160 to the power 100 = 2.6×10^{220}.

Compare this to the fact that there are only 10^{80} atoms in the whole universe. And if you think that is does not matter that these chances or so small, because there is so much time to make it possible, consider that – as per Big Bang cosmology – the universe is "only" about 15 billion years old. This is "only" about 4×10^{17} seconds. Therefore, all the available atoms in the universe combined with the total time the universe has existed so far does not give enough opportunity to statistically justify the random assembly of just one single protein molecule! Do you remember our previous illustration with the silver dollars? It would require doing the "silver dollar experiment" about nine times successfully in a row simulate the probability of assembling a protein by mere coincidence.

And that still only gives you one single protein molecule. For the simplest cell, you will need at least about 200 of these proteins molecules!

These chances are so small that even evolutionists do not believe anymore that any proteins have ever formed just by chance! [40]

THE MILLER EXPERIMENT

But wait, how about the Miller experiment? Did not Stanley Miller show that if you have a "soup" of early earth materials and you add energy that the building blocks of life are spontaneously formed?

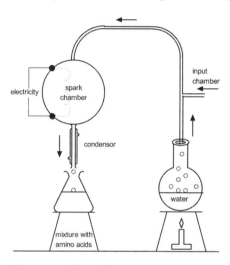

Figure 5-1: The Miller Experiment

Indeed, in 1952, Stanley Miller, a graduate student in the chemistry department of the University of Chicago, conducted his famous *spark-chamber experiment*, the so called *Miller-Urey experiment*. After attending a lecture by Nobel laureate Harold Urey on the conditions on early earth, Miller decided to re-create those conditions in the lab. He connected water ("the ocean") via glass tubing to a mixture of methane, ammonia and hydrogen, the chemicals supposedly present in early earth's atmosphere. Using electrodes, he simulated lightning. After a week, the water had turned yellow-brown and was coated with an oily scum. Analysis showed that the water contained glycine and other amino acids, the building blocks of proteins. With further improvement of the experiment, Miller was ultimately able to produce small amounts of about half of the twenty amino acids required for building proteins.

Time Magazine, Life, and many newspapers heralded Miller's achievement with headlines such as *"Test Backs Theory That Life Began as Chemical Act."* But, of course, all Miller had done was synthesize a few amino acids. Bricks alone do not make a house. Like house bricks, the amino acids would have to be assembled in a very specific way before they became a protein.

Current scientific knowledge has revealed some serious problems with the Miller experiment. These give a clear indication about the complexity and improbability of the "building by chance" theories:[41]

• First of all: Miller "stacked the deck" in his spark-chamber. The "atmosphere" in his chamber was composed only of the "perfect" components selected to react the right way (ammonia, methane, and hydrogen). Real earth's atmosphere likely had only small, if any concentrations of those gases. Scientists now believe the early atmosphere was mainly composed of water, carbon dioxide, and nitrogen. Those gases would not produce any reaction in the spark-chamber whatsoever. Various evolutionary origin-of-life scientists confirm that Miller used the wrong gas mixture: "the early atmosphere looked nothing like the Miller-Urey simulation."

- Only 2% of the amino acids Miller made are potentially usable to build the proteins needed in a living cell. The rest is useless for life building and actually mostly destructive to any evolving life (as they tend to react more readily with the amino acids than the amino acids react with each other).

- Even the "right" molecules formed in the spark-chamber are far more likely to react in "wrong" than "right" ways with the other "right" molecules.

Even today, despite many, many efforts and dollars spent, modern science has not been able to get better results for creating "life in a test tube." Now 50+ years after this "breakthrough in evolution science," Miller's spark-chamber only shows us, more than ever before, how extremely improbable (impossible is a better word) it is to create just a simple protein molecule by chance.

Actually the Miller-Urey experiment has backfired and has become a piece of evidence for the Creator model: it shows that if you leave the process just to chance, it will not produce any workable results. Only if you stack the deck and control the results, you can produce (some) amino acids – that is applying "intelligent interference" – the concept behind the Creator model.

BUILDING DNA

DNA (Deoxyribo-Nucleid Acid) contains the blueprint of a living organism. It is the set of detailed instructions that specifies and regulates what the organism is and will be. If the proteins are the building materials for a house, the DNA is the set of home building plans. Working together with *RNA (RiboNucleid Acid)*, the DNA directs the correct sequencing of amino acids in proteins during the cell replication process. It is able to do this through biochemical instructions – information – that is encoded on the DNA.

The making of DNA and RNA would be an even greater problem than assembling proteins. These molecules are far more complex than our "simple" protein molecules. DNA is built like a string of pearls with the main chain consisting of sugars and phosphate groups. Each link in the chain has a base connected that actually spells a letter of the genetic code. There are four kinds of bases that can spell the genetic letters *G (Guanine), C (Cytosine), A(Adenine),* and *T(Thymine).* And just like our alphabet, combinations of these four DNA "letters" can spell any genetic instruction.

Figure 5-2: A Pair of Chromosomes

DNA makes is possible for a cell to build functional protein molecules from the available pool of amino acids. For this purpose, certain parts of the DNA specify the order of the amino acids in the protein. When the protein molecule is built, the DNA code is unraveled into RNA strands, which contains words – one word per amino acid. Each three letter word represents a specific amino acid.

DNA is combined with protein into structural units called *chromosomes*, which usually occur in identical pairs (23 pairs in a human cell). The chromosome is like a single, very long, highly coiled molecule of millions and millions (up to 250 million in human chromosomes) of DNA base letters. The DNA bases link the two chromosomes together (see figure 5-2).[43]

In every chromosome pair, a "T" base in one of the chromosomes links always to an "A" base in the other. Likewise, a "C" links to a "G." This way each chromosome is the mirror image of the other one. The links are called the *DNA base pairs*. On the chromosome, large groups of DNA base pairs form functional sub-units called *genes*. A gene occupies a certain place on the chromosome. It is basically a sequence of DNA base pairs (each base pair specifying a DNA letter) that work together as one unit of genetic information (an average gene in the human body is about 3,000 DNA base pairs long). Each gene embodies the encoded instructions for the assembly of proteins and the inheritance of a particular characteristic or group of characteristics that are passed on from one generation to the next. Together the chromosomes contain all the information needed to build an identical functioning copy of the cell.

The information stored in human DNA is almost incomprehensible. Each of us starts at conception as a tiny little ball about the size of a period on a printed page. In that tiny ball, there are over six feet (!) of DNA. That DNA specifies our (future) characteristics (brown hair, blue eyes, etc.) in a manner that can be read like a book. Every cell in the human body contains these same DNA strands. Therefore each cell has about three billion DNA base pairs comprising an estimated 20,000-25,000[44] genes. Compare that to an average page of text of 2,000 to 2,500 letters. Just the DNA letters in each individual cell of our body is equivalent to the information of a book with a whopping 1.5 million pages. That is equivalent to a pile of paper of about 625 feet high, and that is just for one cell. The estimate for the number of cells in an average human body is in the range of 50 trillion (that is a 5 with fifteen zeroes, or 5×10^{15}). So the total amount of information written into all the cells of an average person would be a stack of paper as high as 625 feet multiplied by 50 trillion = 5 trillion miles. To try to understand this humongous number, it helps to consider that the distance between us and the farthest planet in our solar system, Pluto is about five billion miles. Therefore the pile of paper written with the DNA letters of every cell in an average person would be about 1,000 times the distance between us and Pluto!

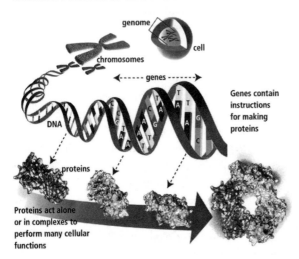

genome

cell

chromosomes

genes

DNA

Genes contain instructions for making proteins

proteins

Proteins act alone or in complexes to perform many cellular functions

Figure 5-3: DNA is stored in chromosomes. Genes on the chromosome specify the assembly of proteins. Proteins work together to build new cell material or perform specific functions[46]

Completed in 2003, the *Human Genome Project*,[45] coordinated by the US Department of Energy and the National Institutes of Health, took 13 years to determine the sequences of the base pairs on the 26 chromosomes of the human DNA (referred to as the *human genome*) and store this information in a giant database. This gigantic effort only gave us a map of all the genes/DNA letters; for the most part we still do not know what controls what characteristics, nor how it works. Subsequent efforts are ongoing to use this information to complete the identification of all the genes in the human genome.

Could such an almost unimaginably complex chemical compound ever be formed by mere chance and time? We've seen how unlikely it is for a "simple" protein molecule to be formed just by chance. It is hard to make a calculation for the statistical chance of a DNA molecule to just "assemble" under the right conditions. Estimates for the probability of random assembly of DNA[47] present in a one-cell living organism (about 100 genes) range from 1 in $10^{3,000}$ to 1 in $10^{100,000,000,000}$. Whatever the exact number, these chances are all basically non-existent.

MOLECULAR MACHINES

In home construction it is not enough to dump all required building materials (lumber, rafters, nails, concrete, sheetrock, and so on) and a set of plans at the building site. Obviously nothing will happen until the workers arrive. Labor is required to read the plans, cut the materials, and put it all together.

So it is also in a living cell. If the amino acids and the proteins are the building materials, and the DNA is the blueprint, then the so called *molecular machines* are the workers. They perform the labor needed to actually construct the different components of the living cell from the building materials according to the DNA blueprint.

These machines, made from proteins, use the information from the DNA/RNA to assemble and shape proteins, copy DNA, build new cells, and also build other molecular machines. Molecular machines operate in the cell and haul the amino acids to protein assembly lines. These assembly lines, which are also molecular machines, are called *ribosomes*. Other molecular machines turn cellular switches on and off, sometimes killing the cell or causing it to grow. Solar-powered molecular machines capture the energy of light and store it in chemicals. Electrical machines allow current to flow through nerves. Manufacturing machines build other molecular machines as well as themselves. Cells swim using machines, copy themselves with machinery, and ingest food with machinery. In short, mind-boggling, highly advanced molecular machines control every cellular process.

Needless to say these machines are extremely sophisticated and complex. The molecular machines are the robots that, without any outside interference, build new cells and new robots.

We now have the technology at the cellular level to study and see these machines in action. Molecular biologists can analyze their composition, understand their function, and marvel at their complexity. Evolutionary scientists have yet to offer any explanation for their existence.

"Can all of life be fit into Darwin's theory of evolution?... If you search the scientific literature on evolution, and if you focus your search on the question of how molecular machines – the basis of life – developed, you find an eerie and complete silence. The complexity of life's foundation has paralyzed science's attempt to account for it... I do not think [Darwin's mechanism] explains molecular life." [48]

SOME MORE COMPLICATIONS

In *Origins of Life* (2004)[49] the authors identify a significant number of additional challenges for the evolutionary "origins of life" model that cannot be explained by modern science. Some of these problems are:

- **Finding enough time.** Based on studies of the fossil records, paleontologists claim that first life in its most primitive form was present on earth about 3.8 billion years ago. Geologists have concluded that earth was heavily bombarded by comets and asteroids until about 3.9-3.85 billion years ago. During these bombardments it would not have been possible for life to have developed or existed. Therefore the window for the first life to develop was less than 100 million years, probably closer to only 50 million years. In evolutionary thinking, that is an impossibly small time to produce life by chance.

- **Only left-handed amino acids**. Amino acids are the building blocks of proteins. As mentioned earlier, amino acids exist in both so called left-handed and right-handed orientations (this property is called *chirality*). These orientations are determined by how the different chemical groups are attached to the central carbon atom. For not-yet-understood scientific reasons, only chains of left-handed amino acids are able to produce a working protein molecule. Therefore right-handed amino acids in any "soup" are a serious challenge for life developing by evolution (a combination of chance and time). However all known amino acids producing reactions furnish chiral molecules in equal proportion – 50% left-handed and 50% right-handed. Scientists agree the odds of finding any "soup" that consists of only left-handed amino acids is implausible. As such a "soup" is a prerequisite to even consider evolutionary assembly of protein molecules, the chirality problem has presented itself as an impenetrable roadblock.

- **The search for chemical pathways.** Evolutionary models require the existence of so called *chemical pathways* (chains of subsequent chemical reactions). These chemical pathways should explain how basic elements available on early earth are able to form and assemble proteins and DNA/RNA. Over the past 50 years, researchers have achieved little to no progress with respect to identifying any of these pathways. Pre-life pathways to crucially important biochemical compounds have yet to be discovered and the real possibility remains that these undiscovered pathways just do not exist. More problematic, however, is the total failure of the naturalistic models to identify any pathways that would operate efficiently under the conditions of primordial earth. The conditions of early earth are incompatible with many key prebiotic routes advocated by the origin-of-life community. Given these chemical problems several origin-of-life researchers have concluded that for fundamental chemical reasons, undirected chemical processes cannot lead to life.

HOW DOES EVOLUTION EXPLAIN THIS?

Ever since Darwin published his book, scientists have struggled with how to explain the beginning of life. And as time has progressed and we have acquired more knowledge, it has become a more and more complex problem.

There are at least a dozen explanations proposed by evolutionists to explain first life. The following are the most widely accepted and well known theories:

1. Life just formed by chance

This is the traditional explanation by evolutionists. It claims that simple living organisms on early earth came into existence by natural processes, random chance, and lots of time. But as we have seen, modern science teaches us that this is inconceivable. As discussed, to form one single protein molecule of about 100 amino acids has a probability of 1 in 10^{220}. The prospects for a complete cell to assemble by chance are even much smaller. In other words, the odds are effectively zero. That's why only people who are not educated about this subject still believe life emerged by chance. Objective scientists simply don't believe this anymore, even if they don't believe in a Creator. In the words of late mathematician, physicist, and professor of astronomy, Fred Hoyle:

"At all events, anyone with even a nodding acquaintance with the Rubik cube will concede the near-impossibility of a solution being obtained by a blind person moving the cube faces at random. Now imagine 10^{50} blind persons each with a scrambled Rubik cube, and try to conceive of the chance of them all <u>simultaneously</u> arriving at the solved form. You then have the chance of arriving by random shuffling of just one of the many biopolymers [= a protein] on which life depends. The notion that not only the biopolymers but the operating programme of a living cell could be arrived at by chance in a primordial organic soup here on the earth is evidently nonsense of a high order." [50]

2. Chemical affinity

One of the first theories – still taught in many textbooks – argues that the emergence of life actually might have been *biochemically predestined* because of chemical bonding preferences. According to this theory, some kind of inherent attraction would cause amino acids to spontaneously link up in the right sequence, creating the protein molecules.

However, more extensive experiments and computer models have demonstrated conclusively (1986) that the sequencing has nothing to do with chemical preferences. Now, even Dean Kenyon, one of its biggest early proponents, has repudiated the idea. [51]

3. Panspermia – life from space

Desperate for a secular explanation for the origins of life on earth combined with the relatively short amount of time available for life to develop ("only" about 50-100 million years), some scientists have turned to space. They seriously consider the possibility that life might have started somewhere else in the universe and was brought ("hitchhiked") to earth on a rock or rocks that hit our planet. This idea is labeled *Panspermia*.

A related idea is that life formed first on early Mars. Some of these life forms were blasted off Mars by an asteroid or comet impact. Over time this material landed on earth and was the beginning of life (Sounds like the basis for a script for the movie *Mission to Mars [2000]*).

Both of these theories are even more difficult to find evidence for and may have to wait for samples to be taken from comets and Mars for further study. Noteworthy is that neither of them actually answers the question of how life first originated, but merely shifts it to another planet or a comet, still leaving the real question of origins of life unanswered.[52]

4. RNA world

By far the most popular line of thinking in the scientific evolutionary world today is the concept that life must have originated in an *RNA world*. If you recall, RNA is a sub-string from the DNA containing a detailed set of instructions to build molecules, like proteins. The idea is that if RNA would be present, part of the problem of building proteins would be solved (you would still need the molecular machines to read the RNA code and build the proteins). The theory claims that simple RNA was assembled by natural processes and chance/time from the early "soup" on earth. This simple RNA subsequently evolved by replicating itself into more and more advanced structures, able to produce proteins and ultimately evolve into DNA.

Today, research in the RNA world is a medium-sized industry. Scientists in this field can demonstrate that random sequences of RNA sometimes exhibit useful properties. However despite the vast amounts of money spent on experiments and research since the mid 1980s, no hard evidence has been produced about how any RNA could evolve into a complete simple living cell.

And obviously, nobody is able to explain how even the simplest RNA strain could form by chance from the "soup"! A recent quote illustrates the lack of progress:

"Is this a fact or a hope? I would have thought it relevant to point out for 'biologists in general' that not one self-replicating RNA has emerged to date from quadrillions (10^{24}) of artificially synthesized, random RNA sequences." [53]

A short and honest summary of the above theories and explanations would be "*they do not know.*" The more we learn about how a living cell works, the less we can scientifically understand how this all could have come about. If one does not want to consider God as the Creator, evolutionists are at a dead end. Secular explanations are harder and harder to develop. It's amazing to observe to what extent evolutionary scientists are willing to push their theories into the realm of ridiculous extremes in order to avoid a supernatural explanation. Anything goes, no matter how extravagant, as long as a Creator is not involved.

As an illustration of an honest confession of "*we just do not know,*" please read the following excerpt from an interview by (PBS) NOVA published on their website with Dr. Andrew Knoll (emphasis added):[54]

NOVA: *In a nutshell, what is the process? How does life form?*

Knoll: *The short answer is* <u>we don't really know how life originated</u> *on this planet. There have been a variety of experiments that tell us some possible roads, but we remain <u>in substantial ignorance</u>. That said, I think what we're looking for is some kind of molecule that is simple enough that it can be made by physical processes on the young earth, yet complicated enough that it can take charge of making more of itself. That, I think, is the moment when we cross that great divide and start moving toward something that most people would recognize as living.*

NOVA: *Will we ever solve the problem?*

Knoll: *I don't know. I imagine <u>my grandchildren will still be sitting around saying that it's a great mystery</u>, but that they will understand that mystery at a level that would be incomprehensible to us today.*

As Klaus Dose, a biochemist considered one of the foremost experts in this area, stated:

"More than thirty years of experimentation on the origin of life in the fields of chemical and molecular evolution have led to a better perception of the immensity of the problem of the origin of life on earth rather than to its solution. At present <u>all discussions on principle theories and experiments in the field either end in stalemate or in a confession of ignorance</u>."[55]

And finally in the words of Harvard biologist Marc Kirschner and Berkeley biologist John Gerhard who wrote as recently as 2005:

"Everything about evolution before the bacteria-like life forms is sheer conjecture," because "evidence is completely lacking about what preceded this early cellular ancestor."[56]

CHAPTER 6

From Bacteria to Human Beings

"So God created man in his own image,
in the image of God he created him;
Male and female he created them."
GENESIS 1:27

Suppose simple life forms exist on a life-supporting planet. How could these develop into more complex life forms and ultimately into human beings? This was the focus of Darwin's theory in *The Origin of Species*. He claimed (as evolutionists still insist) that, given enough time, more complex life forms evolve merely by chance and natural processes. Now, 150 years later, has modern science discovered the mechanisms that made this happen? Have intermediate species been found that support the model? Or does the evidence point the other way?

The evolutionary textbooks offer various examples of "evolution" within species as proof of their theory. These include the beaks of finches, fruit flies, and bacteria resistant to antibiotics. But are these genuine examples of evolution? To get a better grasp of the process that makes these changes occur, it is necessary to understand the difference between changes of characteristics within the same species and changes that transform one species into another species. These two kinds of changes, respectively called *natural selection* (or also *survival of the fittest*) and *genetic mutations* prove to be quite different.

NATURAL SELECTION OR SURVIVAL OF THE FITTEST

Traditional evolutionary theory – also called *Darwinism* – considers *natural selection* the driving force behind evolution. It is the observation that individual organisms with favorable characteristics are more likely to survive and reproduce than those lacking these traits. As a result, subsequent generations are largely composed of the organisms with favorable traits, so these traits will occur more and more. After a number of generations, all organisms will have the favorable traits, and those without them will have died out. Hence, natural selection is also a *survival of the fittest*, as Darwin liked to call this process.

Darwin's research was based on breeding. He himself was an active breeder of pigeons and vigorously researched the principles behind breeding, which he called *controlled selection*. This combined with his observations of unusual variations in animals on the Galapagos islands in South America, while traveling on the *HMS Beagle* in the 1830s lead him to his theory of natural selection.

One of his most famous illustrations from *The Origin of Species* has come to be known as *Darwin's Finches*, and it is still used in most evolutionary textbooks. Darwin noticed that the beaks of the Galapagos finches were distinctively different than those of finches in England. The Galapagos beaks were longer and more pointed. He concluded that the sustained periods of drought and the rocky terrain of the islands were such, that only finches with long beaks could survive. To secure food, these birds had to dig deeper into harder soils than the finches in England. So he reasoned that finches with short beaks on the Galapagos would not last long. After natural selection through numerous generations, only a population with the longer, more pointed beaks could remain.

DOES NATURAL SELECTION LEAD TO NEW SPECIES?

There are many other illustrations of natural selection. For instance, today there are as many as 200 breeds of dogs. Did you know that most of these breeds did not exist in the days of Jesus? Likely all dogs then were similar in terms of size, hair, color, behavior, etc., and looked like what we now would call "a common street dog." So does this mean that in only 2,000 years dogs have evolved into 200 new species? If so, this, like Darwin's Finches, would be convincing evidence for evolution.

That, however, is not the case. Genetics has taught us how natural selection works. Every organism has unique DNA, grouped in genes on chromosomes. The genes are the units of genetic information that specify the "blueprint" for a particular characteristic of the organism. For instance in human beings, certain combinations of genes will control eye color, hair color, skin color, height and blood group, as well as tendencies for high blood pressure and heart disease.

Through breeding and/or natural selection, certain genetic characteristics are favored over others. As these characteristics are controlled by genes, the organisms with these traits have their genes "set" to produce these characteristics. Therefore, offspring in subsequent generations are likely to have these same gene settings, resulting in a dominance or even exclusivity of these favored characteristics. So in a pure-breed dog, the genetic information passed down from the parents is set to the desired characteristics of the breed. The genetic information that would produce the non-desired characteristics has disappeared through the selective breeding of the previous generations. Hence in terms of genetic information, pure breeds have less genetic diversity than "street dogs." Let me illustrate. A pure breed Labrador will have only the genetic information that produces the characteristics of a Labrador. In a similar way, a pure breed German Shepherd has only the genetic information for the characteristics of a German Shepherd. A dog from the local dog pound, however, with a Labrador and a German Shepherd as his parents will have genetic information from both breeds. This animal might be less appealing to dog owners, but from a genetics standpoint, it is actually "richer" in genetic information than the pure breed.

Thus natural selection or breeding does NOT lead to new species. It only emphasizes certain characteristics selected through controlled breeding (dogs) or the natural environment (Darwin's Finches). It is always reversible. That is, if controlled breeding stops and the various breeds of dogs are allowed to mate together, in just a few generations all dogs once again will appear to be quite average.

Or in the case of Darwin's Finches, it has been observed on the Galapagos Islands that the beaks of the finches do not continue to grow. Actually the opposite happens – in rainy periods, the beaks grow smaller, more like the "traditional" finch beaks observed in Europe.[57]

As nicely summarized by Dr. Elmer Noble:[58]

"Natural selection can act only on those biological properties that already exist; it cannot create properties in order to meet adaptational needs."

Natural selection is widely observed in the world around us. Unfortunately it is often misused as evidence for evolutionary changes. Most evolutionary textbooks claim Darwin's Finches as well as peppered moths, bacteria resistant to antibiotics, and insects resistant to insecticide as evidences for evolution. However these are mere examples of natural selection. By favoring certain existing characteristics, the offspring of the organism has a better chance of survival. No new characteristics are formed, and over time, if the condition that favors these characteristics disappears, the suppressed characteristics begin to appear once more.

To make things even more confusing, these variations within a species are also dubbed *micro-evolution*, suggesting permanent changes in the species on a small scale. As explained, these changes might appear significant and permanent, but they are not. No new genetic information is added, actually the opposite happened – genetic information is lost.

☼ EXHIBIT #6: NO MECHANISM FOR SPECIES TO EVOLVE

For real evolution to occur, however, one species must change – evolve – into another species. This new species needs to have a set of genes different from that of the original species. Evolution claims that when small errors occur (also called *genetic mutations*) genetic information (DNA/genes) from the parents to the offspring is changed, deleted, or added. Mutations can be caused by copying errors in the genetic material during cell division and by exposure to radiation or viruses. Genes are changed or deleted, or new ones are created. These revised/new genes allow new characteristics to develop in the species. This process is controlled wholly by chance. Errors in the copying process can be neutral, positive, or negative.

If these characteristics are beneficial (*favorable mutations*), evolution claims that natural selection will ensure that these new characteristics will be favored and the species will evolve. The *less favorable mutations* are removed from the gene pool. In evolutionary biology, natural selection is the force that transforms species into other species by helping select/keep favorable changes caused by mutations which occur during reproduction.

Neutral mutations are the genetic changes that do not influence the fitness of either the species or the individuals within the species. The *overwhelming majority* of mutations have no significant effect, since *DNA repair* is able to reverse most changes before they become permanent mutations, and many organisms have mechanisms for eliminating otherwise permanently mutated cells.

DNA repair is a built-in mechanism that "proofreads" itself during replication. During reproduction, the offspring gets a complete set of DNA from each parent. Of the two strands on the pair of chromosomes, one strand is passed from the father and one from the mother. If a gene on one strand is "damaged," it is neglected and only the healthy genetic instructions on the other strand will be used. If both strands are healthy, various dominancy mechanisms control how the characteristics of parents are passed on to the offspring. Only if both strands are damaged at the same location on the DNA, will there be a possible mutation effect.

This immediately raises an important question: If genetic mutation is the mechanism of change, why would this process essential to make evolution possible develop a mechanism that would repair itself and actually prevent change? That just does not seem to make any logical sense.

It is very important to understand that each of these mutations is a very small step and occurs completely randomly at the level of DNA base pairs (DNA letters). For any new characteristic to form, a significant number of subsequent mutations are needed to evolve into a new gene or significantly revised gene. Since this is controlled only by random chance, many generations would be required, spanning extremely long periods of time.

For this to occur, the DNA of the original species must mutate – by chance or mistake in the copying process – into a new set of DNA with better, more complex, characteristics. On the surface this may sound reasonable, but this process (also known as *macro-evolution*) has <u>never</u> been observed in nature. When mutations are observed, almost uniformly they result in reduced and damaged genetic information.

Let's read what some experts have to say about genetic mutations:

"But in all the reading I've done in the life-sciences literature, I've never found a mutation that added information... All point mutations that have been studied on the molecular level turn out to reduce the genetic information and not increase it." [59]

"Mutations are almost universally harmful. In human beings, they are classified as 'birth defects.' They result in death and sterility. People today suffer from more than 4,000 disorders caused by gene mutations. Down's syndrome, cystic fibrosis and sickle cell anemia are familiar examples." [60]

"Mutations are rare phenomena, and a simultaneous change of even two amino acid residues into one protein is totally unlikely... One could think, for instance, that by constantly changing amino acids one by one, it will eventually be possible to change the entire sequence substantially... These minor changes, however, are bound to eventually result in a situation in which the enzyme has ceased to perform its previous function but has not yet begun its 'new duties'. It is at this point that it will be destroyed – along with the organism carrying it." [61]

Mutations occur, but only rarely. Can we quantify how rare this really is? Research[62] shows most non-lethal mutations are neutral. That is, they have no discernible effect on the characteristics of the organism. Of the remaining mutations, the vast majority are harmful to the species. Depending on the species, the ratio of harmful to favorable mutations falls between 10,000 to 1 and 10,000,000 to 1.[63]

This is why inbreeding in humans (having children with close relatives) increases the chances of genetic diseases quite dramatically. Damages ("mutations") of the DNA of related people are likely to occur at the same location on their chromosomes. So if they would have children, these children would have a significantly increased chance of a mutation that could not by corrected by DNA repair. You could say: good news for evolution, as that would surely increase the opportunities to "evolve" the human species. However as the results are universally negative and manifest themselves as genetic disorders and diseases, it is better to avoid these situations.

Confusing terminology

Is micro-evolution evolution? The evolution debate often becomes quite foggy by the careless use of terminology. For example, *micro-evolution* describes small changes within a species, while *macro-evolution* is the dramatic change from one species to another. Talk about micro-evolution might suggest that macro-evolution happens, but that is not the case. Micro-evolution is only another term for natural selection. The fact that modern humans are getting taller is often said to be an example of micro-evolution. Subsequently this is cited as proof of Darwinian evolution.

Not valid! First – and this might surprise you – humans are not necessarily getting taller. Yes, statistically the average height of people in industrialized nations has increased by about four inches (10 centimeters) during the last 150 years. However, examination of skeletons shows no significant differences in height from the Stone Age through the early 1800s. Even the Middle Ages produced numerous accounts of people taller than six feet, and that was not considered an exceptional height. Most scientists today believe this increase in height simply occurred thanks to better nutrition. This is supported by the fact that height seems to be leveling off.[64]

Second, even if this is micro-evolution (natural selection), it is no proof of evolution. As we have extensively demonstrated, micro-evolution only optimizes existing genetic information in an organism to maximize its opportunity in its environment – nothing more. It adds nothing to a species, there is no new genetic information, no mutations occur, and its changes can easily be reversed. A taller-than-average person is not a new human species, just as a Chihuahua and a German Shepherd are quite different, but are both dogs.

This confusing terminology seems to be deliberately used by many evolutionists in text books, articles, and debates to suggest that micro-evolution is evidence of evolution from one species into another. In many textbooks, the illustrations are drawn from natural selection. The authors then claim that macro-evolution is a fact because micro-evolution has been observed. However, trying to prove evolution merely by showing natural selection is intellectual dishonesty.[65]

Based on the above, one can only conclude that the case for mutations as the driving force behind the evolution of one species into another more advanced species is on very shaky ground and lacks support from factual evidence. First, the mechanism of DNA-repair prevents a mutation at one of the DNA bases (the DNA letter level) to have any effect unless the corresponding base on the other chromosome is also damaged. Second, even if the mutation is not corrected by DNA-repair, the vast majority of these mutations have no effect on the organism. And third, if a mutation is not neutral but has an effect, this effect is almost always harmful. Think about it: about 4,000 years of recorded history of the human race report numerous disorders, or birth defects, but no "*X-men.*"[66]

BUT CHIMPS AND HUMANS ARE 98.77% IDENTICAL!

October 2006 *Time Magazine*[67] reported that after mapping the human genome, scientists also completed the mapping of the genetic record for the chimpanzee. They have concluded that of the approximate three billion base pairs of the human genome (this are all the DNA letters together, forming the estimated 20,000-25,000 human genes) an amazing 98.77% are the same as the chimp genome. In other words, a chimp is only 1.23% genetically different from a human.

Convincing evidence, claim evolutionists, for the idea that man must share a common ancestor with chimpanzees. As the article in *Time Magazine* states: "*Genetic clues would suggest that the last ancestor chimps and humans had in common lived as recently as 6 million years ago.*"

Really? Is that what this proves? The fact that the genetic record of humans has very significant similarities with animals does not by itself prove evolution. Similarity in physical features between animals in general and animals and humans is quite evident. Most animals and humans have one head, one pair of eyes, one mouth, four "arms" and "legs," fingers or claws, skin as well as very similar internal organs, digestive system, lungs, hearth, brains, and ears, so this fact surprises nobody. In many evolutionary textbooks this is often presented as evidence of *homology*, assuming common ancestry and hence proving evolution.

However homology does not prove evolution at all. Evolutionists claim homology shows common ancestry, and common ancestry demonstrates homology; this is no more than a weak case of circular reasoning.[68] Creationists can build a similar case claiming homology as evidence for design. After all, if a Creator designed/created a large variety of creatures would it not be logical to expect them to share a large level of similarity. When engineers design a new transportation vehicle, is it not likely to share many of the characteristics of existing cars such as wheels, engine, brakes, doors, and seats?

For a chimp to evolve to a human being would require a total of 1.23% of 3,000,000,000 mutations of DNA base pairs. That 1.23% is still a whopping

3.69 million mutations of DNA letters! And as Darwinian evolution claims, these mutations are supposed to happen randomly in small steps over many subsequent generations. These numbers and the improbability of mutations to be beneficial make the alleged six million years to a common ancestor sound very, very optimistic!

What about the fruit fly experiments?[69]

In an attempt to provide observational evidence, evolutionists put their hypothesis to the test with what is known as the "genetic workhorse" of evolution: a fruit fly named *Drosophila*. Evolutionary scientists have tried to change Drosophila through various means over the past 75 years in an effort to force it to mutate into some new life form. Even with much intelligent intervention, and under laboratory-controlled conditions, all of the efforts of evolutionists have failed. Yes, Drosophila has changed – from normal to eyeless to orange-eyed to short-winged to yellow, and finally to ebony, but it remains what it has always been – a fruit fly. The changes caused by natural selection (micro-evolution) – changes only within the species – are not changes from one type of life form to another life form. Instead of showing genetic boundaries do not exist, Drosophila has demonstrated just the opposite!

Why can't evolutionary geneticists get Drosophila to become a new life form? The simple answer is that the genetic code of the fruit fly has certain limits, and the information needed to transform that code into a new life form does not exist within the molecular structure or design parameters of Drosophila. Furthermore, a new genetic type requires more than just gene modification – it needs new genetic information/material and the intelligence to construct it. Consequently, if intelligent evolutionists cannot accomplish this task by their own ingenuity, why should it be reasonable that such could happen by accidental genetic variations? The fruit fly experiments provide solid observational evidence confirming the implausibility of both artificial and natural selection as viable mechanisms in support of evolution. In fact, their research serves as a strong case to authenticate the Creator model's claim that micro-evolutionary variation occurs within the range of genetic limits.

A MORE IN-DEPTH LOOK AT DNA

We have seen that cells are the fundamental working units of every living system. All the instructions needed to direct their activities are contained within the chemical DNA stored in every cell.

DNA from all organisms is made up of the same chemical and physical components. The DNA sequence is the particular side-by-side arrangement of bases (DNA "letters") along the DNA strand (e.g., ATTCCGGA). This order spells out the exact instructions required to create a particular organism with its own unique traits.

The *genome* is an organism's complete set of DNA. Genomes vary widely in size: the smallest known genome for a free-living organism (a bacterium) contains about 600,000 *DNA base pairs*, while human and mouse genomes have some three billion. Except for mature red blood cells, all human cells contain a complete genome.

DNA in the human genome is arranged into 23 pairs of *chromosomes* – physically separated molecules that range in length from about 50 million to 250 million base pairs. Each chromosome contains many *genes*, the basic physical and functional units of heredity. Genes are specific sequences of DNA base pairs that encode instructions on how to make proteins. Genes comprise only a small percentage of the human genome (close to two percent); the remainder consists of *non-coding DNA* (also referred to as *junk DNA*), whose functions may include providing chromosomal structural integrity and regulating where, when, and in what quantity proteins are made. The human genome is estimated to contain 20,000 – 25,000 genes.

At the end of the chromosome there is a highly repetitive section of DNA called a *telomere*. Scientists believe these telomeres control the number of times DNA can successfully be copied during cell replication. More about this later.[70]

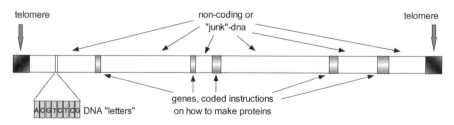

Figure 6-1: A Simplified Chromosome Strand

JUNK DNA, EVIDENCE FOR EVOLUTION OR DESIGN?

In molecular biology, *non-coding DNA*, or *junk DNA*, is a collective label for the portions of the DNA sequence of a chromosome for which no function has yet been identified. Currently of the human genome, about 97% of all DNA has been designated as "junk."

Evolutionists initially considered the presence of junk DNA as a strong argument for the random process of evolution and against involvement of an intelligent Creator: "*Why would a perfect God create DNA which is primarily composed of useless, non-functional sections?*"

According to one evolutionary explanation, the sections of junk DNA consist either of randomly produced sequences that are non-functional or are leftovers from ancestor DNA no longer used. Another evolutionary claim is that the junk DNA is like a parasite, also called *selfish DNA*, because it consists of DNA that preferentially replicated more efficiently than coding DNA.

As knowledge grows, numerous studies find more actual use of large sections of what was previously considered junk material. First it has become clear, using statistical techniques, that the non-coding DNA is actually highly uniform and patterned and by far not just random. Second, more definitive studies have shown that non-coding DNA provides structure to DNA so it can perform functions impossible without some form of structure. Third, it has become evident that the non-coding DNA sections play a role as enhancers for transcription of certain genes. Fourth, the existence of so called *pseudo-genes* (copies of regular genes in the non-coding sections) has proved to play an important role in the proper working of the corresponding regular genes.

Lastly, it now appears that sections of the non-coding DNA play a role as molecular switches to tell genes when and where to turn on and off. Dr C. Owen Lovejoy in the earlier mentioned *Time Magazine* article:[71] "*Take the genes involved in creating the hand, the penis and the vertebrae. These share some of the same structural genes... It is like having the blueprints for two different brick houses. The bricks are the same, but the results are very different.*" The article goes on to say: "*Those molecular switches lie in the non-coding regions of the genome – once known dismissively as junk DNA, but lately rechristened the dark matter of the genome.*"

The "evolution" of junk-DNA from "junk" to "dark matter" illustrates that non-coding DNA is not evolutionary left-over material and that the science of genetics still has a long way to go to understand fully the purpose and working of DNA in the cell replication process.

Berra's blunder[72]

In 1990, Ohio State University biologist Tim Berra published a book intended to refute critics of Darwinian evolution.[73] To illustrate how the fossil record provides evidence of species evolving from less developed and sophisticated ancestors, Berra used illustrations of various models of Corvettes. He wrote: *"If you compare a 1953 and a 1954 Corvette, side by side, then a 1954 and a 1955 model, and so on, the descent with modification is overwhelmingly obvious."* However in evolutionary theory, descent means biological reproduction. Automobiles are designed and assembled, not merely born. So the Corvettes analogy actually proves the opposite of what Berra intended – namely, that a succession of similarities does not provide evidence for biological evolution but shows similarity because of design!

Darwin critic, and major contributor to the current Intelligent Design movement, Philip Johnson called this *"Berra's Blunder."*[74]

☼ Exhibit #7: The Fossil Record

Fossils are the mineralized or otherwise preserved remains or traces of animals, plants, and other organisms. Fossils are found in rock formations and sedimentary layers (also called strata). In many school books the *fossil record* is heralded as strong and objective evidence for the evolution model. Evolutionists claim that the presence of fossils of simpler life forms in older rocks and strata than fossils of more complex life forms proves evolution over time from simple to complex organisms.

However, the fact that older organisms are less developed than more recent life forms is not exclusive evidence for the evolutionary model, but also consistent with a Creator model.

The fossil record, however, does reveal two major discrepancies between the observed fossils and those fossils one would expect to see according to the evolution model: *the lack of fossils of intermediate species* and the so called *Cambrian Explosion.*

Where Are the Intermediate Species?

If evolution is correct, new species gradually develop through subsequent small mutations. If so, it would logically follow that the fossil record would overflow with evidence of a long series of organisms revealing minor changes over time. Yet the evidence shows only the opposite. The fossils reveal the abrupt appearance of new species with no evidence of prior, gradual development. Additionally, most fossils found are not of extinct animals or organisms, but are very similar (and often identical) to creatures living today. All in all, the fossil record shows no signs of change – any change – in species whatsoever. In Darwin's time this was common knowledge, and Charles Darwin himself considered this the most serious challenge to his fabled theory. In his words:

> *"Why is not every geological formation and every stratum full of such intermediate links? Geology assuredly does not reveal any such finely graduated organic chain; and <u>this is the most obvious and serious objection which can be urged against the theory</u>."*[75]

Darwin hoped that over time, with more detailed research through more sophisticated means, the fossil record would expand to include fossils of the intermediate links. However, despite the millions and millions of fossils found and studied (*"97.7 percent of living orders of land vertebrates are represented as fossils"*),[76] fossils of intermediate species have never been found! As Darwin himself acknowledged, this is the most obvious and serious objection against his theory, showing it is flawed! If he would be alive today, based on this statement, he himself would be hard pressed to believe in evolution.

What is the fossil record?
The vast majority of fossils are from marine life:[77]
- 95% of all fossils are marine invertebrates, particularly shellfish.
- Of the remaining 5%, 95% are algae and plant fossils (4.75% of all fossils).
- 95% of the remaining 0.25% are of the other vertebrates, including insects (0.23775%).
- The remaining 0.0125% includes all vertebrates, mostly fish. Of the few land vertebrates 95% consists of less than one bone. For example, only about 1,200 dinosaur skeletons have been found. Of the mammal fossils, 95% have been deposited during the Ice Age.

This, however, has not stopped the authors of evolutionary textbooks. As an example, one textbook boldly claims:

> *"Fishes are considered to be the most primitive living vertebrates… similarities in structure and embryological development show that fishes and modern invertebrate chordates probably did evolve from common invertebrate ancestors that lived many millions of years ago."*[78]

Not a single intermediate fossil is identified in the textbook to support this claim!

The same is true of the famous *"missing link"* or *"common ancestor"* between ape (chimp) and man as claimed by many textbooks and even the above mentioned *Time Magazine* article. If man and ape evolved from a common ancestor millions of years ago, where are the fossils of these ancestors and the transitional life forms, the half ape/half man? Yes, some bones, teeth, and other claimed remains have been found of alleged human ancestors, but closer analysis has shown that they are either very similar to modern men, or apes, or inconclusive, or even hoaxes. Available material is very scarce and highly questionable. The scientific community seems unable to reach any consensus about how to interpret and how to date these findings. In fact, in the absence of the many transitional forms demanded by evolution, most often presented is the "discovery" of a tooth or partial bone fragment, then pronounced to be a transitional form. This is flimsy evidence for what should be untold millions of transitional fossils!

As Jonathan Wells explains in his interview with Lee Strobel in *Case for a Creator* (2004):[79]

> *"One of the major problems with paleo-anthropology is that compared to all fossils we have, only a minuscule number are believed to be of creatures ancestral to humans. Often, it's just skull fragments or teeth. So this gives a lot of elasticity in reconstructing the specimens to fit evolutionary theory. Of course, this lack of fossil evidence also makes it virtually impossible to reconstruct supposed relationships between ancestors and descendents. One anthropologist likened the task to trying to reconstruct the plot of 'War and Peace' by using just thirteen random pages from the book."*

Despite the abundance of fossils and remains of "ancient" apes, men and even dinosaurs, evolutionists have yet to find even one of the evolutionary human ancestors!

THE CAMBRIAN EXPLOSION – BIOLOGY'S BIG BANG

Surprisingly, the recovered fossil record provides compelling evidence for the case of the Creator model, by revealing the *Cambrian Explosion*, or *Biology's Big Bang*.

The Cambrian Explosion was a geological period of about 5-10 million years that started about 530 million years ago. It is called Biology's Big Bang because during this period, suddenly the body design/plans (phyla) of most all the living animals known today came into existence as well as some now extinct. The fossil record shows jellyfish, sponges, and worms prior to the Cambrian Explosion (however no evidence of gradual development). Then in the beginning of the Cambrian period, like a Big Bang, suddenly representatives of all the major body plans turn up in the fossils.

This completely defies Darwin's common ancestor theory. These animals, fundamentally very different from one another in their body plans, appear fully developed, all of a sudden, in what evolutionary paleontologists have called *"the single most spectacular phenomenon of the fossil record."* Renowned paleontologist James Valentine agrees the Cambrian Explosion *"is real; it is too big to be masked by flaws in the fossil record."* Indeed as more fossils are discovered, it becomes clear that the Cambrian Explosion was *"even more abrupt and extensive than previously envisioned."*[80]

Paleontologist Harry Whittington, who extensively studied the Cambrian Explosion in the Burgess Shale in the Rocky Mountains in Western Canada, wrote:

> *"I look skeptically upon diagrams that show the branching diversity of animal life through time, and come down at the base to a single kind of animal…Animals may have originated more than once, in different places at different times."* [81]

CHAPTER 7

Other Compelling Evidences

"In the beginning was the Word, and the Word was with God,
and the Word was God. He was with God in the beginning.
Through Him all things were made."
JOHN 1:1-3

At this point it has become evident that the Big Bang model and its evolutionary timeline are in serious trouble. The evolution model does not provide an explanation for the cause of the Big Bang event, nor can it explain the apparent design of the laws and constants of nature. If it all happened by chance, the universe should be bubbling with life; however, earth has emerged as potentially the only planet where life is possible and it seems uniquely "prepared" for observation of our solar system, our galaxy, and the rest of space. Even if earth was the result of "winning the cosmic lottery" against inconceivable odds, after decades of intense research scientists have made no progress on their quest to explain how the first living organisms came into existence. The previous chapter showed that there is no viable mechanism for simple life forms to evolve to more complex ones. As the final nail in the coffin of the evolutionary timeline, the fossil record does not confirm the existence of intermediate species. On the contrary, it shows the abrupt occurrence of completely formed phyla during the Cambrian Explosion.

Still, there is more evidence to share. In this chapter, we will examine another cluster of exhibits that reveal divine involvement in the creation of our universe and our very existence.

☼ EXHIBIT #8: THE AGE OF THE HUMAN RACE

Through the last decades science has struggled to estimate the age of the human race. Obviously, evolution would insist this occurred a long time ago, as it would take an incredible span of time for the first human-like creature (the *cave man* or *monkey man*) to develop into the sophisticated humans of today.

First, it must be observed that current estimates for the age of mankind are still all over the board. The lack of reliable dating methods for organic material is a serious challenge for all paleo-anthropologists.[82] This might surprise you, but the only reliable dating method for organic material is *Carbon-14 dating*. This procedure can date organic material such as bones and teeth accurately but only to a maximum of 25,000-30,000 years. Dating older organic material is nothing more than guesswork. In many cases these guesses rely on "leap of faith" assumptions by dating the rocks found near the organic material in question, wildly asserting these rocks were formed at the same time as the bones/skull/teeth were deposited. Obviously that is not science, but only wishful thinking.

BIOCHEMICAL DATES FOR EARLY MAN AND WOMAN

Recently the advance of genetics has opened a new pathway to estimate the age of mankind through the analysis of human organic material.[83] By comparing samples of currently living humans with well dated DNA samples from the past, an estimate can be made for the rate the human DNA record changes.[84] Applying this estimated natural mutation rate to a representative sampling of the DNA of today's world population allows one to estimate how much time would be required for today's human DNA to mutate ("deteriorate") from a common ancestor. As every cell in the human body contains the combined DNA from both the father and the mother, analyzing this DNA would not allow one to trace the separate ancestry of the male or female. However, two portions of human genetic material do not recombine in reproduction, namely:

Mitochondrial DNA (mtDNA) This DNA resides in the so called *mitochondria*[85] structures, outside the cell's nucleus. Both men and women get nearly all of their *mtDNA* only from their mother. In the late 1980s and early 1990s a number of studies examined the mtDNA of women all over the world. These concluded that all women descended from one "Eve" who lived within the last 200,000 years.[86] Refinements in measurements lowered these original estimates to 135,000 years and finally to less than 100,000 years.[87] These studies not only suggest a much younger age for humanity than previously assumed, but also indicate that all humans descend from ONE woman, ruling out that humans would have simultaneously evolved in multiple locations/regions.

A large segment of the Y-chromosome. Only men have a *Y-chromosome*, most of which they receive only from their father. Since 1995 studies have been conducted to trace genes on this Y-chromosome to determine the age and descent of males. Various studies all indicate younger ages for mankind. What may well be the most reliable study published so far,[88] calculates a common ancestor to modern man at between 37,000 and 49,000 years ago.

These studies also indicate that genetically all humans are much more alike than one would predict from Darwinian theory. Examinations of the genetic sequences of diverse modern human populations reveal minor differences, if any at all. One scientist noted:[89] *"It's a mystery none of us can explain."* All this evidence suggests a recent origin for modern humans, far more recent than evolutionary theory would allow.

Evidence from archaeology and anthropology is consistent with such estimates for the age of humanity. Sophisticated works of art first appear about 40,000-50,000 years ago,[90] and evidence of religious relics and altars date back no earlier than 25,000 years.[91]

Table 7-1 is an overview of the various estimates of the age of mankind in the scientific community over the last decades. It shows how dramatically these estimates have changed and how wrong the initial estimates were by "modern" science. This table also shows the age of the oldest evidences of human civilizations and peoples, based on archaeological finds. Most of these ancient leftovers of human habitation date back only 15,000 years ago. Claims for older finds are rarely presented.

Time period	Estimated age of mankind
In the late 1950s	5 - 15 million years old
In the mid 1970s	5 - 7 million years old
In the late 1970s	1 million years old
In the mid 1980s	800,000 years old
In the late 1980s	50,000 – 200,000 years old
In the mid 1990s	43,000 years old
Current estimates	37,000 (or less) – 49,000 years old
Oldest historical record of civilizations	8,000 – 25,000 years old
The Bible	6,000 – 25,000 years old [92]

Table 7-1: Estimated Age of Mankind during the Last Decades

Accounts in the Biblical book of Genesis mention the descendents from the first man, Adam, through Noah, Abraham, and Moses. Based on the literal reading of this data, it can be calculated that Adam was created by God a little over 6,000 years ago. This is also the date claimed by Six Day Creationists for the actual creation of the world. Other scholars point out the common practice of ancient Hebrew culture to skip generations in the genealogical records. Thus it is conceivable there were substantially more generations between Adam and Abraham than recorded in Genesis. These scholars generally theorize that, based on these records, Adam and Eve could have lived 8,000 to even 25,000 years ago. These views are the basis of the suggested range of 6,000 to 25,000 years old for the age of mankind. These Biblical estimates are surprisingly consistent with those supported by archaeology.

Whichever way one looks at the data, one conclusion is inescapable: as time progresses, estimates from science come ever closer to the age implied by the Biblical accounts.

AN ALTERNATIVE REASONING ABOUT THE AGE OF MANKIND

Today's world population hovers near 6.5 billion people, growing at an annual rate of 2.3%. A somewhat mind-boggling observation is that more people are alive today than have ever lived before! Just in the last one hundred years, the world population has increased more than six-fold!

We can use these numbers and attempt to work backwards to calculate how long it would take to grow this world population at different growth rates starting with "Adam and Eve." The result of this exercise has resulted in table 7-2. Assuming a generation to be 25 years, the table also shows the average number of children per family that corresponds with the growth rate.

Growth rate	Average # children[93]	Age of mankind
2 %	3.3	1,150 years
1 %	2.5	2,275 years
0.5 %	2.25	4,550 years
0.25 %	2.12	9,100 years

Table 7-2: Growth Rates Versus the Age of Mankind

This demonstrates that even with a very low growth rate of the population, such as 0.5% (quite low compared to the current 2.3%) and the average number of children per family 2.25, only 4,550 years would be required to grow a population of 6.5 billion from just one original couple. Even with the growth rate at only 0.25%, only 9,100 years would be required to achieve the same.

One might claim that the lack of medical knowledge dramatically lowered the average life expectancy of our "ancient" ancestors, forcing the growth rate to be much lower. However, mankind has a strong drive to populate and continue to preserve and grow the species. As observed often today, areas with the lowest degree of development and by far the lowest life expectancy see their population growing the fastest. Women can bear children in their teenage years, so even a life expectancy of only 25 or 30 years of age, still gives more than enough time to get large families.

The same applies for the aftermath of epidemics (for instance, the plague in Europe in 1347, see figure 7-1)[94] and the effect of major wars or other catastrophes. Historical records show usually a population boom right after the catastrophic event. This boom compensates within a few generations for the more than average loss of life. For instance, the devastating plagues of 1347 killed an estimated 50-75% of the population in many European countries, but in less than 200 years, the dip in population had been completely recovered. That's why the generation born right after WWII is called, *the Baby Boomers.*

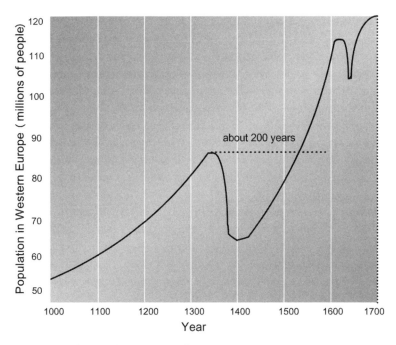

Figure 7-1: The Population Boom after the European Plagues

A similar line of thinking challenges that even the low range of the biochemical estimate of 37,000 years of human habitation might still be too high. If the "first family" was alive that long ago, even at a low growth rate of 0.5% we now should have a world population of 1.4×10^{80} (that would be calculated as $[1 + 0.005$ (the 0.5% growth rate)] $^\wedge$ 37,000 [years]).

Lastly, please notice that the global flood described by the Bible supposedly happened about 4,500-5,000 years ago. This event would be quite consistent with the above calculations of growth rate and size of today's world population.

☀ EXHIBIT #9: IRREDUCIBLE COMPLEX MACHINES

In *Darwin's Black Box*[95] biochemist Michael Behe demonstrates the existence and importance of so called *"irreducible complex molecular machines."* These complicated, microscopically small biological systems cannot have been assembled, evolved, or combined in gradual steps (as the evolution model would claim), because the system works only if all components are present and "connected" correctly. If only one component is missing, the irreducible complex machine will not work. To illustrate, Behe refers to an ordinary mousetrap. The mousetrap works only if all components are present. If the spring or the hammer or any other component is missing, the whole mousetrap would be useless.

Therefore these molecular machines cannot have been assembled "step by step," but had to be fully present from the start. At present the most famous example is the bacterial flagellum (figure 7-2). In the words of Behe:[96] *"Some bacteria boast a marvelous swimming device, the flagellum, which has no counterpart in more complex cells. In 1973 it was discovered that some bacteria swim by rotating their flagella. So the bacterial flagellum acts as a rotary propeller. The flagellum is a long, hair-like filament embedded in the cell membrane. The external filament consists of a single type of protein, called "flagellin." The flagellin filament is the paddle surface that contacts the liquid during swimming. At the end of the flagellin filament near the surface of the cell, there is a bulge in the thickness of the flagellum. It is here that the filament attaches to the rotor drive. The attachment material is comprised of something called "hook protein." The filament of a bacterial flagellum, contains no motor protein; if it is broken off, the filament just floats stiffly in the water. Therefore the motor that rotates the filament-propeller must be located somewhere else. Experiments have demonstrated that it is located at the base of the flagellum, where electron microscopy shows several ring structures occur."*

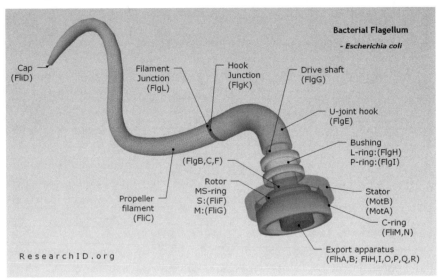

Figure 7-2: The Bacterial Flagellum[97]

The bacterial flagellum uses a paddling mechanism, and it must meet the same requirements as other such swimming systems. It is necessarily composed of at least three parts – a paddle, a rotor, and a motor. It is irreducibly complex. Gradual evolution of the flagellum faces mammoth hurdles.[98]

This illustration has become so well known that it is now considered the poster child of Intelligent Design and is even called the *Icon of Intelligent Design* by evolution supporters.

Other illustrations of irreducible complex mechanisms in the molecular world are the process of blood clotting, the eye's light-sensing mechanism, and the system of transportation of proteins within cells.

In Origin of Species, Darwin writes: *"If it could be demonstrated that any complex organ existed which could not possibly have been formed by numerous, successive, slight modifications, my theory would absolutely break down."* According to Darwin himself, the existence of these irreducible, complex systems is a devastating blow to the model of evolution!

☼ Exhibit #10: Symbiotic Relationships

A symbiotic relationship, or symbiosis, is the cooperation between two organisms (usually two animals or an animals and a plant) that maintain a more or less intimate association that benefits each of them, establishing a real win-win cooperation. Sometimes they bond so closely they interact with the outside world as a single organism.

Hundreds of examples of symbioses found in nature including the following:

The Goby fish and a shrimp: The shrimp digs and cleans a burrow in the sand in which both the shrimp and the Goby fish live. The shrimp is almost blind and this leaves it vulnerable to predators. The goby fish touches the shrimp with its tail to warn it of impending dangers, and both shrimp and goby fish quickly retreat into the burrow.

Clownfish and sea anemones: Another example is the clownfish that lives among the tentacles of tropical sea anemones. The territorial fish protects its host from anemone-eating fish, and in turn the stinging tentacles of the anemone protect the clownfish (mucus on the clownfish protects it from stings).

Egyptian Plover bird and crocodile: A well-known land version of symbiosis is the relationship of the Egyptian Plover bird and the crocodile. The bird preys on parasites that feed on crocodiles and are potentially harmful to the animal. The crocodile openly invites the bird to hunt on his body, even so far as to allow the bird to enter his mouth safely to hunt. This relationship not only brings the bird a ready source of food, but genuine safety, since few predators dare strike at such proximity to its host.

Oxpecker birds and large animals: The oxpecker picks parasites off large mammals such as the buffalo, elephant, and zebra. It was recently discovered that while the birds do this, they also keep skin wounds on the animals open, and feed on the blood. Hence the relationship between oxpeckers and their hosts is sometimes beneficial for both though at times the oxpecker behaves like a parasite.

The bee and the flower: Bees fly from flower to flower gathering nectar, which they make into food, benefiting the bees. When they land in a flower, the bees get pollen on their hairy bodies, and when they move to the next flower, some pollen rubs off, pollinating the plant. This benefits the plants. In this symbiotic relationship, the bees eat and the plants reproduce.

The bacteria and the human: Certain bacteria live in the intestines of humans and many other animals. The human can not digest all of the food eaten. The bacteria eat this food and partially digest it, allowing the human to finish the job. The bacteria benefit by getting food, and the human benefits by being better able to digest his food.

Symbiotic relationships are strong evidences for Intelligent Design. After all, how could two organisms so different from each other independently evolve into a relationship where together they use their individual strengths and complement their weaknesses?

☼ EXHIBIT #11: THE LAW OF ENTROPY

Everyone – and everything – grows older and continuously deteriorates. Anything unattended turns from order to chaos, from a high level of organization to a lower level. This is a universal truth. Consequently, people get sick and die, buildings and bridges collapse, cars break down, landscapes erode, and natural resources deplete. No matter how hard we try, we will never reverse this process and "grow younger and better." Systems constantly spiral downward to greater disorder. Fix the car, paint the house, pave the drive way over and over, yet some counterforce seems to work persistently to undo it all. This tendency is the universal law of physics known as the *Law of Entropy* or *The Second Law of Thermodynamics*.

This principle is widely considered the most thoroughly proven scientific law with overwhelming evidence all around. Its greatest power is its universal predictive quality that disorder will eventually prevail. The implications are enormous for the universe, and devastating for the evolution model.

The universe, at some point in time, will run out of useable energy! One day the sun will simply burn out, and life on earth will cease. In the same way the universe itself will run out of energy to expand, and everything as we know it will end.

This contradicts the claims of evolution. As systems by the second law of thermodynamics all tend to a higher level of chaos/entropy, they can *never* – without help from "outside" – evolve into higher levels of organization and energy. So evolution of any system can lead only to a less organized, less sophisticated, less intelligent, less developed system. Over time humans might evolve into apes (perhaps some do), but not the other way around!

This also explains why researchers have discovered thousands and thousands of species that have become extinct, but they have never found evidence of the beginning of a new species.

☼ EXHIBIT #12: THE WATCHMAKER ARGUMENT

The classic argument for the Creator model is an analogy known as the *Watchmaker* argument.[99] One of its most popular forms was given by William Paley (1743-1805), an English clergyman. Paley insisted that if a person found a watch in an empty field, its obvious design would lead him to rightly conclude that this watch had a *watchmaker*. Likewise, the even more complex design of the world compels us to conclude there is a great Designer behind it:

1. A watch shows it was assembled for an intelligent purpose (to keep time): (a) Its spring gives it motion. (b) Its series of wheels transmit this motion. (c) The wheels are made of brass to prevent rust. (d) The spring is made of steel to be resilient. (e) The cover is glass so that one can see through it.

2. The world shows an even greater evidence of design than a watch: (a) The world is a work of art far greater than a watch. (b) The world has more subtle and complex design than a watch. (c) The world has an endless variety of means adapted to ends.

3. Therefore, if the existence of a watch implies a watchmaker, the existence of the world implies an even greater Intelligent Designer (God).

So how could a person think only time and chance started life?

THE PRINT SHOP ARGUMENT

An alternative illustration is this question: How many explosions must occur in a fully equipped print shop to produce a complete dictionary? One? Two? 50,000?

Obviously the only answer is none, because such a thing could never happen by chance. It's no more possible than for a monkey (or an army of monkeys) at a typewriter to type a copy of Tolstoy's *War and Peace*.

Only the application of intelligence to such processes will produce a dictionary or a novel.

That begs the question how an educated person can actually believe that even the simplest life form (the one-cell organism), itself requiring far more information than a dictionary, can result from chance?

Evidences for design

The 1997 hit movie *Contact* was based on a book by the late Carl Sagan, an outspoken evolutionist. In that story, the reception of prime numbers on a radio wave was convincing evidence of intelligent life. Isn't it ironic that Sagan accepted a simple ordered sequence of radio signals as proof of intelligent life, but he refused the far more complex ordered sequences of DNA molecules as evidence for creation by an intelligent Creator!

Another illustration of the power of the Watchmaker argument is the so called *Antikythera Mechanism*. In 1900, near the Greek island Antikythera, sponge divers discovered at the site of the wreck of a Roman ship a highly sophisticated device. This device – now known as the Antikythera mechanism – dates to 90 BC. It appears to be an analog computer with 37 precision made gear wheels, able to predict for any given date the precise location of the sun, moon, and a number of planets.[100] This discovery has baffled scientists for the last 100 years and has elevated appreciation for the knowledge of the ancient world to a new level. No one, however, doubted this mechanism was produced by an intelligent Greek designer. Even with parts missing, the design was so compelling it fueled a century-long investigation of its purpose.

☼ EXHIBIT #13: THE MORALITY ARGUMENT

All humans are born with a concept of *moral values* – right and wrong, good and evil. Animals do not have this sense; they have no concept of right and wrong choices and are therefore amoral. Animals are driven solely by basic needs such as food, play, and comfort. This concept of morality makes humans different from any other creature on earth.

We all know deep inside what "*is the right thing to do.*" We all agree: a serial killer is an evil man, and Mother Theresa was a good woman.

Why is that? If evolution were true, how can it explain this shared concept of moral values? If humans are nothing more than a cosmic "accident," a fluke of time and chance, why do persons have these moral values? Simply said, how can a vast number of amoral organic components result in a human being with moral values? And how can it be, if we evolved from an amoral ancestor, that we possess these moral values?

A similar reasoning is described by C.S. Lewis.[101] He questions the concept of morality. That is just not possible or logical. The heart of his argument follows this basic structure:

1. Moral laws imply a Moral Law Giver.
2. There is an objective moral law.
3. Therefore, there is a Moral Law Giver.

The first premise is self-evident. Moral laws differ from natural laws. Moral laws don't *describe what is,* they *prescribe what ought to be.* They can't be known by observing what people do. They are what all persons should do, whether or not they actually do it.

The weight of the argument rests on the second premise – the existence of objective moral law. That is, there is a moral law not just prescribed by us, but *for* us as well. Humans prescribe proper behavior for other humans. The question is, is there evidence that a universal, objective prescription binds all humans? The evidence for such a law is strong. It is implied in our judgments that *"the world is getting better (or worse)."* How could we know unless there were some standard beyond the world by which we could measure our progress. Statements such as *"Hitler was wrong"* have no force greater than opinion, leaving us to decide if Hitler's moral judgments are right or wrong depending solely on the cultural norms. If he was objectively wrong, then there is a moral law beyond all of us by which we are all bound. And if there is such a universal law, there must be a universal Moral Law Giver (God).[102]

☼ EXHIBIT #14: THE TESTIMONY OF SILENCE

Perhaps the most overlooked, yet simplest evidence comes from the evolutionist camp itself: their own silence! When was the last major breakthrough in evolutionary science? There has not been one. Since the Miller experiment of the 1950s the evolutionists have been very quiet. Many millions of dollars and thousands of work-years have been spent during the last five decades, all trying to produce a simple life-form in controlled laboratory environments (even just a complete protein molecule). There have been no successes – not even a near success, not even any significant progress. Despite elaborate studies of fossils and bones, no "missing-links" have turned up; in fact, no evidence of evolution in any kind of life-forms has been discovered. The more scientists attempt to prove evolution, the more evidence emerges testifying to the complexity of life and the improbability of (macro) evolution. Evolution textbooks in the year 2000 still have the same manufactured "evidence" as those published in 1960![103]

☼ EXHIBIT #15: EXTRA DIMENSIONALITY

We experience our universe as a "three-and-a-half" dimensional world; that is, three space dimensions (length, width, height) and a "half of a" time dimension (we can only move forward). However, is that really all there is? Or is that just our limited ability to experience our world? [104]

Throughout the 1980s and early 1990s theoretical physicists recognized that there simply was not enough room in the dimensions of length, width, height, and time for the symmetries demanded by both gravity and quantum mechanics.

In 1996 a team led by Andrew Strominger discovered that only in ten space-time dimensions (nine space, one time) gravity and quantum mechanics could successfully coexist at all epochs of cosmic history. This theoretical calculation was subsequently supported by several observational confirmations.

The picture of creation that arises out of this theory proceeds as follows:
- At the creation event (Big Bang) ten space-time dimensions instantly appeared.
- All nine space dimension rapidly expanded.
- At 10^{-43} seconds after the creation event, six of the nine space dimensions ceased to expand.
- Thereafter, the space dimensions of length, width, and height continue to rapidly expand.

Presently, the six tiny space dimensions are very tightly wrapped up around the three large space dimensions. Except for the interiors of black holes, the tiny space dimensions play no role today in the dynamics of the universe.

If God created the universe, He caused the Big Bang and limited human perception to a three-and-a-half dimensional world. However, nothing limits Him to move around in this 10 (or even more) dimensional world. This includes full control over the time dimension. He created time, and it sets no limitations upon Him.

This *extra-dimensional* concept could help us understand many concepts humans struggle with, such as:
- For God, time is a full dimension, not only a one-way dimension; therefore, time has no limitations for Him, and He can move freely back and forth in the past and future and foresee the future.
- God can be close to each of us all the time in an extra-dimensional world without us ever knowing it. Imagine the surface of a table. Suppose you are limited to only live in the two dimensional world of the table surface, so you can only move over the surface (you are a "flatlander"), but can never go up or down. Your perception is limited to this surface and its two dimensions. You cannot be aware of anyone who lives in three dimensions, unless that person is on the table surface. If that person was just 0.0001 inch above the table surface, just above you, you would not

be able to see him (as you cannot experience anything above you), but he would see you and be very close to you.

- The spiritual world (angels, demons) and even the location of heaven and hell could all be simply in another set of dimensions. Death must be just a step into this other dimensional world. For people in heaven, time has no meaning or limitation.

☼ EXHIBIT #16: NEAR-DEATH EXPERIENCES

Thanks to improved survival rates resulting from modern techniques of resuscitation, more and more people experience close encounters with death, but live to tell about it. The current estimate is that as many as 15-20 million Americans alive today have experienced a so called "Near-Death Experience" (NDE). Many claim these experiences actually give a glimpse of what happens at the moment we die and consequently provide insight into God and the afterlife. I would like to emphasize that the presented material in this exhibit is anecdotal and not evidence that can be scientifically verified. But still – as the similarity of experiences is quite impressive – it is worth learning more about.

In 2001 a ground-breaking 13-year study of NDEs in 10 Dutch hospitals was published in the highly respected international medical journal *Lancet*.[105] The study interviewed 344 patients who experienced cessation of heart and/or breathing function and were resuscitated and later interviewed. Through these interviews, the doctors identified that a number of the patients had experienced NDEs. The advantage of this type of study is that it gives scientists a matched comparison group of non-NDE patients against which to compare the near-death experiences. Therefore the data is more reliable about the possible causes and consequences of the NDE.

In the past, some scientists have asserted a NDE is simply a hallucination brought about by the brain, due to loss of oxygen (called anoxia), after the heart has stopped beating. This study casts doubt on that theory, as all patients had a cardiac arrest, and were clinically dead with unconsciousness resulting from insufficient blood supply to the brain. In such circumstances the EEG (a measure of brain electrical activity) becomes flat, and if CPR is not started within 5-10 minutes, irreparable brain damage occurs, and the patient will die. According to the theory that NDE is caused by anoxia, all patients in the study should have experienced a NDE, but only 18% reported having one.

There is also a theory that a NDE is caused psychologically by the fear of death. But only a very small percentage of the patients said they had been afraid seconds before their cardiac arrest – it happened too suddenly for them to realize what was occurring. More patients than the frightened ones reported NDEs. Finally, differences in drug treatments during resuscitation did not correlate with the likelihood of patients experiencing NDEs or with the depth of their NDEs.

Of the 344 patients tracked by the Dutch team, 18% had some memory of unconsciousness, and 12% (1 out of every 8) had what the physicians called a "core" or "deep" NDE.

Dr. Raymond Moody[106] has outlined nine elements that generally occur (in this order) during the near-death experience:

1. A strange buzzing or ringing noise, while the patient has a sense of being dead.

2. A feeling of peace and painlessness.

3. An out-of-body experience – the sensation of rising up and floating above their own body, watching the medical team working on the body.

4. The tunnel experience – being drawn into darkness through a tunnel towards a radiant golden-white light.

5. Some people reported rising suddenly into the sky and seeing the earth as it is seen by astronauts from space.

6. People of light – after step 4 or 5, the dying meet people who glow with an inner light. Often they experience friends and relatives already dead are greeting them there.

7. The "being of light" – after meeting the people of light, the dying often meet a powerful spiritual being whom some have called God, Jesus, or some other religious figure.

8. The life review – the "being of light" presents the dying with a panoramic review of everything they have ever done. That is, they relive every act they have ever done to other people and come away convinced love is the most important experience in life.

9. Reluctance to return – the "being of light" sometimes tells the dying they must return to life. Other times they are given the choice to stay or return. In both cases, they are reluctant to return. The people who chose to return do so only because of loved ones they do not wish to leave behind.

There is much speculation about why some people remember NDE experiences and others do not remember or never had one. No satisfactory explanation is currently available, but it is clear NDEs are real and likely are what they suggest to be: a brief and limited look into life after death.

Apologist and philosopher Peter Kreeft mentions features of a NDE that argue for its truth:[107]

• The pattern of experiences is consistent. It does not vary much by personality.

- The experience is not what one would expect. No "traditional" religious observations of angels, clouds, harps, and halos.
- People who experience a NDE are usually drug free, so the experience is not the result of any drugs.
- There are objectively verified reports of people who had a NDE to have an out-of-body experience where they can see doctors and nurses "working on them" or "seeing" the location of lost objects that later turn out to be true.
- All people who experience a NDE return to life as changed persons, and these changes are for the better. They are convinced there is life after death, they are no longer afraid of death, they have a strong sense of meaning in their lives, and they have a new sense of values claiming the absolute importance of truth and love above all other things.

The NDE experiences seem timeless in duration. The described events should require (in "earth" time) considerable duration; however they are experienced as timeless. In our reality – given the short elapse of "earth" time involved between clinical death and resuscitation – they all happen in only a few moments.

The "being of light" and the "feeling of love being the most important sensation in life" is also experienced by non-believers who experience NDEs. So experiencing the "being of light" seems to be a fact we all face, even if we do not believe in God or accept that love is the most important "sensation in life." This is exactly what Jesus teaches again and again (John 15:17) *"This is my command: Love each other"* plus numerous other Biblical references.

SUMMARY
We Know That God Exists

In this section we have studied the Big Bang model as generally taught by evolutionary scientists. We have seen that evolution is not established fact, no longer even a credible theory, but merely a model used to explain scientific observations of the natural world. A series of exhibits deal devastating blows to the foundations of this evolutionary model, and, in contrast, provide a compelling case for the reality of a Creator:

1. There is no scientific, evolutionary explanation for the cause of the Big Bang. How could something come out of nothing? How could the universe come to exist without a cause? The sudden occurrence of a Big Bang event and the "popping into existence" of space and time can be explained only as caused by a Creator who Himself is beyond and outside space and time.

2. The natural laws that govern the universe and our world are perfectly fine-tuned. Even minor changes in the constants of these laws and/or the natural or chemical properties of the elements critical to life would have destroyed life before it existed. How can these natural laws be so perfectly balanced and designed without a Designer?

3. Earth is a truly privileged planet. Modern astrobiology has identified numerous conditions that must simultaneously be fulfilled on any planet for life to be possible. Chances of meeting all these requirements at the same time are so small that – even with the presence of trillions and trillions of planets in the universe – the probability to find any planet suited for life is extremely small to non-existent.

4. Earth is not only extremely rare as to its suitability for life, it is also likely the best positioned and equipped to allow observations of the rest of the universe.

5. Modern science has reached the unanimous conclusion that life on a planet like earth could not have started by mere chance. The complex building blocks of the simplest living cell – proteins, DNA and molecular machines – do not allow for random assembly even through long periods of time. Despite decades of intense research, origin-of-life scientists have found no explanation to explain how life could have started by natural processes alone.

6. Even if a one-cell life form could have started by natural processes alone, there is no mechanism for this life form to "evolve" into more complex life

forms. All familiar evidences for evolution into more complex species demonstrate natural selection (variation within one species) and not genetic mutation (new DNA as a result of errors during cell duplication resulting in additional, better characteristics for the life form).

7. According to the evolution model, species would evolve to more complex new species by a series of gradual mutations. However, despite of over 100+ years of extensive studies of the fossil record, no intermediate species have been discovered. On the contrary, the Cambrian Explosion shows the almost "overnight" appearance of the body plans of all modern day life forms at about the same moment in time.

The failing case and evidence for evolution is well summarized by the following quotations:

"Evolution is unproved and improvable. We believe it only because the only alternative is special creation, and that is unthinkable." [108]

"I myself am convinced that the theory of evolution, especially the extent to which it's been applied, will be one of the great jokes in the history books of the future." [109]

"Scientists who go about teaching that evolution is a fact of life are great con-men, and the story they are telling may be the greatest hoax ever. In explaining evolution, we do not have one iota of fact." [110]

A series of other evidences supports the case for the existence of a Creator:

8. Through *biochemical dating techniques* (based on DNA), the estimated age of mankind has now been revised to the range of 37,000-100,000 years. The evidences from archaeology and anthropology are consistent with dating in the 40,000-50,000 years range. A much younger than earlier estimated age for mankind is in contradiction with evolutionary ancestry models, but is consistent with the Biblical creation account.

9. The existence of so called *irreducible complex molecular machines* cannot be explained by gradual evolvement of the components of these machines, as these systems can only perform if all components are present.

10. Numerous life forms live together in *symbiotic relationships*. These relationships cannot be explained from gradual, independent development of these species.

11. The universally observed *Law of Entropy* is consistent with a Creator model, but contradicts an evolutionary model.

12. The *Watchmaker Analogy* shows that complex mechanisms and/or organisms are the product of intelligent design, not of random chance and blind forces of nature.

13. All human beings are born with a concept of *morality*; we know what is "right" and "wrong." If humans evolved merely through random chemical processes, why would any morality matter?

14. Despite decades and decades of intense research and multi-billion dollar investments, evolutionary science has not produced any convincing evidences or explanations for the above mentioned challenges to the evolution model. Recent evolutionary textbooks still have the same questionable evidences as presented in the 1960s.

The evidence for the existence of a Creator God is overwhelming. Thanks to the advance of science in studying the universe, as well as the growing abilities to better understand and appreciate the complexity of life and the marvelous design of DNA, astrobiology as well as molecular biology and genetics reveal exciting new discoveries pointing to the design and handiwork of an intelligent Creator. Our generation is better equipped than any generation before us to discover and study previously unknown details of this beautifully and perfectly created world.

Pascal's Wager

If you conclude there is not enough evidence that God exists to be a believer, but on the other hand there are too many indications of God's possible existence to be an atheist, you might consider *Pascal's Wager* (named after Blaise Pascal, a French philosopher (1623-1662).

The wager simply claims: it is safer to choose that God exists than not. If God indeed exists and you choose him, you will be rewarded for your choice in heaven. If you choose Him, but He does not exist after all, you did not lose anything. You will just disappear into nothing. However if you reject God and He exists after all, you will be condemned to hell. And if you would reject Him and He does indeed not exist, you still will just disappear into the empty void.

So you have only to gain and nothing to lose by choosing God.

Section II
Can We Trust the Bible?

CHAPTER 8

How Do We Know That the Bible Can Be Trusted?

"For what I received I passed on to you as of first importance: that
Christ died for our sins according to the Scriptures, that He was buried,
that He was raised on the third day according to the Scriptures."
1 CORINTHIANS 15:3-4

WHAT IS THE BIBLE?

If we believe God, our Creator, indeed exists, then it is only logical to expect Him to communicate with His creation. Therefore, it would be reasonable to conclude that God, either in person or by revelation, or both, has revealed Himself to mankind. In this section we will examine whether the Bible is this revelation.

The word *Bible* is derived from the Greek βιβλιοσ or βιβλια, ("biblios" or "biblia") meaning book or books. The Bible is not a single book, but rather a collection of smaller works, written over a long period of time, all considered part of God's revelation to mankind.

The three main monotheistic religions are Christianity, Islam, and Judaism. Surprisingly, all three recognize parts of the Bible as a true revelation. However, Jews reject the New Testament, and Islam claims the Bible was corrupted over the years by both Christians and Jews. Therefore additional revelation – through the prophet Mohammed – in the Qur'an was given to correct these errors. Still Islam recognizes most of the Bible accounts (with some alterations) to be God's Word.

The Bible is by far the most copied, published, and studied document ever known. According to *Barna Research Group*[111] more than 90% of American households own at least one Bible; however, only 31% read theirs regularly. Worldwide, the Bible has been translated in more than 2,000 languages, and estimates run as high as two billion for the number of copies of the Bible that have been distributed.

The Bible consists of two main sections: The *Old Testament* (OT) and the *New Testament* (NT). All books in the OT were written well before the birth of Jesus of Nazareth and are recognized as genuine by both Judaism and Christianity. The NT, written after Christ, is part only of the Christian Bible and is not recognized by Judaism.

The Protestant Bible contains 66 individual books, 39 in the OT and 27 in the NT. These books were written by 40 (some suggest 44) authors over a period of 1,500 years working in three languages (Hebrew, Aramaic, and Greek) from three continents.

Each Biblical book has been subdivided into chapters and verses. The current Protestant Bible counts a total of 1,189 chapters and 31,102 verses. The original texts had no such divisions; they were added much later to facilitate study. Some appear a bit arbitrary and chapter endings do not always coincide with natural breaks in the Scriptures. Chapter divisions were made in the year 1228 by a British clergyman, Stephen Langton. The OT was divided into verses in 1448 and the NT in 1551. The entire Bible as we know it, divided into chapters and verses, first appeared in the Geneva Bible[112] of the year 1560.

THE OLD TESTAMENT

The *Protestant Old Testament* and the *Hebrew Bible* of Judaism share the same books and texts, but they are organized differently. The Jewish Scriptures number 24 instead of 39 books and are presented in a different order. The Hebrew Bible is called the *Tanakh*. The first five books are traditionally linked to Moses (Genesis, Exodus, Leviticus, Numbers, and Deuteronomy) and are often referred to as the *Law* or the *Torah* (Judaism) or the *Pentateuch* (a Greek term, "penta" meaning five).

The Roman Catholic OT contains additional books unknown to the Protestant OT. These books, also called the *Apocrypha* (literally "hidden" or "concealed"), are not considered part of the Scriptures by all Christians (more about this later).

When the Bible refers to *"the Scriptures,"* reference is always to the OT alone, not the NT (as it was not fully completed and available at that time).[113]

Traditionally the books of the OT fall into five main groups:

The Torah: The first five books, attributed to Moses, describe the creation of the world, Adam and Eve, Noah and the flood, Abraham and the patriarchs, Joseph and the relocation to Egypt, Moses and the exodus from Egypt and 40 years wandering through the desert. In Exodus Moses receives the *Ten Commandments*. The book of Leviticus describes in detail God's instructions for worship and living a holy life. Orthodox Jews still consider the Torah the most important part of the Scriptures and attempt to follow these instructions to the letter.

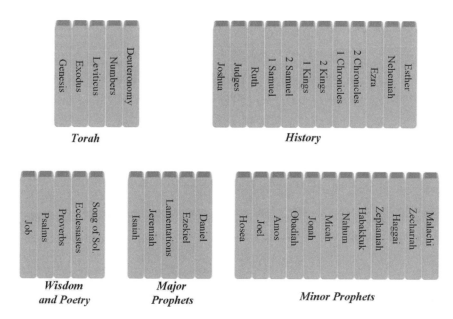

Torah

History

*Wisdom
and Poetry*

*Major
Prophets*

Minor Prophets

Figure 8-1: The Books of the Old Testament

History: The next 12 books, Joshua through Esther, cover 1,000 years of history (roughly 1400 BC through 400 BC): the campaign to conquer the Promised Land; the time of the judges; the reigns of Saul, David, and Solomon; the divided kingdoms of the North (Israel) and the South (Judea); the defeats by the Assyrians and Babylonians; the exile and ultimate return to Judea/Jerusalem.

Wisdom and Poetry: These timeless principles show how to enjoy success and blessing regardless of the political and religious circumstances into which a person is born. These are also called *"books of poetry"* because they are largely written as poetry, especially the books of Psalms and Proverbs.

Major Prophets: Four prophets are designated as the *Major Prophets*: Isaiah, Jeremiah, Ezekiel, and Daniel. They are "major" not because of rank, but due to the length of their prophetic books. Isaiah called Judah to repentance, which postponed the judgment of God for 130 years. Daniel and Isaiah both contain many prophecies about Jesus.

Minor Prophets: The 12 *Minor Prophets* were raised up by God at strategic times during the history of Israel to call people back to Him. They are "minor" only because their books are shorter. Although applications of these books are limited largely to the people to whom they were written, many blessings can be found there.

The complete OT was written over a span of about 1,000 years, from 1400 BC (the books of Moses) through about 400 BC (Malachi). Except for small sections of Daniel and Ezra written in *Aramaic* (the spoken language in Palestine from 200 BC through 200 AD), the OT was completely written in *Hebrew*.

THE NEW TESTAMENT

The 27 books of the New Testament were all written in *Koine Greek* ("street" or common Greek) by eight men, three of whom (Matthew, John, and Peter) were original disciples and eyewitnesses of Jesus of Nazareth. Paul, author of 13 (some suggest 14) of the NT books, was not a personal disciple but had a special post-resurrection encounter with Jesus. Paul also had numerous meetings with the original disciples.

The books of the New Testament cover a little less than 100 years, from the birth of Christ to John's vision of triumph in the book of Revelation. Most emphasis, from a historical perspective, is upon the three-year ministry of Jesus from 30-33 AD.

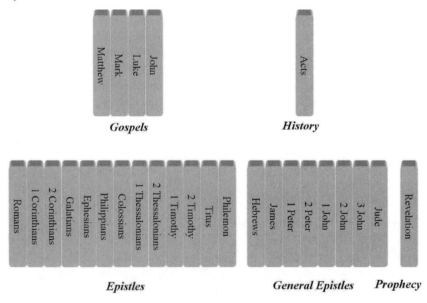

Figure 8-2: The Books of the New Testament

The books of the NT can be divided into five groups:

The Gospels: The New Testament begins with four records (books) of the life and teachings of Jesus, called the *gospels*. Most of what is known about the life of Jesus of Nazareth is found in these four books. That's why we will analyze in depth the background, dating, authorship, and reliability of these books. Each one describes the life, ministry, death, and resurrection of Jesus of Nazareth. Some events are recounted in all four, but each biography presents Jesus in a slightly different light; the variations are determined by the audience and the writer's intent. The four gospels provide a comprehensive, multi-facetted view of Jesus of Nazareth, known better as Jesus Christ.

Church History: The 28 chapters of the book of Acts record the birth of the church (after Jesus' resurrection), how the faith was introduced to the non-Jewish believers, and the spread of the new faith through the Roman Empire through the efforts of Paul.

The Pauline Epistles: The majority of books in the New Testament are the 13 Pauline epistles. These were written by Paul (in the period 49-62 AD); some to churches he started, some to individuals, and others had a special message for a general readership. Paul, *"the apostle born out of due time,"* was the intrepid missionary of the early church who did more to spread Christianity than any man on record in the Bible. His dramatic conversion is a classic testimony to the power of Jesus Christ to change lives, for he was transformed from a Christ-hating opponent to a Christ-serving advocate.

His letters, which can be traced in history by linking them to events described in the book of Acts, give profound answers to questions and solutions to problems in the early Christian church. Almost every human need is covered.

The General Epistles: This collection of letters, written for a specific need or to a group not reached by Paul, cover general truths needed by God's people of every era. Authors include James and Jude (both brothers of Jesus) as well as the apostles Peter and John.

Prophecy: The last book is a book of prophecy about the coming judgment of Christ, and is called Revelation, also the Apocalypse.

ORIGINAL TEXT VERSUS TRANSLATIONS

Later we will discuss compelling evidences that indicate the careful preservation of the original Bible texts, the historical reliability of the accounts, and the divine inspiration for the Scriptures, but that relates only to original texts.

Many translations have been made over the years. In the early days of Christianity the Hebrew OT was usually read in a Greek translation. As the church spread, the need for translations grew, taking the sacred text into widely accepted languages as well as local tongues. The Bible was soon translated into Latin (the language of the Roman Empire), Syriac (an Eastern Aramaic language), Coptic (Egyptian), and Arabic. By 500 AD, some estimate, scripture could already be found in more than 500 languages. Unfortunately, translations were not always accurate and errors were made. For this reason – and also because they did not want "ordinary" people to be able to read the Bible – the (Roman) Catholic Church banned any further translations and used only a particular Latin text known as the *Vulgate,* which had been translated from the Greek around 600 AD. In the 1380s the first English translations were made by John Wycliffe. By 1455 the printing press was invented (Gutenberg), and mass-production capabilities made additional English versions and other language translations more readily available.

Hundreds of translations into English (estimated around 450) have been made over the years. Some of the best known are: the King James (KJV, 1611), the New International Version (NIV, 1978), the New King James (NKJV, 1982), the New American Standard Bible (NASB, 1971) and the English Standard Version (ESV, 2001). This large number of translations is usually grouped into three main categories:

Literal translations: These translate the original texts word for word into the best English equivalent words. These translations are sometimes also referred to as *interlinear translations,* placing the English rendering along side the original Hebrew and Greek. Although they are undoubtedly the most accurate translations, they can be difficult to read because the flow of language follows the original Hebrew and Greek, quite different from modern English. The *NASB* as well as the *ESV* are good examples of literal translations.

Dynamic equivalent translations: These translations attempt to be as literal as possible, but restructure sentences and grammar from the original language to English. They attempt to capture thought and intent of what writers wanted to say. As a result, these are more readable in English, but have a higher degree of subjective interpretation than the literal translations. These translations include the *KJV, NKJV,* and *NIV.*

Contemporary language translations: These translation paraphrase the thought and intent of the original text into contemporary English. The result is easy to read, but the text is largely a subjective interpretation of the translator. These versions, such as the well known *The Message* and *The New Living Translation,* should be approached with great care. Use them perhaps for supplementary readings, but be aware that these texts can (and often do) differ significantly from the original Bible texts.

Every translation requires interpretation. Why? Languages do not translate one on one. That is, not every word has a unique word to match it in the other language. Also some tongues are richer in expression than English (such as Greek) or smaller in vocabulary (such as Hebrew). A translator must interpret the original meaning and find an equivalent wording, but this makes the result subject to the biases of the translator. Bottom line: interpretations differ and errors can occur. When translations differ significantly, research into the original language can help clarify the message.

To complicate things a bit, a small number of NT verses are not supported by all ancient manuscripts; this forces translators to decide which verses to incorporate. Most translators are cautious to err on the safe side and note for the reader any verse not supported by the majority of manuscripts.

As an illustration, following (table 8-1) is the Lord's Prayer from Matthew 6:9-13 in the New International Version and the King James Version. Apart from "old" English versus more modern English style, notice the two differences in the last verse:

"The evil one" versus "evil." The KJV asks for deliverance from *"evil"* while the NIV asks to deliver us from *"the evil one."* There is no little difference between the two. The original Greek text actually uses an adjective with an article, making *"the evil one"* the only correct translation. We pray to be delivered from the evil one, not from any danger, disaster, or from the general ugliness of the world.[114]

KJV versus NIV Translation		
Matthew	**King James Version (KJV)**	**New International Version (NIV)**
6:9	*"After this manner therefore pray ye: 'Our Father which art in heaven, Hallowed be thy name.*	*"This, then, is how you should pray: 'Our Father in heaven, hallowed be your name,*
6:10	*Thy kingdom come. Thy will be done in earth, as it is in heaven.*	*your kingdom come, your will be done on earth as it is in heaven.*
6:11	*Give us this day our daily bread.*	*Give us today our daily bread.*
6:12	*And forgive us our debts, as we forgive our debtors.*	*Forgive us our debts, as we also have forgiven our debtors.*
6:13	*And lead us not into temptation, but deliver us <u>from evil</u>: For thine is the kingdom, and the power, and the glory, for ever. Amen.'"*	*And lead us not into temptation, but deliver us <u>from the evil one</u>.'"*

Table 8-1: All Translations are Interpretations

An extra sentence. Compared to the NIV, the KJV has an extra sentence at the end: *"For thine is the kingdom, and the power, and the glory, for ever, Amen."* This is a good illustration of a later addition to the oldest preserved Greek manuscripts. As the NIV mentions in a footnote: *"some late manuscripts: for yours is the kingdom and the power and the glory forever. Amen."* Other verses in the NT have similar additions. None of these are of vital theological consequence, but it is important to be aware of these variations.

SCHOLARS AND THE SCRIPTURES

Before diving into the evidence, this is a good point to reflect on how scholars in the last few centuries, and especially nowadays, approach the Scriptures.

A significant number of recognized Bible scholars, however surprising it might be, do not classify themselves as believing Christians. Many presume that supernatural events in the Bible cannot be true; hence, those documents cannot be reliable. This relates not only to recorded and later fulfilled prophecies but to miracles as well, and especially the resurrection. The general approach of these more liberal scholars is to declare miracles to be only legends and to date writing of prophecy after its fulfillment. The underlying philosophy assumes *"any Bible story/account to be false unless proved over and over again to be true."*

Just as evolutionary scientists reject evidence for an intelligent Creator, even so secular, liberal scholars reject evidence for the supernatural events and prophecies as described in the Bible. Therefore, one should not be surprised to find large numbers of scholars reject the authorship and date of the Pentateuch (the first five Bible books) as well as the books of Joshua, Isaiah, and Daniel in the Old Testament. These books contain important revelation (Pentateuch and Joshua) and prophecy (Isaiah and Daniel), so we will discuss evidence for their historical reliability in the next chapters.

For the New Testament the secular worldview of many scholars will drive them to claim that:
- None of the gospels was written by an eyewitness.
- All gospels are dated after 70 AD or even much later.
- All recorded miracles are mere legend.
- The resurrection never happened.

Most modern scholarly focus on the New Testament follows the so called *"third quest for the historical Jesus"*[115] and emphasize anchoring Jesus against the backdrop of His own time, with special regard to the Jewish setting and context for His life and teachings. This third quest, fueled by non-believing scholars, is actually a quite positive development. Much of the gospel text is now considered *"historically reliable"* because of its consistency with what is now known about first century Palestine through other sources. Even so, sections that present miraculous power over nature (such as walking on water and stilling of the storm), claims of deity for Jesus, and the resurrection are still rejected as legend and considered unreliable.

Another extreme group of scholars has united themselves as *The Jesus Seminar* under the leadership of ultra-radical scholars such as John Dominic Crossan and Marcus Borg (I mention these because these men often appear in documentaries presented by the Discovery Channel, the History Channel and so on, and their views are portrayed as the *"consensus scholar opinion"* about Scripture). Be aware, that this group is not at all representative of any significant segment of the scholarly community. Of the 74 members, only 14 have an established New Testament scholarly reputation; the rest are only students of the others. The sole reason the Jesus Seminar is worth mentioning is that it commands serious media attention, giving the impression that they represent the majority consensus. Not long ago, the Jesus Seminar published *The Five Gospels.*[116] Here the four Biblical gospels are discussed together with the so called fifth gospel, the *Gospel of Thomas.* This last "gospel" is widely rejected by the vast majority of other scholars (we will discuss the Gospel of Thomas later in more detail).[117] The Jesus Seminar has – using a voting system – marked all Jesus' sayings in these "five gospels" with a color code, indicating the certainty of whether these were Jesus actual teachings: red if definitely, pink if probably, gray if perhaps, or black if definitely not. The result is dramatic: only 15 of Jesus' sayings in the gospels are coded red, while 82% is rejected altogether. Again, this is only the opinion of this small group of liberal scholars. A group of evangelical scholars has written a response to the *The Five Gospels* titled *Jesus under Fire*[118] – an excellent rebuttal to the claims of the Jesus Seminar.

Recently the bestseller and 2006 movie *The DaVinci Code* set in motion a new wave of attacks on the New Testament credibility. The story's tabloid-like claims about Jesus and Mary Magdalene are based on an extreme and liberal interpretation of gnostic writings found in Nag Hammadi in Egypt in 1999. The *DaVinci Code* claims have been refuted by numerous Christian scholars in various publications.[119]

The Nag Hammadi library also has started what some call *The New School,* including (non-Christian) scholars like Elaine Pagels and Bart Ehrman. This New School seeks to endow these newly discovered "gospels" with the same authority – or even more – as the NT gospels and letters, even though it can be demonstrated these documents were written much later and are not as credible because of gnostic, non-Christian influences.[120] More about the Nag Hammadi library and some of its finds will be discussed in a later chapter.[121]

ANALYZING THE EVIDENCES FOR THE BIBLE

How can we know that the stories we read in the Bible are not legendary accounts, but actual historical facts? Is there any way we can know whether the

Bible is not only factually accurate but also God's word revealed to mankind?

To build the case for the historical reliability and divine inspiration of the Bible, we will study the following topics in subsequent chapters and throughout provide numerous exhibits:

The Texts of the Old Testament: How were the texts transmitted? What is the importance of the Dead Sea Scrolls, the Septuagint, and the Old Testament canon?

Authorship and Dating of the Old Testament: Who wrote the books of the Old Testament, and when was it accomplished?

The Texts of the New Testament: What can be learned from the manuscript evidence, the writings of the Early Church Leaders, and the New Testament canon?

Authorship and Dating of the New Testament: Who wrote the books of the New Testament and when was it completed?

The Lost Books of the New Testament: What are these books? How were they found, and by whom? Were they actually lost at all?

Historical Reliability of the Bible: Do archaeology and historical analysis confirm or contradict the Biblical accounts?

The Testimony of Non-Christian Writers: Do first and second century non-Christian sources mention Jesus and Christianity? And if so, do these sources confirm the New Testament books?

Can We Trust the Witnesses?: Does a detailed analysis of the four gospels, Acts, and Paul's epistles using criteria for credibility and honesty provide us with more insights about the integrity of these writings?

CHAPTER 9

The Texts of the
Old Testament

*"For the Scripture says to Pharaoh: 'I raised you up for this very
purpose, that I might display my power in you and that
my name might be proclaimed in all the earth.'"*
ROMANS 9:17

The original manuscripts of all 39 OT books have long since been lost. This presents a crucial concern: With no original documents, not even fragments, can we reconstruct them from the oldest manuscripts available? Can we be confident that, over time and numerous copies, the original texts have not been altered, or even lost? Extensive research and close analysis of many ancient manuscript discoveries have yielded much information about the reliability of the copying of the old manuscripts.

PAPYRUS, PARCHMENT AND SCROLLS

Failure to preserve the original texts and the very limited number of ancient OT *manuscripts* (a manuscript is literally "a hand-written copy") is the result of the perishable writing materials. Most common was *papyrus*, a type of paper made from the papyrus reed. In a dry climate papyrus is stable, but in more humid conditions the material is easily destroyed and lost within a few centuries.

By the time of Jesus, *parchment*, a writing material of animal skins had become popular. The parchment was stretched, scraped, and dried. Like papyrus it is vulnerable to humidity, but is a more durable alternative. Vellum was a parchment made from calf skin. By the fifth century parchment had replaced papyrus, far and wide.

Both papyrus and parchments were used as large sheets that were rolled around a stick to create a *scroll*. The average scroll ranged between 20 and 30 feet long, occasionally exceeding 140 feet. Usually writing was limited to one side of the sheet only.

In the second century scrolls began to be replaced by *codices*. To make reading easier and the scroll less bulky, the papyrus/parchment sheets were inscribed on both sides, then assembled in leaf form, forming a primitive book known as a *codex*. The introduction of paper in the later half of the Middle Ages, caused widespread use of parchment to be abandoned.[122]

HOW ACCURATE WAS THE COPYING PROCESS?

To preserve the integrity of the OT, its text had to be copied onto new scrolls again and again through the centuries. The undertaking was assigned to devout Jews known as *scribes*. A scribe was considered a professional person in antiquity. In the absence of printing as known today, people were trained to copy documents. Scribes reverently believed these scrolls were the very Word of God; thus they were extremely careful in copying. They were not hasty or rapid in their work. In fact, they trained for long years, working up from an apprenticeship. Their penmanship was meticulously checked and rechecked for error. Even slight errors would cause their work to be rejected.

From generation to generation a succession of scholars and scribes were charged with preserving a standard Biblical text. During the early Middle Ages, scribes that copied the Hebrew Bible were called *Masoretes*. The Masoretes were charged with preserving the sacred OT texts during the period from 500 to 950 AD. These Jews were meticulous in their copying. The earliest complete copy of the Hebrew Old Testament dates from this period and is called the *Masoretic Text*.

The Masoretes would for example copy the book of Isaiah. When the project was completed, they would total up the number of letters of the copy and compare that to the number of letters in the original. Next they would locate the middle letter of the book and compare that to the original. If variations were found, the copy would be discarded and the copying would begin again.

Up to this time written Hebrew had only 22 consonants and no vowels. The texts were all in capital letters, only consonants, with neither punctuation nor paragraphs. Vowels were only implicitly implied. The Masoretes are credited with devising the Hebrew vowel point system. Adding this to the original OT texts gave each word its exact pronunciation and precise grammatical form.

All present copies of the Hebrew text from this period are in remarkable agreement. Comparing the Masoretic text to the earlier Latin (Vulgate) and Greek (Septuagint) has revealed careful copying. The evidence suggests little deviation during the thousands of years previous to 900 AD. Until recently there was only scant material in Hebrew from antiquity to compare to Masoretic texts of the tenth century. This lack of older Hebrew texts persistently challenged confidence in the accuracy of the copying process until the *Dead Sea Scrolls* were found in 1947.

☼ EXHIBIT #1: THE DEAD SEA SCROLLS

In 1947 a young Bedouin goat herdsman found strange clay jars in caves at Qumran near the valley of the Dead Sea. Inside were leather scrolls. This led to the discovery of 40,000 fragments from about as many as 870 separate scrolls in 11 different caves, all between 1947 and 1956. Carbon-14 dating (very reliable for organic material of this era) as well as textual analysis and handwriting analysis, suggest the scrolls were written in the period 250 BC to 68 AD.

The *Dead Sea Scrolls* have been hailed as one of the most outstanding archaeological discoveries of the twentieth century. The scrolls have revealed that a community of farmers, likely a Jewish, strict Torah-observant sect called the *Essenes*, flourished in the area from 150 BC to 70 AD.

The Essenes are mentioned by Jewish historian Josephus and by a few others, but not in the New Testament. Evidently when they saw the Romans invade the land, they put their sacred scrolls in the jars and hid them in the caves in the cliff region northwest of the Dead Sea.

The scrolls are most commonly made of animal skins (about 85%), but also papyrus (15%) and even one of copper. They are written with a carbon-based ink, from right to left, using no punctuation except for an occasional paragraph indentation. In fact, in some cases, there are not even spaces between the words. Most of the texts are in Hebrew, some in Aramaic, and a few in Greek.

The Dead Sea Scrolls can be divided in four groups:

Old Testament texts: Roughly 30% of the Dead Sea Scrolls are Biblical texts containing (partial) copies of every OT book, except for Esther. The best preserved scroll contains the book of Isaiah, consisting of one complete copy of the book and 21 other fragmented manuscripts. Others fragments include 39 manuscripts of the book of Psalms, 33 of Deuteronomy, 24 of Genesis, 18 of Exodus, 17 of Leviticus and 1 to 10 (fragments of) manuscripts from all the other books of the OT.

Apocrypha: Also found were partial copies of known as apocryphal ("hidden") books, including Enoch, Tobit, Jubilees, and Sirach.

Religious, non-Biblical texts: Scattered among the scrolls were numerous religious writings, including commentaries on the OT, psalm-like hymns, prayers, and prophecies.

Sectarian texts: Lastly, numbers of writings about the beliefs, regulations, and membership requirements of the sect were found, including the *Manual of Discipleship*, *The War Scroll*, and *The Copper Scroll*.

The Dead Sea Scrolls gave new insights into the daily life of a Jewish community in the days of Jesus, but by far *their greatest value is their confirmation of the reliability of the Old Testament texts* as they were copied over the centuries.

As such, the scrolls are like a time machine that provides access to extensive manuscripts of the Hebrew OT as much as 1,100 years older than the Masoretic texts. Comparing these texts reveals that the copying process was indeed accurate with no changes or additions. There were few or no textual changes found in those Masoretic texts where comparisons were possible. Therefore, it would be fair to conclude that the Masoretic scribes had probably been just as faithful in their copying of the other Biblical texts not found with the Qumran material.

The significance of the find, and particularly the complete book of Isaiah, was recognized by Merrill F. Unger when he said,[123] "*This complete document of Isaiah quite understandably created a sensation since it was the first major Biblical manuscript of great antiquity ever to be recovered. Interest in it was especially keen since it antedates by more than a thousand years the oldest Hebrew texts preserved in the Masoretic tradition.*"

What was learned? A comparison of the Qumran manuscript of Isaiah with the Masoretic text revealed that both were extremely close in accuracy to each other. "*Of the 166 words in Isaiah 53, there are only seventeen letters in question, Ten of these letters are simply a matter of spelling, which does not affect the sense. Four more letters are minor stylistic changes, such as conjunctions. The remaining three letters comprise the word "ligh," which is added in verse 11, and does not affect the meaning greatly...Thus, in one chapter of 166 words, there is only one word (three letters) in question after a thousand years of transmission – and this word does not significantly change the meaning of the passage.*"[124]

World-renowned archaeologist Gleason Archer states that the Isaiah copies of the Qumran community "*proved to be word for word identical with our standard Hebrew Bible in more than 95 percent of the text. The five percent of variation consisted chiefly of obvious slips of the pen and variations in spelling.*"[125]

In his book, Can I Trust My Bible, R. Laird Harris concluded,[126] "*We can now be sure that copyists worked with great care and accuracy on the Old Testament, even back to 225 BC ... indeed, it would be rash skepticism now to deny that we have our Old Testament in a form very close to that used by Ezra when he taught the word of the Lord to those who had returned from the Babylonian captivity.*"

The Dead Sea Scrolls overwhelmingly confirm that the Old Testament has navigated the centuries well. As Notre Dame professor Eugene Ulrich, chief editor of the Qumran Biblical texts for the Oxford Discoveries in the Judean Desert series, observed:[127]

"*The scrolls have shown that our traditional Bible has been amazingly accurately preserved for over 2,000 years.*"

☼ EXHIBIT #2: THE SEPTUAGINT OR LXX

After the Northern Kingdom (Israel) was captured by the Assyrians (722 BC) and the Southern Kingdom (Judah) was destroyed by the Babylonians (586 BC) the Jewish population was deported. Many returned to their homeland upon their release, but others spread throughout the world. Far removed from Judea, many Jews lost their Hebrew mastery as Greek became their main language. This created a growing need for a Greek translation of the Hebrew Scriptures. Alexandria, Egypt, held the largest Jewish community of that era and was also a great center of Greek learning. On request of the Alexandrian Jews, according to tradition (supported by the legend of Ptolemy and other scholars), some 70 Hebrew scribes traveled to Alexandria in 285-270 BC where they produced a translation now known as the *Septuagint*. That name derives from the Greek word for 70 and is also designated as *LXX* (the Latin numeral for 70).

Overall the translation was executed with great care, given the means of those days and the challenges that faced translators. Still, when comparing the LXX and the Hebrew (Masoretic) texts, a number of small differences between the texts can be noted. Through the Dead Sea Scrolls, many of these differences are now identified as being caused by the fact that translators likely followed a different Hebrew text belonging to what now is called the *Proto-Septuagint* family.[128]

In addition to the 24 books of the Hebrew OT, the LXX contains additional books as well as add-ons to books circulated in the Greek-speaking world, but were not included in the Hebrew texts. These books are now known as the Apocrypha of the Old Testament.

The LXX was held with great respect in ancient times; Philo and Josephus ascribed divine inspiration to its authors. It formed the basis of the Old Latin versions and is still used intact within the Eastern Orthodox Church. Besides the Old Latin versions, the LXX is also the basis for Gothic, Slavonic, old Syriac, old Armenian, and Coptic versions of the Old Testament.

Significant to all Christians and Bible scholars is the fact that the LXX was quoted both by the writers of the New Testament and by the leaders of the early church. Christians naturally used the LXX since it was the only Greek version available to the earliest Christians, who, as a group, had rapidly become overwhelmingly Gentile and, therefore, unfamiliar with Hebrew. While Jews have not used the LXX in worship or religious study since the second century AD, recent scholarship has brought renewed interest toward it in Judaic Studies. The oldest surviving LXX codices date to the fourth century AD.

The importance of the LXX as evidence for the reliability of the texts of the Old Testament is two-fold:

Confirmation of the Masoretic texts: Although there are textual differences between the LXX and the Masoretic texts, generally these differences are small. In the words of Norman Geisler and William Nix: "*The LXX was generally loyal to the readings of the original Hebrew text, although some have maintained that the translators were not always good Hebrew scholars. The importance of the LXX may be observed in several dimensions. It bridged the religious gap between the Hebrew- and Greek-speaking peoples as it met the needs of Alexandrian Jews. It bridged the historical gap between the Hebrew Old Testament of the Jews and the Greek-speaking Christians who would use the LXX with their New Testament. It set a precedent for missionaries to make translations of the Scriptures into various languages and dialects. It bridges the textual criticism gap in its substantial agreement with the Hebrew Old Testament text (א, A, B, C, etc.). Although the LXX does not measure up to the excellence of the Hebrew Old Testament text, it does indicate the purity of the Hebrew text.*"[129]

Confirmation of early texts: The LXX was translated from the Hebrew Scriptures in the years 285-250 BC. It includes all 24 books of the Hebrew Old Testament. The existence of the LXX proves that the OT was widely available in written form before this time. Therefore the prophecies in the book of Daniel about the Greek and Roman empires as well the extensive prophecies about the Messiah in Daniel, Isaiah, and especially Psalm 22 were written well before the actual events happened.[130]

☼ Exhibit #3: The Canon of the Old Testament

The word *canon* is derived from the Greek word *kanon* ("kanon"), a rod, ruler, staff, or measuring rod. The Biblical canon is the list of books recognized by the leaders of the church, based on objective criteria, to be inspired by God and to authoritatively and accurately express the historical relationship between God and His people.

For the Old Testament, the canon was initially implicit and undisputed. When the Torah was written, it was immediately recognized as inspired by God, handled with great reverence, maintained by the priests, and stored in the Ark of the Covenant. Most other books of the Old Testament were handled in the same manner. While the Jewish nation was flourishing under judges and kings, and prophets were recognized as men from God, their history and prophecies were written and protected by the priests and scribes. After the captivities of the two Jewish kingdoms and the scattering of the people, this became problematic. Even so, the work was still manageable as the priests in Jerusalem continued to maintain the Scriptures.

The first serious discussion about the canon began with the translation of the LXX. A number of texts included in the LXX were not part of the

Scriptures recognized by Jerusalem. These are mostly writings after 400 BC, whereas Jews in Jerusalem considered Malachi (ca. 450 BC) the last prophet. The Hebrew canon had informally been established before 150 BC; this is corroborated by various rabbinical writings of those days[131] stating *the voice of God had ceased to speak directly.* In other words, the prophetic voice had gone quiet, as without prophets there is no new scriptural revelation.

The rise of Christianity (which, in its earliest days, used only the LXX) caused Jewish leaders to recognize the need for a formal canon. Likely by the end of the first century the canon of the Hebrew Old Testament had been officially closed.[132]

The completed canon of the Hebrew Bible contains the same books and texts (in a slightly different order) as the modern Protestant Old Testament. However, in 1546 the Roman Catholic clergy accepted the entirety of the Septuagint as the canon for its Old Testament. Therefore Roman Catholic Bibles contain additional books of the OT Apocrypha (also known as *deuterocanonical* – "second canon"). These are Tobit, Judith, Wisdom of Solomon, Ecclesiasticus (also called Sirach or Ben Sira), Baruch (including the Letter of Jeremiah), First and Second Maccabees, and additions to the books of Esther and Daniel.

The Eastern Orthodox Church has accepted the Septuagint as the definition of the canon for its Old Testament, adding further the books of First Esdras, the Prayer of Manasseh, Psalm 151, and Third Maccabees, with Fourth Maccabees as an appendix.

CHAPTER 10

Authorship and Dating of the Old Testament

"Then the Lord said to Moses, 'Write down these words, for in accordance with these words I have made a covenant with you and with Israel.' Moses was there with the Lord forty days and forty nights without eating bread or drinking water. And he wrote on the tablets the words of the covenant – the Ten Commandments."
EXODUS 34:27-28

WHO WROTE THE OLD TESTAMENT?

In the strictest sense, many of the writings of the Old Testament are anonymous. Few books explicitly identify their authors. Only by tradition do most books have an assigned author. Take the Pentateuch (the first five books of the Bible), also known as the Torah (from the Hebrew word for "the Law"). The text itself makes no claims to be written by Moses. Solid tradition suggests that Moses wrote these books during the 40 years in the desert, in part recording instructions from God, in part preserving the history of the Jewish people.

The question of authorship is no simpler in the remainder of the OT. Talmudic traditions do link some books to well-known Biblical figures, yet most of the books do not directly identify their writers, and there is no unambiguous external evidence of authorship.

The only support for the traditional claims for authorship (and also dating) of the books is found by searching the texts themselves for confirmations through style, details, and historical references.

The 17 major and minor prophetic books seem to lay the strongest claims on authorship, as most identify those said to have received the divine words or visions that the books contain. Critical scholars find various reasons to doubt the authenticity of these claims.

The bottom line is that, working only with the best evidence available, the OT authors almost "A-to-Z" must be viewed as anonymous. The authority of the ancient sources and the integrity of the writers who drew upon them to compile the Hebrew Scriptures are not diminished by this formal anonymity.

The scope of this book does not allow an extensive examination of the issues of authorship and dating of each book Old Testament book. We will, however, discuss the case for authorship and dating for the most disputed and vigorously attacked books: the Pentateuch-Torah and the prophets Isaiah and Daniel.

☼ EXHIBIT #4: AUTHORSHIP OF THE PENTATEUCH

The Pentateuch records the creation of the earth, the flood, God's covenant with the Patriarchs, the exodus, the history of Israel, and the laws revealed to Moses. As a result, its authorship and historical reliability have been and will continue to be subjected to much scholarly attention.

The author of the Pentateuch is not unambiguously identified. Tradition undisputedly has suggested Moses as the writer around 1400 BC. Obvious puzzling passages are found, such as in Genesis 12:6: *"at the time the Canaanites were in the land"* – how could Moses know? Or even more challenging, how could Moses record his own death in Deuteronomy 3:4-5? On the other hand, Moses is clearly the leading character from Exodus on.

In the early twentieth century scholars developed the *Documentary Hypothesis.*[133] This theory claims the Pentateuch was written by four different individuals, each from a different period of Israel's history, long after Moses. The authors are identified by the different names used for God. This theory postulates the oldest document was produced in the ninth or tenth century BC and the latest one during the Babylonian exile as late as the fourth century BC.

A related extreme theory even suggests final authorship is to be assigned to Ezra in the middle of the fifth century BC. This theory claims that many accounts (such as that of the flood) were copied and edited from similar stories from the Babylonian history and culture.

But others have produced strong evidence for Moses as the author. As Gleason L Archer states:[134]

> *"When all the data of the Pentateuchal text have been carefully considered, and all the evidence, both internal and external, has been fairly weighed, the impression is all but irresistible that Mosaic authorship is the one theory which best accords with the surviving historical data. For the purposes of a convenient survey, and without elaborate demonstration or illustration at this point, we shall list the various areas of evidence which point to this conclusion."*

A summary of Archer's evidences includes:

1. The Pentateuch itself implies authorship by Moses (Exodus 7:14, Exodus 24:4, Exodus 34:27. Deuteronomy 31:9).

2. The unity of the first five books suggests a single author.

3. Tradition (including references in the New and Old Testament) uniquely identifies Moses as the author.

4. Moses is the main character.

5. The abundance of irrelevant details points to eyewitness testimony. A wealth of especially irrelevant detail in ancient writings and testimonies is generally accepted as strong evidence of honest and reliable eye-witness testimony.

6. The author is well acquainted with Egypt and the desert, but not with Palestine/Canaan.

7. Many 2nd millennium BC customs (like the blessings of the first born son) are correctly described.

8. A relatively large percentage of Egyptian words is used.

9. Moses had the qualifications (education, background, experience) to be the author.

10. Archaeological and historical discoveries[135] confirm details, such as the existence of the Hittites, Ur, Bethel, Shechem, Sodom and Gomorrah, the use of camels, price of a slave in the days of Joseph, Moses as an Egyptian name, etc.

The discovery of the *Silver Scrolls* in 1979, dated earlier than 586 BC (more about this archaeological discovery later)[136] and containing a text from the book of Numbers, strikes a major blow to the late date argument for the Pentateuch, as this particular section was supposed not to have been written before 500 BC.

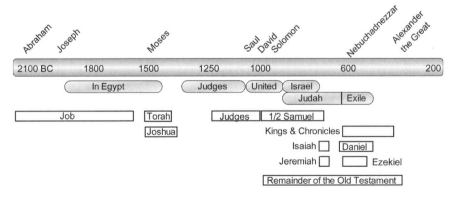

Figure 10-1: Overview of Dating of Books of the Old Testament

The dominant Jewish tradition attributes the Pentateuch to Moses. In addition, the fact that he certainly is the main character in these recordings leads to a conclusion supported by a majority of Biblical scholars that:[137]

"Whether or not Moses can be called the author in a literal sense of anything in the Pentateuch, it is reasonable to hold his work and teaching as the initial stimulus for the creation of the Pentateuch."

The strongly supported and widely accepted role of Moses in the composition of the Pentateuch also implies that at least part of the books dates from the period of the exodus from Egypt: approximately 1440-1400 BC.

☼ EXHIBIT #5: AUTHORSHIP OF THE BOOK OF ISAIAH

Like the Pentateuch, Isaiah has also received significant scholarly scrutiny because of its numerous prophecies about Israel, Babylon, and the Messiah.

The author is identified as Isaiah, son of Amoz (Isaiah 1:1: *"The vision concerning Judah and Jerusalem that Isaiah son of Amoz saw during the reigns of Uzziah, Jotham, Ahaz and Hezekiah, kings of Judah."*). That pinpoints the writing to the period from 790 BC through 686 BC, at least 100 years before the fall of Jerusalem to the Babylonians and the resulting exile of 70 years. Isaiah extensively prophesied about this event as well as about God's judgment on the Assyrians (who conquered the Northern Kingdom of Israel in 722, during Isaiah's lifetime) and on the Babylonians.

Because liberal scholars are skeptical about anything that points to supernatural inspiration of the Bible, they have tried to explain the fulfilled prophecies in this book by re-dating it to after the events. The theory of *Deutero-Isaiah* (or Second Isaiah)[138] emerged near the end of the eighteenth century. According to this theory, Isaiah himself wrote only the first 39 chapters, leaving one of his students to pen the second part (chapters 40-66) after the Babylonian captivity started (so, after 586 BC). This later date would explain explicit predictions of *"Cyrus, King of Persia"* in Isaiah 44:28-45:1.[139]

The Deutero-Isaiah theory claims Isaiah chapters 40-55 contain no personal details of the prophet Isaiah, in strong contrast to Isaiah 1-39. The first section relates numerous stories of Isaiah, especially his dealings with kings and others in Jerusalem. The style and language of Isaiah 40-55 are said to be quite different from the earlier chapters (interestingly, an argument for similarity of styles is advanced by scholars who support one author for Isaiah). The assertion is that specific references to Cyrus originated in the experiences of the exiles in Babylon.[140] This last argument is supposedly the strongest, yet it seems more wish than fact! It claims the second part of Isaiah was written later because only a later date can explain the accuracy of the prophecy.

Many scholars reject the Deutero-Isaiah theory. A long list of arguments includes the similarity of writing styles in both sections, the consistent use of the same words throughout, and the familiarity of the author with Palestine but not Babylon. Jewish tradition uniformly ascribes the entire book to Isaiah. The Dead Sea Scrolls contain a complete scroll of Isaiah dated from the second century BC that indicates the book as one unit (the end of chapter 39 and the beginning of chapter 40 are in one continuous column of text). Evidently scribes who produced this scroll never doubted the singular unity of the book. Neither did the New Testament authors nor the early church, as quotations from both sections are attributed only to Isaiah.[141]

Isaiah contains extensive and explicit prophecies about the coming of the Messiah as well as the life and crucifixion of Christ. Briefly these include:[142] the reign of Christ in the kingdom (2:3-5), the virgin birth of Christ (7:14), the reign of Christ (9:2,7), His rule over the world (9:4), Christ as a descendant of David (11:1,10), Christ to be filled with the Spirit (11:2; 42:1), Christ to judge with righteousness (11:3-5; 42:1, 4), Christ to rule over the nations (11:10), Christ to be gentle to the weak (42:3), Christ to make possible the New Covenant (42:6; 49:8), Christ to be a light to the Gentiles and to be worshiped by them (42:6; 49:6-7; 52:15), Christ to be rejected by Israel (49:7; 53:1-3), Christ to be obedient to God and subject to suffering (50:6; 53:7-8), Christ to be exalted (52:13; 53:12), Christ to restore Israel and judge the wicked (61:1-3).

Messianic prophecy is strong and important evidence for Jesus' claims to be God (more about prophecy when we discuss the evidence for Christ).[143]

These prophecies cannot be ignored since Isaiah's writings were completed many centuries before Jesus Christ was born. Remember, the Dead Sea Scrolls contained more than one complete scroll of this book composed well before the birth of Christ. And the book of Isaiah was included in the LXX translated at least 300 years earlier.

✲ EXHIBIT #6: AUTHORSHIP OF THE BOOK OF DANIEL

The book of Daniel contains three detailed predictions of the overthrow of the Babylonian empire by Medo-Persia. It also prophesies the Greek empire under Alexander the Great, the breakdown into four smaller powers after Alexander's death, and the subsequent rise of Rome (Daniel chapters 7-12).[144] As the book of Daniel is claimed to be written by Daniel in Babylon, during the exile around 535 BC, these prophecies were made centuries before the events.

Liberal critics push the date for the composition of Daniel to near 165 BC, in an effort to discredit the book's prophecies about the Greek and Roman empires. Their claim, however, stretches far beyond available evidence. The case for an early date includes the detailed knowledge of sixth century BC events not known by a later author, various archaeological discoveries that confirm the names of characters/kings in the book, the use of early Aramaic language by the author, and the similarity of theology between Daniel and the other books of the Old Testament written in the 700-500 BC period.[145] Ezekiel, the sixth century prophet known to be a contemporary of Daniel, refers to Daniel three times in his book (Ezekiel 14:14, 14:20, and 28:30) and these references are convincing evidence for the traditional view.[146] Considering that Daniel was included in the LXX (translated before 250 BC) it becomes obvious the 165 BC date simply will not work. Lastly, among the Dead Sea Scrolls eight manuscripts of Daniel survive, one of these was dated to the late second century BC. It is highly unlikely the book would have been accepted as Scripture by the Qumran community and placed along side other sacred books only a few years after its composition.[147]

Even if the 165 BC date were to be considered, the prophecies about *"the fourth beast"* (Rome) would still have been recorded about 100 years before the events (the rise of the Roman Empire occurred around 60 BC).

Besides its many prophecies of world events, Daniel contains accurate predictions about Christ. As we will discuss in detail later,[148] Daniel 9:24:27, the "Seventy Sevens" Prophecy, predicts the exact day for Palm Sunday, the triumphant entrance of Jesus into Jerusalem. As with Isaiah, the Dead Sea Scrolls and the LXX present undisputed evidence that this book was written centuries before the birth of Christ.

Chapter 11

The Texts of the
New Testament

*"In addition, for the proof of our statements, we take testimonies from
that which is called the Old Testament and that which is called the
New – which we believe to be divine writings."*
Origen, ca. 225 AD[149]

While the Old Testament was compiled over many generations and
records the history of thousands of years, the New Testament covers only one
century at most and was completed within a single lifetime.

The evidence for the reliability of the texts is quite different and far more
extensive than for the Old Testament. It comes from two main sources: Greek
manuscripts and translations, and the testimony of the leaders and writers in
the early Christian movement.

☼ Exhibit #7: The Manuscript Evidence

The New Testament is by far the most reliable ancient writing known
today. There exist as many as an astounding 25,000[150] ancient manuscripts that
contain all or portions of the New Testament.

Counting Greek copies alone, the texts are preserved in 5,366 partial and
complete manuscripts hand copied from the second through the fifteenth century. A few New Testament fragments are very early, dating from the second
century. At least 362 New Testament manuscripts and 245 lectionaries (collections of Scripture texts grouped together for reading in public worship services)
date from the second through the tenth centuries, constituting nearly 11% of
all New Testament and lectionary manuscripts. Such early manuscripts are valuable in establishing the original text of the New Testament. The other 89% of
manuscripts are minuscule, dating between the ninth and fifteenth centuries.[151]

Add to these Greek manuscripts the more than 10,000 Latin Vulgate and
at least 9,300 early translations, and we approach the earlier mentioned number of 25,000.

By contrast, the manuscripts for most other ancient books date from about
a thousand years after their original composition. To compare this to the other
ancient writings: Homer's *Iliad* is in "second place" behind the New Testament

with no more than 643 copies. And of Plato's *Tetralogies* only seven copies are known. Also the earliest copy of Plato's work is dated about 1,200 years after he produced the original. The oldest copy of the *Iliad* dates about 500 years after the original. This is a dramatic contrast to the oldest papyrus text of the New Testament, a part of chapter 18 of the Gospel of John, dated at near 125 AD.

The importance of the vast number of manuscripts copies cannot be overstated. This abundance of manuscripts makes it possible to reconstruct the original with virtually complete accuracy.[152]

OVERVIEW OF THE NEW TESTAMENT MANUSCRIPTS

An overview of the most important New Testament manuscripts, sorted by age:[153]

125 AD – Oldest Fragment (P_{52}): Perhaps the earliest section of Scripture to survive is a fragment of a papyrus codex containing John 18:31-33 and 37 of about 2 1/2 x 3 1/2 inches. Known as the *Rylands Papyrus* (P_{52}), it dates from the first half of the second century, as early as 117-138 AD. Found in Egypt (some distance from the probable place of composition in Asia Minor), this little piece of papyrus has forced the critics to place the fourth gospel in the first century, abandoning previous assertions that it could not have been written by the apostle John.

250 AD – Chester Beatty Papyri (P_{45},P_{46},P_{47}): This collection of three codices contains most of the New Testament. P_{45} consists of pieces of 30 leaves of a papyrus codex: two from Matthew, two from John, six from Mark, seven from Luke, and thirteen from Acts. P_{46} contains 86 slightly mutilated leaves (11 by 6 1/2 inches), stemming from an original that contained 104 pages of Paul's epistles, including Romans, Hebrews, 1 Corinthians, 2 Corinthians, Ephesians, Galatians, Philippians, Colossians, 1 Thessalonians, and 2 Thessalonians. P_{47} is made up of 10 slightly mutilated leaves of the book of Revelation.

Second-third century AD – Bodmer Papyri (P_{66},P_{72},P_{75}): P_{66}, dating from about 200 AD or earlier, contains 104 leaves of John. P_{72} is the earliest known copy of Jude, 1 Peter, and 2 Peter. It dates from the third century and also contains several apocryphal books. P_{75} is a codex of 102 pages (originally 144); it contains most of Luke and John, and dates between 175 and 225 AD. This is the earliest known copy of Luke. Actually, in this collection are some 88 papyri manuscripts of portions of the New Testament, of which the foregoing are merely the most important representatives. The papyri witness to the text is invaluable, dating as far back as the threshold of the second century – within a generation of the autographs (original copies penned by the author) and including most of the New Testament. All are extant (that is, available as manuscript) from within the first 200 years after the New Testament itself was written.

325-350 AD – Codex Vaticanus (B): The Codex Vaticanus is perhaps the oldest codex on parchment or vellum (ca. 325-350). It is one of the most important witnesses to the text of the New Testament. This manuscript of the whole Bible was likely written by the middle of the fourth century; however, it was not known to textual scholars until after 1475, when catalogued in the Vatican Library. It includes most of the LXX version of the Old Testament and most of the New Testament in Greek. Missing are Timothy through Philemon, Hebrews 9:14 through Revelation, and the general epistles.

340 AD – Codex Sinaiticus ($\aleph$): This fourth century Greek manuscript is generally considered the most important witness to the text because of its antiquity, accuracy, and lack of omissions. It contains over half the Old Testament (LXX), and all of the New Testament, with the exception of Mark 16:9-20 and John 7:53-8:11.

From five of the early manuscripts alone ($P_{45}, P_{46}, P_{47}, P_{66}, P_{75}$), it is possible to construct all of Luke, John, Romans, 1 and 2 Corinthians, Galatians, Ephesians, Philippians, Colossians, 1 and 2 Thessalonians, Hebrews, and portions of Matthew, Mark, Acts, and Revelation. Only the "pastoral epistles" (Titus, 1 and 2 Timothy), the general epistles (James, 1 and 2 Peter, and 1, 2, and 3 John), and Philemon are excluded.

Overview of NT Manuscripts versus other Writings of the same Period[154]					
Author and Work	Date of events	Date of writing	Earliest text[155]	Event to writing	Event to text
Matthew, *Gospel*	4 BC -30 AD	55-70	ca. 200	<50 years	<200 years
Mark, *Gospel*	27 - 33 AD	50-70	ca. 225	<50 years	<200 years
Luke, *Gospel*	5 BC -33 AD	55-70	ca. 200	<50 years	<200 years
John, *Gospel*	27-33 AD	85-95	ca. 130	<80 years	<100 years
Paul, *Letters*	33 AD	50-65	ca. 200	20-30 years	<200 years
Josephus, *War*	200 BC -70 AD	ca. 80	ca. 950	10-300 years	900-1,200 years
Josephus, *Antiquities*	200 BC -65 AD	ca. 95	ca. 1050	30-300 years	1,000-1,300 years
Tacitus, *Annals*	14-68 AD	100-120	ca. 850	30-100 years	800-850 years
Seutonius, *Lives*	50 BC -95 AD	ca. 120	ca. 850	25-170 years	750-900 years
Pliny, *Letters*	97-112 AD	110-112	ca. 850	0-3 years	725-750 years

Table 11-1: Comparing NT Manuscript to Other Ancient Writings

The amount of manuscript evidence for the New Testament (see table 11-1) makes it by far the most reliable of all ancient books.

INTEGRITY OF THE MANUSCRIPT TEXTS

The texts of New Testament manuscripts were not copied and maintained as meticulously as those of the Old Testament. As strange as it may appear, the texts for the Old Testament – especially the oldest books in the Torah – are the very texts likely to be the most accurate when compared to the original. This is because they were recognized as the sacred Word right from the beginning; as a result they were carefully protected and copied by scribes. The New Testament manuscripts, however, were copied by the early Christians. Not all text was immediately acknowledged as Scripture, but also the early Christians were not well-trained scribes. They did not do the extensive error checking like the Masoretes and other Jewish scribes and were under much more time pressure to get the texts reproduced and distributed among the fast-growing number of eager disciples of Christ.

Errors in copying, mistranslations, and some scribal editing and additions to many manuscripts have resulted in numerous *variant readings*.

Norman Geisler[156] cites widespread misunderstanding among critics as to "errors" in the Biblical manuscripts. Some estimated as many as 200,000 variant readings. First, these are not "errors" but only variations, the vast majority of which <u>are strictly grammatical</u>. Second, these readings are spread over more than 5,300 manuscripts, so that a variant spelling of one letter of one word in one verse in 2,000 manuscripts is counted as 2,000 "errors." Textual scholars Westcott and Hort estimated only one in 60 of these variants has significance. This would leave the text 98.33% pure. Philip Schaff calculated that of the 150,000 variants known in his day, only 400 altered the meaning of the passage, only 50 were of real significance, and *not even one* affected *"an article of faith or a precept of duty which is not abundantly sustained by other and undoubted passages, or by the whole tenor of Scripture teaching."* [157]

Most other ancient books are not so well authenticated. New Testament scholar Bruce Metzger estimated that the *Mahabharata* of Hinduism has been copied with only about 90% accuracy and Homer's *Iliad* with about 95%. By comparison, he estimated the New Testament is about 99.5% accurate.[158]

It is safe to summarize that less than one percent of the New Testament text as we know it today is under competent dispute. No doctrine taught in the Bible depends on the turn of any of these disputes.[159]

In the words of Dockery, Mathews, and Sloan: *"For most of the Biblical text a single reading has been transmitted. Elimination of scribal errors and intentional changes leaves only a small percentage of text about which any questions occur."* [160] They conclude: *"It must be said that the amount of time between the original composition and the next surviving manuscript is far less for the New Testament than for any other work in Greek literature...Although there are certain differences in many of the New Testament manuscripts, not one fundamental doctrine of the Christian faith rests on a disputed reading.*" [161]

And finally, the conclusion of the renowned Bible scholar F.F. Bruce: [162]

"*The variant readings about which any doubt remains among textual critics of the New Testament affect no material question of historic fact or of Christian faith or practice.*"

☼ EXHIBIT #8: EARLY CHURCH LEADERS' LETTERS

Another great attestation for the authority of our New Testament is the huge number of quotations found in letters and other writings from the leaders of the early church. [163] Dean Burgon's research found more 86,000 quotations from this vast body of information. [164]

Harold J. Greenlee points out "*these quotations are so extensive that the New Testament could virtually be reproduced from them without the use of other New Testament manuscripts.*" [165]

Despite the extensive quotations, early church writings must be used with caution. The *Early Church Leaders* in general did not have access to much written material from the NT. As a result quotations were often used loosely (although some writers were very accurate), but they at least reproduced the substantial message of the original text. Additionally, some writers were prone to make mistakes or even occasionally to make intentional changes. Therefore the integrity of the quotations is too low to prove useful in accurate analysis of variant readings in the NT texts.

The testimony of the early church however is quite valuable for two other reasons:

Early dating of the New Testament: Quotations of NT texts – especially the gospels and Paul's epistles – in letters dated to the early second century or even near the end of the first century provide hard evidence for dating the texts in the early second half of the first century, within a generation of the death of Christ.

Early acceptance as Scripture: Quotations by church writers from the gospels and epistles at such an early date provide clear testimony of widespread recognition that these texts belong to an informally accepted New Testament canon.

AN OVERVIEW OF THE EARLY CHURCH WRITINGS

Below is a summary of the most important early church writings from what is often called the *Age of the Apostolic Fathers* (70-150 AD) and *Early Ante-Nicene Fathers* (150-300 AD) along with some background about the authors (see also table 11-2): [166]

Clement of Rome's epistle to the Corinthian church (ca. 95-97 AD):
Clement (30-100 AD) was likely a Gentile from Rome. As disciple of Paul,
he was likely with Paul at Philippi (57 AD – he is mentioned by name in
Philippians 4:2) and later in Rome. Clement, a bishop (presbyter) in Rome,
wrote to the church at Corinth (as Paul had done before him), quite possibly the earliest Christian writing outside the New Testament. Clement quoted the Old Testament extensively as Scripture, referring also to words of Jesus
found in Matthew, Mark, and Luke. He quoted from Romans, 1
Corinthians, and Hebrews. His letter also provides important evidence for
the martyrdom of the apostles Peter and Paul and for a mission of Paul to the
"western boundary" (Spain?).

Ignatius' seven letters (martyred ca. 107 AD): Ignatius of Antioch wrote
seven letters while en route under armed guard to Rome to be martyred (ca.
107 AD). He wrote to churches in cities through which he passed: Philadelphia
and Smyrna, and to churches that sent delegations to visit him during this final
journey: Ephesus, Tralles, and Magnesia. He sent one letter ahead to the
church in Rome to prevent their intervention with the authorities in deliver-
ing him from martyrdom. Lastly, he also wrote to Polycarp, the bishop of
Smyrna. His references to the New Testament are either loose quotations from
memory or allusions, but include Matthew, Luke and John as well as Romans,
1 Corinthians, Galatians, Ephesians, Philippians, Colossians, and 1
Thessalonians. Some claim also references/allusions to other Pauline letters,
Hebrews, James, and 1 Peter.

New Testament Confirmations from the Earliest Writers			
	Clement of Rome Bishop of Rome	Ignatius En route to Rome	Polycarp Bishop of Smyrna
To who:	Corinth	7 letters	Philippi
When:	95 AD	110 AD	115 AD
Quotes from:	Matthew, Mark, Luke, Romans, 1 Corinthians, Hebrews	Matthew, Luke, John, Romans, Colossians 1 Corinthians, Galatians, Ephesians, Philippians, 1 Thessalonians	Matthew, Mark, Acts, Romans, 1&2 Corinthians, Galatians, Ephesians, Philippians, 1&2 Timothy, 1 Peter, 2 John
Refers to:	John, Acts, James, 1 Peter, Ephesians	Hebrews, James, 1 Peter	

Together they confirm the existence of 20 of the 27 NT books by 115 AD

Table 11-2: Early Confirmations of the New Testament

Polycarp's epistle to the Philippians (ca. 115 AD): Born to a Christian family, Polycarp (ca. 70-156 AD) is said to have been a disciple of John the apostle. The account of his death, recorded in a letter from the church of Smyrna to the church of Philomelium, is the earliest account of martyrdom in early church writings. His letter to the Philippians has been preserved and shows strong apostolic influence. He quotes numerous times from Matthew, Mark, Acts, Romans, 1 and 2 Corinthians, Galatians, Ephesians, Philippians, 1 and 2 Timothy, 1 Peter (10 times), and 2 John.

Epistle of Barnabas (ca. 100 AD): The writer of this epistle is thought to have been an Alexandrian Jew in the times of Trajan and Hadrian. His name might have been Barnabas, but he most likely was not the same as Barnabas known from the book of Acts. Whoever wrote it, it is commonly dated at the end of the first century. Norman Geisler dates this letter even to 70-79 AD.[167] It cites Matthew a number of times and includes several loose quotations of John, Romans, and 2 Peter.

The Shepherd of Hermas (ca. 115-140): The text was written by a certain Hermas in Rome between 140 and 150 AD. "Free" quotations from memory and allusions to the New Testament are evident in this writing more than in earlier works. All three portions of the *Shepherd* cite the New Testament, including Matthew and Mark as well epistles such as 1 Corinthians, Hebrews, James, 1 Peter, and 1 John.

The Didache (ca. 100-150 AD): *The Didache,* or *The Teaching of the Twelve Apostles,* was discovered only in 1873 and was published ten years later.[168] No date is known, but internal evidence suggests the first half of the second century. The Didache was widely used in the early church as a handbook. The pattern of loose quotations and allusions is similar to the *Shepherd.* Numerous references to Matthew, Mark and Luke demonstrate widespread use of the gospels by the middle of the second century. Other citations include Romans, 1 Corinthians, Hebrews, 1 John, and Jude.

Papias (ca. 60-130 AD): The information concerning Papias and his work was provided by Eusebius of Caesarea and Irenaeus of Lyons. According to Irenaeus, Papias heard the apostle John preach and was acquainted with Polycarp. Eusebius mentioned his *Explanation of the Sayings of the Lord.* Papias claimed Mark the Evangelist never actually heard Christ, but was the interpreter of Peter. He gave a careful account of all he remembered from the preaching of Peter. Papias also affirmed that Matthew wrote the sayings of Jesus in Hebrew. Irenaeus understood this to refer to Hebraisms in Matthew's gospel, though Origen thought it meant Matthew originally wrote his gospel in Hebrew. The importance of Papias as an early witness to the existence and authorship of both Matthew and Mark cannot be overstated. Traditionally his writings are dated to 120-130 AD, however, a compelling case can be built for a date as early as before 110 AD![169]

Justin Martyr (ca. 100 - martyred 165 AD): Of Greek descent, Justin was born in Palestine near the modern city of Nablus in Samaria. For awhile he taught Christian philosophy at Ephesus, but left in 135 AD and went to Rome, where he taught and wrote until martyred under Marcus Aurelius. Justin was one of the first apologists to offer Christianity to the world of his day using current Hellenistic modes of thought. Only two or three of his treatises are extant: his first *Apology* (the second may not be authentic) and his *Dialogue with Trypho*. More than 330 citations of the New Testament are in his work, along with an additional 266 allusions.

Other great names in the early church include Clement of Alexandria (ca. 150-215), Tertullian (ca. 160-220), Hippolytus (ca. 170-236), Origen (ca. 185-254), and Cyprian (ca. 195-258). A vast number of their writings have been preserved and thousands of quotations from the New Testament can be recognized. More than 36,000[170] quotations from the NT have been found in writings before the council of Nicea in 325 AD.

The above confirms that the New Testament was available to the church as early as 95-100 AD, so within 65-70 years of the resurrection. These letters also help to establish an absolute latest date at which the documents have been written. We will discuss the dating of the gospels in a later chapter, but for now these letters establish that at least 20 of the 27 books of the New Testament books (all except Titus, Philemon, 2 Peter, 1 and 3 John, Jude, and Revelation) were in wide circulation in the early church by the year 100 AD.

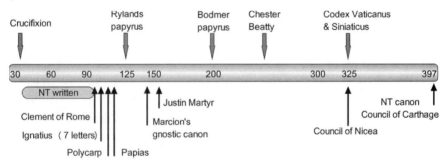

Figure 11-1: Establishment of the New Testament

☼ EXHIBIT #9: CREEDS IN THE NEW TESTAMENT

Even before the books of the New Testament were written, the early church formulated *creeds* to proclaim and share the faith. A creed (from the

Latin "credo" which means: "I believe") is a memorized statement that was declared, shared, and passed among believers at early church meetings. Many of the creeds were incorporated into the New Testament books; some as early as the gospels but others in apostolic letters.[171]

These verbal statements of faith were originally in Aramaic and are easily recognized, because they use a different style than other passages, contain Aramaic words and/or often are introduced by an "*I-pass-on-as-I-received*" construction. If translated back to the original, most creeds exhibit poetic features and sound like old hymns,[172] which made for easier and better memorizing.

By far the most important two creeds are the recollections of the sharing of the bread and wine at the Lord's supper in 1 Corinthians 11:23-29 and Paul's testimony about the resurrection appearances in 1 Corinthians 15:3-8 (we will visit this creed in more detail when we discuss the resurrection evidence in a later chapter).[173]

Other creeds are found in Romans 1:3-4 and 10:9, 1 Timothy 3:16, 2 Timothy 2:8, and Philippians 2:6-11. Creeds can also be found in the sermons of Peter and Paul in Acts.

These creeds are the oldest Christian testimonies to Jesus' ministry, His teachings, and resurrection; some date even to the mid-30s AD, within a few years of the resurrection! Even the most critical scholars acknowledge that these creeds are to be considered reliable eyewitness testimony exceptionally close to the actual events.

☼ EXHIBIT #10: THE CANON OF THE NEW TESTAMENT

Formal creation of Christian Scripture was achieved slowly. In the early years, the message of Christianity was transmitted orally. Preachers, many of whom had seen Jesus and heard him teach, shared vivid memories and proclaimed the message of His death, burial, and resurrection.

As the years passed, however, and the church spread into Asia Minor and Italy, written records about Jesus and the apostles became increasingly important. For instance, as an aging apostle, Peter urged readers to rely heavily upon what he had written (2 Peter 1). Eventually, those writings would assume a status equivalent to the Hebrew Scriptures.

There is little doubt, that the earliest texts of the emerging New Testament canon were the letters by Paul written around and just after 50 AD. Soon the gospels, the apostolic memoirs, became available as well. These texts conformed to the "*rule of faith*" – the Christian truth recognized in the early church. As evidenced from the early church writings, by 100 AD all books of what we now call the NT (except for a few letters and Revelation) had implicitly been accepted as part of the canon.

The first known effort to create an official list occurred in 140 AD (known now as *Marcion's canon*). This list included ten of Paul's letters and the Gospel of Luke. Marcion was a gnostic heretic (he believed the God of the OT was not the God of the NT, and he rejected the humanity of Christ). He strongly disliked the Jewish aspect of the gospels. His list was soon viewed as heretical by Early Church Leaders, but sparked the need for a formal canon.

That second century conflict, scholars say, shaped the church's emphasis on authentic apostolic connection as the main determinant of canonical status. Either a book would be written by an apostle/disciple of Jesus (Matthew, John, Peter, Paul) or by somebody closely associated with an apostle/disciple (Luke via his links to Paul, Peter, and others; Mark as the "voice" of Peter; James and Jude as the brothers of Jesus). Consequently some highly regarded writings from second and third generation Christians were excluded (this includes many of the Early Church Leaders discussed earlier).

In 397 AD (at the *Council of Carthage*) a list was finally compiled and found wide acceptance. There was little disagreement, except for the books of James, Jude (both brothers of Jesus, but not known to be disciples during his lifetime), 2 Peter, 2 and 3 John, and Revelation. These books were later accepted and included in the completed New Testament.

Based on his research of the manuscript evidence for the New Testament, the great classical scholar Sir Frederic Kenyon writes:[174]

> *"The interval then between the dates of original composition and the earliest extant evidence becomes so small as to be in fact negligible, and the last foundation for any doubt that the Scriptures have come down to us substantially as they were written has now been removed. Both the authenticity and the general integrity of the books of the New Testament may be regarded as finally established."*

CHAPTER 12

Authorship and Dating of the New Testament

"So too our Lord Jesus Christ…sent his apostles as priests carrying well-wrought trumpets. First Matthew sounded the priestly trumpet of his Gospel. Mark also, and Luke, and John, each gave forth a strain on their priestly trumpets. Peter moreover sounds with the two trumpets of his Epistles; James also and Jude. Still the number is incomplete, and John gives forth the trumpet sound through his Epistles and Apocalypse; and Luke, while describing the deeds of the apostles. Latest of all, moreover, that one comes who said, "I think that God has set us forth as the apostles last of all", and thundering on the fourteen trumpets of his Epistles he threw down, even to their very foundations, the walls of Jericho, that is to say, all the instruments of idolatry and the dogmas of the philosophers."

ORIGEN, CA. 254 AD[175]

WHO WROTE THE NEW TESTAMENT?

The New Testament has 27 individual books, of which the majority, 21, is a collection of letters to certain individuals, particular churches or the body of Christ in general. Most of the epistles follow a style common in those days, placing the name of the writer at the beginning (exceptions to this are Hebrews and 1,2, and 3 John). In addition, Revelation has several explicit claims to authorship by John the apostle. Thus most of the epistles and Revelation are quite unambiguous as to the identity of the author. We only need to verify whether the name indeed refers to the person we think it is (the absence of surnames makes that a little harder) and that this epistle is genuine and not a forgery.

The gospels and Acts, however, do not mention an author by name. Fortunately, there are early church traditions as well as a number of indications in the documents themselves to give us pointers and clues towards the identity of the writer.

Authorship and date are closely linked. As we have seen, the main criterion for canonizing books in the NT was authorship by either a personal disciple/apostle of Jesus or by somebody closely associated with one of these. The date for the book obviously would need to be within the lifetime of the claimed author. So we will investigate both together.

In contrast to the OT, all NT books were written within one generation. Likely all the writers knew one another; some very well (as Peter and John), some only distantly (as Paul and James). Perhaps some never met in person, but still each would have known about the others.

Logically the books can be divided into the following groups:

- **The synoptic gospels and Acts:** Depictions of the birth, life, ministry, death, and resurrection of Jesus recorded in the gospels by Matthew, Mark, and Luke as well as the history of the apostolic church and Paul's missionary travels.
- **The Gospel of John:** The teachings, ministry, death, and resurrection of Jesus recorded by the apostle John.
- **The Pauline epistles:** A collection of 13 instructional letters by the apostle Paul to seven churches he founded and some of his close disciples.
- **The other epistles and Revelation:** Another eight teaching epistles written to various churches and Christians by the apostles Peter and John, and by James and Jude, both brothers of Jesus. The book of Revelation speaks to churches undergoing intense persecution.

From the perspective of evidence, the most important books are the gospels, Acts and Paul's letters, so we will limit our discussion to these.

WHO WROTE THE GOSPELS?

The gospels (Matthew, Mark, Luke, and John) – regarded by many as the most sacred Christian writings – proclaim through dramatic narrative, recorded sayings, and theological dogma, the story of Jesus and the significance of His life, death, and resurrection. The gospels are largely regarded the authoritative record of Jesus' words and deeds. They are recollections of original disciples (as Matthew and John), or of close associates to the apostles (as Mark and Luke).

But, who wrote the Gospel of Matthew? The obvious answer is Matthew, but not everyone agrees. Many scholars insist there is no convincing evidence that any of the gospels were actually written by the one whose name is attached. The name might have been associated later by some unknown person in an effort to increase the credibility of the text. These claims are made by non-believing scholars who reject the miracles recorded in the gospel and insist the story of the resurrection is only a myth. One can only wonder what evidence could convince such critics. Scholarship does not ensure objectivity and clearly many knowledgeable scholars have personal agendas. Once again, this shows the importance of investigating all the evidence on both sides of each dispute.

Information about authors comes from two sources:

External evidences: Statements made about this gospel by sources outside the Bible, including the Early Church Leaders as well as tradition.

Internal clues: What clues does the gospel itself give us about the author?

☼ EXHIBIT #11: THE SYNOPTIC GOSPELS AND THE BOOK OF ACTS

The first three gospels are Matthew, Mark, and Luke. No in-depth study is needed to notice these three documents share a lot of common information (figure 12-1 shows these relationships). Traditionally, therefore, they are referred to as the *synoptic gospels* as they lend themselves to a synoptic arrangement, a form in which they can be studied together.[176]

Most of the content of 606 out of the 661 verses (approximately 90%) of Mark appears in Matthew. That means that out of the 1068 verses in Matthew, about 500 (close to half) contain information also found in Mark. The same is true of Luke: 350 verses in Mark appear with little change in Luke's gospel. Therefore of the 1149 verses found in Luke, 350 are parallel accounts (about 30%) to Mark. Only 31 verses in Mark are unique to that gospel. This has led to the widely held notion that Mark was the first gospel written, and that both Luke and Matthew had at least a partial copy of Mark available to them, as they wrote their gospels.

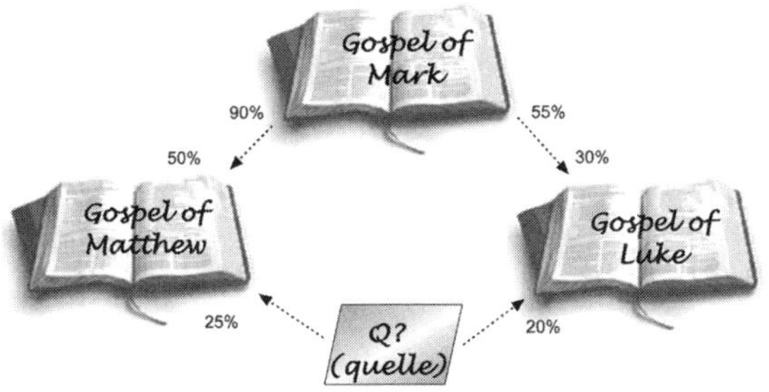

Figure 12-1: The Relationship Between the Synoptic Gospels

When we compare Luke to Matthew (excluding verses similar to Mark), we notice these two have about 250 verses with common material not found in Mark. This leaves about 300 verses unique to Matthew and perhaps 550 unique to Luke. This similarity between the two has led to the popular theory that Luke and Matthew shared a common source that was available to both. This document (or person or even persons) is usually referred to as "*Q*" (or "Quelle," German for "source").

However, it is significant to note that both Matthew and Luke in the verses shared with Mark and/or Q use their own style. Each aims at different readers, and each has details which clearly show personal and/or other eyewitness accounts are incorporated! Yes, there is much similar material, but each gospel seems to access additional information. Even Mark, thought to be the earliest gospel, has occasionally more detailed descriptions than

Luke and Matthew. The puzzle is much more complicated than it appears at first glance.

THE AUTHOR OF THE GOSPEL OF MATTHEW

This gospel probably has the weakest claim to the name associated with the book. Many clues point to Matthew the apostle, but there are conflicting observations. Therefore, the conclusion that Matthew was the author remains somewhat speculative; it is, some might say, a well-educated guess. Let's look at what we know:

External evidences:
- Church tradition has always regarded Matthew as the author. In this context we need to remember he was a tax collector, a profession hugely unpopular in those days. This alone would make him an unlikely candidate if a name was selected later to be attached to this book.
- Already by 120-130 AD, some claim even as early as 110 AD,[177] Papias writes: *"Matthew put together the oracles in the Hebrew language, and each one interpreted them as best as he could."*[178]
- And Irenaeus writes in *Against Heresies* by 170-180 AD: *"Matthew also issued a written gospel among the Hebrews in their own dialect, while Peter and Paul were preaching in Rome."*[179]

Internal clues:
- The gospel is written in well-versed Greek, but not polished so as to suggest Greek was the author's native language. This is consistent with the language level expected of a tax-collector with the skills of a scribe and proficient in Greek.
- The style throughout is Jewish, showing the author was likely a Jew. This includes the lineage of Jesus, many OT quotations, and the emphasis on fulfilled prophecy.
- The gospel has the most extensive record of Jesus' teachings compared to the other gospels. Best known, perhaps, is the complete *Sermon on the Mount*. That would also fit Matthew's scribal skills, which might have included a form of shorthand.

Arguments against Matthew:
- Critics charge that if Matthew the eyewitness was the author, he would have no need for Mark's gospel as a source. However, Mark was not his only source, but one of several. Since Mark (as we will see on the next pages)[180] likely was "Peter's interpreter," it would only make perfect sense

for Matthew to use Mark/Peter's account as an important source. Especially as Peter was one of the three apostles closest to Jesus (together with John and James). He enjoyed private meetings with Jesus and witnessed unique events.

- The above-mentioned references from Papias and Irenaeus suggest this gospel was first written in Hebrew or more likely Aramaic. This has led to the speculation that Matthew might have written an initial version in Aramaic completed by a later writer in Greek.

As well respected scholar Craig L. Blomberg concludes on the authorship of Matthew:[181]

"This author, at least of an original draft of this book (or one of its major sources), seems quite probably to have been the converted toll collector, also named Levi, who became one of Jesus' twelve apostles. But again we present these conclusions tentatively. Little depends on them. Neither inspiration nor apostolic authority depends on apostolic authorship (cf. Mark and Luke), and the church was capable of preserving accurate information outside of apostolic circles."

THE AUTHOR OF THE GOSPEL OF MARK

This gospel is also anonymous, but we have some solid early evidences:

External evidences:
- Papias wrote in 120-130 AD (or even before 110 AD):[182] *Mark having become the interpreter of Peter, wrote down accurately whatsoever he remembered. It was not, however, in exact order that he related the sayings or deeds of Christ. For he neither heard the Lord nor accompanied Him. But afterwards, as I said, he accompanied Peter, who accommodated his instructions to the necessities [of his hearers], but with no intention of giving a regular narrative of the Lord's sayings. Wherefore Mark made no mistake in thus writing some things as he remembered them. For of one thing he took especial care, not to omit anything he had heard, and not to put anything fictitious into the statements."* [183] This quote not only dates Mark as a gospel well known in the beginning of the second century, it also confirms Mark's relationship to Peter the apostle.
- Another early church confirmation is from Irenaeus ca. 170-180 AD: *"Mark, the interpreter and follower of Peter, begins his gospel narrative in this manner."* [184]
- Clement of Alexandria emphasized further the link between Mark and Peter ca. 195 AD: *"Mark, the follower of Peter, while Peter publicly*

*preached the Gospel at Rome before some of Caesar's equites, and adduced
many testimonies to Christ, in order that thereby they might be able to commit to memory what was spoken, of what was spoken by Peter wrote entirely what is called the Gospel according to Mark."* [185]

- Likely the strongest argument for Mark is the unanimity of the early
  church behind the conviction that Mark was the author of a gospel. All
  but Augustine claimed further that Mark wrote in association with Peter.
  The claim for Mark is significant when one realizes he was not prominent in the primitive church; indeed, he had tarnished his reputation by
  deserting Paul and Barnabas in the middle of a missionary campaign
  (Acts 13:13). It is most unlikely the church would have attributed a
  gospel to him without strong evidence he wrote it.[186] If the early church
  would have "made up" a name for the gospel, Mark certainly would have
  been an illogical choice.

Internal clues:
- Only this gospel records the flight of the young man from Gethsemane
  (Mark 14:51-52). The detailed description of the "guest room" in 14:12-
  16 (compare Matt. 26:17-19; John 13:1-12) suggests that Mark was
  writing about his own house.[187]

The lack of alternative candidates has led many scholars to accept Mark as
the writer. Others will conclude that likely Mark is the writer, but technically, the gospel remains anonymous.

THE AUTHOR OF THE GOSPEL OF LUKE AND ACTS

Acts begins, *"In my former book, Theophilus, I wrote about all that Jesus
began to do and to teach until the day he was taken up to heaven, after giving
instructions through the Holy Spirit to the apostles he had chosen"* (Acts 1:1-2).
This former book mentioned by the author is clearly the gospel of Luke, that
starts with: *"Therefore, since I myself have carefully investigated everything from
the beginning, it seemed good also to me to write an orderly account for you, most
excellent Theophilus, so that you may know the certainty of the things you have
been taught."* Both books are addressed to the same Theophilus (literally: "lover
of God," either a real person or a symbolic name for a Christian believer),
strongly suggesting Acts is a sequel to Luke. Acts begins where Luke ends, and
the style and vocabulary of both books are so similar even the most critical
scholars agree that both books were written by the same person.

The case for Luke, the non-Jewish (*Gentile*) companion of Paul, likely a
medical doctor, possibly from Antioch, as the author is not in serious dispute.

Only few scholars even attempt to argue that he was not the author. Let's look at what we know and notice how all clues point to the conclusion that Luke and Acts were indeed both written by *"the beloved physician."*

External evidences:
- Luke has always been associated as the author by church tradition. No alternative has been suggested. As a "make-up" choice, Luke would not be logical, as he is not only a Gentile (the only such to be associated with the origin of any book in the Bible), but also not one of the original disciples of Jesus.
- Irenaeus writes in *Against Heresies* 170-180 AD: *"Luke also, the companion of Paul, recorded the gospel in a book."* [188] Similar references can be found in Clement of Alexandria[189] (ca. 195 AD) and Tertullian[190] (ca. 207 AD).
- The Muratorian Canon (ca. 170-180) reads: *"The third book of the Gospel: According to Luke. This Luke was a physician."* [191]
- The gnostic heretic Marcion (ca. 140 AD) selected Luke by name for his abridged canon for the NT. This shows the gospel was known by Luke's name at that time.

Internal clues:
- Both books were written by a well-educated, native Greek writer.
- An important clue comes from the so called *"we" clauses.* The author traveled with Paul as indicated when the text in Acts changes from the third person to a first person narration. The passages are 16:10-17 (Paul's voyage from Troas to Philippi); 20:5-21:18 (Paul's trip from Philippi to Jerusalem); and finally 27:1-28:16 (Paul's journey from Caesarea to Rome).
- Luke was mentioned by Paul in Colossians 4:14, 2 Timothy 4:11, and Philemon 24. In Colossians Paul identifies Luke as a physician.

DATING THE SYNOPTIC GOSPELS

The dates of the synoptic gospels (Matthew, Mark, and Luke) are critical because the longer the gap between an event and its record, the more distortion can occur. History has shown accounts written more than one generation after an event are quite likely subject to myth development. Illustrations of this are the well-known accounts of *King Arthur and the Knights of the Round Table* and the stories of *Robin Hood.* The accounts of their adventures cherished today were written many generations after these persons lived. During this long time, as the stories passed orally from generation to generation they were embellished and new adventures added. Likely there once was a king named Arthur and a "rebel" known as Robin Hood, but no historian seriously believes they did the heroic deeds found in these records. This is how myths and legends form: by playing the game of "telephone" over multiple generations.

So the closer we can reliably place the gospels to the actual events, the more confident we can be they are historically trustworthy. In this context the term *eyewitness period* is important. Historians consider this the time span following an event during which it can be safely assumed that a significant number of first-hand witnesses are still alive and able to testify. During the first century, that period is generally reckoned to be 40 years. This is quite conservative, as also in Jesus' day people could easily live into their 50s and 60s, or even older. The period from the crucifixion (33 AD) to the destruction of Jerusalem in 70 AD was relatively peaceful. Yes, Jews were oppressed by the Roman occupation, but there was no excessive violence or mass executions. Accurate estimates for natural life expectancy of a first century person are not available, but we do know of the old age of some individuals. For instance, historically reliable information indicates one of the bishops of the early church, Polycarp was well into his 80s when martyred in 156 AD.[192] Augustus Caesar (63 BC-14 AD), the Roman emperor who reigned during Jesus' birth, lived to be 76 years old, while his successor, Tiberius Caesar Augustus (42 BC-37 AD), died a natural death at age 78.

Abundant support suggests a significant number of the personal witnesses to Jesus' ministry and resurrection would still be alive during the eyewitness period of 30-70 AD. Evangelical scholars often date the synoptic gospels to 55-70 AD, 10 years or so earlier than their more liberal counterparts, who prefer 65-90 AD. Let us explore the reasoning and arguments.

The synoptic theory described above proves useful in helping establish a date range for these gospels. This is due to two considerations:

Mark was first: As both Luke and Matthew used Mark as a source, his gospel must have been the first gospel – hence, if we can establish a latest possible date for the composition of Luke and/or Matthew, we logically conclude Mark was written earlier.

Luke and Acts have the same author: As Acts is a sequel to Luke, that logically means that if we can date Acts, we have a latest possible date for Luke and, because Mark was written earlier, we also have a latest possible date for this gospel.

But can we date Acts? Opinions among scholars on the date of Acts vary greatly, ranging all the way from 57 to 150 AD. There are three distinct viewpoints:[193]

Acts was written before 65 AD: Most of the book is occupied with the ministries of Peter and Paul, and much of the action centers in Jerusalem and Paul's missionary travels. Undoubtedly, Luke made an effort to record many events and historical details as accurately as he could. The martyrdoms of Stephen (7:54-60) and James (brother of John, 12:1-2) are recorded, and the book ends with Paul under arrest in Rome (28:14-31) but says nothing about the outcome of his detention. Neither does the book mention the deaths of Paul or Peter (mid 60s AD) or James (Jesus' brother about 62 AD). Nor does it say anything about the Jewish rebellion against Rome (beginning in 66 AD) and the destruction of Jerusalem (70 AD). How could the author omit these events when they seem more important than many of those events that are recorded? These omissions set a strong case for a date 60-62 AD, no later than 65 AD for the composition of Acts. Advocates also appeal to the primitive theology of Peter's speeches and the fact that Luke showed no acquaintance with Paul's epistles. Lastly the use of the *Son of Man* title for Jesus supports the early date, as already by the end of the first century (notice the names for Jesus in the Gospel of John) the title *Son of God* was prevalent.

Acts was written 70-90 AD, probably before 80 AD: Two problems exist with dating the Gospel of Luke as early as 62 AD. First, Luke's gospel might suggest an awareness of the fall of Jerusalem in 70 AD. Luke records three predictions of the city's destruction (19:41-44; 21:20-24; 23:28-31). Critics claim the emphasis on this event suggests it had already happened. The second argument against an early date for Luke is the likelihood that he used the Gospel of Mark as one of his sources. Irenaeus indicated Mark wrote his Gospel based on the memoirs of Peter and after the death of Peter.[194] This text reads: *"…while Peter and Paul were preaching at Rome, and laying the foundations of the church. After their departure, Mark, the disciple and interpreter of Peter, did also hand down to us in writing what had been preached by Peter."* Peter and Paul are thought to have died during persecution by Nero in the mid 60s. This dates Mark after 65 AD and hence Acts even later. Luke might have had immediate access to Mark and composed his Gospel soon after Mark. More likely some time elapsed between the two gospels. This seems to date Luke's gospel after 70 AD and Acts during the decade of 70-80 AD.

Acts was written after 90 AD: Dates after 90 AD are no longer seriously considered. This is because of the authorship by Luke, who, according to tradition, was martyred earlier. Both Acts and Luke claim access to good sources – eyewitnesses no longer available by this time. Lastly, Clement of Rome, Ignatius, and Polycarp all refer to Luke/Acts, which supports a date before 90 AD, and likely even earlier than 80 AD. Scholars who support this late date are in the decided minority.

This lengthy but important discussion leads to two options:
1. Mark (50-60) < Luke (55-62) < Acts (60-62, 65 latest)
2. Mark (65-70) < Luke (70-75) < Acts (70-80, 90 latest)

As for the date of Matthew, it is unanimously thought to have been completed well before 100 AD. If Matthew wrote the entire gospel, a date from 55-70 AD seems logical, especially if we accept the earlier quote from Irenaeus: *"Matthew also issued a written gospel among the Hebrews in their own dialect, while Peter and Paul were preaching in Rome"* (emphasis added). Peter and Paul were thought to have been in Rome in the early 60s. An early date is also supported by abundant quotations and references to Matthew's gospel in most of the Early Church Leaders' letters.

The theory that Matthew wrote the initial version of his gospel in Aramaic to be later completed by another writer seems to fit all the facts as well. This would place the early version easily in the 55-65 range and the complete gospel before 90 or even 100 AD.

In summary, we conclude that both options for the dating of Mark-Luke-Acts as well as the two alternatives for the date of Matthew are supported by solid arguments. Scholarship seems evenly divided. Whichever option one takes, it shows all three synoptic gospels and Acts were written:

- Within 20-60 years after the resurrection.
- During the lifetime of numerous eyewitnesses to Jesus' ministry, crucifixion, and resurrection.
- Much too close to the events for myths and legends to form.
- Early enough for Matthew, Mark, and Luke to be corroborated as the authors.

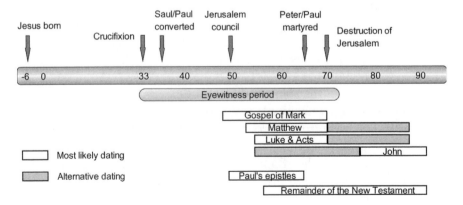

Figure 12-2: Dating of the New Testament

☼ Exhibit #12: Authorship and Date of The Gospel of John

The Gospel of John stands fully independent of the synoptic gospels. The main story lines are shared: John the Baptist, Jesus' ministry, His teachings, the betrayal, Peter's denial, the trials, the crucifixion, and the resurrection. John sketches a less chronological picture of Jesus but provides more explanation, includes instructions to the Christian believer, and presents Jesus' miracles as evidence for the non-believer (John 20:30).

As with the other gospels, it is anonymous, so what links this gospel to John the apostle?

External evidences:

- Irenaeus ca. 170-180 AD: *"Afterwards, John, the disciple of the Lord, who also had leaned upon His breast, did himself publish a Gospel during his residence at Ephesus in Asia."* [195] The context of this quote also confirms John wrote after the synoptic gospels and while he was in Ephesus.
- Muratorian fragment of ca. 200 AD: *"The fourth Gospel is that of John, one of the disciples."* [196]
- Tertullian writes ca. 207 AD: *"Of the apostles, therefore, John and Matthew first instill faith into us; whilst of apostolic men, Luke and Mark renew it afterwards."* [197]
- No early church writer proposed any alternative, and the book is accepted in all of the early canonical lists.

Internal clues:[198]

- The author was a Jew very familiar with Jewish customs and the OT.
- The author was from Palestine: shows knowledge of the geography and topography, particularly of Jerusalem and the surrounding Judean countryside.
- The author claims to be an eyewitness in John 21:24: *"This is the disciple who testifies to these things and who wrote them down. We know that his testimony is true."*
- The author writes as an eyewitness, because of discussed irrelevant details.
- The author refers a number of times to himself as *"the disciple whom Jesus loved."* He was present at Jesus' final supper and throughout that last night. He was part of "the inner circle."
- John and James (sons of Zebedee) are never mentioned by name. Peter and others are mentioned often. James was martyred ca. 44 AD, hence John is the only candidate left.
- John the Baptist is referred to as just "John" in the document, indicating there was no confusion with any other John (John the apostle, i.e., the author).

Arguments raised against John the apostle:

- Why was the early church so quiet about John's gospel? Neither Ignatius nor Polycarp, both disciples of John, mention his gospel in their letters. However, they do not mention any other gospel either, and their letters do not address any other writings.
- If this was John the apostle, why did his account differ so from the synoptics? This assumes John was writing a historical account, which was not the primary purpose of his gospel.
- How could a fisherman from Galilee be so well known and influential in Jerusalem to even gain access to the high priest's courtyard during the trial of Jesus (John 18:15-16)? In this context one needs to realize that in those days fishermen would not necessary be poor and uneducated. To own a boat and a business would require at least a basic education and business skills, plus a successful business would bring wealth. So, perhaps John's family – the Zebedees – were more wealthy and connected than expected and/or even related to a priestly family.

Where does this all lead? Gerald L. Borchert summarized it accurately:[199] *"There seems little reason to reject the idea that the son of Zebedee was the towering figure and the authentic witness involved in the writing of this Gospel. I would not think it necessary that he himself was the actual scribe of this work nor that he himself would have had to refer to himself by the designation of the beloved disciple. Nor would I think it impossible that the Gospel was the combined work of an elderly John and a loving scribe who greatly revered the leader of his church or community."*

As to the date of John, general consensus among scholars places it 85-95 AD. As the Rylands papyrus (P52) with part of John 18 is dated 117-138 AD (and some time would be required for this piece of papyrus to travel to Egypt, where it was found), dating the gospel much later then 100 AD is not consistent with this evidence. That case is strengthened by the freshness and vividness of the book, often lacking in ancient accounts written many years after the events they relate. Background explanation, personal detail, and carefully related private conversation (e.g., John 3, 4, 8-10, 13-17) suggest the work of an eyewitness. Some scholars propose a much earlier date, well before the destruction of Jerusalem, because of the very detailed eyewitness descriptions of parts of the city destroyed in 70 AD, including the use of the present tense in these descriptions (see John 5:2); however, this is a minority opinion.

☼ EXHIBIT #13: AUTHORSHIP AND DATING OF PAUL'S LETTERS

The earliest written books in the New Testament are the letters written by Paul to the churches he established and to some of his personal disciples. The gospel documents give us many details about Jesus' ministry and teachings, but Paul's letters corroborate the main events we know of Jesus: His birth and genealogy through His crucifixion and resurrection.

Paul contributed 13 epistles to the NT, undisputed through most of Christian history. Modern – more skeptical – scholarship has aimed at Paul's work, claiming some of the letters might have not been written by Paul himself, but a close associate.[200] Virtually non-disputed are 1 Thessalonians, Galatians, 1 and 2 Corinthians, Romans, Philippians,and Philemon.

A brief overview of external and internal evidences:

External evidences:
- Clement of Rome testified ca. 95-97 AD: *"Owing to envy, Paul also obtained the reward of patient endurance, after being seven times thrown into captivity, compelled to flee, and stoned. After preaching both in the east and west, he gained the illustrious reputation due to his faith, having taught righteousness to the whole world, and come to the extreme limit of the west, and suffered martyrdom under the prefects."*[201]
- Ignatius wrote to the Romans ca. 105-107 AD: *"I may be found a sacrifice to God. I do not, as Peter and Paul, issue commandments unto you. They were apostles of Jesus Christ, but I am the very least [of believers]: they were free,"*[202]
- Polycarp in his letter to the Philippians ca. 115 AD: *"For neither I, nor any other such one, can come up to the wisdom of the blessed and glorified Paul. He, when among you, accurately and steadfastly taught the word of truth in the presence of those who were then alive. And when absent from you, he wrote you a letter,"*[203]

Internal evidences:
- The opening verses in each letter claim to have been written by Paul the apostle.
- 2 Peter 3:15-17: *"Bear in mind that our Lord's patience means salvation, just as our dear brother Paul also wrote you with the wisdom that God gave him. He writes the same way in all his letters, speaking in them of these matters. His letters contain some things that are hard to understand, which ignorant and unstable people distort, as they do the other Scriptures, to their own destruction."* If Peter was the author of 2 Peter, this letter is to be dated before 65 AD. Most more critical scholars date 2 Peter in the early second

century and consider it the last NT book written. They believe an unknown author claimed Petrine authorship to give his work the authority and tradition of a revered Christian leader.[204]

As we examine the evidence that the Bible, and especially its claims about Jesus of Nazareth, are historically reliable and trustworthy, our discussion will focus on the four letters that provide facts and evidence for this cause. These are:

1 Thessalonians: Paul identifies himself as the author (1 Thessalonians 1:1, along with Silas and Timothy), writing this letter from Corinth during his second missionary trip. His authorship is not disputed. The broad acceptance of the letter as genuinely Pauline, the content of the letter itself, and the date of Paul's encounter with Gallio in Corinth combine to validate a date for 1 Thessalonians of 50 or 51 AD.[205]

Galatians: Galatians 1:1 identifies Paul as the undisputed author. The exact date of this letter has drawn a large variety of scholarly opinion ranging from 49 AD even to the end of his missionary travels about 59 AD. Most likely Galatians was written from Antioch on the eve of the *Council of Jerusalem*, usually dated 49 or 50 AD.[206]

1 Corinthians: Extensive evidence for Christ's life and resurrection comes from this letter which provides rock-solid, early dated, undisputed claims for the resurrection, as we will discuss in later chapters. Its importance cannot be overstated. This letter is one of the undisputed documents written by the apostle Paul (1 Corinthians 1:1, together with Sosthenes). In Ephesus during his third journey (53-56 AD), hearing disturbing news about the church in Corinth he visited a year or two earlier, Paul wrote a number of letters to Corinth. The first letter is believed to be lost, making 1 Corinthians actually his second letter, written 54 or 55 AD.[207]

Romans: Romans was written by *"Paul, a servant of Christ Jesus, called to be an apostle and set apart for the gospel of God"* (Romans 1:1). Through Acts we learn that it was composed between the time when Gallio was proconsul at Corinth (Acts 18:12, 14, 17) and the replacement of Felix by Festus as procurator in Palestine (24:27). This places Romans between 54-58 AD with a likely date of 56 AD.[208]

CHAPTER 13

The 'Lost Books' of the New Testament

"Test everything. Hold on to the good."
1 THESSALONIANS 5:21

What are these *"lost books"* of the New Testament? Could books really be lost to the providence of God? Or perhaps they were never lost at all, only rejected?

With greater access to research tools and ancient texts recently discovered, such as the Dead Sea Scrolls and the Nag Hammadi Library, many scholars are on a quest to find new discoveries while attempting to discredit the New Testament and its claims about Jesus of Nazareth.

This chapter will survey these texts that are in the spotlight of media attention and scholarly arguments. Are they really "once-lost-and-now-found" texts? Are we on the verge of redefining Christianity? Or does the evidence suggest these books, excluded by the Early Church Leaders from the New Testament canon, are not relevant, composed in later generations, or perhaps even from heretical sources?

WHY WOULD THESE BOOKS NOT BE INCLUDED IN THE NEW TESTAMENT?

If a newly "discovered" book has significant spiritual insights or serious historical value, the early church would have known of it. It seems not plausible to conclude a genuine gospel or authentic epistle would have remained unknown and not even considered for the canon.

But, why are these other writings not in the New Testament? Logically there are only three alternatives:

They were written much later: The primary reason to exclude any writing from the New Testament is its date of writing. All documents in the canon were written in the lifetime of the apostles, basically all before 90 AD and surely not later than 100 AD. Many genuine Christian writings (such as the extensively discussed and often quoted correspondence of the Early Church Leaders) were never considered because they were written too late and too removed from the generation of eyewitnesses. A few scholars argue some books in the NT canon were written later as well, but these are minority opinions, not supported by objective investigation. The four gospels, Acts, and Paul's epistles all easily meet this criterion. So any "lost" book not dated to the first century could never be given importance and authority equal to the NT writings.

They were not from apostolic sources: Even if a document can be traced to the first century, another criterion for the NT canon was that its author had to be a close associate of Jesus or someone closely connected to one. This was the only way to ensure correct teaching and avoid myths and legends, even heresies. For instance, Clement of Rome's epistle to the Corinthians was ultimately rejected for this reason. It is genuine, to be sure, but from a source not close enough to Jesus.

They were considered not relevant or heretical: Even if a document dated from the first century and came from someone associated with Jesus, it would still have been rejected if it was considered irrelevant or heretical. Documents in this category are worthy of serious consideration, as these are perhaps new sources of information and/or over the centuries (purposely) suppressed documents.

The apostles warned for false teachings

Even during the lifetime of the apostles, false teachings about Christ and the gospel were rising throughout the young Christian church. Explicit warnings against heresies are found in the writings of Luke, Paul, and John:

"Keep watch over yourselves and all the flock of which the Holy Spirit has made you overseers. Be shepherds of the church of God, which he bought with his own blood. I know that after I leave, savage wolves will come in among you and will not spare the flock. Even from your own number men will arise and distort the truth in order to draw away disciples after them" (Paul's farewell admonition to the elders of the church of Ephesus, Acts 20:28-30).

"Evidently some people are throwing you into confusion and are trying to pervert the gospel of Christ. But even if we or an angel from heaven should preach a gospel other than the one we preached to you, let him be eternally condemned! As we have already said, so now I say again: If anybody is preaching to you a gospel other than what you accepted, let him be eternally condemned" (Paul's opening words to the churches in Galatia, Galatians 1:7-9)!

"Dear friends, do not believe every spirit, but test the spirits to see whether they are from God, because many false prophets have gone out into the world. This is how you can recognize the Spirit of God: Every spirit that acknowledges that Jesus Christ has come in the flesh is from God, but every spirit that does not acknowledge Jesus is not from God" (1 John 4:1-3).

Amid the writings of early Christian leaders discussed earlier, numerous writings also circulated with lofty claims to apostolic authority, but most were clearly spurious. Documents appeared in such numbers one could almost think them produced by a *"apocryphal mill."* Most were likely penned by well-meaning believers who tried to "fill in the gaps" of the New Testament accounts. For instance the *Infancy Gospel of Thomas* (second century, see below) describes the childhood of Jesus. Accounts such as the *Gospel of Nicodemus* (likely third century), the *Acts of John* (second-third century), the *Acts of Peter* (end of second century) and the *Acts of Paul* (second-third century)[209] describe the fictitious but miraculous adventures of the apostles John, Peter, and Paul. These "apocryphal mill" accounts have seldom received serious consideration. Their well documented late dates and wildly exaggerated stories quickly disqualified them.

We will first define Gnosticism, considered the most prevalent heresy to beset the early Christian church. Then we will discuss the source and background of many of the recently discovered writings, the Nag Hammadi Library.

THE GNOSTIC MOVEMENT

The best known movement – considered heretical from the start – is known as the *gnostic* movement. What did its adherents believe? Unfortunately, there is no simple answer. The term is derived from the Greek "gnosis" (*gnosis)* which simply means knowledge. Gnosticism rose in the Mediterranean world and the Near East at the same time as primitive Christianity but independently of it, reaching its zenith in the third century. In its broadest sense Gnosticism is religious dogma based on a view of special knowledge. Over time, the term has become a catchword for any heresy as opposed to orthodox Christianity. A good illustration of this confusion is the Nag Hammadi documents. They are considered gnostic, but reveal significant differences among themselves.

One approach is to define characteristics common to gnostic documents:[210]
- **Dualism:** The true and "good" God differs from the "evil" Creator God in Genesis.
- **Cosmogony:** The physical material world is evil. Light, soul, spirit, and knowledge are good.
- **Salvation:** Salvation and redemption are experienced only by knowledge. The flesh (the physical) is not redeemable. Hence, there is no resurrection of the body from the dead.
- **Eschatology:** Understanding where existence is heading, namely, the redemption of the soul and recovery of creation into the "fullness," being where good dwells (separated from the evil physical world of matter and flesh).

• **Cult and community:** The worship, sacraments, and the people who nurtured such views.

Gnosticism began to influence the widespread Christian community by the end of the first century. Look at 1 John 4:2-3 (emphasis added): "*This is how you can recognize the Spirit of God: Every spirit that acknowledges <u>that Jesus Christ has come in the flesh</u> is from God, but every spirit that does not acknowledge Jesus is not from God. This is the spirit of the antichrist, which you have heard is coming and even now is already in the world.*" Here John the apostle, writing 80-90 AD, denies gnostic claims that a Divine Jesus could not have been human or exist in flesh. They argued that all flesh, indeed the whole physical world, is evil.

The well known *Apostles' creed,*[211] *probably dated in the third century was derived from the Old Roman creed (likely written in the latter half of the second century). The Old Roman creed* developed within the Christian community to fight Gnosticism (underlined are anti-gnostic statements):

"*I believe in God the Father Almighty. And in Jesus Christ <u>his only Son</u> our Lord, who was <u>born of the Holy Spirit and the Virgin Mary</u>; cruci-fied under Pontius Pilate and buried; the third day <u>he rose from the dead</u>; he ascended into heaven, and sits at the right hand of the Father, from thence he shall come to judge the living and the dead. And in the Holy Spirit; the holy church; the forgiveness of sins; <u>the resurrection of the flesh.</u>*"

An even earlier fragment of this creed – probably written as early as the end of the first century simply states (showing again an anti-gnostic emphasis):

"*I believe in God the Father Almighty, and in Jesus Christ <u>his only Son</u>, our Lord. And in the Holy Spirit, the holy church, <u>the resurrection of the flesh.</u>*"

Many early church writers vigorously opposed gnostic influences in their letters throughout the Christian community. Examples of this are seen in two letters of Ignatius[212] (ca. 105-107 AD) and many writings of Justin Martyr (ca. 160 AD), Hegesippus (ca. 170 AD), Irenaeus (ca. 170-180 AD), Clement of Alexandria (ca. 195 AD), and Tertullian (ca. 210 AD).

"GNOSTIC CHRISTIANITY" VERSUS "TRADITIONAL CHRISTIANITY"

A few of today's liberal scholars – referred to by some as *The New School* – claim that at the time of the birth of the Christian faith, modern-day Christianity was not the only interpretation of Jesus' teachings.[213] They assert that alternatives such as the gnostic interpretations ("*Gnostic Christianity*") were also considered. After the struggle of the various concepts for supremacy, the view of "*Traditional Christianity*" "won" and other early forms of

Christianity were suppressed, reformed, or even forgotten. Recent finds, they claim, of new gospels bring these alternative views to light. Many promote a "make-over" of traditional beliefs, as a liberation from current Christianity, said by some to be an old, tiresome, constraining, and narrow faith.

As we have seen, the early church actively fought gnostic claims and influences. However, anti-gnostic statements are found only in the book of 1 John, likely one of the last books, written near the end of the first century. If Gnosticism had been a major concern to the apostles, we would expect many more anti-gnostic statements in the Bible books. Therefore it logically follows that gnostic influences started to interfere with the Christian faith about 50-60 years after the birth of Christianity. This implies that:

- "Traditional Christianity" and "Gnostic Christianity" did <u>not</u> develop in parallel. Traditional Christianity was well established, all (except for very few) books of the NT had been written well before gnostic concepts began to influence the faith. Therefore, Gnostic Christianity is not an alternative interpretation of the teachings of Christ that could be considered in any way on par with Biblical Christian theology. No, it is a cult, claiming additional revelation to justify its changes to the original faith.
- Gnostic Christian "gospels" therefore could not have been written before the end of the first century because Gnostic Christianity did not exist earlier. Our discussion of the various "gospels" and the evidence for their authenticity should verify this conclusion.

THE NAG HAMMADI LIBRARY

In 1945 at *Nag Hammadi,* [214] 300 miles south of Cairo in the Nile River region, two Arab brothers found 13 papyrus codices in a jar. The 52 separate writings contained in these scrolls are now known as the Nag Hammadi gnostic texts. In 1959 the first document from the library appeared – *The Gospel of Thomas.* Publication of the entire collection was completed in 1977.

These texts are all in Coptic, an Egyptian language written with the Greek alphabet. The general consensus is that these Coptic translations from original Greek texts date from 350-400 AD, but agreement between scholars ends right there! The original texts are dated earlier – but how much earlier is sharply disputed. Furthermore, most scholars conclude these Nag Hammadi texts do not compare to the significance of the New Testament texts, while some (such as the Jesus Seminar and the author of *The DaVinci Code*) believe they are more reliable than the NT. This last group even claims that they might contain evidence of a major conspiracy of the (Roman) Catholic Church.

Apart from this discussion, two important issues pertain to the quality of the texts:

- The texts were translated one by one from Greek into Coptic. The translators were not always capable of grasping what they sought to translate. When there are duplications one can sense what a difference the better translation makes in comparison to the poor translation – which leads one to wonder about the bulk of the texts that exist only in a single version.
- There is a similar hazard in transmission of the texts by a series of scribes who copied them, generation after generation, from increasingly corrupt copies, first in Greek, later in Coptic. The number of unintentional errors is hard to estimate. When only a few letters are missing, they can often be filled in adequately, but larger holes must simply remain a blank.

The Nag Hammadi documents can be organized into several categories:[215]
- **Gnostic Texts with Christian Orientation**. Among these, receiving considerable attention is *The Gospel of Thomas*. This series of sayings was thought at first by some scholars to be a source for the canonical gospels of Matthew and Luke (Q?). Another is *The Gospel of Truth,* which might have been written by the well-known heretic Valentinus; *The Gospel of Philip* contains unique teachings related to gnostic sacraments.
- **Gnostic Texts with Less Than Clear Christian Orientation**. Some scholars allege that these texts suggest a pre-Christian Gnosticism, but this seems unsubstantiated. The writings in this category are not considered relevant in the context of looking for new Christian writings.
- **Non-Gnostic, Christian Documents**. There are also several non-gnostic Christian documents in the library. These include: *The Acts of Peter and the Twelve, The Sentences of Sextus*, and *The Teachings of Silvanus*. None of these is considered a newly discovered text.
- **Miscellaneous Documents**. In addition, several documents are neither Christian nor gnostic, but likely were read with great interest by gnostic scribes.

☼ EXHIBIT #14: THE LOST BOOKS WERE NEVER LOST

The "apocryphal mill" mentioned earlier likely produced hundreds of alternative "gospels," "acts," and "apocalypses," during the first centuries of the Christian era. In the ninth century Photius listed 280, and more have been discovered.[216] Some of these gnostic "gospels" discovered more recently have been treated as potential new revelations. Most, however, have been known to exist for centuries and are considered irrelevant. We will survey the most "famous" of these and categorize them, using criteria outlined at the beginning of this chapter:

Written much later than the NT canon (after 100 AD):

The Gospel of Judas (mid to late second century). This gospel was known to Irenaeus and Epiphanius (ca. 315-403), bishop of Salamia. As the product of a gnostic sect it may have contained *"a passion story setting forth the 'mystery of the betrayal'"* explaining how Judas by his treachery *"made possible the salvation of all mankind."* [217] The only available fourth century gnostic re-written text characterizes Judas as Jesus' favorite, most trusted disciple, and that the betrayal was part of God's will. [218]

The Gospel of Philip (second or third century). [219] This gnostic gospel was known only by one citation until a later manuscript was found at Nag Hammadi. It seems to be a collection of diverse materials, most notable for its description of sacraments. In the novel *The DaVinci Code* a passage from this gospel is used to "prove" the close relationship between Mary Magdalene and Jesus as *"the privileged disciple."* [220]

The Gospel of Truth (second century). Another gnostic gospel found at Nag Hammadi. It reflects the significance of the work of salvation by Jesus from a special theological (Gnostic) perspective. [221]

The Gospel of Mary (Magdalene) (second century). Yet another gnostic writing found at Nag Hammadi. It consists only in part and can easily be divided into two sections. The first section describes dialogue between the risen Savior and the disciples. The remainder is Mary's recall of special revelation given her by Jesus. [222] *The DaVinci Code* incorporates a passage to portray *"Peter as complaining about Mary's closeness to Christ."* [223]

The Infancy Gospel of Thomas (second century). This was the popular story of the childhood of Jesus to the age of 12. It depicts Him as a powerful boy with all the features of a supernatural wonder-worker and teacher. It probably originated in Gentile Christian circles in the second century and has no relation to the Gospel of Thomas. [224]

Written before 100 AD, considered genuine, but not from apostolic sources:

The Gospel According to the Hebrews (ca. 65-100 AD). Probably the earliest non-canonical gospel, this text survived only in a few fragmentary quotations by early church writers: Clement of Alexandria (ca. 195 AD) and Origen (ca. 228 AD). According to Jerome, some called it "the true Matthew." This seems unlikely because its quotations bear little relation to the canonical Matthew.

Clement of Rome, Ignatius, Polycarp, the Didache, Epistle of Barnabas. These are all writings by the early church that we discussed earlier.

Possibly initially written before 100 AD, but considered not relevant or heretical:

The Gospel of Thomas (second or end of first century). One of the Nag Hammadi documents, and by far the best-known alternative gospel. Dating is crucial. This we know for sure: *"At least one of these Greek fragments comes from a manuscript that was written before 200 AD; thus the Greek version of this gospel was used in Egypt as early as the second century."* [225] Most place the gospel at the early second century, but some argue a mid- or late first century origin. [226] Some even call this *"The Fifth Gospel."* [227] The author might have been Didymas Judas Thomas, Judas "the twin," an apostle of Jesus.

The Gospel of Thomas is not a narrative like the canonical gospels, but a collection of 114 sayings attributed to Jesus. Many show striking similarities to parts of the synoptic gospels, some appear to have been given a gnostic twist.

The main problem here is that the Nag Hammadi version is the only complete text available. We know it is a translation dated 350-400 AD that had significant gnostic redaction (re-writing, like most if not all documents in the Nag Hammadi library). The earliest Greek texts date from 200 AD, but are too fragmented to reconstruct the original text. The following illustration compares some verses from Matthew to Saying #2 from a third century Greek fragment and the fourth century Coptic Nag Hammadi text. [228] Notice how the text "evolves" between the translations:

Matthew 7:7-8 and 11:28:
"Seek and you will find...he who seeks finds...Come to me...and I will give you rest."

Saying 2 (found in the third century Greek fragment):
"Let him who seeks not cease (seeking until) he finds; and when he finds (he will) be astounded, and having been (astoun)ded, he will reign; an(d reigning), he will (re)st."

Saying 2 (found in the fourth century Coptic document):
"He who seeks should not stop seeking until he finds; and when he finds, he will be bewildered (beside himself); and when he is bewildered, he will marvel, and will reign over the All."

So the Gospel of Thomas might date as early as the writing of the NT. It might have been available as source material (like Q) to writers of the canonical gospels. It could contain some original teachings of Jesus. However, comparison of the Nag Hammadi text to the limited Greek fragments reveals abundant signs of gnostic editing. If those are removed, what is left likely changes nothing that is taught in the New Testament. [229]

The Gospel of Peter (likely second century, some claim second half of first century). Origen (ca. 200 AD) and Eusebius (ca 300 AD) both refer to this gospel but neither gives any of the text. The oldest extant text is from an eight or ninth century manuscript uncovered in 1886. It is a passion narrative describing the suffering and death of Christ. It seems to build upon the synoptic gospels and is not necessarily in conflict with these accounts, except for some Docetic messages (probably later additions during copying). *Docetism* is the heretical belief that Jesus' physical body and his crucifixion were an illusion; that is, Jesus' body and death only seemed real, but in reality He was a pure spirit, and hence could not physically die.

The Gospel of Peter teaches several things that conflict with the New Testament. These include:

- Pilate was innocent regarding the death of Jesus, and only the Jews were responsible for it.
- Jesus felt no pain when crucified.
- Jesus referred to the Father as "my power." And the Lord called out and cried, *"My power, O power, Thou hast forsaken me!"*
- Jesus' "brothers and sisters" were from a first marriage of Joseph, a view long held by Roman Catholic scholars.

In addition, the Gospel of Peter contains an embellished account of the resurrection of Jesus.[230]

So it is possible, though not likely, that this was composed about the same time as the other NT gospels. However, early church writers did not mention it or quote from it. In fact, it was never considered for the canon. The available text is many centuries removed from any original and has likely been edited by Docetic influences.[231]

Q (before Matthew and Luke). To be complete, we also need to list the so called *Q* source here. Although not necessarily a written source – it could also be a person or persons – it would date back to the middle of the first century. Some were quick to claim the Gospel of Thomas was Q, but that is no longer a serious option.

CONCLUSION

As we have seen, the buzz and hype about these "lost books" suggest much more than really is going on. Yes, cable and satellite TV documentaries on the Bible like to mention the "lost books." Indeed, visit a bookstore and you will find significant shelf space devoted to these "new discoveries." One wonders how much is driven by objective scholarship and how much is no more than the pursuit of personal anti-Christian agendas and/or elusive sales targets?

The objective reconstruction of history and available evidence show that the early church knew these "lost books" well. They decided to not include them in the canonical New Testament for several solid reasons: they were written later, not by the apostles, and many were even heretical, touting wildly exaggerated accounts.

The texts today mostly come from the fourth century through the gnostic Coptic translations in the Nag Hammadi Library. These are not reliable translations or copies of the original Greek second century texts. They have been purposely altered to fit gnostic views.

An honest and careful analysis of the "lost books" only increases the strength of the case for the reliability of the canonical New Testament documents.

CHAPTER 14

The Historical Reliability of the Bible

"As a matter of fact, however, it may be clearly stated categorically that no archaeological discovery has ever contradicted a single Biblical reference. Scores of archaeological findings have been made which confirm in clear outline or exact detail historical statements in the Bible."
NOTED ARCHAEOLOGIST NELSON GLUECK[232]

WHAT CAN WE EXPECT?

Blessed in so many ways unknown to the generations before us, we have a large toolkit available to research the historical reliability of the Scriptures. Our tools include:

- **History:** Through sources outside the Bible we can reconstruct the timeline of past events, often with remarkable accuracy. We can pinpoint the dates of empires and kingdoms, rulers and battles, as well as explore discoveries and inventions, early technology, and ancient economies. In doing so, we can determine if the Biblical accounts "fit" into the history of the world, spanning from the political landscape even to particular customs such as the cost of a slave or the price of sharpening plow points.
- **Archaeology:** Painstakingly careful excavations at far-flung sites have verified the Bible's records of cities, fortifications, and structures. Artifacts and documents from distant time periods help evaluate both history and the Biblical record.
- **Other supporting sciences:** A number of additional scientific disciplines support our findings through history and archaeology. These disciplines include geology to date large-scale events, radio-metric dating to determine the age of documents and artifacts, textual scholarship to analyze the background and interpret documents, and so on.

This toolkit gives us a solid base for effective research, but never lose sight of limitations of this exploration. In many cases, this is not solid, objective science, but actually requires lots of subjective interpretation and creative solutions to puzzles so as to define the "total picture" when only a small number of the pieces of the puzzle are present:

- Unlike many fields of science, historical processes cannot be re-created in a laboratory. Archaeologists and historians can only study and interpret the evidence left behind, often after many years. New discoveries can upset many comfortable conclusions.
- Interpretation of archaeological evidence depends on a researcher's presuppositions and worldview. A believer of the Bible searches for evidence that confirms it and interprets all findings within that particular perspective. Many researchers are openly skeptical of the Scriptures and hostile to its worldview. They can be tempted to reach conclusions that discredit Biblical accounts.
- Thousands of documents have been discovered, even whole archives, but a staggering amount of material has been lost. For example, the famous library in Alexandria, Egypt once held more than one million codices and manuscripts; unfortunately, all were destroyed in a seventh century fire.
- Lastly, whatever we find can only corroborate Biblical accounts and events. We can never prove them beyond dispute, nor can any of these discoveries prove the Bible is inspired.

The power of archaeological and historical research is not just the ability to confirm the accuracy of the Biblical record. Its <u>inability to disprove</u> Biblical accounts is an even more significant contribution to the credibility of the Scriptures.

✵ EXHIBIT #15: THE OLD TESTAMENT IS HISTORICALLY RELIABLE

Over the centuries, and especially the last century, numerous artifacts and structures previously lost were uncovered. It is not possible, in the scope of this book, to discuss all discoveries, so we will survey those most important. In this exhibit we will focus on the Old Testament.

THE SILVER SCROLLS, THE OLDEST BIBLICAL TEXT

In June 1986 archaeologists of Tel Aviv University announced discovery of two small silver amulets. These two *silver scrolls* were found in 1979 deep inside a burial cave at a site known as Ketef Hinnom, west of the old city of Jerusalem. They were hidden at the back of the tomb embedded in pottery fashioned as early as the seventh century BC. Seven years later the fragile scrolls were opened and their texts deciphered. The scrolls contain an excerpt from Numbers 6:24-26, also known as the *Priestly Benediction*. In English the verses read: "*The LORD bless you and keep you; The LORD make His face shine upon you, And be gracious to you; The LORD lift up His countenance upon you, And give you peace.*" On the scrolls we find the texts:[233]

Amulet 1: concluding benediction (lines 14-19):

"[...] May Yahweh bless you [and] keep you. May Yahweh cause his face to shine [on you]...]."

Amulet 2: benediction (lines 5-12):

"[...] May Yahweh bless you and keep you. May Yahweh cause his face to shine [on] you and give you peace [...]."

The location of the find and analysis of the Hebrew on the scroll confirm a date close to 600 BC, perhaps earlier – long before the capture of Jerusalem and the Babylonian exile.

The importance of this find can hardly be overstated. It proves this section of Numbers was written at least 2,600 years ago. This Old Testament passage is 400 years older than the oldest Dead Sea Scroll manuscripts, and perhaps even older yet. The age of the text may prove a nail in the coffin of the Documentary Hypothesis[234] theories that the Pentateuch was not written by Moses, or that it was not even known in Moses' time. Those theories speculate that large segments of the first five books of the Bible originated in the period of Ezra: 400-500 BC. In this debate, some of the arguments revolve around the use of YHWH, the divine name of God (often rendered "Jehovah" or "Yahweh"), which is said not to have been in use before this time. The silver scrolls, dated before 586 BC, contain that name. In fact, this is the earliest the name had been found in any dig in Jerusalem.[235]

SODOM AND GOMORRAH

The story of Sodom and Gomorrah has long been viewed as a legend. Critics assume that it was created to communicate moral principles. However, throughout the Bible is referred to the ruin of the two cities as a historical event. The Old Testament mentions the destruction of Sodom several times (Deuteronomy 29:23, Isaiah 13:19, Jeremiah 49:18), and these cities play a key role in the teachings of Jesus and the apostles (Matthew 10:15, 2 Peter 2:6 and Jude 7). What has archaeology found to establish the existence of these cities?

Actually Sodom and Gomorrah were only two of five cities close to each other in this region. *"At this time Amraphel king of Shinar, Arioch king of Ellasar, Kedorlaomer king of Elam and Tidal king of Goiim, went to war against Bera king of Sodom, Birsha king of Gomorrah, Shinab king of Admah, Shemeber king of Zeboiim, and the king of Bela (that is, Zoar). All these latter kings joined forces in the Valley of Siddim (the Salt Sea)"* (Genesis 14:1-3). The *"Salt Sea"* is another name for the Dead Sea. To the east six wadies, or river valleys, flow into the Dead Sea.

Along five of these wadies, ancient cities were discovered. The most northern site is *Bab edh-Drha*, which is assumed by many to have been Sodom. Bab edh-Dhra was occupied during the early Bronze Age (third millennium BC). Overlooking the Dead Sea from a height of 550 feet, Bab edh-Dhra was no doubt built on a bluff for defense purposes. The site consists of a town and a large cemetery. In 1924, renowned archaeologist Dr. William F. Albright excavated this site, searching for Sodom and Gomorrah. He discovered it had once been heavily fortified. Although he identified this city as one of the "*Cities of the Plains*" (Genesis 13:11), he found no conclusive evidence to justify this assumption.

More digging was done in 1965, 1967, 1973, and 1979.[236] Archaeologists discovered a 23-inch thick wall that circled the city, along with numerous houses and a large temple. Outside the city were huge grave sites where thousands of skeletons were unearthed. This showed the city was well populated during the early Bronze Age, when Abraham lived. Most intriguing was the evidence that a massive fire had destroyed the city. It lay beneath a layer of ash several feet thick. A cemetery only one kilometer (a little more than half a mile) outside the city contained charred remains of roofs, posts, and bricks that had turned red from intense heat.

It is also significant that only five sites have been located in the Dead Sea area, and each was near a flowing spring. All five date to the early Bronze Age, and there is no evidence of other occupations in the area until the Romans arrived more than 2,000 years later.

The archaeological world is still divided on the identity of this location as Sodom, Gomorrah and other cities of the plain. Some claim the evidence strongly suggests this is the site, but it is not conclusive.[237] Others claim that these are the sites of the cities.[238] Most recently this claim was renewed in 1999 by the Associates of Biblical Research.[239]

THE NUZI OR NUZU TABLETS

The *Nuzu* or *Nuzi Tablets*, found in Nuzi (near Kirkuk, Iraq) on the Tigris in 1925, date to the fifteenth century BC. This small collection of clay tablets confirms the historicity of many customs practiced by Abraham and other patriarchs of that time:[240]

- Abraham's reference to his servant Eliezer as "*son of his house*" in Genesis 15:2 (prior to the birth of Ishmael and Isaac) suggested that he had adopted him as his legal heir. God's rejection of this arrangement (Genesis 15:4) might have caused Abraham embarrassment had it not been customary (as Nuzi texts show) to set aside the claims of an adopted son if a natural heir was subsequently born into the family.

- Several Nuzi texts describe occasions when a barren woman asked her husband to take her slave as a sort of surrogate wife to produce an heir; much as Abraham did with Hagar (Genesis 16:1-16).[241]
- The legitimacy of selling one's birthright (as Esau sold his in Genesis 25:33) was established at Nuzi, for in one case an older brother received a payment of three sheep for selling his younger brother the rights of his inheritance.[242]
- The binding character of a deathbed will (as when Jacob tricked his aged father Isaac) is attested by a case where a man named Tarmiya established his right to a woman he had married by proving that his father on his deathbed had verbally bestowed her to him. This was sufficient to win the lawsuit brought against him by his brothers.
- A plausible motive for Rachel's theft of her father's household gods (Genesis 31:19) is supplied by a Nuzi case where a man was able, in court, to claim the estate of his father-in-law because he possessed the family teraphim (or household gods).[243]

As summarized by H. H. Rowley: *"Their* [the Biblical accounts of the patriarchs] *accurate reflection of social conditions in the patriarchal age and in some parts of the Mesopotamia from which the patriarchs are said to have come, many centuries before the present documents were composed, is striking."* [244]

And in another conclusion from J.A. Thompson: *"The fact that there are so many links with the world of the first part of the second millennium BC is inexplicable if the stories of the Patriarchs are only the inventions of later days. It would seem impossible for the Israelites of those centuries to have access to such information as we now find beneath the earth on thousands of baked clay tablets. The fact that the Bible customs are so close to the contemporary customs is a strong argument either for written records, or for reliable oral traditions. We are compelled to conclude that the narratives of Genesis 12-50 have a solid historical basis."* [245]

THE PRICE FOR A SLAVE

Archaeological finds such as the Nuzi tablets make it possible to track the *price of slaves* in ancient times. Similar to oil prices in our day, in the Old Testament times a slave was traded according to the appropriate price current then.

In *Biblical Archaeology Review* (BAR) and in his book *On the Reliability of the Old Testament*[246] renowned archaeologist Kenneth A. Kitchen analyses the price of a slave mentioned in the Bible compared to the "free market." As he writes in BAR:[247] *"One important item involves the price of slaves in silver shekels. From ancient Near Eastern sources we know the price of slaves in some detail for a period lasting about 2,000 years, from 2400 BC to 400 BC Under the Akkad*

Empire (2371-2191 BC), a decent slave fetched 10-15 silver shekels, though the price dropped slightly to 10 shekels during the Third Dynasty of Ur (2113-2006 BC). In the second millennium BC during the early Babylonian period, the price of slaves rose to about 20 shekels, as we know from the Laws of Hammurabi and documents from Mari and elsewhere from the 19th and 18th centuries BC By the 14th and 13th centuries BC, at Nuzi and Ugarit, the price crept up to 30 shekels and sometimes more. Another five hundred years later, Assyrian slave markets demanded 50 to 60 shekels for slaves; and under the Persian Empire (fifth and fourth centuries BC), soaring inflation pushed prices up to 90 and 120 shekels."

The Bible tells us *"when the Midianite merchants came by, his brothers pulled Joseph up out of the cistern and sold him for <u>twenty shekels of silver</u> to the Ishmaelites, who took him to Egypt"* (Genesis 37:28, emphasis added). In the Mosaic Law we read the price for a slave in the 1450s BC: *"If the bull gores a male or female slave, the owner must pay <u>thirty shekels of silver</u> to the master of the slave, and the bull must be stone"* (Exodus 21:12, emphasis added). And lastly, Menahem, king of Israel ransomed some Israelites from Pul, king of Assyria, *"Every wealthy man had to contribute <u>fifty shekels of silver</u> to be given to the king of Assyria"* (2 Kings 15:20, emphasis added).

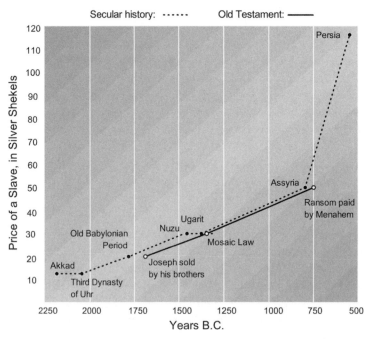

Figure 14-1: The Price of a Slave: the Bible versus Secular History

Figure 14-1[248] presents this data graphically. As one can see, the Biblical accounts are consistent with other ancient sources.

This is extremely significant. If the Torah was written during the Babylonian exile (sixth century BC) or even later as many critical scholars claim,[249] how could its writers have known with accuracy the price of a slave perhaps 1,200 years earlier? They would not have had access to this kind of information and likely would have used the price for a slave common to their own time.

THE CONQUERING OF JERICHO

The Bible suggests the conquest of *Jericho* occurred near 1400 BC. The miraculous aspect of how the city was conquered, causes some scholars to dismiss the account as only folklore. Does archaeology support the Biblical account? Because of its dramatic Biblical history, Jericho has been in the crosshairs of archaeologists for a long time; its first documented excavation began as early as 1867 by Charles Warren. Over the past century four prominent archaeologists have also excavated the site: Carl Watzinger from 1907-1909, John Garstang in the 1930s, Kathleen Kenyon from 1952-1958, and Bryant Wood from 1985-1990. The results of their work have been remarkable, but also have been subjected to much debate and interpretation.

Ancient Jericho is located near a large spring on the western edge of the Jordan Valley, just north of the Dead Sea. This excellent water supply and favorable climate (especially in winter) made it a desirable place to live in ancient times. Archaeologists think it might have been settled as early as 8000 BC, thus making Jericho the world's oldest known city. At 670 feet below sea level, it is also the lowest city in the world.

According to the book of Joshua, the Israelites marched around the town for seven days, increasing their presence by marching seven times around the city on the seventh day. Priests blew trumpets and the walls of the city collapsed (Joshua 6:13-20). After this, the Israelite army *"destroyed with the sword every living thing in it – men and women, young and old, cattle, sheep and donkeys"* (Joshua 6:21).

If this actually happened, we would expect to find two confirmations: evidence that the walls indeed collapsed, and indications this event happened at the time period when Joshua lead the Israelites into the promised land, around 1400 BC.

- **Was the city destroyed as described in the Bible?** The editor of the *Biblical Archaeology Review*, Hershel Shanks, believes so, as he states that fiery destruction did occur at Jericho *"in uncanny detail just as the Bible describes it."*[250] His conclusion followed his review of the vast archaeological data collected over the years. As early as the 1930s John Garstang concluded "*as to the main fact, then, there remains no doubt about it: the walls fell outwards so completely, the attackers would be able to clamber up and over the ruins of the city.*" In the words of Kathleen Kenyon: "*The destruction was complete. Walls and floors were blackened or reddened by fire, and every room was filled with fallen bricks, timbers, and household utensils; in most rooms the debris was heavily burnt, but the collapse of the walls of the eastern rooms seems to have taken place before they were affected by the fire.*"[251] Also remarkable is that both Garstang and Kenyon found large quantities of grain stored in the ground-floor rooms of the houses. The presence of these grain stores in the destroyed city is entirely consistent with the Biblical account. The city did not fall to a starvation siege, so common in ancient times.[252] Therefore it can be safely concluded that the destruction of Jericho was complete and was accomplished without a sustained siege or long battle. Some propose this was a major earthquake, but that is entirely consistent with the Biblical account.

• **When was Jericho destroyed?** This appears the most controversial among archaeologists. John Garstang in the 1930s concluded the destruction occurred in the 1400s BC, consistent with the date of the Biblical account. Kathleen Kenyon however concluded the city fell 150 years earlier. If so, Jericho was only rubble long since abandoned by the time Joshua's armies entered Canaan. From 1985 to 1990 Bryant Wood did additional excavations, re-examining Kenyon's conclusions. He found various mistakes in her analyses and concluded Garstang's original date appears correct.[253]

The disagreements among archaeologists about Jericho are far from settled. There is no unanimous judgment, and future excavations might well lead to new discoveries and new conclusions. Clearly the historical data is friendly to the Bible and definitely does not disprove that Jericho might have fallen in a miraculous way to the Israelites – just as described in the Bible.

THE CITY OF SHILOH

After the conquest of Canaan, Joshua assembled the Israelites at *Shiloh* and erected the Tabernacle (Joshua 18:1). Shiloh was established as the religious center of Israel, a position it held throughout the period of the judges. Its location is described in the Bible as "*Shiloh, to the north of Bethel, and east of the road that goes from Bethel to Shechem, and to the south of Lebonah*" (Judges 21:19).

In the days of Eli and Samuel, the Ark of the Covenant was taken from Shiloh to Ebenezer, where Israel battled the Philistines (1 Samuel 4:1-4). Israel was defeated, and the Philistines captured the Ark. It was displayed in a tour of Philistine cities, unleashing a plague at each. When the Philistines returned the Ark to Israel, it ended up at Kiriath-Jearim (1 Samuel 7:1-2). It was never returned to Shiloh. No explanation is given as to why it was not returned to the religious center, though many conclude from 1 Samuel 4:1-22 that Shiloh must have been destroyed at this time.

The site of Shiloh was still known in the Middle Ages; in the nineteenth century it was identified as Khirbet Seilun, 20 miles north of Jerusalem. The mound covers 12 acres, and contains the remains of Shiloh. The later towns were situated on the southern slope of the mound.[254]

Shiloh (modern Seilun) was excavated by Danish archaeologists in four stages, during the period 1926-1963. In the early 1980s, Israel Finkelstein returned to excavate and reevaluate their findings. His excavation confirmed an earlier conclusion of the Danes, that Shiloh had been destroyed by fire perhaps in 1050 BC. Though the Bible does not record the event, Israel's religious center was destroyed apparently when the Ark had been taken from it, making the return of the Ark not possible.[255]

THE HOUSE OF DAVID

One of the most beloved characters in the Bible is *King David*. Scripture says he was a man after God's own heart, and David's name is the most frequently mentioned name in the entire Bible. He is revered above all Israelite kings and the Messianic covenant was established through his lineage. Despite his key role in Israel's history, until recently, some critics questioned his very existence. In our generation two archaeological discoveries now confirm the existence and reign of this great king of Israel:

- **Tel Dan Stela.** In the summer of 1993, while excavating a site known as Tel Dan (in the Old Testament land of Dan) an impressive royal palace was unearthed. In the ruins archaeologists discovered the remains of a black basalt stela, or stone slab, dated from the ninth century BC. The inscription on the stela refers both to the "*House of David*" and to the "*King of Israel.*" That the inscription, in early Aramaic, refers not simply to David but to the House of David, the dynasty of the renowned king, is even more remarkable.[256]
- The Mesha Stela or Moabite Stone. This monument, dating likely to between 840 and 820 BC, was found 13 miles east of the Dead Sea at Diban in 1868. Since 1875, it has been displayed in the Louvre in Paris. Only during recent research it was (re-)discovered that, like the Tel Dan Stela, the Mesha Stela has similar references to *"King of Israel"* and *"House of David,"* again confirming the reign of the Biblical David.[257]

THE KINGS OF ISRAEL AND JUDAH

The Bible gives a detailed chronology and history of the kings who followed Solomon in the divided kingdom of Israel (the north) and Judah (the south). Can we find archaeological confirmations of their names outside the Bible? Ancient rulers used monuments such as prisms, obelisks and stones to record their exploits. These massive documents of stone and clay have survived for centuries amid the ancient ruins. They provide valuable insights into life during Bible times, confirming and often adding valuable information about Biblical events. This overview sums up finds that confirm the lives of these kings and their enemies as well as their Biblical dates:

- **Black Obelisk of Shalmaneser III.** As early as the mid-nineteenth century, archaeologists uncovered a stone monument south of Mosul in Iraq from the ninth century BC (around 840 BC), now known as the *Black Obelisk*. The four-sided limestone monument is decorated with five registers of relief sculptures, each depicting the bringing of tribute to Shalmaneser. Each register reads around four sides, one panel to a side, portraying a particular tribute and tribute-bearers. The second register from the top shows the tribute of the Israelite king Jehu (ruled 841-814 BC). The central figure on the first panel of this register, presumably Jehu himself, prostrates himself, forehead to the ground possibly kissing the feet of the Assyrian monarch. Some suggest this figure might be Jehu's emissary, but if it is Jehu, this panel provides the only extant picture of a king of ancient Israel.[258] The caption to this scene reads: *"Tribute of Iaua* [Jehu], *son of Omri. Silver, gold, a golden bowl, a golden beaker, golden goblets, pitchers of gold, tin, staves for the hand of the king,* [and] *javelins, I* [Shalmaneser] *received from him."* [259]

- **Moabite Stone.** In addition to King David, Ahab and his father Omri are named on the above mentioned *Moabite Stone* (also known as the Mesha Stele). Mesha, king of Moab (2 Kings 3:4), writes that Omri, king of Israel, and his son Ahab had subdued Moab because Chemosh, the nation's god, was angry with his land. Mesha, however, claims to have found favor with Chemosh, which enabled him to reclaim the land lost to Israel. His rebellion against Israel and Ahab's son Jehoram is recorded in Scripture (2 Kings 3:5-27), but the success he reports contradicts the Biblical record.[260]

- **Sennacherib's Prism or the Taylor Prism.** Scripture reports that in the 14th year of king Hezekiah (701 BC), the Assyrian king Sennacherib (705-681 BC) invaded Judah and marched against Jerusalem (2 Kings 18:13). Having held the city in siege, Sennacherib retreated to Assyria after the death angel killed 185,000 of his men (2 Kings 19:35). At home he recorded his version of the event on a hexagonal cylinder discovered at Kuyunjik (ancient Nineveh) in 1830 by J. E. Taylor. Sennacherib bragged that he had taken 46 walled cities in Judah. And concerning Hezekiah he stated, *"He himself I shut up like a caged bird within Jerusalem, his royal city."* [261] While this siege of Jerusalem is a confirmed historical fact, it is interesting to note Sennacherib's account did not tell how the siege ended. This leads historians to suspect the siege failed, since Assyrians never mentioned defeats in their official records – only victories.

THE CYRUS CYLINDER

In the nineteenth century, Hormuzd Rassam found a nine-inch baked clay cylinder in Babylon that dated to 500 BC. Its inscription is Cyrus's account of how the god Marduk had blessed his efforts to capture Babylon. Then Cyrus tells how his policy permitted former captives in Babylon to return home and restore the temples of their own deities:

"From [Babylon] up to the city of Ashur and Susa, Akkad, to the land of Eshnunna, to the towns Zamban, Me-Turnu, Der up to the region of the Gutians, I returned to (these) sacred cult-cities on the other side of the Tigris, the sanctuaries of which have been ruins for a long time, the gods who live in them and established for them eternal sanctuaries. I (also) gathered all their inhabitants and returned them to their habitations. Furthermore, I resettled upon the command of Marduk, the great Lord, all the gods of Sumer and Akkad whom Nabonidus has brought into Babylon to the anger of the Lord of the gods, unharmed, in their chapels, the places which make them happy." [262]

Realistically, Cyrus merely exploited the occasion to his advantage. He knew that happy subjects would be loyal subjects. So Cyrus's benevolence was part of his international policy. He, however, unwittingly fulfilled Isaiah's pointed prophecy about him (Isaiah 44:28-45:1), that he would be the Lord's *"shepherd"* and *"anointed one"* who would perform His pleasure. The *Cyrus Cylinder* answers doubts raised by Ezra 1:2-4. Ezra states that, in his first year after conquering Babylon, Cyrus acknowledged the Lord God of heaven, who had commanded him to build the Temple in Jerusalem and to permit God's people (the Jews) to return. [263]

SUMMARY OF THE OLD TESTAMENT ARCHAEOLOGICAL CONFIRMATIONS

Table 14-1 summarizes some of the historical and archaeological evidences for the reliability of the Old Testament. Entries in *italics* were not discussed here, but added for completeness.

Archaeological Evidence for the Old Testament

Discovery	Dated	Evidence/Inscription	Significance
Silver Scrolls	Before 600 BC	Numbers 6:24-26	Confirms sixth century BC Torah texts
Sodom and Gomorrah	Around 2000 BC	Excavated "cities of the Plains"	Corroborates Genesis accounts
Nuzi or Nuzu tables	Around 1400 BC	Describe Bronze Age customs	Corroborates Torah accounts and customs
Jericho	Around 1400 BC	Destroyed as described in Joshua chapter 6	Corroborates Joshua's invasion of Canaan
Shiloh	Around 1100 BC	Destroyed around 1050 BC	Corroborates books of Joshua, Judges, Samuel
Tel Dan Stela	ninth century BC	"House of David," "[Jeho]rm," "[Ahaz]yahu"	Corroborates King David, Jehoram, and Ahaziah
Tel Al-Rimah Stela	870-810 BC	"Joash the Samarian"	Corroborates king Joash (805-790 BC)
Moabite Stone	840-820 BC	"House of David," "Omri," "Ahab"	Corroborates King David, Omri, and Ahab
Black Obelisk of Shalmaneser III	840 BC	"the tribute of Jehu, son of Omri"	Corroborates Omri and Jehu
Annals of the king Tiglath-Pileser III	744-727 BC	"the Land of Omri....king Pekah,,,,Hoshea," "As for Menahem....," "..tribute of Azriau...Ahaz of Juda"	Corroborates accounts of Menahem, Pekah and Hoshea of Israel and Uzziah and Ahaz of Judah
Annals of king Sargon II	721-705 BC	"I conquered... the Land of Omri"	Corroborates accounts of king Omri(885-874 BC)
Taylor Prism	700-680 BC	"Hezekiah, the Jew..."	Corroborates Hezekiah
Prism B of king Esarhaddon	680-669 BC	"...Manasseh, king of Judah"	Corroborates Manasseh (696-642 BC)
Rassam Cylinder of Ashurbanipal	668-633 BC	"Manasseh, king of Judah"	Corroborates king Manasseh
Ration documents of Nebudchadnezzar	605-562 BC	"to Jehoichin, king of Judah"	Corroborates Jehoiachin (597-560 BC)
Neo-Babylonian Chronicle	600 BC	Records of Nebudchadnezzar	Confirms Babylonian invasion of Palestine
Cyrus Cylinder	500 BC	Cyrus's victory and decree permitting free worship	Confirms Ezra 1:1-4

Table 14-1: Archaeological Evidence for the Old Testament

☆ EXHIBIT #16: THE NEW TESTAMENT IS HISTORICALLY RELIABLE

There are numerous archaeological and historical confirmations for the New Testament as well. The books of Luke and Acts are like treasure maps for archaeological expeditions because of the large numbers of locations, rulers, and travel routes that are recorded. As with the Old Testament, a overview of discoveries is presented, and discussed.

SIMON PETER'S HOUSE IN CAPERNAUM

Capernaum was a town on the western shore of the Sea of Galilee, situated on the highway from the Mediterranean coast to Damascus. It provided local fishermen with a small port. The town is known from the early Roman period onwards. Josephus describes the area as very fertile and records that its people had taken an active part in the war against the Romans.[264]

This town is frequently mentioned in the gospels. Jesus moved there from Nazareth, on the borders of Zebulon and Naphtali (Matthew 4:13). There He found His first disciples, Peter, Andrew and the two sons of Zebedee (Matthew 4:18-22). He taught in the town's synagogue (John 6:24-59) and directed Peter to find a coin in the mouth of a fish with which to pay the temple tax (Matthew 17:24-7). He lodged there in Peter's house, healing the sick and teaching (Mark 1:29-34; 2:1-12; Luke 4:38-44). Leaving Capernaum, he condemned it along with other cities that had not heeded his calls to repentance (Matthew 11:23; Luke 10:15).

The latest evidence of a living community at Capernaum is a fifth century inscription in Aramaic in the synagogue of el-Hamma (Hammath-Gader). From that time onwards nothing remains intact; only ruins. The most impressive are those of the synagogue, first uncovered by E. Robinson in 1838 and identified as Capernaum by C. Wilson in 1865. In 1894 the Franciscans bought the site and fenced it off to prevent the theft of masonry. It was explored in 1905, excavated in 1921 and partly reconstructed four years later.[265]

The next excavations by the Franciscans (V. Corbo and S. Loffreda) began in 1968, and went well beyond the synagogue, uncovering parts of the town. In this connection they became interested in the remains of an octagonal building, identified as a Byzantine-era church (400-500 AD), 84 feet south of the synagogue, opposite the synagogue façade facing Jerusalem.

Directly beneath the octagonal church building lay remains of another building. It was a house almost certainly used as a church, judging from the graffiti on the walls left by Christian pilgrims. For example, a graffito scratched on a wall reads, *"Lord Jesus Christ help thy servant ... "* A proper name followed but is no longer readable. Another reads, *"Christ have mercy."* On the walls crosses are depicted. The graffiti is predominantly Greek, but some are also in Syriac and Hebrew. The presence of Hebrew graffiti suggests the community might have been comprised of Jewish Christians. According to Franciscan excavators, the name Peter is found at least twice in these inscriptions.[266]

The house was likely built in the first century BC. It was constructed of rough black basalt boulders. There were a number of small rooms, two court-yards, and one large room. When it was built, it was likely indistinguishable from other houses in the ancient seaside town. However it was renovated near the middle of the first century AD. Its walls and floors were plastered – quite unusual for ordinary houses, but common in buildings used for large gather-ings. Experts concluded that the building had been turned into a "house-church," and so used until the fifth century.[267]

While the case is far from airtight, the circumstantial evidence is intrigu-ing, to say the least! Its location, original construction, early conversion into a Christian house-church, and presence of the name Peter in inscriptions have many scholars[268] lead to the conclusion that this house once belonged to Simon Peter.

Joseph, Who was Called Caiaphas

During the creation of a water park in Jerusalem's Peace Forest (just south of the Dome of the Rock) in 1990, workers uncovered a burial cave. It was clearly Jewish, as indicated by its 12 ossuaries. Ossuaries are limestone boxes used to store human bones; such burial procedures occurred mainly near the end of the first century BC and in the first century AD. A date for the burial cave (suggested by a coin found in one of the ossuaries) suggests an early first century AD burial. The most elaborately decorated ossuary contained the bones of a sixty-year old man. This ossuary carries two inscriptions that relate to the Caiaphas family. They are identical except for the addition in one of the names of one letter, a dif-ference in the spelling of the Caiaphas name. The inscriptions read:

אפק רב יׄסוׄה = Yhwsp br Qp' = Joseph, son of Qafa' and

אפיק (or אׄפוׄק) = Qyp' (or Qwp') = Qafa' (or Qayafa')

The name אפק (Qafa) or אפיק (Qayafa) is an Aramaic form. The name *"Joseph, son of Caiaphas"* does not necessarily mean that Caiaphas was Joseph's father. Caiaphas may designate simply a family nickname. Thus the inscription may well be understood as Joseph of the family Caiaphas. The elderly man buried in the highly decorated ossuary was Joseph, probably a forefather who had acquired this nickname, which then became a sort of family name – inher-ited by his descendants.[269]

The gospels refer to the high priest only by the name Caiaphas, but the first century Jewish historian Josephus mentions his name as "Joseph, who was called Caiaphas": *"Besides which, he also deprived Joseph, who was called Caiaphas, of the high priesthood, and appointed Jonathan, the son of Ananus, the former high priest, to succeed him. After which he took his journey back to Antioch."* [270]

Just coincidence? Or could this be the remains of the old high priest himself?

THE PILATE INSCRIPTION

Evidence for *Pontius Pilate*, the Roman governor who presided at the trial of Jesus, was discovered at the seaside ruins of Caesarea Maritima, the ancient seat of Roman government. In 1961, an Italian archaeologist uncovered a fragment of a plaque near steps leading to the Caesarea Theater. Though it is believed to have been placed there during fourth century renovations, experts say it was originally a first century dedicatory plaque at a nearby temple honoring emperor Tiberius. The inscription, written in Latin, contained the phrase:

"Pontius Pilatus, Prefect of Judea has dedicated to the people of Caesarea a temple in honor of Tiberius." [271]

Emperor Tiberius reigned from 14-37 AD. This fits well with the New Testament chronology and both Philo and Josephus record Pilate was procurator/governor from 26-36 AD.[272]

THE CRUCIFIED MAN OF GIVA'AT HA-MITVAR

Historians estimate that as many as 100,000 people might have been crucified during the Roman Empire. Crucifixion was the preferred execution by the Romans because its gruesome, slow death instilled the maximum fear in the hearts of the suppressed people. During the siege of Jerusalem in 70 AD alone, as Josephus reports, thousands of Jews were crucified (as many as 500 a day for several months) by the Roman army along the walls of Jerusalem.[273]

In 1968 an ancient burial site at Giva'at ha-Mitvar near the Nablus road outside of Jerusalem was uncovered containing 35 bodies. Most of these died violently in the uprising against Rome in 70 AD. One was a man named Yohanan Ben Ha'galgol (Yehohanan, son of Hagakol). He was about five foot six inches tall and between 24 and 28 years old. He had a cleft palate, and a seven-inch nail was still driven through both his feet. The feet had been turned outward so that the square nail could be hammered through at the heel, just inside the Achilles tendon. This would have bowed the legs outward as well so that they could not have been used for support on the cross. The nail had gone through a wedge of acacia wood, then through the heels, then into an olive wood beam. There was also evidence that similar spikes had been put between the two bones of each lower arm. These had caused the upper bones to be worn smooth as the victim repeatedly raised and lowered himself to breathe (breathing is restricted with the arms raised). Crucifixion victims had to lift themselves to free the chest muscles and, when they grew too weak to do so, died by suffocation.[274]

Further study revealed Yohanan's lower leg bones had been broken. The left tibia and fibula bones and the right tibia bone were apparently crushed by a common blow, with the legs sawed off later.[275] This "breaking of the legs" is consistent with common Roman practice of crucifragium mentioned in the Gospel of John: *"Because the Jews did not want the bodies left on the crosses during the Sabbath, they asked Pilate to have the legs broken and the bodies taken down. The soldiers therefore came and broke the legs of the first man who had been crucified with Jesus, and then those of the other"* (John 19:31-32). By breaking the leg bones, death was hastened because the victim was not any longer able to push himself up to breath.

Numerous critical scholars[276] accept the fact that Jesus was crucified, but take the position that after his crucifixion, his body was devoured by wild animals or tossed into a common grave. They claim this was the Roman practice; therefore the burial by Joseph of Arimathea (recorded in all four gospels) is mere fiction. These scholars insist that this explains why Jesus' body was never produced. The man Yohanan gives factual evidence that disproves this theory. The fact that he was crucified by the Romans but subsequently buried according to Jewish tradition establishes the legitimate possibility that Jesus' body was buried just as described in the New Testament.

THE POOL OF BETHESDA

A number of scholars consider the Gospel of John a second century document and hence not written during the lifetime of John the apostle. However, archaeological excavations and research concur in detail with the landscapes and structures described in the book of John. This is especially relevant because some of these buildings were destroyed in Jerusalem in 70 AD by the Romans. It is quite unlikely that a second century author could have had the knowledge necessary for such an accurately detailed description.

An illustration is John's description of the pool of Bethesda: *"Now there is in Jerusalem near the Sheep Gate a pool, which in Aramaic is called Bethesda and which is surrounded by five covered colonnades"* (John 5:2).

Excavations between 1914 and 1918 have laid bare a double pool surrounded by four porticoes, with a fifth on a rock gangway between the two pools. The pool was approximately 16 meters (53 feet) deep, making it necessary for a crippled person not only to be assisted to the water, but also supported in it. It is not doubted that this is the very site described by John.[277]

ERASTUS, TREASURER IN CORINTH

In Romans 16:23 (*"Erastus, who is the city's director of public works,*[278] *and our brother Quartus send you their greetings."*) Paul conveys greetings to the Roman church from several people, one of whom is identified as *"Erastus, the city's director of public works."* Since the apostle almost certainly wrote this letter from Corinth, Erastus was probably the treasurer of Corinth. Erastus is even specifically associated with Corinth in 2 Timothy 4:20 (*"Erastus stayed in Corinth"*). This same Erastus is likely also referred to in Acts 19:22 (*"He sent two of his helpers, Timothy and Erastus, to Macedonia"*) as the helper of Paul, whom Paul sent from Ephesus (near Corinth) to Macedonia.

In 1929 a limestone slab that was part of the pavement near the theater in Corinth was discovered. A Latin inscription found on it has been dated to the second half of the first century AD. Originally it consisted of letters cut into limestone paving blocks and then inlaid with metal. Only two metal punctuation marks remain, however, although most of the inscription itself is still in a small plaza just east of the theater. It reads as follows:

[...] ERASTVS PRO AEDILIT[AT]E S P STRAVIT
"Erastus in return for his aedileship laid [the pavement] at his own expense." [279]

No other person with this name is known to have been an official in Corinth, and since the name itself is not common, it would appear that this Erastus is the same one whom Paul mentioned. Although an *aedile* was not a city treasurer, but more like a commissioner of public works, one did not attain an aedileship without having first served the city in other important capacities. In the case of Erastus the *aedile*, we may suppose one of those earlier offices was that of *quaestor*, or municipal financial officer.[280]

SUMMARY OF THE NEW TESTAMENT ARCHAEOLOGICAL CONFIRMATIONS

Below is a table (table 14-2) of some of the evidences that support the historical reliability of the New Testament. Entries in *italics* were not discussed in detail and are added for completeness.

Archaeological Evidence for the New Testament			
Discovery	**Location**	**Evidence/Inscription**	**Significance**
Excavated house	Capernaum	first century house church	Peter's house in Capernaum
Ossuary of Caiaphas	Jerusalem	"Joseph son of Caiaphas"	Bones of Caiaphas the High priest
Fragment of plague with inscription	Caesarea Maritima	"Pontius Pilatus, Prefect of Judea"	Confirms Pilate as governor
Bones of crucified man	Giva'at ha-Mitvar	Bones of crucified man	Confirm crucifixion details
Pool of Bethesda	Jerusalem	Pool with 5 porticoes	Confirms John 5:2
Pool of Siloam	*Jerusalem*	*Pool with inscription*	*John 9:7-11*
Slab with "ordinance of Caesar"	*Nazareth*	*Strict prohibition against disturbing of graves*	*Confirms early Christian claims of resurrection*
Galilean boat	*Sea of Galilee*	*first century fishing boat*	*Corroborate gospel accounts*
Golden Gate	*Jerusalem*	*Ancient gate under current Golden gate*	*Mark 11:11?*
Slab of limestone in pavement	Corinth	"Erastus in return for his aedileship…"	Romans (16:23), 2 Timothy (4:20)
Temple inscription	*Damascus*	*"Lysanias the tetrarch"*	*Luke 3:1*
Dated Greek inscription	*Delphi*	*"Lucius Junios Gallio… Achaia"*	*Acts 18:12-17*

Table 14-2: Archaeological Evidence for the New Testament

Distinguished Roman historian A. N. Sherwin-White concludes about the writings of Luke:[281]

"*For Acts the confirmation of historicity is overwhelming… Any attempt to reject its basic historicity even in matters of detail must now appear absurd. Roman historians have long taken it for granted.*"

American Biblical archaeologist and Middle Eastern scholar William F. Albright writes:[282]

"*The excessive skepticism shown toward the Bible by important historical schools of the eighteenth- and nineteenth centuries, certain phases of which still appear periodically, has been progressively discredited. Discovery after discovery has established the accuracy of innumerable details, and has brought increased recognition to the value of the Bible as a source of history.*"

☼ Exhibit 17: The Testimony of the Ancient Chinese Characters

Additional confirmations for the historicity of the Genesis accounts come from a rather unexpected source: the written characters of the ancient Chinese. The pictorial Chinese language was composed an estimated 4,500 years ago (that is about 2,500 years before the birth of Christ and 500 years or so before Abraham left Ur and made his covenant with the Lord). As still used today, written Chinese employs pictures to express words or ideas. Simple pictures were combined to express more complex thoughts or concepts. Well known history and everyday things were used to make a word easier to remember.

By studying the composition of the symbols for some of the Chinese words some remarkable observations can be made:[283]

- **The symbol for "God."** Genesis 1 says God "*spoke*" the world into existence. The Chinese symbol for God reflects this concept as it is composed of the symbols for "to show," "revelation," and "to say" (see figure 14-2a):
- **The symbol for "beginning" or "first."** In Genesis we read that God created Adam and Eve as the first couple. In Chinese the symbol of "first" or "beginning" is built from the symbols for "two" and "people" (see figure 14-2b).
- **The symbols for "forbidden" and "desire."** Genesis 2:8-9 relates that in the center of the Garden of Eden two special trees, the "*tree of life*" and the "*tree of knowledge of good and evil*" were present. So these two trees symbolize the Garden of Eden.

(a) 示 + 申 = 神

to show, revelation — to say — God

(b) 二 + 儿 = 元

two — people — beginning, first

(c) 林 + 示 = 禁

two trees — command — forbidden

Figure 14-2: Chinese Symbols Related to the Bible (1)

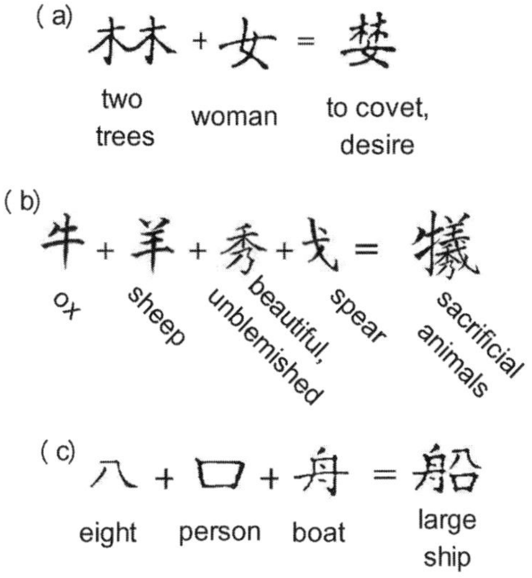

(a) 林 + 女 = 婪

two trees — woman — to covet, desire

(b) 牛 + 羊 + 秀 + 戈 = 犠

ox — sheep — beautiful, unblemished — spear — sacrificial animals

(c) 八 + 口 + 舟 = 船

eight — person — boat — large ship

Figure 14-3: Chinese Symbols Related to the Bible (2)

Subsequently in Genesis 2:16-17 God forbids Adam and Eve in the Garden of Eden to eat fruit from the tree of knowledge. In the Chinese the symbol for "forbidden" is composed of the symbol for "two trees" and "command" (figure 14-2c) and the symbol for "desire" consists of symbols for "two trees" and "woman" (figure 14-3a).

- **The symbol for "sacrificial animals."** In the Torah God established the sacrificial system.[284] By the sacrifice (killing) of an unblemished sheep or ox the patriarchs and Jews – by faith – could have their sins forgiven. This concept is symbolically summarized in the Chinese symbol for "sacrificial animals" (see figure 14-3b).
- **The symbol for a "large ship."** According to Genesis 6:15-16, God commanded Noah to build a huge, container-like ship, the ark. He and his wife, their three sons along with their wives, a total of eight people, were to enter it when the flood started. As figure 14-7 shows, the Chinese symbol for "large ship" is composed of a combination of the symbols for "eight," "person" and "boat" – "eight people on a boat."

This overview is just an illustration of the numerous Chinese characters that can be broken down into the meanings of sub-characters. Words describing concepts such "to talk," "to create," "first," "happiness or blessing," "West," "devil," "tempter," and "flood" can all be broken down in other symbols related to the Biblical accounts in Genesis.

Is this coincidence? Is this perhaps creative imagination? Skeptics will argue this proves nothing but that some religious fanatic had too much time and imagination. On the other hand, how many symbols does one need to find to demonstrate this is no mere coincidence? Five ? Ten? Perhaps twenty-five? The discovery of the Biblical roots of the Chinese pictorial characters points to a common bond between Chinese and Jewish people. This could well be explained by the accounts of the creation, the flood, and the tower of Babel outlined in the first 11 chapters of Genesis.

CHAPTER 15

The Testimony of Non-Christian Writers

*"Christus, from whom the name had its origin, suffered the
extreme penalty during the reign of Tiberius at the hands
of one of our procurators, Pontius Pilate"*
Roman historian Tacitus (55-120 AD)

Exhibit #18: Confirmations from Non-Christian Sources

Some folks have the impression that the only evidence for the Christian faith is the Bible itself (along with other Christian sources, of course). Skeptics suggest that this evidence can't be trusted because the writers are biased in favor of the Christian message.

It is true that only few references to Christian origins have been located outside the Bible and the Christian church. This should not surprise us; after all, documents available today are only a fraction of what was written then, a fairly random selection at that. Remember also that the early stages of the Christian movement were quite obscure and certainly "low profile." These events occurred in a forgettable province on the eastern edge of the Roman Empire.

Even so, more than a dozen non-Christian (Roman, Greek and Jewish) sources refer to Christian origins. Writers include ancient historians such as Tacitus, Suetonius, and Thallus; Jewish sources such as Josephus and the Talmud; Roman government officials such as Pliny the Younger and Emperor Trajan; and the Greek writer Lucian. Combine these sources and the reader has ample confirmation of the historical picture presented in the Bible.

Flavius Josephus (37 – ca. 100 ad)

Flavius Josephus was a Jewish military officer and historian. He was born in 37 AD, and raised as a Pharisee. Later he joined the Zealots who rebelled against Roman rule in 66 AD, and the Sanhedrin (the Jewish governing body) appointed Josephus commander of Galilee. After the defeat at Jotapata and his surrender to the Romans, his life was spared through a friend's intervention. When Vespasian became emperor in 69 AD Josephus became his advisor, even adopting Vespasian's family name, Flavius. In the year 70 AD, when Vespasian's

Testimony from Flavius Josephus

Date	Event	Bible text	Josephus text
4 BC	Archelaus ruler of Judea	"But when he heard that Archelaus was reigning in Judea..." Matthew 2:22	"So Caesar, ... gave the one half of Herod's kingdom to Archelaus, by the name of Ethnarch...." [286]
6,7 AD	Roman annexation	"This was the first census that took place while Quirinius was governor of Syria." Luke 2:2	"...and Cyrenius [is Quirinius], one that had been consul, was sent by Caesar to take account of people's effects in Syria..." [287]
6,7 AD	Revolt of Judas the Galilean	"...Judas the Galilean appeared in the days of the census..." Acts 5:37	"...a certain Galilean, whose name was Judas, prevailed with his countrymen to revolt..." [288]
28 AD	Pontius Pilate	"In the fifteenth year of the reign of Tiberius Caesar—when Pontius Pilate was governor of Judea..." Luke 3:1	"Now Pilate, who was sent as procurator into Judea by Tiberius..." [289]
29,30 AD	John the Baptist	"King Herod..... sent an executioner with orders to bring John's head. The man went, beheaded John in the prison..." Mark 6:14-29	"...a punishment of what he did against John, that was called the Baptist... who was a good man, and commanded the Jews to exercise virtue... and so to come to baptism ...Herod, ...thought it best, by putting him to death..." [290]
30-33 AD	Jesus' crucifixion	All gospels, book of Acts	"Now, there was about this time Jesus, a wise man... he was a doer of wonderful works... He drew over to him both many of the Jews, and many of the Gentiles. ... when Pilate, at the suggestion of the principal men amongst us, had condemned him to the cross, those that loved him at the first did not forsake him.... and the tribe of Christians, so named from him, are not extinct at this day." [291]
ca. 36 AD	Joseph, also called Caiaphas	All gospels mention Caiaphas	"... he also deprived Joseph, who was called Caiaphas, of the high priesthood..." [292]
ca. 36 AD	Aretas IV, king of Nabateans	"In Damascus the governor under King Aretas had the city of the Damascenes guarded in order to arrest me." 2 Corinthians 11:32	"About this time Aretas (the king of Arabia Petrea) and Herod had a quarrel, on the account following: Herod the tetrarch had married the daughter of Aretas." [293]
44 AD	Death of Herod Agrippa I	"...Herod, ...did not give praise to God, an angel of the Lord struck him down, and he was eaten by worms and died." Acts 12:20-23	"Agrippa ... that he was a god... When he said this, his pain was become violent.... he had been quite worn out by the pain in his belly for five days, he departed this life..." [294]
ca. 47 AD	Ananias the high priest	"At this the high priest Ananias ordered those standing near Paul to strike him on the mouth." Acts 23:2	"Herod, king of Chalcis, removed Joseph, the son of Camydus, from the high priesthood, and made Ananias, the son of Nebedeus, his successor." [295]
ca. 57 AD	James, the brother of Jesus	"The next day Paul and the rest of us went to see James, and all the elders were present." Acts 21:18	"Ananus... assembled the Sanhedrin of judges, and brought before them the brother of Jesus, who was called Christ, whose name was James, and some others, ..., he delivered them to be stoned." [296]

Table 15-1: Testimony of Josephus Compared to the Bible

son Titus marched on Jerusalem, Josephus accompanied him. Several times Josephus tried unsuccessfully to persuade the Jews to surrender to end the siege and avoid the massacre and destruction of the city.

Josephus produced a number of books of considerable historical value. In *The Jewish War* (77-78 AD) Josephus described the Roman-Jewish conflict from the time of Antiochus Ephiphanes to just after the fall of Jerusalem. Perhaps his greatest work was *The Antiquities of the Jews* (ca. 94 AD), a 20-volume work tracing Jewish history from creation to the outbreak of war with Rome in 66 AD. Six books in this work cover the reign of Herod the Great, the very period when Jesus lived.[285]

The most intersections with the accounts of the New Testament of any non-Christian writer are found in the work of Josephus. Most of these confirm Biblical events, and some even add information. Table 15-1 is an overview of Biblical accounts and names in Josephus' writings.

Note how well Josephus' accounts match the New Testament documents. Be sure to observe the corroborative details in Josephus: the high priests Caiaphas ("*also called Joseph*") and Ananus (Annas); various Roman rulers including Pontius Pilate; John the Baptist and his execution by Herod; Jesus (twice, including explicit mention of the crucifixion by Pilate), James ("*the brother of Jesus, who was called Christ*") and his execution by the Sanhedrin and Herod Agrippa including the details of his death that are consistent with the book of Acts.

CORNELIUS TACITUS (CA. 55-120 AD)

Little is known of the Roman historian *Cornelius Tacitus*, but his surviving writings present an invaluable picture of Roman life in the first century AD. He lived through the reigns of over a half dozen Roman emperors and has been called the "greatest historian" of ancient Rome. In his *Annals* (ca. 116 AD) he describes the Christian persecution under Nero:

"Consequently, to get rid of the report, Nero fastened the guilt and inflict-ed the most exquisite tortures on a class hated for their abominations, called Christians by the populace. Christus, from whom the name had its origin, suffered the extreme penalty during the reign of Tiberius at the hands of one of our procurators, Pontius Pilatus, and a most mischievous superstition, thus checked for the moment, again broke out not only in Judaea, the first source of the evil, but even in Rome, where all things hideous and shameful from every part of the world find their centre and become popular. Accordingly, an arrest was first made of all who pleaded guilty; then, upon their information, an immense multitude was convict-ed, not so much of the crime of firing the city, as of hatred against

mankind. Mockery of every sort was added to their deaths. Covered with the skins of beasts, they were torn by dogs and perished, or were nailed to crosses, or were doomed to the flames and burnt, to serve as a nightly illumination, when daylight had expired. Nero offered his gardens for the spectacle, and was exhibiting a show in the circus, while he mingled with the people in the dress of a charioteer or stood aloft on a car. Hence, even for criminals who deserved extreme and exemplary punishment, there arose a feeling of compassion; for it was not, as it seemed, for the public good, but to glut one man's cruelty, that they were being destroyed." [297]

GAIUS SUETONIUS TRANQUILLAS (CA. 130 AD)

Little more is known of the Roman historian *Gaius Suetonius Tranquillas* than that he was the chief secretary of Emperor Hadrian (117-138 AD) with access to imperial records. Suetonius makes two references to Christ and Christians:

"Because the Jews at Rome caused continuous disturbances at the instigation of Chrestus [Christus], he [Claudius] expelled them from the city." [298]

This quote refers to an uproar in the Jewish community in Rome in 49 AD that caused Claudius to expel all Jews. This is what apparently had happened to Aquila and Priscilla in Acts 18:2: *"There he [Paul] met a Jew named Aquila, a native of Pontus, who had recently come from Italy with his wife Priscilla, because Claudius had ordered all the Jews to leave Rome."*

Suetonius' second reference is to Nero's persecution of Christians:

"After the great fire at Rome...Punishments were also inflicted on the Christians, a sect professing a new and mischievous religious belief." [299]

In these two references Suetonius confirms that:
- In 49 AD Jews in Rome caused "disturbances" because of Christ. Likely there was already a Christian church in Rome at that time (only 16 years after the resurrection).
- Christians were persecuted by Nero in 64 AD (and that there must have been a large enough Christian population in Rome to have them be identified as such).

THALLUS (CA. 52 AD) VIA JULIUS AFRICANUS (CA. 221 AD)

A questionable reference to events surrounding the crucifixion comes indirectly through the third century early church writer Julius Africanus who refers to a lost historical work from the first century Samaritan-born historian *Thallus*. Julius Africanus (160-240 AD) writes:

"On the whole world there pressed a most fearful darkness; and the rocks were rent by an earthquake, and many places in Judea and other districts were thrown down. This darkness Thallus, in the third book of his History, calls, as appears to me without reason, an eclipse of the sun…Phlegon records that, in the time of Tiberius Caesar, at full moon, there was a full eclipse of the sun from the sixth hour to the ninth – manifestly that one of which we speak." [300]

Apparently, in 52 AD Thallus tried to explain a mysterious darkness (the one mentioned in Matthew 27:45 during the crucifixion?) as an eclipse of the sun. Julius Africanus argues that in the middle of the lunar month (the 14th of Nisan, the Passover) a solar eclipse is not possible. Additionally he refers to a writing of Phlegon, also lost, that records this eclipse.

The indirect reference and its link to the crucifixion leave this quote subject to questions. Still, it is quite intriguing to find a supernatural event referred to by a non-Christian source.

PLINY THE YOUNGER (CA. 61-113 AD)

Roman administrator *Pliny the Younger* (Gaius Plinius Caecilius Secundus) became consul by the year 100 AD. Ten years later Emperor Trajan sent him to Bithynia (present-day Turkey) to look into irregularities in its administration. During this time he wrote to the emperor for advice about how to deal with Christians in his province, because he was executing so many of them. Pliny wrote around 112 AD (extract from much longer letter):

"They [the Christians] were in the habit of meeting on a certain fixed day before it was light, when they sang in alternate verses a hymn to Christ, as to a god, and bound themselves by a solemn oath, not to any wicked deeds, but never to commit any fraud, theft or adultery, never to falsify their word, nor deny a trust when they should be called upon to deliver it up; after which it was their custom to separate, and then reassemble to partake of food – but food of an ordinary and innocent kind." [301]

From Pliny's letter it follows that:
• The Christians worshiped Christ as a god.
• They committed themselves to high ethical values.
• Likely they celebrated communion on a fixed day before it was light.
• By early second century a fairly large Christian community existed in Bithynia.

Emperor Trajan replies to Pliny's letter by writing:

"The method you have pursued, my dear Pliny, in sifting the cases of those denounced to you as Christians is extremely proper. It is not possible to lay down any general rule which can be applied as the fixed standard in all cases of this nature. No search should be made for these people; when they are denounced and found guilty they must be punished; with the restriction, however, that when the party denies himself to be a Christian, and shall give proof that he is not (that is, by adoring our Gods) he shall be pardoned on the ground of repentance, even though he may have formerly incurred suspicion. Informations without the accuser's name subscribed must not be admitted in evidence against anyone, as it is introducing a very dangerous precedent, and by no means agreeable to the spirit of the age." [302]

Trajan's letter does not yield additional confirmations of the Biblical text or the early church, but these valuable insights into official Roman views about the growing movement are vital. It also shows that the persecutions occurred and Christians were martyred during the days of Trajan with some slight moderation and consideration.

THE JEWISH TALMUD (CA. 70-200 AD)

The Talmud is a collection of oral Jewish traditions (the Mishnah) and commentaries (the Gemaras). Talmudic writings of most value to Christian history are from 70-200 AD. By far the most significant text is Sanhedrin 43a:

"On the eve of the Passover Yeshu [Jesus] was hanged [crucified]. For forty days before the execution took place, a herald went forth and cried, 'He is going forth to be stoned because he has practiced sorcery and enticed Israel to apostasy. Any one who can say anything in his favour, let him come forward and plead on his behalf.' But since nothing was brought forward in his favour he was hanged on the eve of the Passover!" [303]

The mentioned 40 day period of announcement is not found in any of the other crucifixion accounts, but it confirms the execution by *"hanging"*, a word to mean crucified *"on the eve of the Passover"* (see similar words in Galatians 3:13 and Luke 23:39).

LUCIAN OF SAMOSATA (SECOND CENTURY AD)

A second century Greek writer, *Lucian of Samosata*, wrote a rather sarcastic critique of Christianity:

"The Christians, you know, worship a man to this day – the distinguished personage who introduced their novel rites, and was crucified on that account. . . . You see, these misguided creatures start with the general con-

viction that they are immortal for all time, which explains the contempt of death and voluntary self-devotion which are so common among them; and then it was impressed on them by their original lawgiver that they are all brothers, from the moment that they are converted, and deny the gods of Greece, and worship the crucified sage, and live after his laws. All this they take quite on faith, with the result that they despise all worldly goods alike, regarding them merely as common property." [304]

Lucian's satire shows that:
• The Christians worship a crucified man, Christ.
• Christ introduced new teachings for which He was crucified.
• The Christians follow Christ's laws and are willing to die for it.

SUMMARY OF THE NON-CHRISTIAN TESTIMONIES
In the words of Dr. Gary Habermas:

"Overall, at least seventeen non-Christian writings record more than fifty details concerning the life, teachings, death, and resurrection of Jesus, plus details concerning the earliest church. Most frequently reported is Jesus' death, mentioned by twelve sources. Dated approximately 20 to 150 years after Jesus' death, these secular sources are quite early by the standards of ancient historiography." [305]

These writings confirm first of all that Jesus of Nazareth, also known as Christ or Christus, was a historical person. And He performed miracles, led disciples, and was worshiped as God. The non-Christians also mention that He was a good teacher or sage (philosopher) and that His teachings included conversion, denial of other gods, meetings and fellowship and life after death. Lastly, there are multiple confirmations of Jesus' crucifixion under Pontius Pilate in the reign of Tiberius and the claims of His followers that He was still alive.

Additionally Flavius Josephus also confirms the existence of more than half a dozen New Testament people and various events described in the Scriptures. His confirmations include the deaths of John the Baptist and James, the brother of Jesus. From the Roman and Greek writers we learn additional details about the early spread of Christianity and how the first century world reacted to the fast growing faith.

CHAPTER 16

Can We Trust the Witnesses?

"We did not follow cleverly invented stories when we told you
about the power and coming of our Lord Jesus Christ,
but we were eyewitnesses of his majesty."
2 PETER 1:16

As we are preparing to discuss the evidence for the claims of Jesus of Nazareth, in this chapter we will further research the quality of the witness' accounts that the Bible gives us about Jesus. As we will see, these witnesses are the four gospels (including the book of Acts, which we will consider as an integral part of the Gospel of Luke) and Paul's testimony, relayed to us through his letters.

THE WITNESSES – ONCE AGAIN, THE GOSPELS

No other books in the entire Bible have been more studied, memorized, quoted, scrutinized, criticized, questioned, discussed, praised, and rejected as the first four books in the New Testament, the good news about Jesus, called the Gospels of Matthew, Mark, Luke, and John. And for good reasons. Not only do these books contain valuable information about the birth, ministry, and teachings of Jesus, but they also record His miracles and His resurrection. These supernatural events proclaim and point to Jesus as part of the Trinity, fully God and fully man.

In previous chapters, we have already established compelling evidence for the authorship of these books by the names associated with these gospels as well as the date of writing. Due to their importance, below is an evaluative list of some other general observations about each of the gospels.

Gospel of Matthew:
- Matthew – Levi – the tax collector, and one of the twelve disciples is the author of the whole, or at least the first draft, of the gospel. It was likely written in the 55-70 AD time period. [306]
- (Parts of) the original gospel may have been written in Aramaic. All extant manuscripts are in well-versed Greek. The writer was well-educated in Greek, but it was probably not his native tongue.

- It describes the calling of Matthew as a disciple in Matthew 9:9: *"As Jesus went on from there, He saw a man named Matthew sitting at the tax collector's booth. 'Follow me,' He told him, and Matthew got up and followed Him."* It is interesting to note that it is only in Mark and Luke he is called Levi; Matthew's gospel does not use that name.
- The Gospel of Matthew is also known as the *Gospel of the Church* or the *Gospel of the Kingdom* as it has extensive references to God's Kingdom and mentions the building of Christ's church on Peter *"the rock"* (Matthew 16:18).
- Matthew was the most used gospel in the early church. It is likely that it was therefore made the first book of the New Testament. It was also considered a "natural bridge" between the Old and the New Testament because of its emphasis on OT prophecies.
- It is the most structured of all gospels and can be divided into an introduction (1:1-4:11), followed by groups of five narratives and discourses (4:12-7:29; 8:1-11:1; 11:2-16:12; 16:13-20:28 and 20:29-27:66), and a conclusion (28:1-28:20).
- It contains the *Sermon on the Mount*, the most extensive sermon of Jesus ever recorded.
- The character of the gospel is convincingly Jewish, written by a Jew for Jews.
- Matthew's Jewish genealogy of Jesus takes us back to the father of the Jewish nation, Abraham, and follows the royal bloodline through the male ancestors of Joseph.
- It presents Jesus as Israel's promised Messiah, the King. To prove his case, Matthew uses more Old Testament quotations and allusions (almost 130) than any other NT book.
- He also emphasized Jesus as a teacher and as an authoritative interpreter of the Law of Moses and the will of God (Matthew 4:23, 5:2, 7:28-29).
- As a tax collector, Matthew would likely have the background of a scribe. This would make him the most logical candidate within the group of disciples to make notes during Jesus' teachings, which he could have included in this gospel later. That would explain why Matthew's gospel has the most extensive record of Jesus' sayings and teachings, including the Sermon on the Mount.
- As one of the synoptic gospels, about 50% of Matthew has significant similarities to about 90% of Mark.
- The source known as Q (shared with Luke) represents about 25% of Matthew's material.
- About 25% of Matthew remains that is unique to this gospel and not found in any of the other gospels.

Gospel of Mark:

- The widely accepted author Mark or John Mark wrote this gospel likely sometime between 50-70 AD.[307]
- The gospel is written in fairly basic Greek (less elaborate that Matthew's Greek).
- John Mark's two names suggest a Hebrew (John) and Greek (Mark) background.
- It is the briefest, most action packed, very factual gospel.
- Mark was evidently directed to a Roman audience, and early tradition indicates that it originated in Rome. It omits strictly Jewish concepts (like Jesus' genealogy, fulfilled prophecy, Mosaic Law, etc.), gives interpretation for Aramaic words (like in Mark 3:17, 5:41, 15:22), and uses Latin terms in place of Greek equivalents (as in 4:21, 6:27, 6:42, 15:15-16 and 16:39).
- The detailed description of the *"guest room"* in 14:12-16 (compare Matthew 26:17-19; John 13:1-12) suggests that Mark was writing about his own house.
- Given the somewhat odd details mentioned in Mark 14:51-52, John Mark was probably the young man mentioned in these verses.
- The house of his mother was apparently a major meeting place for the early church (Acts 12:12-17).
- The presence of a maid (Acts 12:13) suggest a substantial, perhaps even wealthy family.
- John Mark was the cousin of Barnabas (Colossians 4:10).
- He was travel companion to Paul for his first mission trip, then got into a dispute with Paul (Acts 15:37-39), but this was later resolved (Philemon 23 and 2 Timothy 4:11).
- Peter calls John Mark *"my son"* (1 Peter 5:13).
- The "they" form used often in the gospel (like Mark 1:29-31, 8:22, 9:30, 11:15) and the description of Jesus' emotions, supports the theory of Mark describing Peter's account. As a comparison, the other gospels use "he" and "we" forms in these situations.
- About 90% of Mark's material is also found in Matthew and Luke (synoptic gospels).
- Jesus' resurrection appearances mentioned in Mark 16:9-20 are not in the oldest extant codices (340 AD – Codex Sinaiticus) and therefore not generally believed to have been part of the original gospel. Some suggest that Mark just ended with the women's discovery of the empty grave (Mark 16:1-8); others believe the original ending was lost at a very early date.

Gospel of Luke (and Acts):

- Luke is the accepted author for both Luke and Acts written in the 55-90 AD time period.[308]
- The gospel is written in elegant, sophisticated Greek, supporting the claim of an educated native Greek writer.
- The gospel is addressed to a Greek audience, proclaiming Jesus as savior to the whole world (2:3, 24:27) and tracing his genealogy all the way back to Adam, the first human.
- Luke was a travel companion of Paul to Rome and is, as such, mentioned in the books of Acts, Colossians (4:10), and Philemon (24).
- He was a Gentile. In Colossians 4:10-14, Paul lists three companions, who are "*the only Jews among my fellow workers*" and he includes Luke's name with two other Gentiles.
- Luke probably met John Mark (and possibly also Peter) in Rome in the mid 60s AD.
- The "we" clauses used in the later chapters of Acts support Luke's authorship and his presence during those travels:
  - Journey from Troas to Philippi (Acts 16:10-16)
  - Journey from Philippi to Jerusalem (Acts 20:5-21:17)
  - Journey from Caesarea to Rome (Acts 27:1-28:14)
- Early tradition asserts that Luke was a native from Antioch in Syria.
- Luke was a physician (Colossians 4:14) by profession, focused on accurate details. His descriptions of geographical locations, cities, travel routes and customs are accurate and again and again confirmed by what we know via other sources in every detail. This builds a very strong case for the preciseness and completeness of the remainder of this gospel.
- Luke himself was not an eyewitness to Jesus, but scholars believe that Luke "interviewed" many of Jesus' disciples and followers as sources. This probably took place when he was in Jerusalem with Paul from 58-60 AD. Sources likely have included Jesus' brother James and Philip the deacon.
- Compared to the other gospels, Luke pays particular attention to Jesus' ministry to the poor and outcasts, and women play a more significant role.
- About 30% of Luke's gospel is based on about 50% of Mark.
- About 20% of Luke's gospel is shared with Matthew via Q.
- Luke's unique material (about 50% of the gospel) is very detailed and shows extensive research of its sources.
- The nativity chapters (Luke 1 and 2, about 10% of the total gospel) due to their style and vocabulary are considered to have originated from a unique source (Mary, the mother of Jesus?).

The Gospel of John:

- The author is most likely the apostle John, brother of James and son of Zebedee. The gospel is probably written in the 80-90 AD period.[309]
- He was an eyewitness to Jesus' life, referring to himself as "*the disciple whom Jesus loved.*" It is traditionally assumed that he wrote the gospel in Ephesus at an older age.
- Together with his brother James and Peter, he was part of Jesus' inner circle, making him a privileged witness to some unique events (including the transfiguration) and special teachings of Jesus.
- John (and his brother James) is not mentioned by name in the gospel.
- John the Baptist is referred to merely as "John" in the document, indicating that there was no confusion with any other John (John the apostle, i.e., the author).
- The book is intended primarily to teach (already converted) Christians to better understand Jesus' teaching and mature in their faith. Right from the start Jesus is declared to be God (John 1:1-4). The divine character of Jesus remains a main theme throughout.
- The book only lists seven (eight) miracles, called signs, selected by the author to demonstrate the divine nature of Jesus, The author also mentions that Jesus did many more signs, which are not mentioned (John 20:30-31).
- The author seems to assume that the readers are familiar with the other gospel accounts – therefore he is not repeating that information again – pointing to a later dating of this gospel than the synoptic gospels.
- However, this book also contains lively, and correct in every detail, eyewitness descriptions of Jerusalem in the present tense (as especially John 5:2). Also mentioned is the fact that it has "*taken forty-six years to build this temple*" (John 2:20) suggesting that this document (or at least part of it) was written before 65-70 AD (destruction of Jerusalem and all these locations).
- The oldest papyrus fragment of some verses of John 18 is the Ryland papyrus, dated back to around 125-130 AD.
- John 7:53-8:1-11 (the account of the adulterous woman) is not believed to have been in the original gospel as it is not in the earlier codices (Codex Sinaiticus).

Comparing the Four Gospels

| | **The Synoptic Gospels** | | | |
	Matthew	**Mark**	**Luke**	**John**
Author	Disciple	"Peter"	"Paul"	Disciple
Likely date	55-70 AD	50-65 AD	55-70 AD	80-90 AD
Place of writing	Syria, Palestine	Rome	Rome/Greece	Ephesus
For who	Jews	Romans	Greeks	Christians
Theme	Messiah	Redeemer	Perfect man	(Son of) God
Emphasis	Prophecies	Actions	Humanity	Divine
Genealogy	Abraham – Joseph	-	Adam – Mary	The Word = God
Perspective	Historical			Theological
Material	Shared and Unique (Matthew 25%, Mark 10%, Luke (50%)			Mostly unique (> 90%)
Chronology	Only one Passover mentioned			Three Passovers
Geography	Judea and Galilee (Galilee more emphasis)			Mostly Judea
Relationship to other gospels	Complementary			Supplementary

Table 16-1: Comparing the Four Gospels

ANOTHER IMPORTANT WITNESS – PAUL

The evidence for the life, teachings, and resurrection of Jesus is not limited to "only" the four gospels; the other New Testament books are also written by witnesses of Jesus. The large number of Pauline epistles, along with their independent testimony to Christ, makes Paul an important corroborating witness. Most of what we know about Paul comes through Scripture:

The Apostle Paul:
- Born as a Jew in a family of Pharisees (Acts 23:6) of the tribe of Benjamin (Philippians 3:5) in Tarsus of Cilicia (Acts 9:11). He was also a Roman citizen (Acts 16:37, 22:25).
- His name was Saul (after the first king of Israel), but he was also called Paul (Acts 13:9).
- He was well-educated, spoke different languages (Aramaic, Hebrew, and Greek) and was well-trained in the Jewish Law (Galatians 1:14, Philippians 3:5-6). He was even trained by the well-respected Pharisee, Gamaliel (Acts 22:3).
- Paul was a tentmaker by profession (Acts 18:13), which allowed him to support himself financially (Acts 20:34).
- When the Christian movement began to spread in Jerusalem, Paul was a leading figure in the growing persecution by the Jews. He was present at

the stoning of Stephen (Acts 7:58), where he *"persecuted the church of God and tried to destroy it"* (Galatians 1:13). He obtained letters of recommendation from the high priest in Jerusalem and traveled to Damascus for further persecutions (Acts 9:1-2).

- On the road to Damascus (around 34/35 AD, one or two years after the resurrection),[310] he met the resurrected Jesus and was converted to Christianity (Acts 9:3-19).
- During the next period of about 13 years (Galatians 1:18-2:1), he met with Peter and James in Jerusalem and spent time in Syria and Cilicia.
- Together with Barnabas and John Mark (who left them halfway), Paul traveled through the Asia Minor mainland to start churches in Gentile territory. This *First Missionary Journey* must have taken place in the 46-48 AD timeframe (Acts chapters 13-14).
- This resulted in the now famous *Jerusalem council of* 49 AD in which the church reached agreement about how to integrate Gentiles into an originally Jewish religion (Acts 15).
- The *Second Missionary Journey* in 49-52 AD (Acts 16-18:22) brought Paul, traveling together with Silas and Timothy, even further west into Greece. During the subsequent *Third Missionary Journey* in 53-57 AD (Acts 18:23- 20), Paul and his travel companions revisited the churches planted during his previous trips.
- After his return, Paul was arrested in Jerusalem (Acts 21-23), remained a Roman prisoner in Caesarea (Acts 24-26), and ultimately arrived in Rome (Acts 27-28) where he remained under house arrest.
- Tradition (also confirmed by Clement of Rome)[311] tells us that Paul was ultimately martyred during Nero's persecutions in Rome around 66/67 AD.

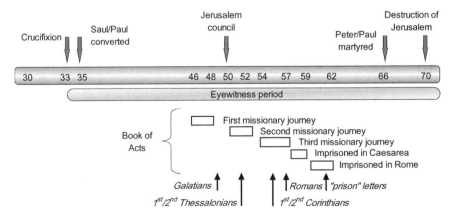

Figure 16-1: Paul's Ministry and Writings

Paul himself was not one of Jesus' personal disciples, however his personal encounter with Jesus and his numerous meetings with the other disciples make his epistles and the detailed travel accounts in the book of Acts valuable testimony. He was not only recognized as one of the key figures in the apostolic church, he was also recognized as a true apostle by the other apostles. Through Paul's writings,[312] we have confirmation from a source independent of the gospels of a number of key facts and events about Jesus (see table 16-2). In many ways Paul is our "fifth witness."

Paul's Testimony about Jesus Christ	
Facts and events from the life of Jesus[313]	Reference
He descended from Abraham	Galatians 3:16
He was a Son of David	Roman 1:3
He was born of a woman, born under Jewish law, the Son of God	Galatians 4:4
He welcomed people	Romans 15:5,7
His lifestyle was one of humility and service	Philippians 2:7-8
He was abused and insulted during His life	Romans 15:3
He had a brother named James	Galatians 1:19
He has also other unnamed brothers	1 Corinthians 9:5
His disciple Peter was married	1 Corinthians 9:5
He instituted a memorial meal of bread and wine, on the night of His betrayal	1 Corinthians 11:23-25
He was betrayed	1 Corinthians 11:23
He gave testimony before Pontius Pilate	1 Timothy 6:13
He was crucified under Roman law	1 Corinthians 1:23, Galatians 3:13, 6:14
He was killed by Jews of Judea	1 Thessalonians 2:14-15
He was buried, rose on the third day, and was seen on a number of occasions by numerous witnesses of whom the majority were still alive at the time this letter was written (20 years later)	1 Corinthians 15:4-8

Table 16-2: Paul, the Fifth Witness, his Testimony about Jesus

☼ EXHIBIT #19: THE WITNESSES ARE HONEST AND TRUSTWORTHY

Writing a historically reliable account does not make the accounts of the witnesses to Jesus also honest and trustworthy. Before we can use the accounts as reliable evidence, we need to evaluate whether these testimonies about Jesus are truly honest and not biased representations or exaggerations or just made up with good intentions.

In his book, *Letters from a Skeptic*,[314] Dr. Gregory Boyd suggests a set of criteria that historians apply to ancient documents in order to examine their credibility. They can be divided into two groups: internal and external criteria. The "internal" criteria apply to the content of the documents themselves; the "external" criteria deal with the corroborating evidence from the outside world in order to confirm the accuracy of the texts. In many ways these criteria also make plain common sense.

At the end of this discussion you will hopefully agree that the gospels, Acts, and Paul's letters pass all these tests and criteria with remarkable ease and high scores, building a well grounded base for the conclusion that these witnesses indeed are honest and trustworthy.

INTERNAL #1: DID THE AUTHOR KNOW WHAT HE WAS TALKING ABOUT?

In order for an account to be trustworthy we must have some solid confirmation that the author of the document is able to provide qualified testimony. The author needs to be either an eyewitness or someone who had access to sources who were eyewitnesses.

As we have seen, the gospels are technically anonymous, but as discussed earlier, there are compelling evidences verifying the names associated with the gospels. As the Gospels of Matthew and John are written by disciples of Jesus who were eyewitnesses themselves, these authors are surely qualified to give testimony. John Mark was not a disciple, but it is likely that he was present at a number of events during Jesus' ministry when he was a young man. He spent considerable time with the other disciples after Jesus' resurrection, traveled with Paul and Barnabas, and later spent serious time in Rome with Peter while writing his gospel. Many even claim that Mark's gospel was written in behalf of Peter. Therefore the Gospel of Mark is written by a qualified witness beyond any serious dispute.

The Gospel of Luke and the book of Acts were written by Luke, the Gentile travel companion of Paul. Luke was not an eyewitness to any events of Jesus' ministry nor the resurrection. It is possible that he was a convert of Paul in Antioch. However, his gospel reveals many evidences of detailed resources and use of qualified sources. He even makes that statement himself at the beginning of his account: *"Many have undertaken to draw up an account of the things that have been fulfilled among us, just as they were handed down to us by those who from the first were eyewitnesses and servants of the word. Therefore, since I myself have carefully investigated everything from the beginning, it seemed good also to me to write an orderly account for you, most excellent Theophilus, so that you may know the certainty of the things you have been taught"* (Luke 1:1-2). His claim of *"careful investigation"* is backed up by many details of people, their titles and positions, and events and locations that have been verified through historical, non-Biblical references and archaeology. Luke is certainly a qualified author.

How about Paul's epistles? As we have discussed earlier[315] – from an evidence perspective – in all his letters, Paul claims to be the author in the first verses of his writings. Also, all these letters are from the 49-55 AD period and are not under dispute.

INTERNAL #2: IS THERE SPECIFIC AND ESPECIALLY IRRELEVANT MATERIAL?

Have you ever noticed that if you ask someone to tell you "what happened?", you often also get a lot of information that is irrelevant to the actual story? The recollection of specific, and many times irrelevant, details is powerful evidence of an actual eyewitness account. If people fabricate stories they will only invent the major story line and stick to that. However, if someone talks or writes about actual events that happened, expanding on details and providing additional, often unnecessary and irrelevant, information comes naturally. How do the gospels and Paul's writings match up with this criterion?

The Gospel of Mark has a powerful illustration of this point. Mark 14:32-52 describes how Jesus and the disciples went to Gethsemane after the Last Supper. In verses 32-42 we read about how Jesus takes Peter, James, and John along with Him and asks them to keep watch. Three times Jesus prays by Himself and returns to find the disciples asleep. The third time, Judas and a crowd sent from the chief priests arrive to arrest Jesus (Mark 14:43-50). This account is also found in the other synoptic gospels (Matthew 26:36-56 and Luke 22:39-53). However, at the end of this section Mark adds: "*A young man, wearing nothing but a linen garment, was following Jesus. When they seized him, he fled naked, leaving his garment behind*" (Mark 14:51-52). This "*young man*" (John Mark himself?) was not part of the previous account on how Jesus was praying and arrested, nor is the young man mentioned at any time later in the gospel. These two verses are completely irrelevant. In addition, the detail about "*wearing nothing but a linen garment*" (who cares?) and that "*he fled naked, leaving his garment behind*" (who would even want to know that?) shows specific irrelevant detail consistent with honest eyewitness recollection.

In the Gospel of Matthew we find examples of specific and irrelevant detail in the various narrative sections. As an illustration, let's look at the description Matthew gives of John the Baptist: "*John's clothes were made of camel's hair, and he had a leather belt around his waist. His food was locusts and wild honey*" (Matthew 3:4). Very specific information and also mostly irrelevant for Matthew's account. The point Matthew is trying to make is that John the Baptist was fulfilling OT prophecy (Isaiah 40:3), was preaching to the people to repent from their sins and be baptized as a sign of repentance. How John the Baptist was clothed and what he ate is interesting to know, but irrelevant detail to Matthew's account.

Being a physician, Luke has an eye and attention for historical details. His gospel is loaded with specific (and sometimes irrelevant) material. Right in the very first chapter we find his introduction of Zechariah and his wife Elizabeth, the parents of John the Baptist: *"In the time of Herod king of Judea there was a priest named Zechariah, who belonged to the priestly division of Abijah* [not relevant information] *; his wife Elizabeth was also a descendant of Aaron* [is this important to know?]. *Both of them were upright in the sight of God, observing all the Lord's commandments and regulations blamelessly* [very specific, nice to know, but really irrelevant]. *But they had no children, because Elizabeth was barren; and they were both well along in years.* [more very specific details] *"* (Luke 1:5-7). Or look at this section in Acts describing how Paul's party, on their way to Rome is shipwrecked on the island of Malta: *"When daylight came, they did not recognize the land, but they saw a bay with a sandy beach* [is all this really important information?] *, where they decided to run the ship aground if they could. Cutting loose the anchors, they left them in the sea* [who cares?] *and at the same time untied the ropes that held the rudders* [do we need to know?]. *Then they hoisted the foresail to the wind and made for the beach. But the ship struck a sandbar* [more and more details] *and ran aground. The bow stuck fast* [relevant?] *and would not move, and the stern was broken to pieces by the pounding of the surf* [details and more details] *"* (Acts 27:39-41). These three verses sound more like the lines of a movie script than the account of Paul's travels and all this information can be summarized in a short sentence: the ship sank.

How about the Gospel of John? Let's read John's account of the morning on resurrection Sunday.[316] John 20:1-8: *"Early on the first day of the week, while it was still dark* [lots of details], *Mary Magdalene* [incriminating detail, because she is a woman. This would be a very bad choice in the Jewish culture, more about this later] *went to the tomb and saw that the stone had been removed from the entrance. So she came running to Simon Peter and the other disciple, the one Jesus loved* [John being too modest to mention his own name throughout this gospel], *and said, "They have taken the Lord out of the tomb, and we don't know where they have put him!"* [Mary seems to have thought somebody moved Jesus' body instead of understanding that the resurrection took place] *So Peter and the other disciple started for the tomb. Both were running, but the other disciple outran Peter and reached the tomb first* [now we know that John is a faster runner than Peter]. *He bent over* [a historically correct detail as tomb entrances were low] *and looked in at the strips of linen lying there but did not go in* [why not?]. *Then Simon Peter, who was behind him, arrived and went into the tomb* [fits the personality of Peter of being bold (blunt sometimes) as described in all gospels] *. He saw the strips of linen lying there, as well as the burial cloth that had been around Jesus' head* [again, lots of details]. *The cloth was folded up by itself,* *separate from the linen* [more and more specific information that is not relevant to the story line]. *Finally the other disciple, who had reached the tomb first, also went inside* [is it important to know the exact order they entered the tomb?]."

Analyzing the narrative sections in the gospels and Acts uncovers abundant evidence of very specific information and many details irrelevant to the main story. Even in the few sections of Paul's writings that are more descriptive than instructive we find similar patterns. This material does not add to the main message of the accounts, except it is just part of what happened; therefore, the authors wrote it down as they recalled the events.

INTERNAL #3: IS THERE SELF-DAMAGING INFORMATION?

If an account is written to "make the writer look good" or to "please the intended readers," it is to be expected that events are portrayed through tinted glasses. This behavior is seen almost continuously in modern day political speeches or debates, but also in many ancient non-Biblical historical authors such as Josephus who wrote for his Roman masters (and himself). In the words of Dr. Paul Barnett:[317] "*His* [Josephus'] *Jewish War is thinly veiled propaganda. His* Antiquities of the Jews *and* Against Apion *are romantic apologetics for Judaism. His* Life *is sickeningly self-serving.*" How do the New Testament accounts compare? Are its writers self-serving, or do they cast a realistic, at times even negative image on themselves? If the "heroes" of Christianity are portrayed as normal people with common flaws and given to occasional stumbling, this would be a good indicator of honesty and a solid basis for trustworthiness, because it would show the Bible is recording real events as they happened to real people.

No more than a casual reading of the gospels is sufficient for many readers to notice abundant evidence of self-deprecating descriptions of Jesus' followers. They seem not to miss any chance to give a wrong answer when quizzed by Jesus. Asked to make a choice, theirs is often wrong. Also there are numerous examples of "politically incorrect" events and even quite confusing statements and actions from Jesus. For a sampling of illustrations, see table 16-3.

The last two illustrations in this table require more explanation.

The Jewish world in the first century was "a man's world." Although numerous positive statements about women are found in the Old Testament, first century Jewish men generally considered their wives to be inferior to them because men were by nature women's superiors. Many Jews believed women had to cover their mouth, legs, and hair at all times. They believed a woman's mouth could speak folly and embarrass her husband. With her legs she could seduce men, and any wife who appeared in public with loose hair was believed to be challenging her husband's authority. Jewish law would not even accept a woman's testimony in court, as women were considered unreliable witnesses. Perhaps that is why, for instance, in Paul's testimony about the resurrection (1 Corinthians 15:3-8) he names only men to whom Jesus appeared and seems deliberately to ignore the women. The Mishna, a collection of Jewish oral traditions and laws compiled around the third century of the Christian era, forbids women to study the law with men. One rabbi even said that a woman was like a piece of meat with which a man could do as he pleased. Also in the Graeco-Roman world, where women were generally more emancipated than in the Jewish world, the husband was still the undisputed head. Roman philosopher Seneca wrote that the man was made to rule and the woman to be silent and to obey.[318]

Self-Deprecating Information in the New Testament	
Event or Statement	Reference
The disciples argue about who would be the greatest in heaven	Matthew 18:1-6
James and John ask a privileged position for themselves	Mark 10:35-42
The disciples forbid others to use the name of Jesus	Luke 9:49-50
Many disciples desert Jesus	John 7:60-71
At the mount of transfiguration Peter makes the profound suggestion to "pitch a tent" for Moses and Elijah	Matthew 17:1-13, Luke 9:28-36
Peter does not have enough faith to walk on the water with Jesus	John 6:16-21
When asked to watch with Jesus, the disciples fall asleep again and again	Luke 22:39-46
When Jesus is arrested all disciples flee and hide	Mark 14:43-50
After a bold statement, Peter still denies Jesus three times	John 18:25-27
Paul is introduced as a Christian killer	Acts 8:1
Paul and Peter have a public argument	Galatians 2:11-13
Paul considers John Mark unreliable after he deserts him on Cyprus	Acts 15:36-41
Paul goes to Jerusalem in spite of the Holy Spirit urging him not to	Acts 21:4,10-14
Jesus' family opposed His ministry during much of His life	Mark 3:31-34, John 7:5
Jesus is rejected and cannot do miracles in His home town	Luke 4:16-30
Jesus' statement on the cross "My God, my God, why have you forsaken me" is not what one would expect the Messiah to say	Matthew 27:46
Women (who were considered socially inferior in Jesus' day) played a role in His ministry, and it was Mary Magdalene who found the empty grave	All gospels
Jesus was born of a virgin	Matthew & Luke

Table 16-3: Self-Damaging Information in the New Testament

With this background the role of women in Jesus' ministry clearly indicates the gospel writers (such as Matthew, a Jew writing to a Jewish audience) may have felt uncomfortable and reluctant to describe female participation. Still, all the gospels include the supporting roles of Martha and Mary in Bethany, and all agree that Mary Magdalene was the first to discover the empty grave on resurrection Sunday.

The claim that Jesus was born of a virgin is even more "unexpected." In those days a girl's greatest asset was considered to be her sexual purity. Only a young woman who retained her virginity could expect to secure a good man for a husband. Mothers kept their daughters out of the public eye as much as possible to not expose them to temptation.[319] A pregnant unmarried woman was considered a grave insult to the honor of her family. As still seen today in many Arab countries (whose citizens still live under the Islamic laws and culture as it was in the ancient middle east) such pregnancies would often lead to honor killings. The father and/or her brothers, lamenting her inability to marry, could kill her to avoid the disgrace.

Against this background Jesus' virgin birth was not heralded as a miracle. Actually apart from the brief accounts in Luke and Matthew, the Bible says nothing about it. Both gospel writers testify about Jesus' birth independently of one another. Each drew upon unique material,[320] yielding two independent testimonies to this event. For Matthew, writing about Jesus' birth must have presented a real dilemma. As a devout Jew, Matthew's decision to record that Joseph, representing the royal bloodline of Jesus, was not Jesus' natural father, could open up a potential flood of compromising criticisms that Jesus was born out of wedlock. This account in Matthew's gospel shows his unconditional commitment to writing the truth without altering any of it.

INTERNAL #4: ARE THE DOCUMENTS CONSISTENT?

Five different sources (the gospels and Paul) give testimony about Jesus. Are these consistent, or do they contradict? It seems both. There are numerous events mentioned in more than one or even all accounts, but there also seem to be significant differences or even contradictions. For many skeptics, it is a favorite criticism that the gospels frequently contradict each other. Some have written books[321] about it, and others keep lists of contradictions.[322]

Before pursuing this discussion, step aside for a moment to consider what one would expect to find. We are looking at testimonies from (eye) witnesses to events that happened 20 years earlier (Paul and Mark) to even 50 years (John) earlier. Many studies have been done about how people remember events from the past.[323] The general (and quite logical) conclusion is that people are well able to remember unique events over time that are significant to their personal lives. Memories are even better retained if the person is also emotionally involved in the events. Accurate memories are usually character-ized by strong visual imagery and irrelevant details from a personal point of view. The "gist" (the sequence or structure that makes the event meaningful to the person) of the memory is likely to remain accurate, even when the details are not. Frequent rehearsal is an important factor in both retaining the mem-ory and retaining it accurately. In other words, people tend to accurately remember the main storyline of the event, especially if it is life changing, and frequently rehearsed or recalled. Only limited (irrelevant) details are remem-bered, sometimes not entirely accurate and often just from the point of view of the observer.

Quite obviously, the accounts as recorded in the gospels were in many forms already circulating orally amongst the Christian community before they were written down. As explained, that is a big "plus" for accurately remember-ing the events. Also if we look at the various writings, they are remarkably con-sistent in the gist of their recordings:

All Writings Agree on the Main Events					
	Matthew	Mark	Luke	John	Paul
Event recorded about Jesus					
Jesus' virgin birth	X		X		
Jesus is a Son of David	X	X	X	X	X
The ministry of John the Baptist	X	X	X	X	
The baptism of Jesus by John the Baptist	X	X	X	X	
The calling of the twelve disciples/Jesus had disciples	X	X	X	X	X
Jesus walking on water	X	X	X	X	
The feeding of the 5,000	X	X	X	X	
Jesus performing many more miracles/signs	X	X	X	X	
Jesus' teachings about the nature of God, humanity, salvation etc.	X	X	X	X	X
Jesus' interpretation of the Sabbath law	X	X	X	X	
The reaction of the religious and political leaders	X	X	X	X	
Jesus' entry into Jerusalem on Palm Sunday	X	X	X	X	
The Last Supper, a memorial meal with bread and wine	X	X	X	X	X
The betrayal (by Judas)	X	X	X	X	X
The denial by Peter	X	X	X	X	X
Jesus was put on trial (before Pontius Pilate)	X	X	X	X	X
Jesus was crucified under Roman law	X	X	X	X	X
The burial (by Joseph of Arimathea)	X	X	X	X	X
The empty grave	X	X	X	X	X
The resurrection appearances	X	X	X	X	X

Table 16-4: All Writers Agree on the Main Events

There are no serious disagreements in the New Testament books concerning major events in Jesus' life, His crucifixion, or His resurrection. The differences, or as some prefer to call them, the contradictions, always deal with the details. Many of these alleged contradictions are explained by paraphrasing, abridgment, explanatory additions, selection, omissions, or just using different names for the same location or participants. As explained earlier, over time, people remember details differently, due either to the fact that they remember them from their unique perspective or just do not remember them accurately.

Without going into too much detailed analysis of alleged contradictions,[324] I would like to address the two most often mentioned "major" discrepancies in the gospel accounts.

The first one deals with the different genealogies for Jesus in Matthew 1:1-16 and Luke 3:23-37. It is perfectly clear that the two genealogies differ widely from one another, and yet each is given as the line of ancestry for Christ. How can they both be true?

There is a simple answer to this alleged contradiction. Matthew, as we know, wrote as a Jew for Jews. Therefore his genealogy starts with Abraham, the father of all Jews. With the Jewish culture, only the man represents the official line of descent. The father passes his rights on to the son he selects, usually his oldest son, but sometimes another son. David for instance had multiple wives and sons. David chose Solomon (a son of Bathsheba) over his oldest living son Adonijah as his successor (1 Kings 1). That makes the line through Solomon the Jewish legal or royal line. Joseph's father Jacob was a descendant from Solomon. And as Matthew makes the link: *"Jacob the father of Joseph, the husband of Mary, of whom was born Jesus, who is called the Christ"* (Matthew 1:16). So Joseph, who Matthew states is the husband of Mary, not the father of Jesus, is the legal and royal father of Christ, and therefore through Joseph's lineage, Matthew establishes Jesus to be a son of David and Abraham.

Luke however approaches Jesus' genealogy from a Gentile, "mankind" perspective. Therefore, he starts with Adam (the first human) through Abraham (the first Jew) to David. From David he descends through Nathan (2 Samuel 5:14) to Heli the father of Mary and subsequently to Mary the mother of Jesus. That is the natural line of descent. Also Mary herself was through her father Heli a descendant of David.

How it all fits together!

Readers of the Old Testament might wonder how Jesus could have been the Son of David because of God's curse on king Jehoiachin. We read in Jeremiah that no descendant of Jeconiah (or Jehoiachin) could ever ascend to the throne of David: *"This is what the Lord says: 'Record this man as if childless, a man who will not prosper in his lifetime, for none of his offspring will prosper, none will sit on the throne of David or rule anymore in Judah'"* (Jeremiah 22:30).

Joseph was of the line of Jehoiachin, and his genealogy furnishes the royal line of Jesus, who was his son under the law. Nevertheless Jeremiah's prediction is fulfilled to the very letter. Jesus was not of the seed of Joseph and therefore was not of the seed of Jehoiachin.

Jesus is from the royal line of David through the line of Jehoiachin and Joseph, but He is a natural son of David through Nathan and His mother Mary.

The other favorite "discrepancy" is the apparent contradictions between the gospels as to the discovery of the empty tomb and those to whom Jesus appeared after the resurrection. When reading the gospels, all seem to disagree. For instance in Matthew the empty grave is discovered by Mary Magdalene and the other Mary (Matthew 28:1). Mark tells us it was Mary Magdalene, Mary the mother of James and Salome (Mark 16:1). Luke mentions only *"the women"* (Luke 24:1). Later they are named Mary Magdalene, Mary the mother of James, Joanna, and *"the others with them"* (Luke 24:10). Lastly John only mentions Mary Magdalene (John 20:1). Who was or were there? On the surface, apart from Mary Magdalene, they all seem to disagree.

Similar confusion seems to exist about those to whom Jesus appeared. Was it Peter or John or all disciples with and without Thomas? Was it in Jerusalem or in Galilee?

Many have written books about how these accounts can be harmonized.[325] Without going into extensive details, the different women at the empty tomb might well be explained by how our memory remembers different specific details as explained earlier. Each gospel writer gives his own testimony about how he remembered this miraculous morning, and as often seen in (eye) witness testimony, they agree on the gist but have a somewhat different recollection on the peripheral details. Additionally, these details are not necessarily in conflict. The other Mary of Matthew is likely Mary the mother of James and Joses (Matthew 27:55). So those are the same

Mary's mentioned by Mark and Luke. The differences can also all be explained by omissions. Some writers just decided not to mention them all or only to mention Mary Magdalene. These omissions of the names of some of the other women also fit well the Jewish views of those days about the unimportance of women.

As for the resurrection appearances, no one's story contradicts earlier other accounts. They seem to differ only in order. For instance, it is plausible that Jesus appeared to the eleven in Jerusalem, then later in Galilee when they had gone home after the Passover, and then once again in Jerusalem upon their return in preparation for the feast of Pentecost.[326]

SOME REMARKS ABOUT JOHN VERSUS THE SYNOPTIC GOSPELS

Many books explore the differences and similarities between the Gospel of John and the synoptic gospels. This has launched a wide range of opinions about the credibility of John. In general, the more critical scholastic community raises serious doubt or even rejects altogether the historical credibility of John. However, detailed analysis based on more recent information (especially also from historical information about the first century Jewish society derived from the Dead Sea scrolls) builds a strong case for the historical reliability of this gospel.[327]

Before discussing differences, I'd like to emphasize the consistency of the gist of John and how well it lines up with the synoptic gospels and the Pauline epistles.

John's description of the passion narrative in the last chapter of his book is not only consistent with the synoptic gospels, but it also provides many details missing from the other gospels. John completes these accounts (and has proved himself historically correct). For example, John says that the Jews no longer could exercise capital punishment. Therefore the Roman authority/Pilate had to be involved. This fact, verified as historically accurate, explains the trial before Pilate as also described in the synoptic gospels.[328]

What would happen if all accounts were in perfect harmony?

We've spent considerable time explaining and analyzing the discrepancies between the various gospels. However, can you imagine how skeptics and critical scholars would react if all accounts were in perfect harmony? What if all details about Jesus' life, the disciplines, the locations, the miracles, the resurrection and so on, were to line up perfectly?

At best, that would have caused critics to (rightly) claim that all gospel accounts are "synoptic," i.e., using the same sources and therefore represent only a single independent testimony. Likely, however, critics would also claim that it is all fabricated testimony, that everyone agreed upfront in detail what to write down. If all books in the NT would be in complete agreement on every detail, the whole NT would have to be rejected as an elaborate hoax.

The fact that there are discrepancies in the details but fabulous agreements in the general storyline is the best evidence one can find for honest, reliable, and independent witness accounts!

Major criticism between John and the synoptic gospels is in four different categories:
- John's selection of material (not much overlap/confirmation of the synoptic accounts).
- John's different theological style (Jesus is directly identified as fully divine).
- An apparent contradiction of chronology. Most important here are the cleansing of the temple (happens in John at the beginning of Jesus' ministry but in the other gospels it is described to have happened during the last week of Jesus' life) and the number of visits by Jesus to Jerusalem (John mentions numerous times, the other gospels only once).
- The different style of Jesus in John versus the other gospels.

Analyzing these similarities and differences, different scholars reach different conclusions. For many of the differences, possible explanations can be given,[329] especially remembering that John wrote his gospel after the synoptic gospels were already completed and in circulation. He had no intent to write another similar account; his objective was to teach Christians about Jesus' divinity as the Son of God.

INTERNAL #5: IS THERE EVIDENCE OF EXAGGERATION?

How realistic are the descriptions of events in the NT? Are they clearly exaggerated to make them more compelling and impressive, or do the accounts describe real-life situations?

The presence of "larger than life" features in a document indicates the formation of myths and legends and point to a later time of writing. Great illustrations of this type of exaggerations are found all throughout the "apocryphal mill gospels" of the second or third century.

For instance, in the well-known, second century *Infancy Gospel of Thomas*[330] we read: *"When this child Jesus was five years old...He made soft clay and modeled twelve sparrows from it...Jesus clapped his hands and cried to the sparrows, "Be gone." And the sparrows flew off chirping."* [331] And as another illustration: *"After some days Jesus was playing upstairs in a certain house, and one of the children playing with him fell from the house and died...Then Jesus leaped down from the roof and stood by the body of the child and cried out lout in a great voice, saying 'Zenon!' – that was his name – 'rise up and tell me, did I thrown you down?' He immediately rose up and said: 'No, Lord, you did not throw me down, but you raised me.' The parents of the child glorified God because of this sign that happened, and they worshiped Jesus."*[332]

Another unrealistic "larger than life" story is found in the end of the second century *Acts of Paul*. We read that Paul is beheaded by order of Nero, and milk flows from his neck: *"But when the executioners struck of his head, milk spurted upon the soldiers clothing."*[333] Next, Paul is resurrected from the dead and visits Nero: *"...he* [Paul] *stood before him* [Nero] *and said: 'Caesar, here I am – Paul, God's soldier. I am not dead, but alive in my God. But for you, unhappy man, there shall be many evils and great punishment, because you unjustly shed the blood of the righteous.'"* [334]

What a difference between these second century "gospels" and authentic New Testament texts. Comparing these colorful, fanciful, and clearly imaginary accounts from later generations of Christians to the careful, sober, and precise witness testimonies from the New Testament shows the lack of creative exaggeration in the canonical documents.

The gospels, Acts, and Paul's epistles describe real life events, not fancy fiction. Yes, miracles are recorded here, and all miracles are beyond the laws of nature, such as walking on water, calming a storm, and feeding thousands of people with a single lunch. Yet still His miracles are "in character," they do not portray a flying Jesus, talking crosses, or other outrageous events, but just Jesus responding compassionately to the needs of the people.

External #1: Is There a Motive for Fabrication or Falsification?

Would the authors have a motive to fabricate their account? Did they have any personal gain from writing? Obviously, if a motive can be established for inventing the testimonies, the trustworthiness of the document becomes more questionable. Conversely, if the authors had nothing to gain, or even something to lose, the document's credibility is increased.

So what happened to John Mark, Matthew, Luke, John, and Paul after writing their gospels and letters? Although there is only limited historical record about what happened to these men after completing their writings, one can with certainty state that none of them retired wealthy from the proceedings of any of their books. Contrary to that, the historical record shows that the early Christian church and their leaders went through centuries of persecution, and the apostles spent their days traveling in poverty proclaiming their message.

More specifically, after completing his gospel and the death of Peter in Rome (66-67 AD), tradition claims that John Mark went to Alexandria in Egypt where he was martyred in 68 AD. According to the research of Dr. William Steuart McBirnie:[335] *"In the year 68 AD Easter fell on the same day as the Serapis festival. The furious mob had gathered in the Serapion and then descended on the Christians while they were celebrating Easter at Baucalis. St, Mark was seized, dragged with a rope around his neck in the streets and then incarcerated for the night. In the following morning the same ordeal was repeated until he gave up the ghost."* Other sources confirm this account as well as his burial site.[336]

What happened to Matthew, the tax collector, is subject to multiple conflicting traditions.[337] His name is linked to various travels throughout Greece and Asia, but most agree on Asian Ethiopia, Persia, Macedonia, and Syria. All but one of these traditions claim an untimely death as a martyr for Christ. Unfortunately, none of these traditions are supported by convincing objective evidence.

According to Catholic tradition,[338] Luke was martyred or died a natural death and was buried in Greece. In 356-357 AD his relics were taken to Constantinople. Later his head was supposedly taken to Rome where it is kept in St. Peter's Basilica.

Before writing his gospel at an advanced age, John moved to Ephesus in Asia Minor shortly before the destruction of Jerusalem. At this strategic location he had a special relationship with other churches in the area, as we know through his letters to the seven churches in the book of Revelation as well as through references in writings of the early church. After a period of exile to the island of Patmos, he is believed to have died of old age, around 100 AD, in Ephesus, where he was buried. The ruins at the Basilica of St. John are claimed to mark the site of the tomb.[339]

As for Paul, some claim that after his imprisonment as described at the end of the Book of Acts, he visited Spain for a period of at least two years.[340] Subsequently, he returned to Rome where during Nero's persecution in 66/67 AD (about the same time as Peter) he was beheaded.

So no lucrative book deals for these writers, no lofty retirement on the French Riviera. The testimony of these men did not end with the completions of their gospels and letters. Their subsequent lives continued to proclaim the message. They lived in poverty, under the continuous threat of persecution, and at the end, most of them paid the ultimate price of an early death by martyrdom. What earthly motive could any of them have ever had for fabrication or even making the smallest change to the truth in their testimonies? They were writing for their Lord; they were writing to built treasures in heaven. Lying, exaggerating, spinning the truth, becoming famous, or gaining any wealth, was not on their agenda.

EXTERNAL #2: ARE THERE EXTERNAL SOURCES FOR CONFIRMATION?

Are there any other sources from outside the Bible that corroborate the accounts and/or that substantiate the genuineness of the documents? Confirmations from extra-Biblical sources will enhance the credibility significantly. Contradictions from other sources would, however, be devastating to the trust factor. It takes considerable effort to build respect and credibility with other people; it; however; only takes one mistake to lose it completely.

As we have already studied,[341] there are more than a dozen non-Christian writers confirming various details and events in the gospels and Paul's writings. And perhaps even more important, none of these sources ever contradict any of the accounts. As these writings are from neutral or most often from unfriendly sources to Christianity, the weight of their testimonies is significant.

We have already met Flavius Josephus and his extensive confirmations of the Biblical accounts. Because of its far reaching importance, following is Josephus extensive quotation about Jesus (emphasis added):

> *Now, there was about this time Jesus, a wise man, if it be lawful to call him a man, for he was a doer of wonderful works – a teacher of such men as receive the truth with pleasure. He drew over to him both many of the Jews, and many of the Gentiles. He was [the] Christ; and when Pilate, at the suggestion of the principal men amongst us, had condemned him to the cross, those that loved him at the first did not forsake him,* for he appeared to them alive again the third day, as the divine prophets had foretold these and ten thousand other wonderful things concerning him; *and the tribe of Christians, so named from him, are not extinct at this day.*[342]

The text is obviously an amazing confirmation from a Jewish contemporary of the apostles, who was not a Christian, but still confirms Jesus as the Messiah (the Christ) and the resurrection. However, it is too good to be true. It is just unlikely that a man like Josephus (not a Christian) would write this about Jesus. Therefore the vast majority of scholars agree that the basis of the text is genuine and originally from Josephus, but that likely over the centuries Christian sources have added the statements about Christ and the resurrection. The text accepted as original is underlined in the above quotation, and it confirms that:

- Jesus was a wise man, a teacher and a "doer of wonderful works".
- Jesus attracted both Jews and Gentiles to be His followers.
- He was condemned to the cross by Pilate at suggestion of the Jews.
- His followers are now called Christians and they are "not extinct at this day."

Even in its "reduced" form, this text from this non-Christian Jew is an invaluable confirmation of the reliability and truth of the gospel accounts.

Additionally, the writings of the Early Church Leaders confirm the early existence and circulation of the New Testament books as well as their authorship.

EXTERNAL #3: DO ARCHAEOLOGY AND HISTORY SUPPORT THE ACCOUNTS?

If archaeological findings and/or the historical record can substantiate the testimonies, the document's trustworthiness is obviously increased. If any of these findings would contradict the accounts, their credibility would be dramatically challenged.

We have already discussed these evidences earlier,[343] therefore I would just like to share a few quotations from renowned archaeologists and Bible scholars to summarize the conclusions:

"Luke is a historian of the first rank; not merely are his statements of fact trustworthy…this author should be placed along with the greatest of historians…Luke's history is unsurpassed in respect of its trustworthiness" [344] (Sir William Ramsay, 1959-1939, New Testament scholar and archaeologist).

"Archaeological discoveries of the past generations in Egypt, Syria and Palestine have gone far to establish the uniqueness of early Christianity as a historical phenomenon" [345] (W.F. Albright, 1891-1971, archaeologist and Biblical scholar).

"Archaeology has in many cases refuted the views of modern critics. It has shown in a number of instances that these views rest on false assumptions and unreal, artificial schemes of historical development. This is a real contribution, and not to be minimized" [346] (Millar Burrows, 1869-1980, professor of Biblical literature).

"Where Luke has been suspected of inaccuracy, and accuracy has been vindicated by some inscriptional evidence, it may be legitimate to say that archaeology has confirmed the New Testament record" [347] (F.F. Bruce, 1910-1990, Biblical scholar).

EXTERNAL #4: COULD CONTEMPORARIES VERIFY THE TESTIMONIES?

When the documents were written and circulated, were there people around who could verify the accuracy and/or raise objections against any mistakes or fabrications? This all boils down to dating and timing. For each event in history one can establish what is often called *the eyewitness period*, a time period of about 40 years (an average adult lifespan in those years) from the actual event. In that time period it is reasonable to assume that there will be a significant number of eyewitnesses still alive to testify to the accuracy or inaccuracy of the described event. In case of the gospels and Paul's letters, this period would be from around 30 AD (the start of Jesus ministry) until about 70 AD (the end of the 40 year period). Obviously, some people grow older than others, so even after 70 AD some eyewitnesses would still be alive (like the apostle John), but on average the population of eyewitnesses would have been significantly reduced at the end of the eyewitness period.

Earlier[348] we have discussed and analyzed the dating of all gospels, Acts, and Paul's epistles. All (except for John's gospel) are likely dated in the range 49 through 70 AD, 80 AD at the latest. John is likely more in the 80-90 AD range. This places most accounts (all but John) safely in the eyewitness period, allowing verification by both friendly as well as hostile contemporaries.

From friendly contemporaries (other Christians) we see positive confirmations by the end of the century and early second century through Papias, Clement of Rome, Epistle of Barnabas, etc.[349]

From the unfriendlies we do not hear much in terms of refuting the events and claims. As we have seen, there are quite a few extra-Biblical confirmations, but there are no contradicting claims. That is quite significant if you realize the hostile environment in which Christianity was born. The whole movement could have been stopped in its tracks almost right from the beginning if anybody would have ever claimed that the resurrection did not happen and/or, even better, would have produced Jesus' body. This did not happen, nor do we find any writings that make these claims. Indirectly, this is strong testimony to the validity of the resurrection claims.

SUMMARY

The Bible is a Historically Reliable Document

The Bible is much more than an ordinary book. It is a collection of ancient writings penned by 40 men spanning 1,500 years, proclaiming to be the Word of God *in toto*. In this section we studied a large collection of evidences and observations that set apart the Bible as a historically reliable document, strongly supported by ancient manuscript evidences and (recent) archaeological discoveries. The following exhibits were presented:

On the texts of the Old Testament:

1. When comparing the 2,000-year-old texts of the Hebrew Old Testament found in the Dead Sea Scrolls to the 1,100-year-old Masoretic texts that form the basis of our modern-day Bibles, hardly any differences are observed. This builds strong confidence that over the centuries the Bible texts, with high dedication and accuracy, were reliably copied and preserved by generations of scribes.

2. The first translation of the Hebrew Old Testament into Greek stems from the 295-270 BC era. This proves the texts of the Old Testament existed at least 300 years before the birth of Christ. Additionally, the preservation of this Greek translation (called the Septuagint) is another evidence for accurate copying over the centuries.

3. The canon (list of books) of the Hebrew Old Testament was closed around 400 BC, the so called apocryphal books of the Old Testament that are in Bibles used by some Christians (including Roman Catholics) are not part of the original Hebrew Scriptures.

4. Because of their prophetic content, the authorship of the Pentateuch or Torah (the first five books of the Bible) and the books of Isaiah and Daniel have been subject of numerous scholarly attacks. Even though the authorship of most Old Testament books cannot be conclusively proved, analysis of the content of the books in relationship to the knowledge derived from secular history builds a strong case for the authenticity of the authors that are usually associated with these books.

On the texts of the New Testament:

1. The existence of thousands and thousands of ancient manuscripts of the New Testament makes it by far the most accurately preserved ancient writing in existence today.

2. Tens of thousands of New Testament text quotations found in the preserved correspondence of the Early Church Leaders provide additional evidence for the preservation of the texts, the early dating of its writing and early acceptance as Scripture of the texts of the books of the New Testament.

3. A significant number of verses in the New Testament can be traced back to be used by the Christian church in its very first years of existence as oral declarations (called creeds) of faith and confirmations of the resurrection.

4. The official canon of the New Testament was not agreed upon until 397 AD; however, already at the turn of the first century, all the gospels, Acts, and most of Paul's epistles were recognized and set apart as Scripture.

5. The four gospels and the books of Acts do not make explicit claims about authorship; however, early and undisputed traditions, confirmations from the Early Church Leaders, and intrinsic analysis of the texts build a strong case for the authorship by Matthew, Mark, Luke (who also wrote Acts), and the apostle John. Additionally, the choice of Matthew with the background of a widely despised tax collector; Mark, who was not even an apostle; and Luke, who was not even a Jew, would not have made the top of any list of potential names to be associated with made-up gospels.

6. Analysis of the synoptic relationship between the first three gospels as well as various details recorded in the texts and the dating of the oldest extant manuscripts support the writing of these documents during the lifetime of the apostles and other eye-witnesses.

7. About half of the New Testament consists of thirteen letters written to various churches. All these letters explicitly claim to be written by Paul, the apostle. Their authorship as well as the composition of these letters in the period 50-65 AD, within 20-30 years of the resurrection, are not under competent dispute.

Archaeology, history and other observations:

1. Over the centuries, and especially during our generation, many other documents have been "discovered" and are now claimed by some as "lost" and "new" or even "more reliable" gospels about Christ. However the vast majority of these "gospels" can be traced to be written generations after the apostles. Of the few documents that might be dated back to the first century, the recently discovered texts from the fourth century show well documented evidences of editing during translations by heretic (especially gnostic) groups.

2. Dozens of significant archaeological discoveries of especially the last 50 years corroborate significant details of described customs, events, names. and locations of accounts in the Old and New Testament. Even more important, no archaeological find has ever been discovered that conclusively disproves any of the recorded accounts in the Bible.

3. Analysis of a number of compounded symbols in the oldest, pictorial language in world history, the ancient Chinese alphabet, show remarkable consistency with the accounts as recorded in the first chapters of the book of Genesis.

4. The writings of more than a dozen non-Christian first century authors and historians confirm many of the historical events as described in the New Testament. This includes multiple confirmations and details about Jesus' crucifixion.

5. Detailed analysis of the gospel texts against commonly accepted criteria of honest and trustworthy testimony shows the truthful intent of the gospel writers. They recall the events as they remembered them, including description of irrelevant details, without evidences of exaggeration or attempts to avoid self-damaging information.

We do not possess the original manuscripts of the Bible books unambiguously signed by the author, nor do we have detailed and accurate non-Biblical confirmations of the events that happened so long ago; therefore it is technically not possible to prove beyond skeptical criticism that the Bible is 100% historically reliable and accurate. However, we are given an astounding amount of clues, details, and observations from archaeological discoveries and (secular) history that again and again confirm the correctness of the accounts. These evidences not only make the Bible unique compared to any of the other ancient (religious) writings, but also build a compelling case to accept the Biblical texts as accurately preserved, written by the proclaimed authors and dated accordingly, being historically accurate and reliable, and additionally truthful and honest.

Section III
Is Jesus God?

CHAPTER 17

Is Jesus God?

"Jesus answered, 'I am the way and the truth and the life.
No one comes to the Father except through me.'"
JOHN 14:6

WHO WAS THIS JESUS?

Who was Jesus? This is likely one of the most frequently asked questions in all history. By far He has the highest name recognition throughout the world. Fully one-third of the world's peoples call themselves Christian, that is about 2.2 billion people. Islam (another 1.3 or so billion people) recognizes Him as the second greatest prophet after Mohammed. Of the remaining 3.2 billion people (roughly half the world's population), most have heard of Him and/or know about Him.

His résumé probably wouldn't have been impressive. After all, there is not much to say about His earthly life. He was born of Jewish parents in Bethlehem, a small town south of Jerusalem, while the territory was under Roman occupation. His parents moved north to Nazareth, where He grew up; hence He came commonly known as Jesus of Nazareth. His father was a carpenter, so Jesus likely learned that trade in His early years. At around thirty years of age He began a public ministry. He chose a dozen disciples to mentor and worked out of Capernaum on the coast of the Sea of Galilee. He traveled and taught throughout Galilee, occasionally moving among neighboring Gentiles and Samaritans with occasional trips south to Jerusalem. His unconventional teachings startled many; with this and an occasional miracle, a following began to take shape. His reception grew so strong that it caught the eye of established leaders of the Jewish faith. Many of them were offended by Jesus and even felt threatened. They soon decided to do away with Him. Working their contacts with the Roman rulers, they had Him arrested, and after a hastily arranged mock trial, He was executed by crucifixion.

That's it. Here the story of Jesus of Nazareth should have ended, hardly worth mentioning a footnote in history.

Unlike any other, His death was not the end, it was only the beginning. We are now discussing Him not merely because of His life, but because of His death. Christianity exists only because of what happened once Jesus died. Three days after His death, His disciples and many others began to claim He had returned to life from the dead. His grave was empty, the body gone, and numerous appearances were averred by different groups, at different locations, amid different circumstances.

As a result of this, followers began to proclaim that He was the Christ, or the Messiah. They claimed His resurrection validated the message of forgiveness of sin through His sacrifice. Initially they proclaimed this gospel in Jerusalem, the same city where He was put to death. The movement, known also as *"the Way"* (Acts 9:1, 19:9), grew rapidly. Only a short time later the faith spread outside the country, soon reaching Rome and the outskirts of its vast empire.

What is in a name?

In the days of Jesus people only had one name. Last names were not introduced before the time of Napoleon. To differentiate between people with the same name a unique characteristic was attached to the name, like the place they were from (Jesus of Nazareth or Mary of Magdalene), names of family members (such as Jesus, son of Joseph; or Mary, the mother of Jesus), professions (like Joseph the carpenter; or Cuza, the manager of Herod's household) or some other feature (such as John the Baptist; or Simon who was also called the Zealot).

In Hebrew Jesus would have been called Yeshua (Jeshua) or Joshua which literally means "Yahweh saves" or "Yahweh is savior." The Greek word *Christ* or the Latin *Christus* both translate the Hebrew *Messiah*, which means in English "the Anointed One."

So, Jesus Christ literally means *"Jesus, the Messiah"* or *"Jesus, the Anointed One."*

CAN WE DATE THE BIRTH AND CRUCIFIXION OF JESUS?

Our current *Anno Domini* (Latin for *"in the year of our Lord"*) calendar year system is based on taking the birth of Christ as the year one. Events after Jesus' birth are dated AD (Anno Domini); time before His birth looks back from this moment and is identified as BC (Before Christ). There is no year 0, after 1 BC follows 1 AD. However, unfortunately, when the year 1 was calculated in 525 AD by a monk named Dionysius Exiguus in Rome he miscalculated at least a few years, so therefore Christ is generally believed to have been born a few years BC.

Herod died in 4 BC, so Jesus was born before that, perhaps in 7 or 6 BC as seen in Matthew's record of Herod's killing boys up to two years old (Matthew 2:16). Luke mentions the decree by Caesar Augustus to take a census while

Quirinius was governor of Syria (Luke 2:1-2). This caused serious criticism, as historical records show that Quirinius was governor from 6-9 AD, but this is at least 10 years too late. Was Luke wrong? Some claim he was and therefore reject the remainder of his gospel as well. Wouldn't it be odd for such a detailed and careful writer as Luke to make such a careless mistake? Because he also reveals John the Baptist was born six months before Jesus in the days of Herod (Luke 1:5, 1:26-38). Instead of taking cheap shots at Luke, give him credit for his scholarship and integrity. After all, there could well be another explanation. Quirinius was a well respected, senior official who previously served in provinces adjacent to Syria. The registration of Jews may have begun while Quirinius held a roving command prior to his formal appointment in Syria.[350] Another explanation might be that a better translation of the text would be *"this census took place before Quirinius became governor."*[351] Or it might have been that Quirinius was governor in two periods, the earlier term around 7 BC. This assumption is supported by a Latin inscription found in 1764 in Antioch ascribing a post to Quirinius.[352] A fourth alternative is that from about 7 to 4 BC Quirinius oversaw the census in the politically volatile Palestine, effectively superseding the weak Quintilius Varus, who was governor in name only.[353] Whatever the explanation, if we take Matthew and Luke seriously, the most plausible date for the birth of Jesus would be 6 or 5 BC.

By studying historical references in Luke and Acts, we can fix the time John the Baptist began his ministry. John began to prophesy *"in the fifteenth year of the reign of Tiberius"* (Luke 3:1). Caesar Augustus died August 19, 14 AD, and Tiberius was proclaimed emperor September 17 of that same year. Tiberius' fifteenth year would have been 29 AD,[354] the very year John began his public ministry. Since Jesus was baptized by John, the earliest date for His ministry is sometime in 29 AD. Astronomical considerations have established that Jesus' death must have occurred either in 30 or 33 AD.[355] Thus – unless one takes the view that Jesus' ministry only lasted one year – it follows that Jesus' ministry extended beyond 30 AD. Therefore the most logical and likely date for the crucifixion is the Passover of 33 AD.

PROVING THAT JESUS IS THE SON OF GOD

There is little doubt that Jesus really lived about 2,000 years ago in Palestine under Roman rule. Few question that He was considered a wise rabbi (teacher) who preached a message of love for one another. Even other religions (Islam) accept that. However, none of this proves Him to be the Son of God. It is one thing to claim to be God, it is quite another to back up the claim. The four most important lines of evidence to support Jesus' claim as the Son of God (Lord) and the Son of Man (Savior) are:

Lord, Liar, or Lunatic? Who did Jesus Himself claim to be? Did Jesus Himself believe and teach that He was the Son of God, or was this invented later by the Christian church? If Jesus taught that He was the Son of God – and He did – was He a liar or a lunatic? Or is the only logical conclusion that He indeed is the Son of God?

Miracles, Signs of Divine Powers. All the gospels report numerous miraculous deeds of Jesus. From healing the sick to controlling the forces of nature, His miracles show compassion and set forth evidence for His divine powers. Do these miracles provide us convincing evidence?

Fulfillment of Messianic Prophecies. Jesus fulfilled hundreds of Old Testament prophecies. Well before Jesus was born, the Jews realized that the Old Testament had numerous references to a Messiah who would save the world. These references contained numerous predictions about the life and the death of the Messiah. Just coincidence? Are there other explanations, or is this a confirmation of Jesus' divine nature?

Did the Resurrection Really Occur? The cornerstone of the evidence of Jesus' claims to be God is the resurrection. Despite all other evidences, if the resurrection is not a well-proved, historical event, the whole system of belief falls apart. The fact that both the Old Testament and Jesus predicted in advance that He would rise from the dead makes the resurrection that much more powerful. Proving (or disproving) the resurrection proves (or disproves) the truth of the Christian faith. Jesus' resurrection is the convincing evidence that He is God, and through that, it opens the door to redemption with God the Father. Great claims demand great evidence. We will spend serious time researching the facts and proofs that build the foundation for our faith in the resurrection.

CHAPTER 18

Lord, Liar or Lunatic?

"'But what about you?' Jesus asked. 'Who do you say I am?' Simon
Peter answered, 'You are the Christ, the Son of the living God.'"
MATTHEW 16:15-16

WHO DID JESUS SAY HE WAS?

What did Jesus claim for Himself? If anybody knew with certainty that Jesus was the Son of God, it obviously would be Jesus Himself. Many people do not realize, however, that Jesus made very strong and clear claims as to His deity throughout His ministry. Jesus was not confused or doubtful; He knew His divine identity and communicated that carefully to His followers.

Jesus had to make His claims carefully. People were looking for the Messiah, but they expected and longed for an earthly king, a general like King David, to liberate them from Roman occupation. Few realized that God's Kingdom is not invested in earthly ambitions. So Jesus had to ensure that His disciples would recognize His divinity and learn God's plan for mankind, while at the same time carefully transforming their own expectations.

In Matthew 16:13-17, Jesus explicitly confirms His identity. Once across the Sea of Galilee, Jesus and His followers headed north along the Jordan River to its headwaters near Caesarea Philippi, approximately 25 miles beyond the lake into Gentile territory. The gospel texts focus closely on the dialogue between Jesus and the Twelve. He questions their perception of the crowds' views of His identity to correct any misconceptions that might have arisen (Matthew 16:13-15):

"When Jesus came to the region of Caesarea Philippi, He asked His disciples,
'Who do people say the Son of Man is?' They replied, 'Some say John the
Baptist; others say Elijah; and still others, Jeremiah or one of the prophets.'
'But what about you?' He asked. 'Who do you say I am?'"

People in general seemed to view Him as a spokesman for God. Many thought His association with John the Baptist marked Him as an extraordinary prophet. Elijah, considered the greatest OT prophet, was the Messianic forerunner of Old Testament prophecy. It would be natural as well to think of Jesus as a kind of Jeremiah, a preacher of judgment and repentance widely rejected by leaders of His nation. When Jesus pressed the small band of men further for *their* response, Peter answered quickly (Matthew 16:16, emphasis added):

" *You are the Christ, the Son of the living God.* "

For the first time in Matthew's gospel someone has unambiguously acknowledged Him to be "*the Christ*," the Messiah, the Anointed One, and "*the Son of the living God.*" Notice Jesus' response, as He validated Peter's statement (Matthew 16:17):

"*Jesus replied, 'Blessed are you, Simon, son of Jonah, for this was not revealed to you by man, but by my Father in heaven.'*"

So Jesus knew quite well who He was. Read the gospels carefully, and notice numerous confirmations by Jesus of His identity:

- **Jesus called himself "Son of Man."** Jesus referred to Himself using this title 80 times in the gospels. "*Son of Man*" refers to Daniel's vision: "*In my vision at night I looked, and there before me was one like a son of man, coming with the clouds of heaven*" (Daniel 7:13). It was commonly understood this title belonged to the Messiah.
- **Jesus called himself "I AM."** Another direct claim to deity is found in John 8:56-58 (emphasis added). Speaking to the Jews, Jesus said, "*Your father Abraham rejoiced to see My day, and he saw it and was glad...before Abraham was, I AM.*" "*I AM*" is derived from the divine name Yahweh ("YHWH" in Hebrew), by which God revealed Himself to Moses at the burning bush. The word emphasizes eternal self-existence. It is evident that the Jews understood this claim. Verse 59 shows that they picked up stones to throw at Him for what they considered a blasphemous self-affirmation. Jesus used the "I AM" name seven times in John.
- **Jesus claimed to forgive sins.** Obviously only God can forgive sins, but multiple times – frustrating and angering both Pharisees and Sadducees – Jesus said "*your sins are forgiven,*" as when He cured the paralytic: "*Since they could not get him to Jesus because of the crowd, they made an opening in the roof above Jesus and, after digging through it, lowered the mat the paralyzed man was lying on. When Jesus saw their faith, he said to the paralytic, 'Son, your sins are forgiven.' Now some teachers of the law were sitting there, thinking to themselves, 'Why does this fellow talk like that? He's blaspheming! Who can forgive sins but God alone?'*" (Mark 2:4-7, emphasis added). Notice the reaction of the teachers of the law; they called this blasphemy.
- **Jesus claimed to be equal with God.** Jesus said: "*'My sheep listen to my voice; I know them, and they follow me. I give them eternal life, and they*

shall never perish; no one can snatch them out of my hand. My Father, who has given them to me, is greater than all; no one can snatch them out of my Father's hand. I and the Father are one.' Again the Jews picked up stones to stone him, but Jesus said to them, 'I have shown you many great miracles from the Father. For which of these do you stone me?' 'We are not stoning you for any of these,' replied the Jews, 'but for blasphemy, because you, a mere man, claim to be God'" (John 10:27-33, emphasis added). Once more, note the reaction of the Jews. They wanted to stone Jesus because He claimed to be the Son of God.

- **Numerous other statements in the Gospel of John.** Because of its audience of Christians, John is bold to mention Jesus' statements about His claims to deity. Some examples are:
  - John 1:1-3: *"In the beginning was the Word, and the Word was with God, and the Word was God. He was with God in the beginning. Through him all things were made; without him nothing was made that has been made."*
  - John 8:19: *"'You do not know me or my Father,' Jesus replied. 'If you knew me, you would know my Father also.'"*
  - John 14:6: *"Jesus answered, 'I am the way and the truth and the life. No one comes to the Father except through me.'"*

Consider too that Jesus never denied His divinity. On trial by the highest authority of the Jews (the Sanhedrin) for claiming to be the Son of God, He could have easily denied the allegations – yet He did not. He remained silent until the high priest put Him under oath to answer. Then Jesus confirmed His identity (Matthew 26:63-66, emphasis added):

"The high priest said to him, 'I charge you under oath by the living God: Tell us if you are the Christ, the Son of God.' 'Yes, it is as you say,' Jesus replied. 'But I say to all of you: In the future you will see the Son of Man sitting at the right hand of the Mighty One and coming on the clouds of heaven.' Then the high priest tore his clothes and said, 'He has spoken blasphemy! Why do we need any more witnesses? Look, now you have heard the blasphemy. What do you think?' 'He is worthy of death,' they answered."

The death sentence came after interrogation and another trial – where once more Jesus could have denied the charges when He faced the Roman procurator Pilate. Jesus was then executed by being nailed to a cross. The accusation attached to the cross read:

The King of the Jews

☀ EXHIBIT #1: NOT A LIAR, NOT A LUNATIC, BUT THE LORD.

Since Jesus identified Himself as the unique Son of God, there are only two alternatives: He is God or He is not. If He knows He is not God and still teaches He is, then He is lying, and that, of course, makes Him a liar. If, however, He is not God but He thinks that He is, then He is deluded; He is a nut and He is a lunatic.

These are simply the only three options:
• He is who He claims to be – Jesus is Lord.
• He knows He is wrongly claiming to be God – Jesus is a liar.
• Or He just thinks He is God, but He is not – Jesus is a lunatic.

Many people try to define another Jesus, one who will not fit the above logical reasoning. History has beyond doubt (as we have seen from Biblical and non-Biblical sources alike) established that Jesus was a historical person who preached throughout Judea and round about. He was acknowledged as a great moral teacher and miracle worker. Denying His very existence is not realistic. Amazingly, many non-Christians will agree that Jesus was a great teacher of moral values but, they will say, He was not God. He was merely a man with great teaching skills, and His moral and wise teachings started a world religion. Nothing new here, though. Why? The same can be said for Buddha, Mahatma Gandhi, and Mohammed.

However, this logic falls apart for one important reason: none of these great teachers claimed to be the unique Son of God. Their message was considered by many of great importance and moral content. Jesus, however, taught He was God. So no one can logically accept Jesus as a great teacher of moral values and reject His teachings that He is God. That does not make sense. How can anyone be a great moral teacher if a significant part of his teaching is false?

No one has said this better than the renowned agnostic-turned-Christian author and scholar C.S. Lewis (1898-1963), in his book *Mere Christianity:*[356]

> *"I'm trying here to prevent anyone from saying the really foolish thing that people often say about Him: 'I'm ready to accept Jesus as a great moral teacher, but I don't accept His claim to be God.' That's the one thing we must not say. A man who was merely a man and said the sort of things Jesus said wouldn't be a great moral teacher. He'd either be a lunatic – on a level with the man who says he's a poached egg – or else he'd be the Devil of Hell. You must make your choice. Either this man was, and is, the Son of God: or else a madman or something worse. You can shut Him up for a fool, you can spit at Him and kill Him as a demon; or you can fall at His feet and call Him Lord and God. But don't let us come with any patronizing nonsense about His being a great human teacher. He hasn't left that open to us. He didn't intend to."*

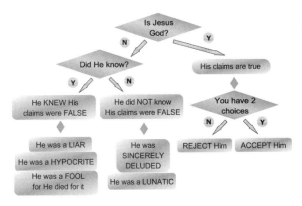

Figure 18-1: Jesus was a Liar, a Lunatic or the Lord

JESUS WAS NOT A LIAR

If Jesus claimed to be God and yet knew He was not, He was lying. In fact, He would be a liar of the worst kind because He tricked people into accepting a religion that, if not true, would inevitably lead them away from the true God and into eternal damnation. He would also be a hypocrite because He taught honesty, whatever the cost, while living a colossal lie. Above all, He would be an incredible fool. As we have seen, His claims to deity were the reason He was crucified. During the trials He was quiet, not responding to His accusers. He spoke only to confirm their accusations that He claimed to be God. A simple denial would have set Him free. If He knew He was lying, He was a fool to die for it. He would be tortured and subjected to an excruciating execution by crucifixion, and for what? To maintain that lie? Someone may die for something he thinks is true, but surely not for something he knows is false.

Given what the Bible reveals about Jesus' teachings and His life, He could not have been a deceiver. Nor is it likely a liar would have had such profound and lasting influence. He taught disciples to be truthful at all costs, to give sacrificially, and to share unconditionally. Jesus not only taught these things, but lived them. He did not have the character of a liar.

In the words of church historian and theologian Philip Schaff (1819-1893):[357]

"The hypothesis of imposture is so revolting to moral as well as common sense that its mere statement is its condemnation...No scholar of any decency and self-respect would now dare to profess it openly. How in the name of logic, common sense, and experience, could an imposter – that is a deceitful, selfish, depraved man – have invented, and consistently maintained from the beginning to end, the purest and noblest character known in history with the most perfect air of truth and reality? How could he have conceived and successfully carried out a plan of unparalleled beneficence, moral magnitude, and sublimity, and sacrificed his own life for it, in the face of the strongest prejudices of his people and ages?"

JESUS WAS NOT A LUNATIC

Perhaps Jesus thought He was God, but in truth He was self-deluded? Many people have claimed divine status, but their madness is usually quite transparent. A self-deluded person, or lunatic, is mentally ill, often dangerous, quite foolish and thoroughly unpredictable. Does what we know about Jesus fit this image?

Neither the Bible nor history bears the slightest hint that Jesus was a lunatic. He showed no symptoms of madness common to those who suffer from mental disorders or hallucinations. His teachings were not the ravings of a madman. He showed no signs of paranoia or schizophrenia. He was neither rash nor impulsive. In each circumstance, even the anguish of the cross, Jesus appeared self-assured and in full possession of emotion and reason. It mattered not on which subject He spoke, His advice was profound, insightful, intelligible, and reliable. His instructions in all areas of human relationships (religious, moral, political, psychological, social) were so reliable that they have molded and shaped Western civilization for nearly 20 centuries. Jesus set thousands of people free from the bondage to mental illness, drugs, and alcohol. There is not a scintilla of evidence that Jesus Christ was anything less than fully sane.[358]

Once again in the words of Philip Schaff:[359]

"Is such an intellect – clear as the sky, bracing as the mountain air, sharp and penetrating as the sword, thoroughly healthy and vigorous, always ready and always self-possessed – liable to a radical and most serious delusion concerning His own character and mission? Preposterous imagination!"

THEREFORE HE IS LORD!

Research far and wide uncovers virtually nobody who seriously claims Jesus was a liar or a lunatic. No realistic person could support either conclusion. Logic and the preponderance of evidence force even the most skeptical and critical to eliminate the liar and the lunatic alternatives.

Therefore, logically Jesus must be who He claims to be – He is the Lord!

How do persons escape this undeniable conclusion? They introduce a fourth alternative: Legend. They claim that Jesus is not Lord, because He never claimed to be such. This is the view that the New Testament texts are not historically true. The Jesus of the gospels, the Jesus who claimed to be God and to save us from sin, the Jesus who performed miracles, and rose from the dead, is a legend very different from "the historical Jesus." Thus, the New Testament tells the truth about Jesus' human personality, but not about His divine nature or His miracles. Those who hold this position discard from the gospels what they dislike and declare that only what remains is historical truth. Thus, Jesus was neither God nor a bad man because He never claimed to be God, as the New Testament says He did. His claim is neither true nor false; it is simply fraudulent.

As we have discovered in previous chapters, the Bible texts are reliable, the gospels are founded in history, written by credible, reliable, and honest eye-witnesses, circulated well within the eyewitness period and corroborated by archaeological discoveries as well as contemporary, non-Christian sources. Dismissing a most significant part of the texts as legend is a weak attempt to deny the evidence.

So, the only way out of the dilemma is simple: deny the data. Because if you admit the data, then you must deal with Jesus' claim to be God, for that is the essence of the New Testament. Then only two options remain: If His claim is true, become a Christian and worship Him; if His claim is false, denounce Him as a blasphemer or lock Him up as a madman.[360]

CHAPTER 19

Miracles, Signs of Divine Powers

"This, the first of his miraculous signs, Jesus performed
at Cana in Galilee. He thus revealed his glory,
and his disciples put their faith in Him."
JOHN 2:11

MIRACLES ARE SUPERNATURAL ACTS OF GOD

What is a miracle? As evidence to the deity of Jesus, a miracle is simply a supernatural act of God. To avoid confusion and bypass non-constructive debate whether specific events are truly miraculous, we limit our discussion to acts that meet the following four characteristics:

- **Significant:** An event must be significant to be considered a miracle. There has to be a dramatic result that belies the charge of a "remarkable coincidence."
- **Immediate:** The effect has to be immediate. If it takes hours, days, weeks, or longer to occur, the change likely can be caused by other factors.
- **Defying the laws of nature:** A real miracle cannot be explained by any natural law or phenomena. Breaking or superseding these laws proves it was a supernatural act.
- **Witnessed by multiple people:** As miracles are extraordinary events, they require an extraordinary burden of proof, so multiple witnesses.

Anyone who does not believe in God finds the concept of a miracle, any event that contradicts and even suspends the laws of nature, impossible to accept. That is, if God does not exist, only nature controls life. Therefore no miracle is possible and any account of a miracle cannot be true. This logical argument against miracles was first formulated by Benedict Spinoza (1632-1677). Spinoza's argument can be summarized as follows:[361]

- A miracle violates natural laws.
- Natural laws are immutable.
- It is impossible to violate immutable laws.
- Therefore, miracles are impossible.

However, if God exists, He created the natural laws, so it should be no problem for Him to move beyond or outside these laws, nor can He be restrained by these laws.

WHY AND WHEN DID JESUS PERFORM MIRACLES?

Jesus used miracles as signs to His credentials as the Son of God. Without miracles it would be exceptionally difficult to believe His claims. As John wrote in John 20:30-31:

"Jesus' disciples saw Him do many more other miraculous signs besides the ones recorded in this book. But these are written so that you may believe that Jesus is the Messiah, the Son of God, and that by believing in Him you will have life."

Observe that the miracles of Jesus not only showed His power over nature, but also revealed His approach to ministry: helping others, speaking with authority, and connecting with people. The keyword is *compassion*. Almost all His miracles were driven by compassion. He healed people who sought His help. He raised the dead to comfort grieving families. He quieted storms to calm the fears of His friends. He fed multitudes to avert their hunger. Don't fail to notice that Jesus never performed a miracle for His own benefit or gain. The miracles aided others, not Him. On five occasions Jesus performed a miracle as a sign solely for the disciples: walking on water; cursing of the fig tree; both miraculous catches of fish by the disciples; and the coin for the temple tax. All other miracles sprang from compassion for the people around Him.

As F.F. Bruce remarks:[362]

"In literature there are many kind of miracle stories; but the Gospels do not ask us to believe that Jesus made the sun travel from west to east one day, or anything like that; they do not even attribute to Him such monstrosities as we find in the apocryphal writings of the second century. In general, the miracles are 'in character' – this is to say, they are the kind of works that might be expected from such a person as the Gospel represents Jesus to be."

☼ EXHIBIT #2: JESUS' MIRACLES PROVE HIS DIVINE POWERS

The following table shows an overview of all thirty-five of His miracles (omitting only the resurrection) found in the gospels, each of which meets our criteria. Only one miracle (the feeding of the five thousand) is described in every gospel. About half of the miracles are recorded in two or more of the gospels. As expected, quite a few, eleven in fact, are shared among all the synoptic gospels, but only seven are recorded in only two of the three synoptic accounts. Two miracles in John also appear in one or more of the synoptic gospels. Matthew has three unique miracles, Mark has two, while Luke and John each record six.

Miracle	Matthew	Mark	Luke	John	Compassion	Nature
Five thousand men are fed	14:15-21	6:35-44	9:12-17	6:5-14	X	X
The storm is calmed	8:23-27	4:35-41	8:22-25		X	X
Demons are sent into the pigs	8:28-34	5:1-20	8:26-39		X	
Jairus' daughter is raised from death	9:18-26	5:22-43	8:41-56		X	
A sick woman is healed	9:20-22	5:25-34	8:43-48		X	
A paralytic is healed	9:1-8	2:1-12	5:17-26		X	
A leper is healed at Gennesaret	8:1-4	1:40-45	5:12-15		X	
Peter's mother in law is healed	8:14-17	1:29-31	4:38-39		X	
A shriveled hand is restored	12:9-13	3:1-5	6:6-11		X	
A boy with an evil spirit is healed	17:14-21	9:14-29	9:37-42		X	
Jesus walks on water	14:22-33	6:45-52		6:17-21		X
Blind Bartimaeus receives sight	20:29-34	10:46-32	18:35-43		X	
A girl is freed from a demon	15:21-28	7:24-30			X	
Four thousand men are fed	15:32-38	8:1-9			X	X
The fig tree is cursed	21:18-22	11:12-24				X
A centurion's servant is healed	8:5-13		7:1-10		X	
An evil spirit is sent out of a man		1:23-27	4:33-36		X	
A mute demoniac is healed	12:22		11:14		X	
Two blind men find sight	9:27-31				X	
Jesus heals the mute man	9:32-33				X	
A coin is found in a fish's mouth	17:24-27					X
A deaf and mute man is healed		7:31-37			X	
A blind man sees at Bethsaida		8:22-36			X	
The first miraculous catch of fish			5:1-11			X
A widow's son is raised			7:11-16		X	
A crippled woman is healed			13:10-17		X	
A sick man is healed			14:1-6		X	
Ten lepers are healed			17:11-19		X	
A man's ear is restored			22:49-51		X	
Water is turned into wine				2:1-11	X	X
An official's son is healed at Cana				4:46-54	X	
A lame man is healed				5:1-16	X	
A man born blind is healed				9:1-7	X	
Lazarus is raised from the dead				11:1-45	X	
The second miraculous catch of fish				21:1-14		X
Total:	35	20	18	20	8	30	9

Jesus' Miracles as Recorded in the Gospels

Table 19-1: Jesus' Miracles as Recorded in the Gospels

This distribution once more demonstrates Matthew, Mark, and Luke are personal testimonies. Even Mark, the gospel "copied" by Matthew and Luke, has two miracles not mentioned in the other two. Why are they omitted if Matthew and Luke leaned on Mark as their primary source as the synoptic theory claims?

As miracles are evidence of Jesus' deity, it is useful to categorize them into:

- **Healing miracles:** The vast majority (26) of miracles in which Jesus heals one person or more or even raises (Jairus' daughter, a widow's son, and Lazarus) from the dead.
- **Nature miracles:** Nine miracles are recorded where Jesus does something impossible within our natural world. He defies the laws of nature.

The healing miracles are easy targets for critics. Many simply insist that the healed person was not ill, the person might be "self-healed" (the "power of positive thinking") or there might even have been a type of hypnosis or other "magic." Obviously our ancestors did not have our knowledge of science, but they were not stupid either! Even first century uneducated Jews could distinguish between a magician's trick and a genuine miracle. They would have identified a fake healing. The healed people were not selected from the audience, willingly participating in a performance. These were locals, known by the community for their handicaps, perhaps long-term blindness or injury. Resurrecting someone moments after his death would suggest he had not actually died. Lazarus, however, was in the grave four days (John 11:39: *"'But, Lord,' said Martha, the sister of the dead man, 'by this time there is a bad odor, for he has been there four days.'"*), so one can hardly argue that "he was not really dead."

Still, from an evidence perspective, the most awesome confirmations of Jesus' deity are the nature miracles. There is just no explanation for walking on water, calming a storm, feeding huge crowds from a single lunch basket, or turning water into wine. Such events are real miracles and they show Jesus' divine power. Keep in mind that such miracles have never been claimed by other professed miracle workers. Only Jesus has displayed such power. Look closely at the nature miracles and probe them for the characteristics for a genuine miracle. We learn:

- **Significance:** There is no doubt the nature miracles are significant. It is unlikely that anyone present was not awed! This is clear from people's reactions, such as when Jesus climbed into the boat after walking on the water: *"Then those who were in the boat worshiped him, saying, 'Truly you are the Son of God'"* (Matthew 14:33). After Jesus calmed the storm: *"In fear and amazement they asked one another, 'Who is this? He commands even the winds and the water, and they obey him'"* (Luke 8:25).
- **Immediate:** All of Jesus' miracles had immediate results. Both healings and nature miracles were instantaneous.
- **Defy the laws of nature:** This cannot be disputed, for this is the exact definition of a miracle.

• **Multiple witnesses:** As a last resort, non-believing critics try to refute Jesus' nature miracles by dismissing them as myths or legends. However, the evidence is overwhelming. First, the miracles were done before groups of varying sizes, either the disciples (one can argue they are not objective) or a crowd of several thousands. Second, five of the nature miracles are recorded in multiple gospels, one even in all four gospels. Third, Jesus' opponents never denied or even disputed his miracles. They admitted Jesus performed miracles and tried to claim Jesus had teamed with the devil: "*But when the Pharisees heard this, they said, 'It is only by Beelzebub, the prince of demons, that this fellow drives out demons'*" (Matthew 12:24). Or they tried to destroy the evidence: "*So the chief priests made plans to kill Lazarus as well, for on account of him many of the Jews were going over to Jesus and putting their faith in him*" (John 12:10-11).

THE FEEDING OF THE FIVE THOUSAND

Among all miracles the astonishing feeding of a crowd of five thousand men plus women and children, likely a total of ten to twelve thousand or more people, stands out.

This may well be the most impressive nature miracle of all. Some see a symbolic link between Jesus as the "*Bread of Life*" and God's gift of manna to the Israelites in the desert long before.

Second, it is the only miracle found in all four gospels. Each describes the events on that hillside near the Sea of Galilee: only five loaves and two fishes to feed the large gathering. Jesus broke the bread and the disciples handed out the food. There was enough for everybody, and the leftovers filled twelve baskets. Comparing the four accounts is rewarding. As we saw in the criteria for honest eyewitness testimony,[363] they describe the same storyline, but each provides different details. For instance, Mark and John estimated "*eight months of a man's wages*" would be necessary to feed all the people. All gospels relate that the people were to be seated, but only Mark and Luke tell they sat in groups of "*fifties and hundreds.*" John mentions the Sea of Galilee, Mark and Matthew just mention a boat, and Luke adds that they are close to a town called Bethsaida. John also reveals it was a boy who had brought along the Barley loaves and fishes. John identified a number of disciples by name. Again there is a random pattern of details in the various gospels. Contrary to synoptic theory, Mark, supposed to be the briefest and simplest gospel, actually has the most extensive account with the most details. A total of four independent witness accounts to this remarkable event.

Third and last, this miracle is performed in the presence of five thousand men, not counting women and children. Nothing was done in secret. It was born out of compassion for the hungry crowd, but the number of witnesses is momentous. And as at least three of the four gospels were written within a generation of this event, many of these witnesses were still alive as these accounts began to circulate. There were plenty of opportunities for someone to confirm or deny this miracle.

In the words of famous Christian philosopher, theologian, and author G.K. Chesterton:[364]

"The most incredible thing about miracles is that they happen."

CHAPTER 20

Fulfillment of Messianic Prophecies

*"He said to them, 'How foolish you are, and how slow of heart
to believe all that the prophets have spoken! Did not the Christ have
to suffer these things and then enter his glory?' And beginning with
Moses and all the Prophets, he explained to them what was said
in all the Scriptures concerning himself."*
LUKE 24:25-27

THE ADDRESS THAT IDENTIFIES THE MESSIAH

Today more than six and a half billion people live on earth. You can send
any one of them a letter, but first you must specify his or her address. Only
then are postal services around the world able to find any person anywhere. For
instance, while we lived in the Netherlands our address was:

Van de Weghe family

Westeinde 8

Oud Alblas

The Netherlands

Each line adds specific information about where a person can be found. The
country specified one certain nation out of more than 200 countries. The city
identified one particular area in that country, a small village of about 2,250 inhabitants. Next the street address pinpointed the name of the street and the number
of the house on that street. Lastly the family's name cut through any confusion
with any others at that address and it verified that the address is indeed correct.

This simple example shows that, with only a few clues, it is possible to locate
any particular person anywhere in the world, even among billions of people.

Like this postal address, the Old Testament is a specific identifier, telling
where, when and how to find the Messiah, the Christ. These address lines are
the *Messianic prophecies*, specific passages written hundreds of years before the
Messiah was born, each one foretelling details about His birth, His family, His
ministry, His betrayal and trial, and His death and burial.

Jesus of Nazareth fit this Old Testament "profile" of the Messiah so well that
New Testament writers (especially and most explicitly Matthew) used prophecy as key evidence to prove His divine identity. As A. T. Pierson put it, the Old

Testament writers added *"feature after feature and touch after touch and tint after tint, until what was at first a drawing without color, a mere outline or profile, comes at last to be a perfect portrait with the very hues of living flesh."* [365]

☼ EXHIBIT #3: JESUS FULFILLED ALL MESSIANIC PROPHECIES

In Biblical context a prophecy means the forth-telling of truth in the future, present or past. A Messianic prophecy thus foretells the profile or the characteristics of the Messiah.

There are hundreds of prophecies about the Messiah in the Old Testament. Counts range from 100[366] to 191[367] to *"nearly 300"*[368] and to even 456 passages of Scripture labeled Messianic according to ancient Jewish writings.[369] These are found all through the Old Testament from Genesis through Malachi, however the most significant ones are found in Psalms and Isaiah.

Not all prophecies are clear, and some can be interpreted to describe either one event seen in the text or to predict exclusively the coming Messiah, or even both. I would like to encourage you not to accept a text as a Messianic prophecy just because others claim it is. Challenge it. Read the relevant Old Testament passage for yourself and draw your own conclusions about how to interpret this text. If you are unconvinced, just remove this prophecy from your list and look at the next one. There are so many prophecies that you can afford to be selective. The remaining prophecies will still identify Jesus as the Messiah, and the evidence is still overwhelming and statistically significant. The proof is in the pudding, as they say, so let us examine a number of the prophecies in more detail:

BORN OF A VIRGIN

Prophecy	Fulfillment
Isaiah 7:14: *"Therefore the Lord Himself will give you a sign: The virgin will be with child and give birth to a son, and will call him Immanuel."*	Matthew 1:18,24,25: *"She was found with child of the Holy Spirit .... Then Joseph ..... but he had no union with her until she gave birth to a son. And he gave him the name Jesus."* Luke 1:26-35: *"In the sixth month, God sent the angel Gabriel to Nazareth, a town in Galilee, to a virgin pledged to be married to a man named Joseph, a descendant of David. The virgin's name was Mary. The angel went to her and said, ... 'Do not be afraid, Mary, you have found favor with God. You will be with child and give birth to a son, and you are to give him the name Jesus.........', 'The Holy Spirit will come upon you, and the power of the Most High will overshadow you. So the holy one to be born will be called the Son of God.'"*

Some believe Isaiah referred only to a local situation where a young woman, still a virgin, was soon to be married and would later bear a child, fulfilling the prophecy. Others believe that the prophecy is exclusively Messianic and predicts that Mary, while still a virgin, would be the mother of Christ as Matthew explicitly claims. Still others see a double fulfillment in this prophecy; that is, predicting both a child described in Isaiah chapter 8 and the birth of Christ.[370] Many prophecies did have two fulfillments: one quite soon, another much later.

Additional evidence for the Messianic aspect of this well-known prophecy is early Christian tradition, the build-up in the preceding verses, and the parallels between Isaiah chapter 9 and Isaiah chapter 11.[371] Other support for this conclusion is the name *"Immanuel,"* which means *"God with us."* Since Jesus is God, that part of Isaiah's prophecy was literally fulfilled. It should be noted that this verse was not identified as Messianic by early Jewish commentaries.

Selection of Old Testament Prophecies about the Messiah

Prophecy	Prediction	Fulfillment[372]
Prophecies about the birth of Jesus		
He is born of a virgin and His name shall be Immanuel	Isaiah 7:14	Matthew 1:18-25
He is the Son of God	Psalm 2:7	Matthew 3:17
He is from the seed of Abraham	Genesis 22:18	Matthew 1:1
He is from the tribe of Judah	Genesis 49:10	Matthew 1:2
He is from the family line of Jesse	Isaiah 11:1	Matthew 1:6
He is from the house of David	Jeremiah 23:5	Matthew 1:1
He is born at Bethlehem	Micah 5:2	Matthew 2:1
He is to be proceeded by a messenger (John the Baptist)	Isaiah 40:3	Matthew 3:1-2
Prophecies about the ministry of Jesus		
His ministry is to begin in Galilee	Isaiah 9:1	Matthew 4:12-13
He will heal the blind, the deaf and the lame	Isaiah 35:5-6	Matthew 9:35
He will teach in parables	Psalm 78:2	Matthew 13:34
He is to enter Jerusalem on a donkey	Zechariah 9:9	Matthew 21:6-11
He is to be presented as the Messiah on a certain day	Daniel 9:24-27	Matthew 21:1-11
Prophecies about the betrayal and the trial of Jesus		
He will be the rejected cornerstone	Psalm 118:22	1 Peter 2:7
He is to be betrayed by a friend	Psalm 41:9	Matthew 10:4
He is to be sold for 30 pieces of silver	Zechariah 11:12	Matthew 26:15
The money is be thrown into the house of the Lord	Zechariah 11:13	Matthew 27:5
He is to be silent before his accusers	Isaiah 53:7	Matthew 27:12
Prophecies about the crucifixion and the burial of Jesus		
He is to be crushed for our transgressions	Isaiah 53:5	Matthew 27:26
His hands and feet are to be pierced	Psalm 22:16	Matthew 27:35
He is to be killed with the transgressors	Isaiah 53:12	Matthew 27:38
He is to make intercession for the transgressors	Isaiah 53:12	Luke 23:34
He is to be rejected by his own people	Isaiah 53:3	Matthew 21:42-43
He is to be hated without a cause	Psalm 69:4	John 15:25
His friends are to watch from a distance	Psalm 38:11	Matthew 27:55
His garments are to be parted and cast lots for	Psalm 22:18	Matthew 27:35
He is to suffer thirst	Psalm 69:21	John 19:28
He is to be offered gall and vinegar	Psalm 69:21	Matthew 27:34,48
He is to commit his spirit to God	Psalm 31:5	Luke 23:46
His bones are not to be broken	Psalm 34:20	John 19:33
His side is to be pierced	Zechariah 12:10	John 19:34
Darkness is to come over the land	Amos 8:9	Matthew 27:45
He is to be buried in a rich man's grave	Isaiah 53:9	Matthew 27:57-60

Table 20-1: Selection of Old Testament Prophecies about the Messiah

FAMILY LINE OF JESUS

Prophecy		Fulfillment
Seed of Abraham	Genesis 22:18: *"and through your offspring all nations on earth will be blessed, because you have obeyed me."*	Matthew 1:1: *"The book of the genealogy of Jesus Christ, the Son of David, the Son of Abraham."*
Son of Isaac	Genesis 21:12: *"But God said to him [Abraham] ... it is through Isaac that your offspring will be reckoned"*	Luke 3:23,34: *"Jesus, ... The son of Isaac."* See also Matthew 1:2
Son of Jacob	Numbers 24:17: *"I see Him, but not now. I behold Him, but not near; A star will come out of Jacob, a scepter will rise out of Israel. He will crush the foreheads of Moab, the skulls of all the sons of Sheth."*	Luke 3:23,34: *"Jesus, ... The son of Isaac."* See also Matthew 1:2
Tribe of Judah	Genesis 49:10: *"The Scepter shall not depart from Judah, nor a lawgiver from between his feet, until Shiloh comes; and to Him shall be the obedience of the people."*	Luke 3:23,34: *"Jesus, ... The son of Judah."* See also Matthew 1:2
Line of Jesse	Isaiah 11:1: *"A shoot will come up from the stump of Jesse; from his roots a Branch will bear fruit."*	Luke 3:23,32: *"Jesus, ... The son of Jesse."* See also Matthew 1:6
House of David	Jeremiah 23:5: *"'The days are coming,' declares the LORD, 'when I will raise up to David a righteous Branch, a King who will reign wisely and do what is just and right in the land.'"*	Luke 3:23,31: *"Jesus, ... The son of David."* See also Matthew 1:1 and many more references.

The bloodline of the Messiah is narrowed down through this line of prophecies. As a son of Abraham, the Messiah is a Jew, but He is also a son of Isaac, a son of Jacob, of the tribe of Judah (one of the twelve sons of Jacob), of the line of Jesse (the father of David) and from the house of David (the youngest of the eight sons of Jesse).

All texts above are widely accepted as references to the Messiah's family line. Even early Jewish rabbinic writings concur, such as the Targum in Jeremiah 23:5 *"And I will raise up for David the Messiah the Just."* This is one of the passages from which, according to rabbinic views, one of the Names of the Messiah is derived: Jehovah our Righteousness.[373] Throughout the Jewish Talmud are references to *"Son of David"* as the Messiah.

Lastly, we also hear the Jews dispute that Jesus was the Messiah because: *"How can the Christ come from Galilee? Does not the Scripture say that the Christ will come from David's family and from Bethlehem, the town where David lived'"* (John 7:41-42)? This confirms that the Jews knew the prophecies about the bloodline as well as the birthplace (see below) of the Messiah.

BORN IN BETHLEHEM

Prophecy	Fulfillment
Micah 5:2: *"But you, Bethlehem Ephrathah, though you are small among the clans of Judah, out of you will come for me one who will be ruler over Israel, whose origins are from of old, from ancient times."*	Matthew 2:1: *"Jesus was born in Bethlehem of Judea"* See also Matthew 2:4, Luke 2:4-7, John 7:42.

Micah, a seventh century BC prophet, predicted the birth of the Messiah would occur in the village of Bethlehem. This tiny town was uniquely connected to David since it was both his birthplace and the home of Jesse his father (1 Samuel 15:16: *"The Lord said to Samuel, '… I am sending you to Jesse of Bethlehem. I have chosen one of his sons to be king.'"*). The birthplace of the Messiah would be a humble place, a town forgotten by the rich and the powerful. Bethlehem was, and is yet today, a forgettable village, hard to locate on a map.

There is also no doubt that the rabbinical authorities of the time of Jesus clearly understood Bethlehem would be the Messiah's birthplace. This was confirmed by the magi's visit with Herod on the way to find Jesus (Matthew 2:4-5), *"When he [Herod] had called together all the people's chief priests and teachers of the law, he asked them where the Christ was to be born. 'In Bethlehem in Judea,' they replied, 'for this is what the prophet has written.'"* Look also once again at John 7:41-42. The rabbinic traditions, oral and written, testify to the Messianic nature of Micah's prophecy.[374]

PRECEDED BY A MESSENGER

Prophecy	Fulfillment
Isaiah 40:3: *"A voice of one calling: 'in the desert prepare the way of the Lord; make straight in the wilderness a highway for our God'"* Malachi 3:1: *"'See, I will send my messenger, who will prepare the way before me. Then suddenly the Lord you are seeking will come to his temple; the messenger of the covenant, whom you desire, will come.' Says the Lord Almighty."*	Matthew 3:1,2: *"In those days John the Baptist came, preaching in the Desert of Judea, and saying, 'Repent, for the kingdom of heaven is near.'"* See also John 1:23 and Luke 1:76-79 and Mark 1:1-4.

All four gospel writers identify this text in Isaiah as an allusion to John the Baptist as the forerunner of Christ, and it is referred to as Messianic in Jewish sources.[375]

ENTER JERUSALEM ON A DONKEY

Prophecy	Fulfillment
Zechariah 9:9: *"Rejoice greatly, O Daughter of Zion! Shout, Daughter of Jerusalem! See, your king comes to you, righteous and having salvation, gentle and riding on a donkey, on a colt, the foal of a donkey."*	Luke 19:29-37: *"He [Jesus] sent two of his disciples, saying to them, 'Go to the village ahead of you, and as you enter it, you will find a colt tied there, which no one has ever ridden. Untie it and bring it here'……They brought it to Jesus, threw their cloaks on the colt and put Jesus on it. As he went along, people spread their cloaks on the road."* Also Matthew 21:1-11, Mark 11:1-11, John 12:12-19.

This is the only Messianic prophecy recorded in the gospels deliberately fulfilled by Jesus. It is also linked to the one day and single event when Jesus deliberately drew attention to Himself on what is known as Palm Sunday.[376] Numerous Jewish sources confirm the recognition of this text as Messianic during the time of Jesus.[377]

SOLD FOR THIRTY PIECES OF SILVER

Prophecy	Fulfillment
Zechariah 11:12: *"I told them, 'If you think it best, give me my pay; but if not, keep it.' So they paid me thirty pieces of silver."*	Matthew 26:15: *" 'What are you willing to give me if I hand him over to you?' So they counted out for him thirty silver coins."* Also Mark 14:10-11 and Luke 22:3-6.

Thirty pieces of silver was the price of compensation for a slave injured by an ox as specified in the Mosaic Law (Exodus 21:32). A Jewish commentary recognizes this as Messianic;[378] however, many do disagree if this points to Judas or whether it is out of context. All synoptic gospels mention Judas received money, but only Matthew tells the price: thirty silver coins.

GARMENTS PARTED AND LOTS CAST

Prophecy	Fulfillment
Psalm 22:18: *"They divide My garments among them, and cast lots for My clothing."*	John 19:23-24: *"When the soldiers crucified Jesus, they took his clothes, dividing them into four shares, one for each of them, with the undergarment remaining. This garment was seamless, woven in one piece from top to bottom. 'Let's not tear it,' they said to one another. 'Let's decide by lot who will get it.'"*

Psalm 22 is considered a stunning account of the crucifixion, and we will discuss this in detail later. At first glance the prophecy appears to contradict itself. John's account of the scene at the foot of the cross explains how Jesus' clothes were divided, but a seamless undergarment was awarded by the casting of lots.

TO SUFFER THIRST, GALL AND VINEGAR OFFERED TO HIM

Prophecy	Fulfillment
Psalm 69:21: *"They put gall in my food and gave me vinegar for my thirst."*	John 19:28: *"Later.... Jesus said, 'I am thirsty.'"* Matthew 27:34: *"There they offered Jesus wine to drink, mixed with gall; but after tasting it, he refused to drink it."* Also John 19:28-29, Mark 15:23, Luke 23:36.

The details of the gall and vinegar offered to Jesus on the cross are mentioned in all four gospels. In that respect it fits remarkably with the passage from the psalm. Early Jewish sources however, quite understandably, did not recognize this verse to speak of the Messiah.

BONES NOT BROKEN

Prophecy	Fulfillment
Psalm 34:19-20: *"A righteous man may have many troubles, but the LORD delivers him from them all; he protects all his bones, not one of them will be broken."*	John 19:33: *"But when they came to Jesus and found that he was already dead, they did not break his legs."*

Just as with the previous prophecy, this passage was not seen to be Messianic by the Jewish commentators in Jesus' generation. However, the exact details are quite astounding. For instance, Jesus' bones were not broken, though the legs of criminals crucified next to Him were broken by the Romans to speed up their death. In order for Jesus to fulfill the requirements of the Mosaic Law to be the perfect Passover lamb, He would have to be "unblemished," i.e. without physical deformity.[379]

HIS SIDE PIERCED

Prophecy	Fulfillment
Zechariah 12:10: *"They will look on me, the one they have pierced..."*	John 19:34: *"Instead, one of the soldiers pierced Jesus' side with a spear,"*

The Roman soldier pierced Jesus' side with a spear to make sure that He was indeed dead.

PSALM 22 AS MESSIANIC PROPHECY

Both Mark 15:34 and Matthew 26:46 record that Jesus cried out on the cross: *"My God, my God, why have you forsaken me."* It is remarkable to learn that these words were actually quoting the first verse of Psalm 22, written 1,000 years earlier by David. The Bible does not record the circumstances under which David wrote this psalm, but clearly he felt abandoned and desperate at the time. However, despite his despair, David firmly clung to the truth that God was still his God, and he lost neither his hope nor his faith.

Some depictions in Psalm 22 go far beyond any sufferings David himself experienced. There is no known incident in the life of David that exactly corresponds to the words of this psalm. What might have been true of David as a type of one who suffered was literally fulfilled by the sufferings of Christ. Knowing what we know now about Jesus' crucifixion, the text of Psalm 22

Prophecy in Psalm 22		Fulfillment
1	*"My God, my God, why have you forsaken me"*	Matthew 27:46: *"About the ninth hour Jesus cried out in a loud voice, 'Eloi, Eloi, lama sabachthani?'—which means, 'My God, my God, why have you forsaken me?'"* Also Mark 15:34.
6-8	*"But I am a worm and not a man, scorned by men and despised by the people.* *All who see me mock me;* *they hurl insults, shaking their heads:* *'He trusts in the LORD;* *let the LORD rescue him.* *Let him deliver him,* *since he delights in him.'"*	Luke 23:35-39: *"They said, 'He saved others; let him save himself if he is the Christ of God, the Chosen One.' The soldiers ..... said, 'If you are the king of the Jews, save yourself.' ..... One of the criminals who hung there hurled insults at him: 'Aren't you the Christ? Save yourself and us!'"*
14	*"I am poured out like water, and all my bones are out of joint. My heart has turned to wax; it has melted away within me."*	John 19:34: *"Instead, one of the soldiers pierced Jesus' side with a spear, bringing a sudden flow of blood and water."*
15	*"My strength is dried up like a potsherd,* *and my tongue sticks to the roof of my mouth; you lay me in the dust of death."*	John 19:28: *"Later.... Jesus said, 'I am thirsty.'"*
16	*"Dogs have surrounded me;* *a band of evil men has encircled me,* *they have pierced my hands and my feet."*	Luke 23:33: *"When they came to the place called the Skull, there they crucified him, along with the criminals—one on his right, the other on his left."* Also John 20:25.
17	*"I can count all my bones;* *people stare and gloat over me."*	Luke 23:35: *"The people stood watching, and the rulers even sneered at him."*
18	*"They divide my garments among them* *and cast lots for my clothing."*	John 19:23-24: *"When the soldiers crucified Jesus, they took his clothes, dividing them into four shares, one for each of them, with the undergarment remaining. This garment was seamless, woven in one piece from top to bottom. 'Let's not tear it,' they said to one another. 'Let's decide by lot who will get it.'"*

described details of a crucifixion in remarkably accurate detail. This is even more fascinating when one considers that in the days of David, stoning was the accepted method of execution, and death by crucifixion was not even invented until 600 years later – 400 years before Jesus!

Isaiah 53, The Servant Song as a Description of Jesus

If you were impressed with Psalm 22, take a seat as you get ready to read Isaiah chapter 53. The nature and meaning of the Messiah's death are nowhere described more significantly than in this magnificent chapter. All Biblical scholars, no matter what the theological persuasion, recognize it as one of the true high points of Biblical revelation. Old Testament commentator Franz Delitzsch called it *"the most central, the deepest, and the most lofty thing that the Old Testament prophecy, outstripping itself, has ever achieved."* [380]

Here's a summary of Isaiah's classic prophecy:[381]

- In the prologue (Isaiah 52:13-15), the prophet Isaiah asserted on behalf of God that the Lord's Servant would ultimately be exalted (verse 13) as well as honored among the Gentiles (verse 15), but only after dreadful personal suffering (verse 14).
- In the body of the song (53:1-9), Isaiah confessed on behalf of his people that (1) Israel utterly rejected the Servant of the Lord in his life (verses 1-3) (2) as well as in his death (verses 7-9) because (3) the nation misjudged his death and assumed he died for his own sins rather than for the nation's transgressions (verses 4-6).
- In the epilogue of (53:10-12), the prophet asserted on behalf of God that the Servant's completed work of atonement would exalt God (verse 10), believers would be justified (verse 11), and the Servant himself would be honored (verse 12).

As you read through Isaiah's much-loved chapter, realize this was written around 700 BC, more than seven full centuries before Jesus' death. Therefore, this passage was completed hundreds of years before crucifixion was invented. Also, in the Dead Sea Scrolls, several Isaiah scrolls were discovered, including more than one complete copy of this chapter, thus providing undeniable, physical evidence these writings existed more than 150 years before Jesus' crucifixion.

Prophecy in Isaiah 53	Fulfillment
3	*"He was despised and rejected by men, a man of sorrows, and familiar with suffering. Like one from whom men hide their faces he was despised, and we esteemed him not."*	Matthew 27:39-44: *"Those who passed by hurled insults at him....."* Matthew 26:38: *"Then he [Jesus] said to them, 'My soul is overwhelmed with sorrow to the point of death.'"* Mark 8:31: *"He then began to teach them that the Son of Man must suffer many things."*
4	*"Surely he took up our infirmities and carried our sorrows, yet we considered him stricken by God, smitten by him, and afflicted."*	Matthew 8:16-17: *"he [Jesus] drove out the spirits with a word and healed all the sick."* Also Mark 1:29-34 and Luke 4:38-41.
5	*"But he was pierced for our transgressions, he was crushed for our iniquities; the punishment that brought us peace was upon him, and by his wounds we are healed."*	John 19:33-37: *"But when they came to Jesus and found that he was already dead, they did not break his legs. Instead, one of the soldiers pierced Jesus' side with a spear,....."* Matthew 20:28: *"the Son of Man did not come to be served, but to serve, and to give his life as a ransom for many."*
6	*"We all, like sheep, have gone astray, each of us has turned to his own way; and the LORD has laid on him the iniquity of us all."*	
7	*"He was oppressed and afflicted, yet he did not open his mouth; he was led like a lamb to the slaughter, and as a sheep before her shearers is silent, so he did not open his mouth."*	Matthew 26:63: *"But Jesus remained silent."*
8	*"By oppression and judgment he was taken away. And who can speak of his descendants? For he was cut off from the land of the living; for the transgression of my people he was stricken."*	1 Corinthians 15:3: *"For what I received I passed on to you as of first importance : that Christ died for our sins according to the Scriptures,"*
9	*"He was assigned a grave with the wicked, and with the rich in his death, though he had done no violence, nor was any deceit in his mouth."*	Matthew 27:57-60: *".....Joseph took the body, wrapped it in a clean linen cloth, and placed it in his own new tomb."* Also 1 Peter 2:21-25.
12	*"For he bore the sin of many, and made intercession for the transgressors."*	Luke 23:34: *"Jesus said, 'Father, forgive them, for they do not know what they are doing.'"*

DID THE JEWS ALSO RECOGNIZE THE MESSIANIC PROPHECIES?

As the Jewish ideas about the Messiah were based on the same Old Testament passages studied by Christians, we need not wonder why they also embodied the chief features of the Messianic history. Careful analysis of their Scripture quotations shows that the main Messianic claims made by the New Testament writers concerning Christ are fully supported by the statements of the Jewish rabbis. The list is quite long. It includes doctrines such as the *pre-creation existence* of the Messiah; His *elevation* above Moses, and even above angels; His *representative* character; His cruel *sufferings*; His *violent death*, and that *for His people*; His *work* on behalf of the living and of the dead; His *redemption*, and the *restoration* of Israel; the *opposition* of the Gentiles; their partial *judgment* and *conversion*; the *prevalence* of His *Law*; the *universal blessings* of the latter days; and His *Kingdom*. All this can be clearly deduced from the ancient Jewish writings. Only, as we might expect, all is much less developed than as in the Christian view where we have the advantage of 20/20 hindsight. Jewish commentaries see these passages as nothing more than unfulfilled prophecy – the haze of the sun about to rise, not the blaze once it has risen. Indeed, the writings of the Jewish rabbis frequently refer to the sufferings, and even the death of the Messiah, and these are connected to our sins – how could it be otherwise in view of Isaiah 53? In one most remarkable comment, the Messiah is seen willingly to take upon Himself all these sufferings, all on the condition that all Israel – the living, the dead, and those yet unborn – should be saved, and that, in consequence of His work, God and Israel should be reconciled, and Satan cast into hell. Reference to the removal of sin by the Messiah, in the sense of vicarious sufferings, is only dimly portrayed, if at all.[382]

COULD THIS HAVE BEEN MERE COINCIDENCE?

Could Jesus have fulfilled these prophecies only by chance? Did He just happen to be at the right place at the right time? How unlikely this is can be illustrated by making simple calculations.

Let us limit ourselves to just a few prophecies, and estimate the probability that these would be fulfilled simultaneously:[383]

- **A Son of David.** What is the chance for any person alive, or who ever has lived in world history, to have been a descendant of David? To make an estimate, let's assume that only one in 100 of people have been Jews. That is likely much too high, but let's be safe. Next assume one in every 100 of these is a descendant of David (again the actual number is likely less, but let's stay on the safe side). That means one in every 100x100 = one out of every 10,000 people alive today or who has ever lived, could have had David as his (grand, grand, grand...grand) father.
- **Born in Bethlehem.** What were the chances that a "son of David" would be born in the tiny village of Bethlehem? Assume descendants of David are statistically evenly spread across Israel. In Jesus' generation, Bethlehem

might have had some 500 inhabitants. Of the estimated 500 million people alive then, about five million would have been Jews. Any Jew would have had a chance in the order of magnitude of 500/5,000,000 or one in 10,000 to be born in Bethlehem. This was in Jesus' days, but as Bethlehem is still a small town, these numbers are not likely to have improved much.

- **To be crucified.** Jesus was crucified and the Messianic prophecies predict in detail a death much like a crucifixion (Psalm 22, Isaiah 53, etc.). Historians estimate throughout human history as many as 100,000 people may have suffered Roman crucifixion. Let's assume any descendant of David had statistically the same chance as being crucified as any other person. To be safe we'll use the 100,000 number and compare that not to the total number of people who ever lived, but to only the 500,000,000 people estimated to be alive in the days of Jesus. We use that number because crucifixion was abandoned only a few centuries later and we want our estimates to be as conservative as reasonably possible. That means anybody would have a chance of 100,000 in 500,000,000 or one in 5,000 to die by crucifixion.

Where does this exercise lead? We can now calculate the statistical probability for any person who ever lived to meet the above three conditions simultaneously: descendant of David, born in Bethlehem, died by crucifixion. As the individual probabilities were estimated as independent chances, the probability of all three conditions being fulfilled at the same time is the product of these individual chances. This is a chance of one in 10,000 (10^4) x 10,000 (10^4) x 5,000 (5×10^3) = one in 500,000,000,000 = one in 500 billion. Compare that to the 500 million people estimated to be alive in the time of Jesus or even the 10 billion people who ever lived and/or are alive today on our planet. Fulfilling even these three conditions merely by chance becomes quite unlikely!

In his classic work, *Science Speaks,*[384] mathematician Peter W. Stoner presents detailed calculations for the probabilities that anyone would fit the Messianic profile by chance. He shows that the chance for fulfilling just eight prophecies is in the order of magnitude of one in 10^{28} (to refresh your memory: that is 10 with 28 zeroes, or 10,000 trillion trillion).

Since the best estimate for the number of people who have ever lived and are now alive on earth is around 10 billion (10^{10}), the probability is one in 10^{18} (1 million trillion) for anybody to fulfill just these eight prophecies purely by random chance.

Stoner goes on to explain the chances for 16 prophecies fulfilled in anyone's life are 1 in 10^{45}. For 48 prophecies, the chances skyrocket to an even more amazing one in 10^{157}.

To illustrate how unlikely it is that Jesus, by mere chance, became the "right" person we will do one other calculation. Assume there are only 100 Messianic prophecies (the lowest number of any list). Assume also that each prophecy has a chance of one in 10 to be fulfilled. So we simply estimate that one man in 10 is a descendant of David; one man in 10 was born in Bethlehem; one man in 10 was born of a virgin; one man in 10 was preceded by a messenger and so on; obviously grossly overestimated probabilities. Even this approach would lead to a chance of one fulfilling all 100 prophecies to be one in 10x10x10x...x10 (hundred times) = one in 10^{100}.

Recall the silver dollar illustration.[385] A chance of one in 10^{25} is the equivalent of a blindfolded person finding, on the first try, one certain coin on the total land surface of the U.S.A. where every available square inch is covered with a pile of silver dollars 10 miles high.

A one in 10^{100} chance is like performing this experiment successfully – four times in a row!

OBJECTIONS AGAINST THE EVIDENCE OF THE PROPHECIES

Of course critics have worked hard and been very creative in challenging the claim that Jesus indeed fulfilled the Old Testament Messianic prophecies. Let's have a look at the most common objections.

- **It is all just coincidence.** This argument claims Jesus merely fulfilled all prophecies by accident. He could even be one of many in history who might have fit the prophetic fingerprint. In the previous paragraph we examined the improbability (no, impossibility would be a better word) of such an astounding coincidence.

  And ... Jesus is the only person in history who claimed to have fulfilled all prophecies.

- **The altered gospel argument.** Is it possible the gospel writers fabricated details to make it appear Jesus fulfilled prophecies? For example: prophecies predict the Messiah's bones would remain unbroken, so maybe John invented the story about the Romans leaving His legs unbroken even thought they broke the legs of the thieves crucified with Jesus. And prophecies speak of betrayal for 30 pieces of silver. Was Matthew creative with the facts and invented the account of Judas selling out Jesus for that same amount?

  This argument, however, makes little sense once we realize the weight of evidence presented earlier for the reliability and accuracy of the gospel accounts. When they were first circulated, the generation that personally experienced Jesus was still alive and would have objected to the record of any events that never occurred.

What's more, disbelievers would have jumped on any opportunity to discredit the gospels by pointing out such false claims. Even though documents of the Jewish Talmud, for instance, refer to Jesus in derogatory ways, they never once claim the fulfillment of the prophecies was falsified. Not one time!

- **The intentional fulfillment argument.** Some skeptics assert that Jesus merely maneuvered His life to fulfill prophecies. They argue, *"He must have read Zechariah, so he just arranged to ride a donkey into Jerusalem in order to fulfill the prophecy."*

  For a few prophecies this argument might be conceivable, such as riding a donkey into the city, being silent before His accusers, and quoting scripture texts while on the cross. However, the vast majority of prophecies were not under His control.

  How could Jesus control the Sanhedrin's offer to Judas of 30 pieces of silver? How could He arrange His ancestry, or the place of His birth, or the method of His execution, or that soldiers gambled for His clothes, or that His legs remained unbroken? How could He arrange to work miracles in front of skeptics? How could He arrange His resurrection? How could He arrange His conception? … Only if He were God – then He could!

- **The context argument.** Do passages Christians see as Messianic prophecies really point to the Messiah, or do Christians misinterpret them out of context?

  This argument sounds, on the surface, reasonable. However, with deeper analysis it does not go very far. Most of the prophecies about the Messiah were already known quite well by Jews centuries before Jesus. They were not always completely and correctly understood, but they were well-known.

The strongest counter argument to any claim of manipulation of the Messianic prophecies is the invitation to do personal research. All information is present in the Bible – spend the time and energy to research for yourself. You will find all the evidence you need!

"Everything must be fulfilled that is written about me in the Law of Moses, the Prophets and the Psalms" (Luke 24:44).

It has all been fulfilled, but only in Jesus – the sole individual in history who has matched the prophetic profile of God's anointed one.

CHAPTER 21

Did the Resurrection Really Happen?

*"The angel said to the women, 'Do not be afraid, for I know
that you are looking for Jesus, who was crucified.
He is not here; he has risen, just as he said.'"*
MATTHEW 28:5,6

WITHOUT THE RESURRECTION OUR FAITH IS FUTILE

Believing Jesus to have been a great moral teacher implies His teachings are true. Since He taught that He Himself is God, He logically must be God. The thirty-five miracles in the four gospels prove Jesus had powers beyond our human limitations. The nature miracles provide strong confirmations of His divine claims. The hundreds of prophecies of the Messiah in the Old Testament were all fulfilled by Jesus of Nazareth, and that far beyond coincidence.

However, not to diminish the importance of this evidence, all claims of Jesus stand or fall with His resurrection. Without the resurrection, His claim to be the Son of God; that is, deity in human flesh, vanishes into thin air. Without the resurrection, His death as payment for our sins is meaningless. Without the resurrection, we are wasting our time.

The importance of the resurrection was immediately recognized by the apostles, and we find statement after statement in the New Testament emphasizing the importance of Jesus' full and complete victory over death. In the words of Paul (1 Corinthians 15:13-22, emphasis added):

"If there is no resurrection of the dead, then not even Christ has been raised. And if Christ has not been raised, our preaching is useless and so is your faith. More than that, we are then found to be false witnesses about God, for we have testified about God that he raised Christ from the dead. But he did not raise him if in fact the dead are not raised. For if the dead are not raised, then Christ has not been raised either. And if Christ has not been raised, your faith is futile; you are still in your sins. Then those also who have fallen asleep in Christ are lost. If only for this life we have hope in Christ, we are to be pitied more than all men.
But Christ has indeed been raised from the dead, the first fruits of those who have fallen asleep. For since death came through a man, the resur-

*rection of the dead comes also through a man. For as in Adam all die, <u>so
in Christ all will be made alive.</u>"*

The resurrection is the ultimate miracle provided for us by God in order
to prove beyond any doubt that Jesus is indeed the Son of God. No one in history successfully claimed to have resurrected himself from death. Nor does any
other world religion claim a miracle such as the resurrection, or anything even
near this magnitude.

Respected Christian scholar William Lane Craig writes:[386]

*"Without the belief in the resurrection the Christian faith could not have
come into being. The disciples would have remained crushed and defeated men. Even had they continued to remember Jesus as their beloved
teacher, His crucifixion would have forever silenced any hopes of His being
the Messiah. The cross would have remained the sad and shameful end of
His career. The origin of Christianity therefore hinges on the belief of the
early disciples that God had raised Jesus from the dead."*

The existence of a spiritual world

The resurrection proves Jesus' deity, but also gives us a glimpse
into the existence of another world, a spiritual one. As we studied earlier[387] the scientific analysis of Big Bang creation points to the existence of at least six other dimensions. Their presence can be shown
theoretically, but we have no ability to observe them. Likewise, Jesus'
resurrection gives us insight into other dimensions beyond our comprehension. Jesus went there when He died and returned when He
resurrected. The resurrection accounts in the gospels tell that afterwards Jesus had a physical body, but He could appear and disappear
instantaneously (John 20:19-29).

HOW DOES ONE PROVE THE RESURRECTION?

How does one prove one of the most extravagant claims in human history?
How does one prove that 2,000 years ago a carpenter executed as a criminal
came back to life after three days and then appeared to many of His followers?
Despite the fact that written historical accounts of those days are few, it is still
possible to build a strong compelling case on a solid foundation of factual evidence for the resurrection of Jesus. The case is made in three logical steps:

• **Jesus died on the cross.** To prove the resurrection, we first must establish that Jesus did indeed die on the cross. If He survived, any attempt

to claim a resurrection could have been only gross deception. Only if we can prove it was not possible for Him to have survived the cross, can we take the next step in our investigation.

- **Three days after He was buried, His grave was found empty.** What happened to Jesus' physical body after His death? Could it have been stolen or perhaps eaten by animals? Or was it buried as the gospels claim. And if so, was that grave empty the following Sunday? If so, what happened to the body? The missing body alone proves nothing, but the empty grave is a necessary condition for the resurrection claim. If an alternative explanation is supported by the evidence, or even, if His body was located and identified, then the whole claim for the resurrection collapses.
- **He appeared before eyewitnesses to prove that He was alive again.** To prove that He returned to life after His death, it is imperative to investigate the encounters of the witnesses who saw Him alive. Outrageous claims require outrageous testimony. So to validate the resurrection claim, we must examine the testimonies of as many witnesses as possible. Get ready for a real surprise. Not only do the gospels tell about Jesus' resurrection, but there are also testimonies from the other New Testament writers, Early Church Leaders, and the conversions of some remarkable individuals.

First we will systematically present the evidences for the resurrection. Next we will investigate the possible alternative explanations that try to explain the resurrection "away."

✻ EXHIBIT #4: JESUS WAS CRUCIFIED UNDER PONTIUS PILATE
Both Biblical and non-Biblical sources provide numerous confirmations that Jesus of Nazareth was crucified under the Roman governor Pontius Pilate:

Biblical sources:
- **Gospel of Mark:** *"Wanting to satisfy the crowd, Pilate released Barabbas to them. He had Jesus flogged, and handed him over to be crucified"* (Mark 15:15).
- **Gospel of Matthew:** *"Then he released Barabbas to them. But he had Jesus flogged, and handed him over to be crucified"* (Matthew 27:26).
- **Gospel of Luke:** *"When they came to the place called the Skull, there they crucified him, along with the criminals – one on his right, the other on his left"* (Luke 23:33).
- **Gospel of John:** *"Finally Pilate handed him over to them to be crucified"* (John (19:16).
- **Paul:** *"May I never boast except in the cross of our Lord Jesus Christ, through which the world has been crucified to me, and I to the world"* (Galatians 5:14).

Early Church Leaders:
- **Ignatius writing to the Trallians (ca. 105 AD):** *"On the day of the prepa-ration, then, at the third hour, He received the sentence from Pilate, the Father permitting that to happen; at the sixth hour He was crucified; at the ninth hour He gave up the ghost; and before sunset He was buried."* [388]
- **Justin Martyr's First Apology (ca. 150 AD):** *"Our teacher of these things is Jesus Christ, who also was born for this purpose, and was crucified under Pontius Pilate, procurator of Judaea, in the times of Tiberius Caesar."* [389]
- **Irenaeus Against Heresies (ca. 180 AD):** *"that He was Christ Jesus, who was crucified under Pontius Pilate."* [390]

Non-Biblical Writers: [391]
- **Jewish historian Josephus (ca. 70-90 AD):** *"when Pilate, at the sugges-tion of the principal men amongst us, had condemned him to the cross."* [392]
- **Roman historian Tacitus (ca. 116 AD):** *"Christus, from whom the name had its origin, suffered the extreme penalty during the reign of Tiberius at the hands of one of our procurators, Pontius Pilatus."* [393]
- **The Jewish Talmud (ca. 100-200 AD):** *"On the eve of the Passover Yeshu [Jesus] was hanged [crucified]."* [394]

The historical confirmations are beyond dispute. Even the most critical scholars who argue that the Bible is just a collection of fabricated stories and the resurrection never happened, accept that the crucifixion is a historical fact. John Dominic Crossan, one of the founders of the liberal Jesus Seminar [395] admits the crucifixion is *"as sure as anything historical can ever be."* [396]

✴ EXHIBIT #5: ROMAN CRUCIFIXION INEVITABLY LED TO DEATH

Before looking into the confirmations of Jesus' death in the Scriptures, it is important to know what crucifixion entailed. Death by crucifixion was the method of execution preferred during the Roman Empire, and there are exten-sive historical records about the procedure. [397]

The practice originated with the Persians near 400 BC, and later passed to the Carthaginians and the Phoenicians. The Romans perfected it as a method of capital punishment, which caused maximum pain and suffering over a sig-nificant period of time. In fact, the word *excruciate* (meaning, "to cause great agony, torment") comes from the Latin for *"from, or out of, the cross."* Romans preferred crucifixion over other executions because of its fear effect. The choice of a highly visible site such as near a major city gate (like Calvary) would ensure that the prolonged painful suffering of victims would be seen over and again by large numbers of people. This maximum exposure would cause oppressed people to refuse to risk the same torturous death. The practice was abandoned by Constantine around 400 AD. Historians estimate 10,000 to 100,000 people (likely much closer to the higher number) were crucified by the Romans.

Crucifixion typically started by scourging or flogging the victim's back. This is explicitly detailed in the gospels, such as Mark 15:15 (emphasis added): "*Wanting to satisfy the crowd, Pilate released Barabbas to them. He had Jesus flogged, and handed him over to be crucified.*" The Romans used a whip called a *flagrum*, with small pieces of bone and metal attached to several leather strands. The number of blows given to Jesus is not recorded; however, the number in Jewish law was thirty-nine (one less than the forty prescribed by the Torah to prevent that a counting error would lead to too many blows). The scourging ripped skin from the back, creating a bloody mass of tissue and bone. Extreme blood loss occurred, often causing death, or, at the very least, unconsciousness.

The about seven-foot vertical post, called the *stipes* was usually already in place at the execution site. Often this was a tree, hence the frequent reference to crucifixion as "*hanging on a tree.*" The crossbar or *patibulum*, was often carried to the execution site by the victim. The patibulum could easily weigh 100 pounds. After the flogging, Jesus was in a weakened state, it's no wonder that He needed assistance. Mark 15:21: "*A certain man from Cyrene, Simon, the father of Alexander and Rufus, was passing by on his way in from the country, and they forced him to carry the cross.*" Once the victim arrived at the execution site, the patibulum was placed on the ground, and the victim was forced to lie down upon it. Spikes about seven inches long and about 3/8 of an inch in diameter were driven through the wrists. The patibulum was lifted to the stipes, and the body turned so the feet could be nailed to the stipes. [398]

Beyond the excruciating pain, crucifixion made respiration, particularly exhalation difficult and extremely painful. Adequate exhalation required lifting the body by pushing up on the feet, and by flexing the elbows and adducting the shoulders. However, this maneuver would place the entire weight of the body on the tarsals and produce searing pain. Furthermore, flexion of the elbows would cause rotation of the wrists around the iron nails and cause fiery pain along the damaged nerves. Raising the body would also painfully scrape the scourged back against the rough wooden stipes. As a result, each respiratory effort would become agonizing and tiring and lead eventually to asphyxia (suffocation). [399]

Several factors contributed to the actual cause of death by crucifixion and varied a bit with each case, but the two most prominent were hypovolemic shock (shock cause by reduced blood volumes) and exhaustion asphyxia. Other likely factors included dehydration, stress-induced arrhythmias and congestive heart failure.

☼ Exhibit #6: Jesus Actually Died on the Cross

An idea popular among non-believers over the centuries has been called the *swoon theory*. In different variations this theory claims Jesus did not really die, He only appeared to be dead, possibly because He had been drugged. He was revived while in the tomb. It is no miracle for a living man to walk out of a tomb. Objectively, however, evidence that Jesus really died on the cross is quite overwhelming:

- **The Roman soldiers were professionals.** The success of the Roman Empire was founded upon the iron discipline of its army. Generally, soldiers were lifetime professionals, skilled in dealing out death. The group of soldiers that crucified Jesus was likely a crucifixion team, well experienced in the procedure. So they knew very well what they were doing. They knew how to position and nail a person to the cross and they knew when he had died. Roman army rule would ensure no mistakes. If a soldier made a mistake in properly administering a punishment, Roman rule would impose that same punishment on the fumbling soldier. In other words, if a Roman soldier allowed a victim to survive crucifixion, he would be the next to be crucified. Yes, these soldiers were highly motivated to do their job right! Of the thousands of crucifixions, no case has ever been found, in either written documents or oral traditions, where the victim survived.

- **The Jews wanted Jesus to die.** The opponents of Jesus were watching. They had exerted tremendous effort to have Jesus arrested and convicted. It is no stretch of the imagination to know that they wanted to be absolutely certain that Jesus died. So they likely verified that themselves. The Jews never disputed Jesus' death either.

- **The gospels and Paul testify to his death.** All gospels explicitly mention Jesus' death:
  - Mark 15:37: *"With a loud cry, Jesus breathed his last."*
  - Matthew 27:50: *"he [Jesus] gave up his spirit."*
  - Luke 21:46: *"When he had said this, he breathed his last."*
  - John 19:30: *"With that, he bowed his head and gave up his spirit."*
  - 1 Corinthians 15: *"...that Christ died for our sins..."*

- **The soldiers did not break His legs.** John 19:32-33 reads: *"The soldiers therefore came and broke the legs of the first man who had been crucified with Jesus, and then those of the other. But when they came to Jesus and found that he was already dead, they did not break his legs."* The standard procedure to complete a crucifixion was to break the victim's legs below the knees (called *crucifracture*) so that he could not lift himself to exhale. The victim would then be asphyxiated as his lungs filled with carbon dioxide. They did break the legs of the two criminals. Yet the professional Roman executioners declared Christ dead without breaking His legs. There was no doubt in their minds.

- **The piercing of Jesus.** In John 19:34 we read: *"Instead, one of the soldiers pierced Jesus' side with a spear, bringing a sudden flow of blood and water."* When His side was pierced with a spear, water and blood flowed out. The best evidence suggests that this was a thrust given by a Roman soldier to ensure death. The spear entered through the rib cage and pierced His right lung, the sack around the heart, and the heart itself, releasing both blood and pleural fluids. Medical analysis suggests the flow of water-like fluids indicates Jesus was dead before this wound was inflicted. If not, the final wound to His side would have been fatal in itself.

- **Pilate's reaction to Jesus death.** Mark 15:44-45 records: *"Pilate was surprised to hear that he was already dead. Summoning the centurion, he asked him if Jesus had already died. When he learned from the centurion that it was so, he gave the body to Joseph."* So even Pilate himself made sure Jesus was dead.

☼ EXHIBIT #7: THE EVIDENCE OF THE MISSING BODY

All four gospel writers unanimously agree that Joseph of Arimathea claimed the body of Jesus after His death. Here is the account of Luke 23:50-56 (see also Matthew 27:57-61, Mark 15:42-47 and John 19:38-42):

"Now there was a man named Joseph, a member of the Council, a good and upright man, who had not consented to their decision and action. He came from the Judean town of Arimathea and he was waiting for the kingdom of God. Going to Pilate, he asked for Jesus' body. Then he took it down, wrapped it in linen cloth and placed it in a tomb cut in the rock, one in which no one had yet been laid. It was Preparation Day [the day before the Sabbath], *and the Sabbath* [Saturday] *was about to begin. The women who had come with Jesus from Galilee followed Joseph and saw the tomb and how his body was laid in it. Then they went home and prepared spices and perfumes. But they rested on the Sabbath in obedience to the commandment."*

Also, Paul mentions the burial of Jesus in 1 Corinthians 15:4: *"that he [Jesus] was buried."* Historically, the common practice was to leave the bodies of crucified victims on the cross as a warning for others as they viewed the decaying and mutilated corpses. Ultimately the victim's bodies became prey for birds and beasts or were thrown in a common grave. However there are also records of relatives or even friends allowed to claim the body of a victim.[400] Because of the independent, consistent testimony of all gospels and Paul, there is no reason to reject the burial account as fictitious.

It is important to notice that all gospels also mention the presence of women (Mary Magdalene, Mary the mother of Jesus, Salome, and others) at the burial on "*Preparation Day*" (still Friday, the same day as the crucifixion). As all gospels record, they (Mary Magdalene) are also the ones who discovered the empty grave. Some have claimed that the women found the grave empty on Sunday morning because "they just went to the wrong tomb." That is extremely unlikely if one realizes that all women were present only two days earlier during the burial. Matthew also mentions the posting of guards at the tomb.

Testimony about the Empty Grave			
	Burial	**Guards**	**Empty grave**
Matthew	27:57-61	27:62-66, 28:11-15	28:1-10
Mark	15:42-47		16:1-8
Luke	23:50-56		24:1-12
John	19:38-42		20:1-9

Table 21-1: Testimony about the Empty Grave

Finding an empty grave by itself does not yet prove a resurrection. However the fact that the grave was empty is essential to the resurrection's truthfulness. If anybody would have been able to produce Jesus' body, any resurrection claims would be voided.[401]

Is Sunday the second or the third day?

All accounts of the resurrection claim that Jesus was raised on the third day. However as this was a Sunday and Jesus died on a Friday, should that not be the second day? And was Jesus not effectively in the grave for one and a half day instead of three days?

This apparent contradiction is explained by understanding first century Jewish culture. In those days a new day started at dusk. So Friday would actually have started on Thursday night after sunset and would have ended on Friday at sunset. Additionally, it was custom to count part of a day as a full day. So as Jesus was buried on Friday, before the Sabbath, therefore before sunset, the Friday was counted as the first day, Saturday/Sabbath as the second day and Sunday (morning) as the third day. This same principle applies in the counting of weeks, months, years and so on.

The case for the empty tomb and Jesus' missing body is strongly supported by the evidences:[402]

- **The discovery was made by women.** In the first century women were not considered reliable witnesses. So the fact that women are in all gospels named as the first witnesses to the empty tomb is very significant, since their word would have been widely rejected. If the account would have been invented, surely a man (why not Joseph of Arimathea himself?) would have been chosen to make that discovery.
- **Paul confirms the empty grave.** Paul testifies in 1 Corinthians 15:3-4: *"that Christ died for our sins according to the Scriptures, that he was buried, that he was raised on the third day according to the Scriptures."* Paul does not explicitly mention an empty grave but implies that after burial Jesus rose, hence His body must have been gone.
- **The Jerusalem factor.** Jesus was publicly executed in Jerusalem and it was here the apostles at Pentecost, only 50 days later, began to proclaim the resurrection. It would, for obvious reasons, have been completely impossible for the new faith to get off the ground in Jerusalem if the body had still been in the tomb.
- **The Jews never denied the empty tomb.** There are no recorded accounts of the Jews denying that the tomb was empty. In fact the opposite is true. They confirm the grave was empty, and in order to explain it, they claim that the disciples stole Jesus' body. Matthew 28:12-13: *"When the chief priests had met with the elders and devised a plan, they gave the soldiers a large sum of money, telling them, 'You are to say, "His disciples came during the night and stole him away while we were asleep."'"*

☼ EXHIBIT #8: THE RESURRECTION APPEARANCES

Several appearances of the resurrected Jesus are recounted in the gospels and Acts – some to individuals and others to groups, some indoors and others outdoors, some to softhearted people, and others to skeptical doubters. Some persons touched Jesus or ate with Him, so there is no doubt that He was physically present. The appearances occurred over a forty-day period between his resurrection and the celebration of Pentecost. There are good reasons to trust these accounts as they are not only – as we have proved – by credible witnesses, they are also quite to the fact, devoid of typical "mythical tendencies" one might expect if the account was written to impress the readers.

The following (table 21-2) is a list of all the appearances as listed in the Bible:[403]

Resurrection Appearances in the New Testament	
To whom	**Scripture reference**
Mary Magdalene	John 20:10-18
The "other" women	Matthew 28:8-10
Cleopas and another disciple on the road to Emmaus	Luke 24:13-32
Eleven disciples and others	Luke 24:33-49
Ten apostles and others (without Thomas)	John 20:19-23
Thomas and the other apostles	John 20:26-30
Seven apostles	John 21:1-14
The disciples	Matthew 28:16-20
With the apostles on the Mount of Olives before his ascension	Luke 24:50-52 and Acts 1:4-9
To 500 people, including other appearances and Paul	1 Corinthians 15

Table 21-2: Resurrection Appearances in the New Testament

These ten different accounts of the appearances of Jesus by five different witnesses are strong compelling evidence. Especially, as we should realize, and this cannot be overemphasized:

- We have five (including Paul) independent and reliable eye-witnesses.
- Even with a liberal approach to dating the gospels, all documents were written before the end of the first century (and likely much earlier).[404]
- The accounts are consistent in timing and experience, and they support each other in all the main events. There are variations in the details of the sequence of the appearances, but those differences support the credibility of individual, independent testimony, and can be harmonized.[405]
- The appearances are to various individuals or groups of people, including numerous non-believers.

Also the writings of the Early Church Leaders include accounts of the resurrection. Of greatest interest are letters written by the disciples of the apostles. These men had been personally taught by and were in close fellowship with the apostles. Their writings are not eyewitness testimony, but these personal accounts reveal what the apostles shared regarding their resurrection experiences and how it affected their lives:[406]

Resurrection Confirmations by the Early Church	
Source	**Text**
Clement of Rome writing to the Corinthians (ca. 95 AD)	*"Let us consider, beloved, how the Lord continually proves to us that there shall be a future resurrection, of which He has rendered the Lord Jesus Christ the first-fruits by raising Him from the dead."* [407]
	"Christ therefore was sent forth by God, and the apostles by Christ. Both these appointments, then, were made in an orderly way, according to the will of God. Having therefore received their orders, and being fully assured by the resurrection of our Lord Jesus Christ, and established in the word of God, with full assurance of the Holy Ghost, they went forth proclaiming that the kingdom of God was at hand." [408]
Polycarp writing to the Philippian church (ca. 110 AD)	*"......and in Paul himself, and the rest of the apostles. [This do] in the assurance that all these have not run in vain, but in faith and righteousness, and that they are [now] in their due place in the presence of the Lord, with whom also they suffered. For they loved not this present world, but Him who died for us, and for our sakes was raised again by God from the dead."* [409]

Table 21-3: Resurrection Confirmations by the Early Church

THE RESURRECTION CREED IN 1 CORINTHIANS 15

Here is a surprise for many readers: the earliest testimony in the Bible of the resurrection of Jesus is not found in the gospels, but in Paul's first letter to the Corinthian church. A little bit of background is needed. The book of Acts enables us to determine when Paul started the church at Corinth. When we read about Paul's second missionary journey, Acts 18:1-4 tells us: *"After this, Paul left Athens and went to Corinth. There he met a Jew named Aquila, a native of Pontus, who had recently come from Italy with his wife Priscilla, because Claudius had ordered all the Jews to leave Rome, Paul went to see them, and because he was a tentmaker as they were there, he stayed and worked with them. Every Sabbath he reasoned in the synagogue, trying to persuade Jews and Greeks."* So, Paul visited Corinth for the first time around the year 51 AD. He stayed there about eighteen months, and, as Acts 18:8 says: *"Many of the Corinthians who heard him believed and were baptized."*

At Ephesus during his third missionary journey about three or four years later, Paul heard of problems in Corinth when a delegation from that church visited him for advice. He quickly penned a letter to address his concerns. This is the letter we now know as the New Testament book 1 Corinthians. Scholars almost unanimously agree Paul was the author and the letter was written about the year 55 AD at Ephesus.[410] The writing of this letter was well within the eyewitness period, perhaps only twenty-two years after the crucifixion! In 1 Corinthians 15:1-8 we read:

> *"Now, brothers, I want to remind you of the gospel I preached to you, which you received and on which you have taken your stand. By this gospel you are saved, if you hold firmly to the word I preached to you. Otherwise, you have believed in vain. For what I received I passed on to you as of first importance: that Christ died for our sins according to the Scriptures, that he was buried, that he was raised on the third day according to the Scriptures, and that he appeared to Peter [Cephas, the Aramaic name of Peter is used in the Greek texts], and then to the Twelve. After that, he appeared to more than five hundred of the brothers at the same time, most of whom are still living, though some have fallen asleep. Then he appeared to James, then to all the apostles, and last of all he appeared to me also, as to one abnormally born."*

In the first sentence of above quotation, Paul reminded the Corinthians that "the following" is what he had told them during his first visit about three or four years earlier. That dates this statement only about eighteen years after the resurrection. Therefore it is older and actually closer to the events on Calvary than any other statement about the resurrection in the New Testament.

The passage (first part of verse 3) *"for what I received I passed on to you"* is of high relevance to trace the source of Paul's testimony. By this, Paul uses a traditional introduction that the following statements are passed along through him as a creed.[411] The word *creed* is derived from the Latin "credo," or "I believe." A creed is a confession of faith, a brief, authorized summary of Christian doctrine believed to have been recited in the early church as an affirmation of faith. In the passage, Paul mentions a total of six appearances; some described in the gospels, but some are mentioned only here in this letter. Let's have a look:

- **Jesus appeared to Peter** (or *Cephas* as the original text says). We do not have this appearance to Peter recorded in any of the gospels; however, John's gospel mentions a conversation between the resurrected Jesus and Peter. Luke 24:34 (*"It is true! The Lord has risen and has appeared to Simon."*) mentions it in passing. The use of the Aramaic name Cephas is another indication that Paul, who wrote in Greek, copied a creed used in the spoken language of first century Israel, which was Aramaic.
- **Jesus appeared to "the Twelve."** Verse 5 says *and then to the twelve.* The Twelve designates the apostles as a group and is not to be taken numerically since Judas was no longer part of the group. This event is also recorded in Luke 24:33-49, Matthew 28:16-20, and John 20:19-23.

- **Jesus appeared to more than five hundred at once.** Verse 6 continues: *"After that, he appeared to more than five hundred of the brothers at the same time, most of whom are still living, though some have fallen asleep."* Although this appearance is not found in the gospels, this might be the most daring evidence presented by Paul. He was likely not one of these *"five hundred"*, but clearly he – perhaps even some of the members of the church in Corinth – knew some of them as he mentions, *"most of whom are still living."* This rather bold statement is an invitation for any first century critic to check it out for himself and talk to any of the five hundred to verify the resurrection claim!

- **Jesus appeared to James.** This James is certainly not one of the apostles, since "the Twelve" are mentioned before, and that group would include James the son of Zebedee (the brother of John) as well as the only other apostle, James, the son of Alphaeus. Therefore, this must be James, the Lord's brother.

- **Jesus appeared to all apostles.** Since Paul mentioned "the Twelve" earlier, this must be used more loosely to include others who were part of the total group of Jesus' followers. Again, we find this appearance in some of the gospels as well.

- **Jesus appeared to Paul.** Here Paul refers to his personal encounter with the risen Christ on the road to Damascus in 34 AD, just a year or so following the resurrection, as extensively recorded in Acts chapter 9.

Obviously Paul was only an eyewitness himself to the last appearance, so how did Paul get the information on the other appearances? How did Paul get this creed? Digging further into the New Testament, we find some rather convincing clues.

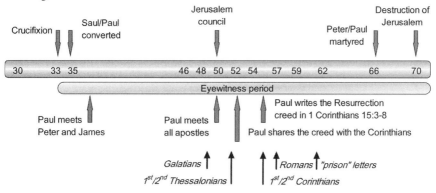

Figure 21-1: Tracing the Resurrection Creed

We need to visit an earlier letter of Paul – Galatians. Just as with 1 Corinthians, this text is widely accepted as genuine. Paul identifies himself as the author at the start of the letter and again in the last chapter. Analyzing clues provided in Acts, we can discover that this letter was written right after the Jerusalem council in 49 AD, so it likely appeared the next year.[412] Read Paul's credentials – in his own words – in Galatians 1:13-19, *"For you have heard of my previous way of life in Judaism, how intensely I persecuted the church of God and tried to destroy it. I was advancing in Judaism beyond many Jews of my own age and was extremely zealous for the traditions of my fathers. But when God, who set me apart from birth and called me by his grace, was pleased to reveal his Son in me so that I might preach him among the Gentiles, I did not consult any man, I did not go up to Jerusalem to see those who were apostles before I was. Instead I went immediately into Arabia and later returned to Damascus. Then after three years, I went up to Jerusalem to get acquainted with Peter and stayed with him for fifteen days. I saw none of the other apostles – only James the Lord's brother."* Then we read in Galatians 2:1: *"Fourteen years later I went up again to Jerusalem, this time with Barnabas. I took Titus along as well."*

What does this tell us? Look at the timeline: Jesus was crucified and resurrected in the year 33 AD; Paul was converted in 34 AD; and he went to Jerusalem as a Christian for the first time three years later, so around 37 AD, where he met with Peter and James. He returned to Jerusalem fourteen years later for the so-called Jerusalem council – a meeting where the church agreed to preach the gospel also to the Gentiles, around 49-50 AD.[413]

Looking back to Paul's testimony in 1 Corinthians 15, notice that Paul claims appearances to Peter and James. When Paul was in Jerusalem three years after his conversion, he only met with Peter and James, so it is not likely to be a coincidence that he mentions both of these men by name in his testimony to the appearances of Jesus. Also, as we found in Galatians 1:18, Paul made it clear that he went to Jerusalem in 37 AD, three years after his conversion, to get *"acquainted"* with the disciples. The Greek word used here is *historeo* – this word is the basis for our English word "history" and means "factual investigation" or "inquiry." So Paul went to Jerusalem not just to hang out with the disciples – he went to talk with them, compare notes and make plans. We know from the record of this same visit in Acts 9:26 that the other disciples were still afraid to meet with Paul, as they were not convinced of his conversion. Therefore Paul only met with Peter and James. This makes it all very probable that Paul's account of the appearances of the resurrected Jesus as described in 1 Corinthians 15 came directly from his main sources: Peter the apostle and James the brother of Jesus.

So, we know with certainty not only that this testimony originates fewer than 20 years from the crucifixion, but we also have "strong circumstantial evidence" that would likely convince a modern-day jury – that Paul received this testimony, also called this early creed, from the apostle Peter and James the brother of Jesus around the year 37, only about four years after the resurrection.[414] Almost as fresh as breaking news!

☼ EXHIBIT #9: WOULD YOU DIE FOR A LIE?

At the beginning of His ministry, Jesus chose twelve disciples, who later served as His apostles. As history and tradition teaches us, likely all but one, John, died a violent death as martyrs for their faith. Theirs is the ultimate testimony. That is actually the origin of our word *martyr*; the Greek verb μαρ–τυρεο ("martureo") means "to be a witness," "to testify."

Skeptics, however, will claim that people die daily for what they believe, either as innocent victims, as a result of persecutions or deliberately, like a fanatic Muslim homicide bomber. So dying for one's faith does not prove anything about the truth of the resurrection.

Wait. Is that correct? What is the difference between an apostle of Christ who was martyred and a fanatic Muslim bomber of today? Yes, both died for their faith. One obvious difference is that Jesus' apostle was killed by others, whereas the suicide bomber took his own life. Also, the apostle acted out of love, while the suicide bomber was motivated by hate. There is one other difference, and this is of huge importance. Both died for what they believed; however, the suicide bomber based his convictions on what others told him to be true, but the apostle based his faith on what he himself had experienced, the resurrection of Jesus! He did not only believe the resurrection was true, he knew it was true.

Remember what happened when Jesus was captured in the Garden of Gethsemane? *"Then all the disciples deserted him and fled"* (Matthew 26:54). They were overcome by fear and afraid they would be captured next. Likely, all ran the other way, racing out of Jerusalem in the direction of Bethany. After this initial cowardly reaction, apparently only Peter and John could muster enough courage to go back to Jerusalem to find out what was happening. When confronted, three times Peter denied any knowledge of Jesus (as foretold by Jesus and recorded in all four gospels). Only John was present at the site of the crucifixion (John 19:25-27).

When Jesus was captured, tried, and crucified, his followers were discouraged and depressed. They no longer were confident that Jesus had been sent by God (how could God allow his Son to be crucified?). They certainly did not anticipate a resurrection. So they hid and dispersed. Just as the Jews had planned, the original Jesus movement had died on the cross.

What is the difference between an apostle and a disciple?

The Bible makes a clear distinction between an apostle (from the Greek word αποστολοσ, "apostolos" which literally means "the one that is sent") and a disciple (a translation of the Greek word ματηυτυσ, "mathutus," meaning "a pupil" or "follower"). Anyone who follows the teachings of Jesus is a disciple; basically all Christians are disciples of Jesus. However, only the Twelve and Paul were considered apostles.

The apostles were each hand-selected by Jesus. The Twelve were personally taught by Jesus. They were promised (John 14:26) and given (Acts 2:3) a special relationship with the Holy Spirit, who empowered them with spiritual gifts. Like "the Twelve," Paul also was filled with the Holy Spirit (Acts 9:7) and received the same gifts.

As we study the Bible, it becomes clear that all Christians receive the Holy Spirit, but only the apostles received directly from heaven the miraculous gifts of tongues (speaking in different languages), healing, prophecy, knowledge and so on, though they were able to endow others with such spiritual gifts. The apostles were the spiritual leaders of the early church and their teachings were considered to have "apostolic authority." They alone had the authority to speak and write the inspired word of God. Therefore only the writings of the apostles themselves or books written on behalf of the apostles were included in the canon of the New Testament.

After only a short time a complete reversal of attitude occurred. Something remarkable transformed these cowards into bold and brave men. We see them abandoning their professions and re-grouping to commit themselves to spread a very specific message: Jesus was the Christ, the Messiah of God, who died on the cross, returned to life, and was seen by them. They invested the remainder of their lives proclaiming this, with no payoff from a human point of view. They faced a life of hardship; often being without food, they slept exposed to the elements, were ridiculed, and faced the constant threat of beatings and imprisonments. Finally, most of them died a hideous death as martyrs.

This change of behavior can only be explained by the fact that they were convinced – beyond any doubt – they had seen Jesus alive from the dead. There is no other adequate explanation.

The Ultimate Testimony of the Apostles

Who	How did he die?	Source
Simon Peter	Crucified in Rome around 67 AD	Tradition, Clement of Rome[415]
James of Zebedee	Killed by Herod Agrippa around 44 AD	Acts 12:1-2
John of Zebedee	Died of old age in Ephesus around 100 AD	Tradition[416]
Andrew	Crucified on an X-shaped cross in Greece, around 69 AD	Tradition/legend[417]
Philip	Died or was martyred in Hierapolis, Turkey	Tradition/legend[418]
Bartholomew	Skinned alive and beheaded in Armenia in 68 AD	Tradition[419]
Matthew	Martyred by spear in Ethiopia in 60 AD?	Legends[420]
Thomas	Speared in India	Tradition/legend[421]
James of Alphaeus	Stoned in Jerusalem or crucified in Persia?	Legends[422]
Jude Thaddaeus	Multiple legends about his martyrdom	Legends
Simon the Zealot	Crucified in Britain or killed in Persia?	Tradition/legend[423]

Table 21-4: The Ultimate Testimony of the Apostles

They were the ones who met the living Jesus in person. They were unique. These men knew the resurrection as <u>fact</u> – and not merely believed it by faith. They were not convinced by someone's testimony, but they had shared time with the resurrected Jesus. Knowing the truth, they were willing to die for it. If they knew it was not true, it is extremely unlikely that all would stick to this deception and would be willing to die for a lie. Would you die for a lie?

The evidence from the changed lives of the apostles after they claimed to have met the resurrected Jesus is a solid historical fact. Their testimony is so sound and convincing that even critical and non-believing scholars accept it: *"The only thing we can certainly say to be historical is that there were resurrection appearances in Galilee (and in Jerusalem) soon after Jesus' death. These appearances cannot be denied."* [424]

☼ EXHIBIT #10: THE CONVERSION OF SAUL TO PAUL

Paul, the great apostle who founded churches throughout Asia and Europe, whose missionary spirit fills the book of Acts, and who wrote much of the New Testament was initially a fanatic Christian killer.

Known originally as Saul of Tarsus, Paul is introduced in the New Testament at the stoning of Stephen (Acts 8:1), one of seven Hellenistic deacons, around 34 AD, only about twelve months after the resurrection.

Next, "*Saul began to destroy the church. Going from house to house, he dragged off men and women and put them in prison*" (Acts 8:3). Extending the vigorous Jewish persecution of the young Christian movement, Saul traveled to Damascus with letters from the high priest to imprison more Christians. However, on the road to the city he encountered the resurrected Jesus. A few days later he was baptized and filled with the Holy Spirit (Acts 9). Paul, in his own words described his dramatic conversion in letters to churches in Corinth (1 Corinthians 15:9-10), Galatia (Galatians 1:12-23), and Philippi (Philippians 3:6-7).

Initially, Paul's conversion was met with suspicion; even the apostles were reluctant to meet with him when he returned to Jerusalem the first time after his conversion: "*Then after three years, I went up to Jerusalem to get acquainted with Peter and stayed with him for fifteen days. I saw none of the other apostles – only James the Lord's brother*" (Galatians 1:18-19, emphasis added). In these days, so soon after the resurrection, the apostles remained in the Jerusalem area, apparently they were still not convinced that Paul's conversion was genuine. Only years later, all apostles felt comfortable with Paul as a fellow Christian and apostle. This might also be one of the main reasons that Paul's ministry was mostly in Gentile territory as far away as possible from his initial anti-Christian, Pharisaic roots.

As we have discussed earlier, Saul/Paul spent the remainder of his life in ministry and church planting until his death as a martyr in Rome around 66/67 AD.[425]

A dramatic conversion as what happened to Paul is not necessarily unique. Critics and skeptics will assert that history shows numerous examples of people who convert from one set of beliefs to another. What makes Paul's conversion such strong evidence is its cause. People usually convert to a particular religion because they have heard the message of that religion from a secondary source and have believed it. Quite similar is how Christians today reach out to non-Christians and share the gospel of Christ. Very contrary to this, Paul's conversion to Christianity did not include any sharing by any Christian. It was based completely on his personal encounter with Jesus. Today, we might believe that Jesus rose from the dead based on secondary evidence, trusting the testimony of the disciples and Paul who saw the risen Christ, but for Paul, his experience came from an unexpected primary source: Jesus appeared to him personally. His conversion was not based on the testimony of someone else.[426]

✳ EXHIBIT #11: THE CONVERSION OF JAMES, THE BROTHER OF JESUS

After the miraculous conception of Jesus, Mary, and Joseph had other children as well. The gospels report that Jesus had at least four brothers and some sisters: "*Isn't this the carpenter's son? Isn't his mother's name Mary, and aren't his brothers James, Joseph, Simon and Judas? Aren't all his sisters with us?*" (Matthew

13:55, also Mark 6:3). And the gospels also record, that while Jesus was alive, his brothers did not believe in Him: *"For even his own brothers did not believe in him"* (John 7:5). The Scriptures do not sugarcoat this. The lack of belief by James and the other brothers is corroborated by the absolute silence about them in the gospels. None of the accounts of Jesus' ministry mentions them in any role.

However, after the resurrection, in the earliest years of Christianity, James, the brother of Jesus, became a significant player in the movement. In Galatians 1:19, Paul explicitly identified him as one of the only two individuals he met with during his 37 AD trip to Jerusalem: *"I saw none of the other apostles – only James, the Lord's brother."* So, there cannot be any doubt that James,[427] Jesus' brother, had within four years of the resurrection not only converted to Christianity; he had become a recognized leader in the early church.

Later on Paul also gives an important clue as to why James became a Christian. In the early resurrection creed in 1 Corinthians 15:3-8, Paul writes that Jesus also appeared to James: *"Then he appeared to James"* (1 Corinthians 15:7). One can argue which James this is (lack of surnames in Bible times can occasionally be quite confusing). However, the context makes it clear, that this is not James the son of Zebedee (the brother of John) or the other apostle James, the son of Alphaeus (as they are mentioned as part of the apostle group before). Therefore this must be James, the Lord's brother.

Subsequently, in Acts 12:17 and 15:13 this same James is recognized after the resurrection as a leader of the church in Jerusalem. And he also wrote the New Testament book by that name.

An important, non-Biblical confirmation comes to us from Josephus: *"Ananus...assembled the Sanhedrin of judges, and brought before them the brother of Jesus, who was called Christ, whose name was James, and some others, ..., he delivered them to be stoned."* [428] This passage does not only confirm that James was the brother of Jesus, it also mentions that he was martyred for his faith by stoning (around 57 AD).

All in all, it is a well-founded conclusion that James, the brother of Jesus – like Paul – made a remarkable conversion from a non-believer during the lifetime of Jesus to a leader in the earliest years of the Christian movement and was ultimately stoned for his faith. Although the personal appearance of the risen Jesus to His brother James is reported only once in the New Testament, this reported encounter is part of the powerful early resurrection creed dated back to only a few years after the resurrection. And one can wonder: What could have ever happened to James that could have converted him to a believer apart from the appearance of the resurrected Christ? James knew Jesus while He was alive and certainly knew about His teachings and even His miracles. None of this, however, convinced him, so what could the apostles have said to convince this man? Logically, only a personal encounter with Jesus, as mentioned by Paul, would explain his 180-degree change in beliefs and actions.

The bone box of James

In October 2002 an ancient ossuary was discovered with the remarkable inscription: *"James, son of Joseph, brother of Jesus."* An ossuary or bone box was commonly used in the first century to give the bones of deceased (after the body had decomposed) a final resting place, usually in a family tomb. Ossuaries were sometimes inscribed, often with the names of the deceased and his father. The 2002 ossuary of James is unusual because it includes the name of the brother, Jesus, which suggests that this brother Jesus must have been an important individual.

Since its discovery the bone box[429] has been the subject of extensive and intense scrutiny, research, and debate. There is unanimous agreement that the box itself is an authentic first century ossuary. The conclusions on the inscription are mixed. The Royal Ontario Museum in Toronto where the inscription was discovered deemed it authentic; members of the Geological Survey of Israel supported this conclusion. However, later a committee of textual scholars and geology specialists appointed by the Israel Antiquities Authority in a majority opinion declared the inscriptions to be a forgery, but at least two members of the committee found the name *"Jesus"* on the box to be authentic.[430]

☼ EXHIBIT #12: NOT ENOUGH FAITH FOR ALTERNATIVE EXPLANATIONS

Ever heard of *Occam's razor*? It is a principle attributed to the fourteenth century English logician and Franciscan friar William of Ockham (later misspelled to Occam). Occam's razor is best described as *"all things being equal, the simplest solution tends to be the best one."* In other words, when competing theories are equal in other respects, the principle recommends selection of the theory with the fewest assumptions and the fewest hypothetical entities. In this exhibit, we will see that it takes more faith to believe an alternative explanation than to accept the conclusion that Jesus actually resurrected from the dead. The evidence is convincing. Logically, Occam's razor does not give you any other choice.

Over the centuries many have proposed alternative explanations to the events in Jerusalem shortly after the execution of Jesus of Nazareth. Wild conspiracy theories, hallucinations, and hoaxes have been suggested. We will assess the basics of these theories. Looking at these alternatives, it is important to realize there is consensus among believers and non-believers that:

- Jesus was executed as a criminal by crucifixion.
- A short time after the crucifixion, the original group of disciples started to boldly proclaim a message of the resurrection of Jesus and founded what we now call Christianity.

ALTERNATIVE #1: THE RESURRECTION IS A LEGEND

Simply stated, many believe "it never happened." The resurrection is just a legend, an embellished account by followers of the initial disciples. A game of "telephone," and at each next link (next generation) the story gets added on to.

Clearly this is not a viable alternative. Legends take several generations to develop (a period of one hundred years or more) and will only be widely accepted once the generation of the original witnesses has died out.

We have seen that the manuscript evidence of the New Testament texts date to within 100 years of writing, as well as confirmations and quotations from the Early Church Leaders. Even today only few words or sentences are challenged by even the most critical scholars.[431] Furthermore, the resurrection claims can be traced back to the original witnesses: the apostles, Paul and James, the brother of Jesus. They were not told about a resurrection that happened years earlier; no, they were witnesses to this event. They proclaimed it, and they gave their lives for it.

Bottom line, the sources for the resurrection claims were too close to the event, and the written accounts appeared much too soon to consider this a serious alternative. It is so much in conflict with the evidence, even well-informed non-believers do not consider this as a serious option.[432]

ALTERNATIVE #2: THE APOSTLES LIED (AND STOLE THE BODY)

The apostles were lying – it is all a hoax. What if the resurrection never happened, but the apostles just pulled off the most elaborate hoax in human history? Perhaps after the crucifixion and death of Jesus, they came together and agreed to claim that Jesus resurrected from the dead. To make this happen, they also would have to steal the body from the tomb to destroy the evidence. After all, this is also what the Jewish priests claimed that happened, as we can read in Matthew 28:12-13: *"When the chief priests had met with the elders and devised a plan, they gave the soldiers a large sum of money, telling them, 'You are to say, "His disciples came during the night and stole him away while we were asleep."'"* There are two major flaws with this theory.

First, there is no evidence to support it. The evidence indicates honest testimony by the original apostles and Mark, Luke, and Paul.[433] Nothing suggests

that immediately after Jesus' death the disciples were capable of the daring ini-
tiative to go the tomb of Jesus (on the Sabbath, the day of rest) and retrieve the
body. These men not only claimed the resurrection, they also believed in it.
Soon after Jesus' crucifixion, they were willing to endure imprisonment, sufferings and even martyrdom. Their claim of the resurrection sprang out of a
strong sincere conviction that they truly had seen Him.[434] In other words: They
not only talked the talk, they also walked the walk. And lastly, why would they
do this? What did they gain from these alleged lies? History and tradition
might not always agree on all the details of the subsequent ministries and martyrdom of the apostles, but all agree that none of them gained any wealth or
luxury. Their only "gain" was poverty, persecution, and a horrendous death.

Second, can you imagine any situation where a large group of people agree
to a lie and maintain it the remainder of their lives, despite torture and death;
and nobody denies it? Just how unlikely this is, is demonstrated by the following illustration by Chuck Colson. Mr. Colson was an aide to President Richard
Nixon and a former accomplice to the 1972-1973 Watergate scandal. As a result
of Watergate, Colson spent time in prison, became a Christian, and founded
Breakpoint Prison Fellowship.[435] He writes in a Breakpoint commentary:[436]

*"I have been challenged myself many times on the resurrection. My answer
is always that the disciples and five hundred others gave eyewitness accounts
of seeing Jesus risen from the tomb. But then I'm asked, 'How do you know
they were telling the truth? Maybe they were perpetrating a hoax.' My
answer to that comes from an unlikely source: Watergate. Watergate
involved a conspiracy to cover up, perpetuated by the closest aides to the
President of the United States – the most powerful men in America, who
were intensely loyal to their president. But one of them, John Dean, turned
state's evidence, that is, testified against Nixon, as he put it, 'to save his own
skin' – and he did so only two weeks after informing the president about
what was really going on – two weeks! The real cover-up, the lie, could only
be held together for two weeks, and then everybody else jumped ship in order
to save themselves. Now, the fact is that all that those around the President
were facing embarrassment, maybe prison. Nobody's life was at stake. But
what about the disciples? Twelve powerless men, peasants really, were facing
not just embarrassment or political disgrace, but beatings, stonings, execution. Every single one of the disciples insisted, to their dying breaths, that
they had physically seen Jesus bodily raised from the dead. Don't you think
that one of those apostles would have cracked before being beheaded or
stoned? That one of them would have made a deal with the authorities?
None did. You see, men will give their lives for something they believe to be
true – they will never give their lives for something they know to be false."*

And we should not forget the testimony from Paul and James, who were not associated with the group of apostles at the time of the resurrection. Paul was even on a mission to kill them all. These men had no reason whatsoever to make up any resurrection stories. Therefore, only a small number of critical scholars have opted for this view during that last 200 years.[437]

ALTERNATIVE #3: THE APOSTLES WERE DECEIVED: JESUS DID NOT DIE

The lives of the Twelve as well as those of Paul and James provide clear evidence they were convinced Jesus really returned from the dead, but perhaps they were deceived. They believed it to be true, but had they been fooled?

Over the centuries there have been several variations of this notion, usually known as the *swoon theory*. All have been abandoned or died a quiet death. The general idea is that Jesus survived the cross and was later revived. His appearances to the disciples were therefore not miraculous, as he never died in the first place.

The theory comes in different flavors, some include:

- *The Passover Plot.*[438] According to its author, Hugh Schonfield, Jesus was a deceiver who carefully plotted His career as Israel's Messiah. Working closely with accomplices Lazarus and Joseph of Arimathea, He planned His survival of the cross. While on the cross, Joseph arranged to have Jesus given a drink to appear dead. On Saturday, Jesus was then removed from the grave and revived.

- *The Jesus Scroll.*[439] Donovan Joyce in 1964 asserted to have been told of a now lost scroll that might have been written by Jesus at the age of 80. He suggests that Jesus never died on the cross, but plotted with the guards that after being drugged He was pronounced dead. In the tomb, a doctor, assisted by Joseph of Arimathea (Jesus' uncle) nursed Jesus back to health. As Jesus recovered, He paid one last visit to His disciples and then lived as a monk at Qumran. Jesus married Mary Magdalene, fathered at least one son, and fought the Roman army at Masada, where He died.

- *Holy Blood, Holy Grail.*[440] This account claims that Jesus was drugged to make Him appear dead. Pilate was bribed to the body's removal from the cross alive. The Essenes (yes, they are part of this as well) then laid His body in the grave of Joseph of Arimathea (a relative of Jesus). Jesus revived and went to France, together with His secret wife Mary Magdalene (remember, this book also inspired Dan Brown's *The DaVinci Code*), Joseph, and Lazarus (Jesus' brother-in-law). There, Jesus and Mary's children started a secret royal bloodline.

These accounts are a great illustration of Occam's razor. How many more wild fantasies have to be invented to explain away the facts? How much better does the resurrection fit the events? The swoon accounts all assume that Jesus was administered some kind of drug to make Him look dead, and a number of unlikely accomplices helped him escape death and revive in the tomb. However, how wild are these speculations? Even with these speculative props, how could Jesus fool the other people at the crucifixion? How could He convince the Jews and Roman soldiers that He was dead when only drugged? And lastly, even for a moment, suppose He swooned, think about the shape Jesus would have been in. He was flogged and had been nailed to a cross for several hours. Even if still alive, Jesus would have been in desperate need of serious medical help. If He would have appeared to the disciples in this shape, they would have not believed for a second this was a glorious resurrection, instead they would have instantly realized that somehow Jesus had survived the crucifixion and needed immediate medical attention.

ALTERNATIVE #4: THE APOSTLES WERE DECEIVED: THEY HAD HALLUCINATIONS

What if Jesus indeed died on the cross and the resurrection appearances are just hallucinations, illusions, and visions? The apostles believed they were telling the truth about the resurrection because of the false notion that they had seen the risen Jesus.

Variants of this hallucination theory seem to be a preferred "way out" of the resurrection evidence for some modern scholars. For instance in *What Really Happened to Jesus?* atheist Gerd Ludemann concludes:[441] "*The critical investigation of the various resurrection appearances produced a surprising result: they can all be explained as visions.*" Or, in the words of atheist Michael Martin: "*A person full of religious zeal may see what he or she wants to see, not what is really there.*"[442]

Jesus seminar co-founder and spokesman, John Dominic Crossan, theorizes that Paul had a vision, a revelation when he met Jesus. The other apostles were making deliberate political dramatizations showing the priority of one leader over another.[443] In Crossan's own words: "*Leaving aside Paul, whose experience was ... an experience of an altered state of consciousness, a vision of Jesus, the other experiences in the last chapters of our New Testament Gospels are not intended to be visions or hallucinations or anything else in that sense. They are calm, serene statements of who is in charge in this community and who is in charge in that other community.*"[444]

There are a number of solid reasons why the appearances cannot be explained by hallucinations:

- Hallucinations are generally experienced by one person alone. In the Bible accounts Jesus also appeared to various groups of people.
- Hallucinations generally develop from hopeful anticipation. They are usually caused by drugs or bodily deprivation. The disciples were grieving in despair after Jesus' death, but they did not meet the medical conditions necessary to expect hallucination.
- It is unlikely that subjective experiences as hallucinations could inspire the disciples' radical transformations, even being willing to die for their faith.
- What grounds do we have to think that James, Jesus' non-believing brother, was in a bodily depraved condition and in a hopeful anticipation, to see Jesus?
- Why would Paul, the persecutor, have yearned to see Jesus?
- Hallucinations cannot explain the empty tomb.
- Hallucinations do not share a meal, nor can they be touched to feel wounds.

ALTERNATIVE #5: OTHER EMPTY TOMB EXPLANATIONS

The empty tomb and the missing body of Jesus are solid corroborations of the resurrection. The empty tomb is strongly supported by the presented evidence,[445] but are there other alternative non-resurrection reconstructions that can explain the missing body?

- **The wrong grave.** Perhaps the women just went to the wrong grave? That wrong grave was empty and they concluded that Jesus had risen from the dead. On the surface this could be possible; however, these same women are mentioned in all gospels to have been present at the burial of Jesus just two days earlier on Friday afternoon. It is not reasonable to assume that all of them developed the same amnesia in such a short period of time. Also, the grave location was well-known. It was, after all, the tomb set aside for Joseph of Arimathea, a wealthy and well-respected individual. It would have been very little trouble to ask him where his grave was, in case they would have been lost. And, after the proclamation of the resurrection surely some people (Joseph, the Jews, or someone else) would have checked Joseph's tomb to look for the body.
- **The body was stolen.** Who would want to steal the body? We have already seen that it is not probable that the disciples deliberately lied about the resurrection and had stolen the body to conceal the evidence. Did the Jews steal the body? They had even fewer reasons than the disciples, and if they would have stolen the body, they certainly would have reproduced it later to stop the Christian movement in its very first days. The last potential thief, the Roman government, is also the most unlikely. These officials had no motive, and the last thing they wanted was more unrest in the city.

- **The body was eaten.** Jesus Seminar founder and spokesman, John Dominic Crossan, claims that, consistent with crucifixion customs, Jesus' corpse remained on the cross to be torn apart by wild beasts or was buried in a shallow grave, dug up, and then eaten by dogs.[446] Either way his conclusion is: *"With regard to the body of Jesus, by Easter Sunday morning, anyone who cared did not know where it was, and anyone who knew did not care. Why should the soldiers, even if they had given him a quick burial and gone home, remember the death and disposal of a nobody?"* [447]

If Crossan is right, why would all gospels claim the women were present at the burial and went to the tomb? Unless of course, as Crossan believes, all gospels are lying. And even if he is right, would the disciples have been so gullible and naive to not have looked for the remains of Jesus near the crucifixion site upon the first claims of a resurrection?

ALTERNATIVE #6: THE TEACHINGS OF THE QUR'AN

We will discuss Islam in more detail in a later chapter, but since Muslims have as unique view of Jesus' resurrection, I'd like to mention their view in this section to be complete. Islam recognizes Jesus as one of the great prophets of Allah. The Qur'an (Islam's most holy book) teaches the virgin birth of Jesus and that He preached the truth. However, according to the Qur'an, Jesus was merely a human being chosen by God as a prophet and sent for the guidance of the people of Israel.[448]

The Qur'an explicitly denies Jesus' crucifixion. In Surah (chapter) 4:157-159 we read:

"That they said (in boast), 'We killed Christ Jesus the son of Mary, The Apostle of God'; – But they killed him not, Nor crucified Him, But so it was made to appear to them, And those who differ therein are full of doubts, With no (certain) knowledge, But only conjecture to follow, For of a surety they killed Him not: – Nay, God raised him up unto Himself; and God is exalted in Power, Wise; – And there is none of the People of the Book but must believe in Him before His death; And on the Day of Judgment He will be a witness against them."

One thing is absolutely certain to Islam: Jesus did not die on the cross. Although they cannot confidently say what did happen, Muslims boldly state what did not happen. Islamic traditions offer multiple possible explanations for what happened on the day of the crucifixion:[449]

- Jesus hid while one of His companions died in his place.

• God made Judas Iscariot to look like Jesus and to take His place.
• Simon of Cyrene replaced Jesus before the crucifixion.

It is quite puzzling to see how Islam ignores the mountain of evidence and confirmations for the crucifixion. As we have seen, even the most critical and atheist scholars confirm Jesus' execution on the cross as a historical event. Claiming that somebody else took His place without the Romans, Jews, disciples, or anybody else noticing seems more than a serious person can imagine. Therefore, from an evidence perspective, the alternative view of the Qur'an on how Jesus supposedly escaped the cross does not seem to bear any significance.

Alternative Explanations for the Resurrection Evidence		
	Alternative theory	**Refutation**
It is a legend	Embellished accounts and fantasy passed on over generations	NT is historically reliable, written by honest witnesses within the same generation
It is a hoax	The disciples conspired and made up the resurrection	Would you die for something you know to be a lie?
The disciples were deceived, Jesus did not die but swooned	Jesus was drugged, appeared to be dead, and was revived	Complicated and unlike conspiracy theories contradict the extensive evidence of His death, and even if He survived, it not have looked like a glorious resurrection
The disciples were deceived, they had hallucinations	Jesus died, but the disciples had visions, dreams, and hallucinations of the risen Jesus	Hallucinations are only individual experiences, require bodily deprivation, do not appear to groups in consistent patterns, visions do not eat meals
The grave was not really empty	The women went to the wrong tomb The body was stolen The body was eaten by beasts	The were present at the burial, Joseph's grave was well known Who would have a motive? Contradicts all the gospels
The teachings of the Qur'an say that somebody else was crucified	Jesus was never crucified	Contradicts the NT and all non-Biblical writings

Table 21-5: Overview of the Alternative Explanations

Jesus is Indeed God

No honest skeptic will doubt that Jesus of Nazareth lived during the first half of the first century in Roman occupied Palestine. Neither does anyone question that this Jesus was a preacher and teacher of rather revolutionary, profound, and life-changing ideas. Many of His contemporaries considered Him to be a worker of miracles and the Messiah as foretold in the Jewish Scriptures. The historical evidence and non-Biblical corroboration for His untimely death by crucifixion is abundant. But was this Jesus also divine? Was He the Son of God and as the Christian faith proclaims, part of the Trinity?

Analyzing the Scriptures, three convincing exhibits were presented to support the claim of Jesus' deity:

1. Reading about Jesus' life, teachings, and ministry has led even the most cynical skeptic to the conclusion that Jesus was an extraordinary teacher of wisdom and moral truths. Studying what Jesus actually did and said reveals that He Himself thought and taught that He was divine. At numerous occasions He claims to be the Son of God, to be sent by the Father, to be the only way to the Father, to forgive sins, to accept worship, refers to Himself by the name Jehovah ("I am"), and so on. Logically this only leaves three alternatives. If Jesus is not God, then He either (a) deliberately deceives His followers and therefore is a liar, or (b) He sincerely believes to be God but is not and therefore He is deluded, He is a lunatic. Or, He indeed is God and therefore (c) He is who He claims to be. Jesus' teachings and actions contradict the liar or lunatic alternatives to such an extent that no serious scholar considers either one to be a valid explanation. Therefore the only logical conclusion left as an option is that Jesus is God. Remarkably, many critics seem to be entangled into a reasoning of intellectual dishonesty by admitting that Jesus was an honest and great moral teacher, while at the same time rejecting the very thing Jesus taught as an essential part of his teachings, namely that He is God.

2. According to the New Testament gospels, Jesus performed numerous miraculous acts during His life and ministry. The four gospels combined describe a total of thirty-five different miracles. The majority of these miracles deal with healings of disabled, sick, or demon-possessed people and from an evidence perspective can be challenged for a lack of objective confirmation and/or other explanations. Nine of the described miracles, however, account events where Jesus' actions defy the laws of nature. Additionally these miracles

were observed by multiple, in some instances even thousands, of witnesses. These nature miracles, of which "the feeding of the five thousand" as described in all four gospels is likely the most impressive illustration, show Jesus' ability to make things happen that can only be explained by His deity.

3. The books of the Old Testament contain hundreds of explicit and detailed prophecies about a promised Messiah (translated to the word Christ in the Greek) who would come to the Jews to be their everlasting King. These prophecies predict the family line of the Messiah, the circumstances and location of His birth, His life and purpose, and in graphic detail His death and burial. Against staggering statistical improbability and beyond His control, Jesus fulfilled all these prophecies to the letter, making Him the only person who ever lived on earth to fit this prophetic fingerprint of the Messiah.

Each of the above-described exhibits strongly supports the case for Jesus' deity and convinced His disciples during His lifetime of who He was. However, despite these evidences, they all deserted Him when He was arrested and later crucified. Something else had to happen to finally convince His followers to commit themselves to His message: the resurrection. Only the resurrection solidifies Jesus as God. Only the resurrection proves the validity of His sacrifice as a payment for our sins. Only the resurrection explains the commitment of the apostles to preach the gospel and their willingness to pay the ultimate price for their missionary work. Only the resurrection could ultimately convince me personally to become a follower of Christ.

The evidence for the resurrection of Jesus of Nazareth on that Sunday morning of the first Easter is remarkably solid and compelling. Logically the resurrection is proved in three steps:

1. The Biblical texts describe in graphic detail Jesus' execution by crucifixion. Secular historical confirmations on the practice of crucifixions as well as extra-Biblical corroboration of the events leave no reasons to doubt that Jesus indeed died on the cross.

2. All gospels describe how Jesus is subsequently buried by Joseph of Arimathea and some of His female followers on the evening of His death. The location of that grave was well-known. On Easter morning, the same women find the grave empty, the body is gone, and has remained missing over the last twenty centuries.

3. Appearances of the resurrected Jesus are mentioned in all four gospels, the book of Acts, and throughout Paul's writings. The most extensive (and non-disputed) creed on the resurrection is found in Paul's letter to the Corinthian church (1 Corinthians 15:1-8). This creed mentions a total of six different resurrection appearances and can be traced back to be composed

within a few years of the date of the resurrection. However, even more compelling than the written accounts about Jesus' resurrection, are the evidences of changed behavior of Jesus' disciples. Before the resurrection, the Twelve lack real commitment and faith. After the resurrection, they become bold; they abandon their professions and possessions and commit the remainder of their lives traveling the world in poverty and under persecution, proclaiming the gospel, ultimately giving testimony through their martyrdom. Dramatic changed behavior is also recorded about Saul-Paul who feverously persecutes Christians until he meets the resurrected Jesus and dramatically transforms into the great missionary to the Gentiles. And also, James, the half-brother of Jesus, is introduced during Jesus' life as a non-believer. Only his encounter with the resurrected Christ can explain his later leading role in the early Christian church in Jerusalem and his subsequent martyrdom.

Various attempts have been made to propose alternative explanations for the radically changed behavior of the first Christians after the crucifixion of Jesus that have led to the remarkable birth and astounding growth of the church in the lifetime of Jesus' initial followers. These alternative explanations include legendary exaggerations, wild conspiracy theories, hoaxes, visions, and hallucinations. However, none of these proposed alternatives can stand the test of objective analysis against the facts. They require such unrealistic and improbable assumptions that logically these alternatives, one by one, have to be rejected.

Only the resurrection of Jesus of Nazareth fits the historically recorded testimony and events. And this resurrection would only be possible if Jesus is who He claimed to be: God Himself!

Section IV
Is the Bible Inspired
by God?

CHAPTER 22

Is the Bible Inspired by God?

"Where do we find God's word except in the Scriptures?"
MARTIN LUTHER (1483-1546)

IS THE BIBLE THE WORD OF GOD?

So far we have built a logical case for the truth of Christianity. 1) By providing evidences from scientific observations, we have shown God's existence. 2) By showing the textual and historical reliability, we have proved the accounts in the Bible are genuine and can be trusted. 3) By analyzing Jesus' life, His miracles, the fulfillment of Messianic prophecies, and, most of all, the historical truth of the resurrection, we have logically concluded that Jesus indeed is the divine Son of God.

The dramatic importance of these conclusions makes it only prudent to take an additional step of verification. Christianity not only claims the Bible is grounded in history, it also claims it is the actual Word of God. That is, the Bible is God's revelation to man. It contains His instructions to us, written in a manner understandable to everyone. And because we have failed (and will continue to fail) to perfectly obey His commands, He has also revealed His plan to save us from His just wrath through the sacrifice and blood of His Son, Jesus Christ.

The Bible is clear about its claims to divine inspiration. Hear the testimony of both Old Testament and New Testament writers:

Moses: "*And God said to Moses, 'I AM THAT I AM. This is what you are to say to the Israelites: I AM has sent me to you'*" (Exodus 3:14).

Joshua: "*After the death of Moses the servant of the Lord, the Lord said to Joshua son of Nun, Moses' aide: ...*" (Joshua 1:1).

The prophet Samuel: "*And the Lord said to Samuel, 'See, I am to do something in Israel that will make the ears of everyone who hears of it tingle'*" (1 Samuel 3:11).

King David: "*The Spirit of the Lord spoke through me; His word was on my tongue*" (2 Samuel 23:2).

The prophet Isaiah: "*The Lord Almighty has revealed this in my hearing: 'Till your dying day this sin will not be atoned for,' says the Lord, the Lord Almighty*" (Isaiah 22:14).

The prophet Jeremiah: "*This is the word that came to Jeremiah from the Lord: 'This is what the Lord, the God of Israel, says: Write in a book all the words I have spoken to you'*" (Jeremiah 30:1-2).

The apostle Peter: *"In those days Peter stood up among the believers (a group numbering about a hundred and twenty) and said, 'Brothers, the Scripture had to be fulfilled which <u>the Holy Spirit spoke long ago through the mouth of David</u> concerning Judas, who served as guide for those who arrested Jesus'"* (Acts 1:15-16).

The apostle Paul: *"<u>All Scripture is God-breathed</u> and is useful for teaching, rebuking, correcting and training in righteousness, so that the man of God may be thoroughly equipped for every good work"* (2 Timothy 3:16).

The apostle John: *"'I am the Alpha and the Omega,' says the Lord God, 'who is, and who was, and who is to come, the Almighty'"* (Revelation 1:8).

So the Bible is boldly and unambiguous when it claims to be the Word of God. Impressive, true, but is there external evidence for this?

HOW DOES ONE PROVE DIVINE INSPIRATION?

It is one thing to claim divine inspiration and quite another matter to prove it. After all, this is a rather outrageous claim. Obviously it will be insufficient to say that merely because the Bible is historically reliable and claims to be the Word of God; it therefore is the Word of God. No, we need more solid and objective evidences. After all, there are other books, such as the Qur'an and the Book of Mormon that claim to be the Word of God, and yet they contradict and even discredit the Bible. God cannot contradict Himself, and His Word cannot contradict itself. Therefore only one of these books can – at best – be the Word of God. Convincing and compelling evidence that the Bible is God's Word will also implicitly demonstrate that other "holy books" cannot be God's Word.

Fortunately, the Lord has given multiple confirmations of the divine authority of His Word. And as with the evidences previously discussed, once again, modern day discoveries, knowledge and science are our allies in this search for the truth. In this section, we will discuss proof for inspiration of Scriptures unknown to many of the generations before us!

These evidences can be grouped into the following categories:

- **Scientific revelations:** The Bible reveals knowledge and scientific insights beyond anything the Biblical author could have known at the time of writing.
- **Prophecies:** The Bible predicts events that are accurately fulfilled later in history.
- **Unity:** Written throughout 15 centuries by more than 40 authors, the Bible presents one, and only one plan for salvation through Christ from the just wrath of God.
- **Ability to transform lives:** Like no other book, the Bible continues to have the power to radically transform the lives of its readers – many times instantly.

• **Testimony of Christ:** The Bible is declared to be the Word of God by the Son of God.

Additionally, some Christian scholars claim that the texts and stories themselves contain evidence of design. That is, there are structures, messages, and symbolic prophecies hidden beneath the surface of Bible texts which cannot be explained by chance and coincidence alone.

CHAPTER 23

Scientific Revelations in the Bible

"The god of this age has blinded the minds of unbelievers, so that they cannot see the light of the gospel of the glory of Christ, who is the image of God. For we do not preach ourselves, but Jesus Christ as Lord, and ourselves as your servants for Jesus' sake. For God, who said, 'Let light shine out of darkness,' made his light shine in our hearts to give us the light of the knowledge of the glory of God in the face of Christ."

2 CORINTHIANS 4:4-6

GOD VERSUS SCIENCE?

God versus Science was found on the cover of *Time Magazine* on November 13, 2006. The cover article questioned *"whether faith and scientific progress and hunger for miracles and for MRI's are incompatible."* [450] In an engaged debate, Oxford professor Dr. Richard Dawkins, who claims Darwinian theory and science can only lead to atheism[451] faced off with Dr. Francis Collins, director of the National Human Genome Research Institute, who is convinced that material signs and design point to God.[452] Apart from name calling ("clowns" as he referred to creationists), Dawkins does not seem to have a problem putting his faith in the existence of billions of parallel universes (of which our universe is just the lucky one) in an attempt to explain the fine tuning of the natural laws.[453] The existence of a God who exists outside of space and time is not a credible option for him, as it is not a scientific alternative.

However, God is not opposed to science. This simply is not a one-or-the-other proposition. Science is only a means to study God's creation, and through it we can learn more about Him. When we discussed the evidences for God's existence, we discovered that recent scientific discoveries in astrobiology, molecular biology, and genetics reveal the work of design by a Creator. Once again, we turn to science to discover that the texts of the Bible reveal scientific knowledge known only in recent times; therefore it was wholly unknown to the authors when the Bible was written.

☼ Exhibit #1: The Genesis Creation Account

*"In the beginning God created the heavens and the earth. Now the
earth was formless and empty, darkness was over the surface of the deep,
and the Spirit of God was hovering over the waters. And God said, 'Let
there be light,' and there was light…By the seventh day God had
finished the work he had been doing; so on the seventh day he rested
from all his work. And God blessed the seventh day and made it holy,
because on it he rested from all the work of creating that he had done."*
Genesis 1:1-31

Scripture was not written by scientists for scientists; it was written by men
living in ancient times. The Genesis account, penned by Moses around 1450
BC, was written when people were living in the late Bronze Age. Primitive stone
and bronze tools were used to work the land, to make weapons, and to build
homes. Writing as we known it was recently introduced, but not a widespread
skill. The great emphasis of day-to-day life was to find food for survival.
Natural science was limited to personal observation. Many in those days were
polytheistic; they worshiped natural phenomena such as the sun, the moon,
stars, fire, and water.

Moses, author of the creation account in Genesis, had been educated in
Egypt. Ancient Egypt flourished from 3000 BC until the first centuries AD. Its
successes were largely based on the irrigation of the Nile valley, early development of basic writing, trade with surrounding regions, and military strength.
Egyptians believed in a complex network of multiple gods and an afterlife that
emphasized the preservation of the body; hence, mummies. Moses' Egyptian
background is also evident in his choice of words throughout the Hebrew text.

This is the background against which the Genesis account should be read
and understood. People 3,500 years ago had no concept of "knowledge" like
we have in our time. That which could not be seen or experienced personally
would be beyond their ability to understand.

In Genesis, much emphasis is placed upon creation "days" (translated from
the Hebrew word *yowm*). In English-speaking circles these days are commonly interpreted to be 24-hour days. As noted above in chapter 2, these "days"
should not be the focal point of discussion. Given the background of Jewish
people, including Moses, events far distant in time would make little sense and
likely could not be understood. The use of yowms to describe the process of
creation seems a logical choice to convey a difficult concept in a language and
account that could be grasped by Moses' contemporaries.

A matter of days?

Genesis depicts how God created the earth and all its inhabitants in six *yowms*. Ancient Hebrew had a very limited vocabulary (about 6,000 words). Moses used this word yowm, commonly rendered "day," though it has several other meanings elsewhere in the Bible:

יﬦ,יוﬦ [*yowm* /yome/] 2,274 occurrences; translated as "day" (2,008 times), "time" (64), "chronicles + " (37), "daily" (32), "ever" (17), "year" (14), "continually" (10), "when" (10), "as" (10), "while" (8), "full" (8), "always" (4), "whole" (4) and translated variously (44).[454]

Therefore, it also denotes "time," "period of time," and similar concepts.

Independent on whether yowm is a 24-hour day or some other expression of time, the text of the first chapter of Genesis shows some remarkable insights:

- **There is one God:** The vast majority of ancient religions are polytheistic, just like the Egyptian beliefs. Genesis sets forth the concept of One God.
- **God is outside His creation:** The gods of the ancients were represented by natural phenomena, usually the sun (the Egyptian god *Ra*) or moon (worshiped as *Thoth* by the Egyptians). In Genesis, God created the universe: *"In the beginning God created the heavens and the earth"* (Genesis 1:1).
- **There was a beginning:** Most ancient religions believed the universe had existed forever. Until the middle of the twentieth century even many scientists still believed the universe had always existed. Only during our generation has science – astronomy in particular – proved conclusively that the universe had a starting point (Big Bang cosmology). How was Moses aware of this?
- **The beginning was not by chance**. The beginning did not just happen; it occurred because God caused it (*"God created…"*). Big Bang cosmology still has no answer to that claim (see Exhibit #1: *How Could the Big Bang Happen?* in chapter 3).
- **Original conditions were not suited for life:** Whatever the precise condition of earth's primordial atmosphere might have been, scientists agree it could not have supported life. Genesis confirms added steps were needed once the earth was created.
- **Non-life preceded life. Vegetation preceded animal life:** According to Genesis, God created plant life at the end of the third day. This is consistent with natural science, which claims[455] amino acids form proteins or RNA, which lead to living organisms. Vegetation is essential to produce oxygen for our atmosphere so that animal life could appear.

Yowm	Genesis event	Verses	Natural science
1	Creation of space – time universe	1-5	Big Bang of cosmology (light bursts forth from darkness)
2	Earth formed/water begins to condense/ global sea emerges/ atmosphere (expanse) created	6-8	Volcanic activity ends/ earth cools/ atmosphere forms over the sea
3	Dry land created/ earth – moon system created/ atmosphere becomes transparent (single – celled plant life created by now)	4, 9-13	Formation of land and ocean(s)/ first plant life forms
4	Creation of sea animals (multi-cellular to amphibians/ reptiles/ winged animals). Creation of the "great reptiles" (dinosaurs?)	14-19	Clearing of the skies/ Cambrian Explosion/ age of fish/ reptiles/ small animals/ birds
5	Creation of land animals (domesticated life stock, non-domesticated, wild)	20-23	Animals
6	Creation of mammals and human life	24-27	More animals, humans

Table 23-1: Genesis' Creation Compared to Natural Science

- **Simple preceded complex:** The fossil record leads to the conclusion of natural science that simple organisms preceded more complex life forms. Genesis describes the same order of events.
- **Mankind appears at the end:** According to scientific observations, modern man appeared only recently in the geological record, later than all other life forms. Genesis teaches that God created mankind on the last day of creation.

Amazing, even mind-boggling! Those words come to mind when one realizes how accurately the 3,500-year-old Genesis account describes what human science has only figured out over the last 50 years or so. More than any generation before us, we have the scientific knowledge that shows that Moses was correct. But how could Moses have known – unless by revelation from God – how our world came to be?

☼ EXHIBIT #2: WE HAVE ALL DESCENDED FROM EVE, ADAM AND NOAH

> *"So God created man in his own image, in the image of God he created him; male and female he created them. God blessed them and said to them, 'Be fruitful and increase in number; fill the earth and subdue it. Rule over the fish of the sea and the birds of the air and over every living creature that moves on the ground.'"*
> GENESIS 1:27-28

> *"The sons of Noah who came out of the ark were Shem, Ham and Japheth. (Ham was the father of Canaan.) These were the three sons of Noah, and from them came the people who were scattered over the earth."*
> GENESIS 9:18-19

When evolution became mainstream science by the middle of the twentieth century, it was widely assumed that humans descended from a single evolutionary lineage: not that we are the result of multiple human evolutions. The consensus is that lower life forms evolved to become man, and one stream of descent flowed forward from that point. Paleo-anthropologists and geneticists speak of *"Mother Eve."* More accurately scientists should speak of "Mother Eve" and "Father Adam" because obviously you need a male and female to have descendents.[456] It is worth noting that this concept of a common male and female ancestor for all human beings is entirely consistent with the Genesis account of Adam and Eve.[457]

But it is even more complicated. As explained earlier,[458] by analyzing the DNA of people from all around the world we can learn about their genetic differences and through statistical analysis of the differences between their DNA, trace back their ancestors. Numerous studies[459] have been done since the end of the 1980s, and these lead to three conclusions:

- Genetically all humans are much more alike than one would expect from Darwinian theory, which suggests a young age of the species.
- Tracing mtDNA (mitochondrial DNA) through females, one learns that all women descend from one female ancestor ("biological Eve") who lived an estimated 100,000 years ago.
- Tracing the Y-chromosome, studies show that all men descend from one male ancestor ("biological Adam") who lived between 37,000 and 49,000 years ago.

Various studies reach different conclusions as to the exact age of "biological Eve" and "biological Adam," but they all agree: the common male ancestor is significantly younger than the common female ancestor. How can this difference in age between "biological Adam" and "biological Eve" be explained? How can "Eve" be 50,000 years older than "Adam"? Evolutionary science does not seem to have an answer to this well documented conundrum. Likely most believe that more study and research will ultimately reveal an answer.

However, there is a good explanation for this. The genetic observation that the common male ancestor of modern man is much younger than the common female ancestor is perfectly explained by the flood account of Noah. Genesis 9:18-19 teaches there were only eight flood survivors who repopulated the earth: Noah, his three sons, his wife and his three daughters-in-law. Noah and his sons were the only surviving males, all related and shared the same Y-chromosome DNA. So if genetics traces back the male Y-chromosome DNA, the found common ancestor for all males would be Noah. This situation is different for the four surviving females. They were not related to each other, thus, their common ancestor mtDNA will not be found at the flood, but much earlier. It is very likely to assume that their common ancestor (female) mtDNA would go back all the way to the first woman, "biological Eve." So, "biological Eve" is the same as "Genesis' Eve," but Genesis would point to Noah as "biological Adam."

Once again modern scientific observations cannot be explained by evolutionary models but confirm the Biblical accounts of creation and the flood!

ADAM AND EVE PROBABLY NEVER MET

It is a rewarding and educational to read the following article with the above mentioned title. It is an excerpt from a press release and publication in *Nature Genetics* (emphasis added):[460]

"In an international collaborative effort, Peter Underhill of Stanford University and colleagues have carried out a study of human Y-chromosome variation, by far the most comprehensive and informative ever conducted. Whereas <u>it confirms the 'out-of-Africa' origin of modern humans, it suggests that our most recent common paternal ancestor ('Y-chromosome Adam') would have been about 84,000 years younger than our maternal one ('Mitochondrial Eve').</u> ...Fossil records have suggested that Homo Sapiens of the sapiens variety, to which all of us belong, first appeared in Africa or South-West Asia, about 150,000 years ago, a time when the current brain size is also thought to have been fixed. It is thought that they later left Africa for Asia and Europe where the earliest fossils of our kind are about 50,000 years old. This out-of-Africa hypothesis was confirmed by studies of mitochondrial DNA, a peculiar part of our genome that comes exclusively

from the mother. Based on these studies, our most recent common ancestor is thought to be a woman who lived in Africa about 143,000 years ago. Through a detailed analysis of the paternal lineage of more than 1,000 men from 22 different geographic areas, researchers propose that our most recent common ancestor was a man who lived in Africa around 59,000 years ago. How can these studies be reconciled? How could Adam and Eve have ever begotten us if they never met?

Paleontology has always had a problem with dates. However, the thoroughness of the current study as well as 13 years of mitochondrial DNA analysis indicate that fallible interpretations cannot explain the whole discrepancy with the Book of Genesis."

This scientific publication corroborates our earlier discussion of genetic dating of our common ancestors. The article mentions a somewhat earlier date for "biological Eve" or "mitochondrial Eve," 150,000 years, not the earlier-mentioned 100,000 years (which indicates data from different studies). Even so, the numbers are in the same order of magnitude. Estimating age based on DNA remains a mere statistical "best guess," consequently disparity in dates is to be expected. Their conclusions are interesting, in that, as usual, they are slanted to an evolutionary view:

- "Biological Adam" (the article calls him "Y-chromosome Adam") is much younger than "biological Eve" (she is "mitochondrial Eve"). That is consistent with the other studies and confirms that this fact is well documented and corroborated.
- Subsequently the article concludes (and even mentions in the title): Therefore he could never have met her. That is correct, of course. We've also reached that conclusion, and that is the evidence for the flood.
- The article asks, *"How could Adam and Eve have begotten us if they never met?"* Does this indicate a *"discrepancy with the Book of Genesis?"* That attempt to discredit the Bible is false, and not even logical. First, if "biological Adam" and "biological Eve" never met, how is it possible that we even exist? Evolutionary theory assumes the existence of "a first couple." If "biological Eve" lived long ages before "biological Adam," how can evolution explain how Eve got children? Secondly, the Biblical flood resolves any so called discrepancy. The Bible has an answer; evolution has not.

☼ Exhibit #3: Telomeres – We Cannot Live Forever

"Then the Lord said, 'My Spirit will not contend with man forever,
for he is mortal; his days will be a hundred and twenty years.'"
GENESIS 6:3

Telomere, the section of DNA base pairs at the end of the chromosome,[461] functions as a disposable buffer. Each time the chromosome replicates during production of new cells, the complete chromosome is not duplicated; a small section at the end of the chromosome is lost. If it were not for telomeres, this would result in the loss of important genetic information needed to sustain the cell's activity.

Over time, the telomere section gets smaller and smaller. And, if the telomere is all "used up" the cell can no longer successfully duplicate. This process has been referred to as the *"end replication problem."* From a biology/genetics perspective – this is why and how we age: fewer and fewer cells in our body can replicate themselves.

Research in this area is still in an early phase, as the exact working and role of telomere is far from fully understood. Though it is probable that changing telomere lengths will influence the ability of the cell to continue to replicate, it has not been positively proved that telomere shortening is indeed the reason for aging rather than a consequence of it.

Much more research is needed, but the existence of a "life-ending" genetic instruction is surely a confirmation of a design decision made by the Creator to limit the age of mankind!

☼ Exhibit #4: The Ark of Noah

"So God said to Noah, 'I am going to put an end to all people, for the
earth is filled with violence because of them. I am surely going to destroy
both them and the earth. So make yourself an ark of cypress wood; make
rooms in it and coat it with pitch inside and out. This is how you are to
build it: The ark is to be 450 feet long, 75 feet wide and 45 feet high.
Make a roof for it and finish the ark to within 18 inches of the top. Put
a door in the side of the ark and make lower, middle and upper decks.'"
GENESIS 6:13-16

In Genesis chapters 6-9 we read about the global flood and the ark Noah is instructed to build by God in order to save his family (himself, his wife, his three sons, and their wives) and pairs of every kind of animal.

Many Christians have been scorned, because they believe the account of the ark. How gullible must one be to believe pairs of animals just "showed up" to march onto the ark? Can you really believe a pair of polar bears walked all the way from the North Pole to somewhere in the Middle East to board an ark? How about penguins? Or kangaroos?

The Bible does not explain to us how this was accomplished, but if we believe in a God who created our world, it is not too hard to believe this same God could also make the boarding of the ark happen.

The amazing evidence from Noah's account, however, is the ark itself. What did it look like? Genesis records specific dimensions as well as detailed instructions on how the ark should be built. This is not merely a little rowboat. Nor did it look like ships of those days. You do not have to be an expert on "Bronze Age boat building" to realize that marine vessels in those days were likely quite small, not able to carry large loads or many passengers. Likely they were not seaworthy enough to cross large bodies of water. In the New Testament people must have faced the same nautical problems encountered by those in Noah's day. We read about the challenges they met daily while fishing on the Lake of Galilee, and how Paul was shipwrecked in a great storm.

In 1992, archaeologists in Dover, England, unearthed remains of a large wooden boat thought to be 3,550 years old (which would date it near the time of Moses). This boat is called *the Dover boat*.[462] Its size is estimated at 15-18 meters (50-60 feet) long (only about half to two-thirds of the boat has been retrieved), and 2.4 meters (8 feet) wide. It could have crossed the channel, carrying supplies, livestock, and passengers, propelled likely by at least 18 paddlers.

This would have been a fairly large boat for the Bronze Age. Compare this to the ark. The ark was 450 feet long (as much as nine times the length of the Dover boat) and 75 feet wide (again, more than nine times wider). That makes the square footage of the ark about 85 times larger! Plus, the Dover boat is just an open row boat. In contrast the ark is 45 feet (3 decks) high – a veritable monster compared to the Dover boat!

The dimensions and shape of the ark make it actually resemble a modern container ship.

Shaped like a rectangular box with a 6-to-1 (450 feet to 75 feet) dimensional ratio, the ark would have had excellent stability. The normal length-to-width ratio of ancient ships was 10 to 1. However, Noah used the same proportions as we now use in modern ship construction. An interesting parallel to the size of the ark can be seen in the well-known *Titanic*. The *Titanic* was 823 feet long by 98 feet wide (a 9-to-1 ratio) with a cargo capacity of 45,000 tons. It's total capacity was quite similar to Noah's Ark, though *Titanic* was somewhat longer and wider.[463]

Has the ark ever been found?

Our faith does not depend on the discovery of Noah's ark, but one can wonder if it could be recovered.

The first question is, what would be found? The ark was built from cypress wood, and the flood – according to Genesis – occurred 4,500-5,000 years ago. A wooden ship that old, even one as big as the ark, likely would have long since disappeared. That is, unless preserved in ice, like a glacier on a high mountain such as Mount Ararat (that name of the location where the ark landed on solid ground) in modern day Turkey.

Reports over the past century range from aerial photographs to visits to the site to even recovery of timber. Ark-eologists claim that at least a substantial part of the Ark is intact, not on the highest peak, but above the 10,000-foot level. Apparently lost beneath snow and ice most of the year, during certain warm summers the structure can be seen and even approached. Some speak of climbing on the roof, others say they have walked inside. Unfortunately, return visits have produced no further evidence, the whereabouts of all photographs are unknown at present, and different sightings do not suggest the same location on the mountain. An additional complication is the lack of cooperation from the Turkish government. Additional expeditions have not produced new discoveries. More expeditions are pending. If evidence of such a ship is found, the world will certainly hear about it.

Taking the ark's dimensions and using "a sheep" as an average animal, Dr. John Whitcomb and Dr. Henry Morris[464] calculated the ark could have contained as many as 130,500 animals. They estimate the total number at about 17,600 (3,500 mammals, 8,600 birds, 5,500 reptiles and amphibians). They conclude the ark would be filled only to perhaps 27% of its available space.

Obviously many disagree with their calculations, but it is beyond dispute that the ark was large, especially for its time, and its dimensions and ratio's are remarkably consistent with modern-day shipbuilding. Certainly it displayed a technical expertise not known in the days of either Noah or Moses.

Moses lived most of his life in the desert. Likely the only ships he had seen were the small boats that traveled the Nile. How did he know these dimensions? How could a man of the sand conceive of a container ship? And how could he know the preferred ratio of length, width, and height of such a vessel?

☼ EXHIBIT #5: TIMING OF CIRCUMCISION

> *"Then God said to Abraham, 'As for you, you must keep my covenant, you and your descendants after you for the generations to come. This is my covenant with you and your descendants after you, the covenant you are to keep: Every male among you shall be circumcised. You are to undergo circumcision, and it will be the sign of the covenant between me and you. For the generations to come every male among you who is eight days old must be circumcised, including those born in your household or bought with money from a foreigner – those who are not your offspring.'"*
> GENESIS 17:9-12

> *"The Lord said to Moses, 'Say to the Israelites: "A woman who becomes pregnant and gives birth to a son will be ceremonially unclean for seven days, just as she is unclean during her monthly period. On the eighth day the boy is to be circumcised."'"*
> LEVITICUS 12:1-3

Genesis 17:9-12 tells that, as part of their covenant, God commanded Abraham that he and his male descendants had to be circumcised. This would serve as the physical sign that a male was under the covenant of God with Abraham. This command is explicitly repeated in the Mosaic Law in Leviticus 12:1-3.

Many claim circumcision has medical benefits; i.e., it increases hygiene and reduces the chances of urinary tract infections and penile cancer. Recently it has also been thought to reduce the risk of contracting HIV by as much as 70%.[465] Lowering HIV risk is a major benefit, especially in countries where AIDS has become an epidemic. Another recent study of 8,000 adult males in Kenya and Uganda concluded that circumcision reduces risk of HIV infection by half.[466]

However, the medical opinion in the US is not unanimous about benefits. In 1971 the American Academy of Pediatrics claimed that *"there are no valid medical indications for circumcision in the neonatal period."* [467]

There are no recorded potential negative medical effects resulting from circumcision.

Both Genesis and the Mosaic Law explicitly specify that circumcision needs to take place on the eighth day. Why this specific day? Remarkably, various medical doctors[468] indicate that on the eighth day the chance of dangerous bleedings is the smallest. The clotting factor is stronger on this day than on the seventh or even on the ninth. Available thrombin (or prothrombin), a protein that plays a major role in the clotting process, is at 90% of its ultimate level at birth. On the third day following birth it drops to 38%, and then recovers to exceed 100% by the eighth day, later to drop back to 100% levels for the remainder of one's life.

How could Moses have known that the eight day is medically the preferred day for this procedure?

☼ EXHIBIT #6: HYGIENE AND CONTAGIOUS DISEASES

"When someone has a burn on his skin and a reddish-white or white spot appears in the raw flesh of the burn, the priest is to examine the spot, and if the hair in it has turned white, and it appears to be more than skin deep, it is an infectious disease that has broken out in the burn. The priest shall pronounce him unclean; it is an infectious skin disease. But if the priest examines it and there is no white hair in the spot and if it is not more than skin deep and has faded, then the priest is to put him in isolation for seven days. On the seventh day the priest is to examine him, and if it is spreading in the skin, the priest shall pronounce him unclean; it is an infectious skin disease. If, however, the spot is unchanged and has not spread in the skin but has faded, it is a swelling from the burn, and the priest shall pronounce him clean; it is only a scar from the burn."
LEVITICUS 13:24-28

"When a man has lost his hair and is bald, he is clean. If he has lost his hair from the front of his scalp and has a bald forehead, he is clean. But if he has a reddish-white sore on his bald head or forehead, it is an infectious disease breaking out on his head or forehead. The priest is to examine him, and if the swollen sore on his head or forehead is reddish-white like an infectious skin disease, the man is diseased and is unclean. The priest shall pronounce him unclean because of the sore on his head. The person with such an infectious disease must wear torn clothes, let his hair be unkempt, cover the lower part of his face and cry out, 'Unclean! Unclean!' As long as he has the infection he remains unclean. He must live alone; he must live outside the camp."
LEVITICUS 13:40-46

Hygiene is commonly understood as the prevention of infection and contagious diseases by cleanliness. We now consider good hygiene to be common sense, because we know bacteria and infectious diseases spread through physical contact and a wider spread can be prevented by simple techniques such as washing hands, clean food preparation, clean drinking water, burying human waste, burning infected items, avoiding contact with dead bodies, and so on.

This understanding is relatively new. Before the nineteenth century, the importance of hygiene was not appreciated by the Western world. In those days a hospital stay carried the significant risk of disease, as not even doctors would wash their hands between treatments.

A dramatic breakthrough was the work of Dr. Ignaz Semmelweis (1818-1865), a Hungarian physician. He is often referred to as the "Savior of Mothers" because in 1847 he discovered the incidence of childbed fever (puerperal fever, an infection of the mother's genital tract shortly after birth) could be significantly reduced by simple hand-washing. This disease was common up to the mid-nineteenth century, with hospitals recording mortality rates as high as 35%! Even though Vienna General Hospital, where Semmelweis worked, saw mortality rates plummet from 18% to less than 1%, it was only much later that his work was recognized. It was confirmed by Louis Pasteur's germ theory and the invention of pasteurization in 1862.[469]

Many illustrations of bad hygiene and its deadly effects through history are available. One example is the spread of the *Black Death* (the plague) from 1347 to 1352. The plague is estimated to have killed as many as 60 million people in Europe in only five years.[470] A number estimated to be as high as half of Europe's population at that time. As the Black Death ravaged Europe, desperate people turned to the church for guidance. Returning to the laws of Moses, they instituted principles practiced by the Israelites for dealing with diseases such as leprosy, for handling of the dead and waste disposal, and for quarantine as described in Leviticus 13, 14, and 15. It is now understood that these procedures were essential to the control of this tragic epidemic.

Leprosy was far more common in the ancient world, even though there are still millions of lepers today. This disease is contagious during its active phase, but once the disease has run its course, the risk of contamination is over. As Leviticus 13:46 commands: *"As long as he has the infection, he remains unclean."* However, after the infection is over, the person could come back into the camp.[471]

Once again, how could Moses have known this?

☼ EXHIBIT #7: DIETARY RULES FOR A HEALTHIER LIFE

"He said, 'If you listen carefully to the voice of the Lord your God and do what is right in his eyes, if you pay attention to his commands and keep all his decrees, I will not bring on you any of the diseases I brought on the Egyptians, for I am the Lord, who heals you.'"
EXODUS 15:26

"The Lord said to Moses, 'Say to the Israelites: "Do not eat any of the fat of cattle, sheep or goats. The fat of an animal found dead or torn by wild animals may be used for any other purpose, but you must not eat it... And wherever you live, you must not eat the blood of any bird or animal. If anyone eats blood, that person must be cut off from his people."'"
LEVITICUS 7:22-27

The Mosaic Law contains explicit instructions to Israel as to what to eat and what not to eat. These rules, it seems, were intended to set the Israelites apart from their neighbors, the Canaanites, and to break any remaining ties to Egypt. Apart from this, we now know, they also constituted a very healthy diet! [472]

For example, the instructions against eating fat (Leviticus 3:17, 7:23-24) and blood (Genesis 9:4-5, Leviticus 3:17, 7:26, 17:14 and 19:26) in the Old Testament and the New Testament (in Acts 15:29) have obvious health benefits in our culture of clogged arteries and diseases transmitted through blood. Furthermore, we know that only freshly killed meat is healthy, and it makes good sense not to eat "road kill" (Leviticus 7:24, 22:8 and Deuteronomy 14:21) and to avoid scavenger animals (Leviticus 11).

☼ EXHIBIT #8: RULES AGAINST INCEST

"No one is to approach any close relative to have sexual relations. I am the Lord."
LEVITICUS 18:6

Leviticus 18:6-30 reveals a long list of restrictions and warnings of certain sexual relationships. Incest is explicitly forbidden; that is, sexual relationships with close relatives. In our day, the advance of medical science and genetics tells us that incest not only creates numerous psychological problems caused by abuse, but also increases chances of genetic diseases.

Wait! If incest is forbidden – how did Cain get his wife? Through Genesis 5:3-4 we know that Adam had a third son named Seth as well as other sons and daughters. The first sons and daughters of Adam and Eve had to marry each other to populate the earth. Cain probably married a sister or cousin. Assuming the accuracy of the Genesis account, and considering the length of lives recorded (900 years, on average), a sizeable population could have developed quite rapidly.

All this raises the issue of incest. If incest is scripturally forbidden, and it was by the Mosaic Law, how do we explain the marriage of siblings in the days of Adam and Abraham? Again, genetics helps us understand this situation. When Adam and Eve were created, they were created with perfect DNA. No errors were present in their chromosomes.[473] Therefore, the risk of in-breeding caused by both DNA bases (letters) damaged in the same DNA base pair was not present. Over the subsequent generations from Adam through Noah, Abraham (Sarah was Abraham's half-sister!), Isaac, Jacob, and ultimately to Moses, more and more genetic errors crept into the people's DNA, slowly increasing the risk of in-breeding through incest.

Therefore at the time of Moses, God instituted a new law – one that had not been revealed earlier – that sexual relationships with close relatives were no longer allowed.

How could Moses have known this without knowledge of genetics? It is fascinating to see how events described in the Bible perfectly fit the slow degeneration of the human genetic record over multiple generations and the current risk incest imposes for genetic diseases.

ARE THERE MORE SCIENTIFIC EVIDENCES?

The above discussion is not exhaustive. Only evidences that could be objectively supported by scientific data were considered, avoiding objections that the "text does not realty say this." Each of the eight exhibits presented demonstrates a case where the Bible is explicit in its statements, with insight clearly beyond the knowledge of those times. Thus the only explanation is that God inspired these writings.

In table 23-2 is an overview of other Scripture passages considered evidence for the scientific accuracy of the Bible, again, recorded before this information was common knowledge to the world.

Other Scientific Statements in the Bible

Scientific fact/observation	Bible Text	Reference
The universe came into existence out of nothing	*"the universe was formed at God's command, so that what is seen was not made out of what was visible."*	Hebrews 11:3
Moisture goes through a cycle of evaporation and condensation	*"He makes clouds rise from the ends of the earth; he sends lightning with the rain"*	Psalm 135:7
The earth is spherical in shape	*"He sits enthroned above the circle of the earth..."*	Isaiah 40:22
The earth rotates upon its axis	*"The earth takes shape like clay under a seal..."*	Job 38:13-14
The earth is suspended in space	*"He suspends the earth over nothing."*	Job 26:7
Tides vary in the late evening and early morning hours	*"He marks out the horizon on the face of the waters for a boundary between light and darkness."*	Job 26:10
The stars cannot be numbered	*"...as countless as the stars of the sky..."*	Jeremiah 33:22
The stars travel in certain paths	*"From the heavens the stars fought, from their courses they fought against Sisera."*	Judges 5:20
The blood sustains life	*"For the life of a creature is in the blood..."*	Leviticus 17:11
The universe is running down	*"They will perish, but you remain; they will all wear out like a garment."*	Psalm 102:25-26
The stars are a great distance from the earth	*"And see how lofty are the highest stars!"*	Job 22:12
The stars differ in magnitude	*"...and star differs from star in splendor."*	1 Corinthians 15:41
The chemical composition of man and earth are identical	*"...for he knows how we are formed, he remembers that we are dust."*	Psalm 103:14

Table 23-2: Other Scientific Facts in the Bible

CHAPTER 24

Fulfilled Prophecies – Glimpses of the Future

"If what a prophet proclaims in the name of the Lord does not take place or come true, that is a message the Lord has not spoken. That prophet has spoken presumptuously. Do not be afraid of him."
DEUTERONOMY 18:22

"Above all, you must understand that no prophecy of Scripture came about by the prophet's own interpretation. For prophecy never had its origin in the will of man, but men spoke from God as they were carried along by the Holy Spirit."
PETER 1:20-21

WHAT IS A PROPHECY?

A Biblical prophecy is the forth-telling of truth, touching not only the future, but also the present or the past. In apologetics the study of prophecies limits itself to the foretelling of events fulfilled in history, but documented well before they happened.

Throughout history, people have sought to know future events from special individuals or groups said to have the gift of prophecy, such as the *Oracles at Delphi* in ancient Greece or *Nostradamus* (1503-1566). Nostradamus, the Latin name of Michel de Nostredame, has been one of the most famous publishers of prophecies. He is best known for his book *Les Propheties*[474] published in 1555. Since then, many people have been virtually obsessed with his work. His followers claim he predicted numerous world events such as the rise of Adolph Hitler and Nazi Germany. However, his prophecies are questionable, to say the least. They are found in 942 quatrains (four-line poems) which are cryptic, confusing, and quite imaginative. For instance his most famous quatrain about Hitler and Nazi Germany reads as follows:

"Beasts ferocious from hunger will swim across rivers:
The greater part of the region will be against the Hister,
The great one will cause it to be dragged in an iron cage,
When the German child will observe nothing."

What does this mean? Basically, it's anyone's guess. Believers of Nostradamus insist that "*the Hister*" describes Hitler, and the "*Beasts ferocious from hunger*" refer to Germany during WWII. This type of creative interpretation is used to link a number of his many quatrains to world events. However, the great majority of his predictions have not happened yet, and those supposed to have happened are at best dimly vague and darkly cryptic. The vast majority of serious scholars reject them as "*unintelligible and garbled by the uninitiated.*" [475]

Nostradamus demonstrates the ageless intrigue of prophecy. In addition, it also reminds us that a true prophet must present hard, objective, solid, and non-disputed evidence, since accurate prophecies are not possible in the natural world. Only one with perfect knowledge of the future can prophesy correctly. Obviously that is possible only for God.

Fulfilled prophecies can be hotly debated, but they are exceptionally strong evidence for the credibility of the Bible as God's word. Doubted and debated by critics, prophecy demands solid evidence; nothing less is convincing. Fulfilled prophecies contained in the Bible demonstrate that Holy Scripture is truly God's Word. No other book has ever been able – beyond objective, reasonable doubt – to uncover the future.

Since prophecies attract intense skepticism, we will apply some tough criteria:
- **Written before fulfillment**: It has to be proved that the prophecy was written down well before the predicted event would have occurred.
- **Unambiguous:** The prophecy has to be clear, and its meaning beyond dispute. Vague wording open for multiple interpretations could be genuine, but such prophecies will not be considered in this analysis.
- **Historically fulfilled:** The fulfillment of the prophecy has to be historically recorded, not open to misinterpretation, and carry some significance.
- **No intentional fulfillment:** The fulfillment has to be beyond control of any involved party, that is, it could not have been an intentional fulfillment.

Not all prophecies that fail to meet these criteria can be rejected as genuine! Not at all. However, critics will insist that unless it can be demonstrated beyond doubt that a prophecy meets these criteria, it could have been invented by the writer or intentionally fulfilled. Thus it would not "count."

A well-known prophecy written around 520 BC by the prophet Zechariah illustrates this point. The prophet foretold that the Messiah would enter Jerusalem on a donkey: "*Rejoice greatly, O Daughter of Zion! Shout, Daughter of Jerusalem! See, your king comes to you, righteous and having salvation, gentle and riding on a donkey, on a colt, the foal of a donkey*" (Zechariah 9:9). All four gospels record its fulfillment on Palm Sunday, when Jesus rode into Jerusalem on a donkey. However, the gospels are also clear that Jesus initiated the event, intentionally fulfilling this prophecy. Hence this foretold presentation of the Messiah on a donkey remains a genuine prophecy and its fulfillment valid, but critics deny it supports divine inspiration. The fulfillment can be explained by actions of men, they insist, so therefore God is not necessarily behind it.

There are hundreds of prophecies in Christian Scripture.[476] Commonly they are divided into two categories; those related to Jesus (*Messianic prophecies*) and those not related to Jesus (*non-Messianic prophecies*).

Before we continue this discussion, it is beneficial to recall that the following facts and dates are beyond any competent scholarly dispute:

- All books of the Old Testament were written before 250 BC. This is proved by the Septuagint translation, which began as early as 285 BC, so to be safe, set the date of the translation at 250 BC. Any translation demands first an original to-be-translated text.
- The Dead Sea Scrolls contain fragments of every book of the OT, with the single exception of Esther. This provides physical (extant) manuscript evidence, demonstrating these books were available in Hebrew well before the birth of Christ.
- The gospels, Acts, and Paul's epistles were all written before 100 AD. Individual books have earlier non-disputed dates.

FULFILLED NON-MESSIANIC PROPHECIES

The great majority of non-Messianic prophecies deal with predictions and fulfillments in the Old Testament times. The oldest confirmations of the OT texts are the Septuagint and the Dead Sea Scrolls, so it remains a serious challenge to prove these prophecies were written before their fulfillment. Critical scholars simply assert each so called prophecy had to be written after its fulfillment. Why? As it is their assumption that genuine prophecy is not possible, they will only support a late date theory. Examples of this approach are the debates over the authorship and date of the books of Moses, Daniel, and Isaiah.[477]

Table 24-1 gives an overview of a selection of the prophecies that span long periods of time and which are fulfilled in history and/or confirmed by other texts. We will limit our analysis to only a few of these prophecies.

Selection of Non-Messianic Prophecies

Prophecy	Prediction	Fulfillment
Abraham to have numerous descendants	Genesis 12:2	In history
God promised Abraham's descendants the land of Palestine (the "promised land")	Genesis 12:7	In history
David anointed as king while still a young boy	1 Samuel 16:1-23	2 Samuel 2:1-4
David's name would be great	2 Samuel 7:9	In history
Solomon would built the temple	2 Samuel 7:13	1 Kings 6:37-38
Because of its many sins, Israel will be judged by God	Isaiah 1:1-25	2 Chronicles 36
Assyria will invade and desolate the land	Isaiah 7:18-25	2 Kings 17:1-18
Prediction of judgment on Babylon	Isaiah 13:1-22	Daniel 5
Prediction that Cyrus would authorize the rebuilding of the temple in Jerusalem	Isaiah 44:28-45:4	Ezra 1:1-4
The captivity of Israel in Babylon would last 70 years	Jeremiah 25:1-11	Ezra 1, history
Description of the destruction of Tyre	Ezekiel 26:3-14	In 332 BC
Nebuchadnezzar's vision of the four world empires	Daniel 2:1-44	In history
Babylon's fall: the writing on the wall	Daniel 5:25-28	In history
The four beasts predicting the world empires	Daniel 7:1-7	In history
The vision prophesying the future of Persia and Greece	Daniel 8:1-22	In history
The city of Nineveh would be destroyed	Jonah 1:1	612 BC
Jesus predicts the complete destruction of the temple	Mark 13:1-2	70 AD
Jesus predicts Peter's denial	All gospels	All gospels
Jesus predicts Peter's crucifixion	John 21:18-19	67 AD in Rome

Table 24-1: Selection of Non-Messianic Prophecies

✵ EXHIBIT #9: ISAIAH'S PROPHECY ABOUT CYRUS, KING OF PERSIA

> *"The Lord ... who says of Cyrus, 'He is my shepherd and will accomplish all that I please; he will say of Jerusalem, "Let it be rebuilt,"*
> *and of the temple, "Let its foundations be laid." 'This is what the*
> *Lord says to his anointed, to Cyrus, whose right hand I take hold of to*
> *subdue nations before him and to strip kings of their armor, to open*
> *doors before him so that gates will not be shut.'"*
> ISAIAH 44:28-45:1

This prophecy is abundantly clear: A certain man named *"Cyrus"* will authorize the rebuilding of Jerusalem and the temple.

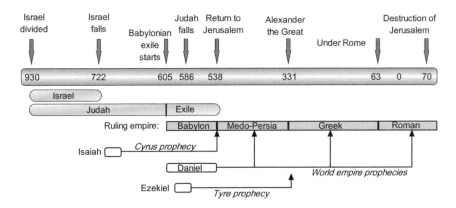

Figure 24-1: Timeline for the Non-Messianic Prophecies

Please check the timeline (see figure 24-1) related to this prophecy. Isaiah prophesied around 700 BC, about 100 years before Babylon destroyed Jerusalem and perhaps 160 years before Cyrus, king of Media and Persia, conquered Jerusalem and Babylon in 539 BC. The following year Cyrus permitted Jews to return to their land and build a temple:

"In the first year of Cyrus king of Persia, in order to fulfill the word of the Lord spoken by Jeremiah, the Lord moved the heart of Cyrus king of Persia to make a proclamation throughout his realm and to put it in writing: This is what Cyrus king of Persia says: 'The Lord, the God of heaven, has given me all the kingdoms of the earth and he has appointed me to build a temple for him at Jerusalem in Judah. Anyone of his people among you – may the Lord his God be with him, and let him go up'" 2 Chronicles 36:22-23 (cf. Ezra 1:1-4).

Analysis of the prophecy:
- The prophecy is crystal clear, historically fulfilled,[478] and beyond control of the Jews.
- The archaeological discovery of the *"Cyrus Cylinder"* confirms Cyrus' policies as to the freedom of religion. It explains why Cyrus let the Jewish captives return to rebuilt the Jerusalem temple exactly as predicted in the prophecy.[479]
- The weakest criterion is the dating of this prediction of Isaiah, given the Deutero-Isaiah alternative. This theory claims the latter part of the book was written later by another author. Actually, the Cyrus prophecy is probably the reason critics have tried to re-date the second half of Isaiah and onwards to around 550 BC or later.[480]

✵ EXHIBIT #10: DANIEL'S PROPHECIES OF THE WORLD EMPIRES

"After you, another kingdom will rise, inferior to yours. Next, a third kingdom, one of bronze, will rule over the whole earth. Finally, there will be a fourth kingdom, strong as iron – for iron breaks and smashes everything – and as iron breaks things to pieces, so it will crush and break all the others."
DANIEL 2:39-40

"Four great beasts, each different from the others, came up out of the sea. The first was like a lion, and it had the wings of an eagle. I watched until its wings were torn off and it was lifted from the ground so that it stood on two feet like a man, and the heart of a man was given to it. And there before me was a second beast, which looked like a bear. It was raised up on one of its sides, and it had three ribs in its mouth between its teeth. It was told, 'Get up and eat your fill of flesh!' After that, I looked, and there before me was another beast, one that looked like a leopard. And on its back it had four wings like those of a bird. This beast had four heads, and it was given authority to rule. After that, in my vision at night I looked, and there before me was a fourth beast – terrifying and frightening and very powerful. It had large iron teeth; it crushed and devoured its victims and trampled underfoot whatever was left."
DANIEL 7:3-7

"The two-horned ram that you saw represents the kings of Media and Persia. The shaggy goat is the king of Greece, and the large horn between his eyes is the first king. The four horns that replaced the one that was broken off represent four kingdoms that will emerge from his nation but will not have the same power."
DANIEL 8:20-22

The book of Daniel contains three distinct prophecies, each different from the others, but all somewhat similar. They concern the future of Babylon and the world empires coming afterward (see figure 24-1 for a historic timeline).

In Daniel chapter 2 the prophecy comes to Nebuchadnezzar *"in the second year of his reign"* (Daniel 2:1; around 604 BC) as a series of dreams about a mysterious stature. Nebuchadnezzar does not share his dreams, yet demands his advisors to explain them. Daniel has the secret revealed to him in a vision and he explains to the king that the different parts of the stature represent a series of world empires to come. The head of gold is Babylon itself; the silver represents the next kingdom (Medo-Persia), a bit weaker than Babylon. The third, the bronze part of the body, would rule the whole earth (Greece/Alexander the

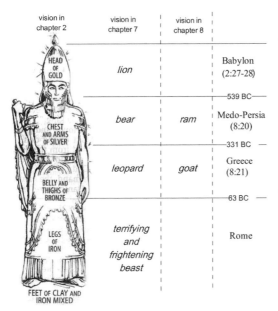

vision in chapter 2	vision in chapter 7	vision in chapter 8	
HEAD OF GOLD	lion		Babylon (2:27-28)
			——539 BC——
CHEST AND ARMS OF SILVER	bear	ram	Medo-Persia (8:20)
			——331 BC——
BELLY AND THIGHS OF BRONZE	leopard	goat	Greece (8:21)
			——63 BC——
LEGS OF IRON	terrifying and frightening beast		Rome
FEET OF CLAY AND IRON MIXED			

Figure 24-2: Overview of Daniel's World Empire Prophecies

Great) and Rome, the final kingdom, strong as iron *"will crush and break all the others."*

In chapter 7 Daniel himself *"in the first year of Belshazzar"* (ca. 553 BC) has a dream of four beasts: a lion, a bear, a leopard, and an unidentified beast, powerful with iron teeth. As in Nebuchadnezzar's dream, the beasts represent the same four kingdoms. The first kingdom is Babylon. The second represents the empire created by the pact between Media and Persia under the leadership of Cyrus; it conquered Babylon in 539 BC. Like a strong bear its power was great, but not as overwhelming as Babylon had been. The greater power of Persia as compared to the Medes is revealed in the bear raising itself up on one side. The leopard depicts the third kingdom, Greece, and the rapid conquest by Alexander the Great of Western Asia. The leopard moves at great speed, just like Alexander's rapid victories. Alexander died in Babylon in 323 BC and his empire was divided among his four generals, represented by the four heads and four wings. The fourth kingdom is not identified by a specific beast, but was historically fulfilled by the Roman Empire.

Finally, in Daniel 8 *"in the third year of King Belshazzar"* (ca. 551 BC) Daniel has another vision of a ram and a goat. As explained in the text itself, the ram represents the empire of the Medes and the Persian, the longer horn is symbolic of the stronger power of Persia. The goat represents the Greek expansion under Alexander the Great (the prominent horn) and attacks and destroys the ram. As it begins to grow, at the very height of its power, this large horn is broken off (as Alexander died in 323 BC at the zenith of his power, only 33 years old).

The three dreams/visions share many similar elements and together prophesy the defeat of Babylon by the combined empire of Media and Persia, and the latter rise of the Greeks under Alexander the Great. Daniel foresaw that the kingdom after Alexander would separate into four main divisions, all of which would ultimately fall to the rising power of the Roman Empire.[481]

Analysis of the prophecy:

- The prophecy is unambiguous (with the exception of Rome, the world empires are mentioned by name), historically fulfilled, and clearly realized beyond control of the Israelites.
- As with Isaiah the date of authorship is subject to debate. The case for dating Daniel in the sixth century BC is rather convincing[482] and trying to reassign its date about 450 years later is quite a stretch – you decide!

☼ EXHIBIT #11: EZEKIEL'S PROPHECY ABOUT TYRE

> *"The Sovereign Lord says: 'I am against you, O Tyre, and I will bring many nations against you, like the sea casting up its waves. They will destroy the walls of Tyre and pull down her towers; I will scrape away her rubble and make her a bare rock. Out in the sea she will become a place to spread fishnets, for I have spoken', declares the Sovereign Lord...'For this is what the Sovereign Lord says: From the north I am going to bring against Tyre Nebuchadnezzar king of Babylon...They will plunder your wealth and loot your merchandise; they will break down your walls and demolish your fine houses and throw your stones, timber and rubble into the sea...I will make you a bare rock, and you will become a place to spread fishnets. You will never be rebuilt, for I the Lord have spoken, declares the Sovereign Lord.'"*
> EZEKIEL 26:3-14

This text was written by the prophet Ezekiel in 590-570 BC. A contemporary of Daniel, Ezekiel was exiled to Babylon in 597 BC (eight years after Daniel); he mentions Daniel three times in his book (Ezekiel 14:14, 14:20 and 28:30). Ezekiel prophesies about the city of Tyre:

- Nebuchadnezzar will take the city.
- Other nations will participate in the fulfillment.
- The city is to be made flat like the top of a rock.
- It is to become a place for spreading nets.
- Its stones and timber are to be laid in the sea.
- The old city of Tyre will never be rebuilt.

Tyre was a city on the north coast of Palestine, an area belonging to the Phoenicians, a strong maritime people greatly feared by their enemies (The king of Tyre supplied timber used by Solomon in building the temple). In 586 BC the king of Babylon, Nebuchadnezzar, besieged Tyre. The siege lasted 13 years; when Nebuchadnezzar took the city in 573 BC, he found the Phoenicians had moved everything of value to an island about one-half mile off the coast. Without a navy the Babylonians could not take the island. Though the city had been taken, the Phoenicians were not conquered. The victory over Tyre by Nebuchadnezzar fulfilled the first part of Ezekiel's prophecy. When it was written Nebuchadnezzar was a recognized world ruler, so this part of the prophecy could easily be discarded as an educated guess. One could even claim that it was written while the Babylonians surrounded Tyre. Notice, however, Nebuchadnezzar only captured the city; he did not destroy it as Ezekiel predicted.

And now the rest of the story. Almost 250 years later, Alexander the Great fulfilled the remainder of the prophecy in 332 BC. Alexander feared the fleet of Tyre might be used against his homeland, so he decided to conquer it. He reached Tyre, now an island city, but as Nebuchadnezzar had learned before him, the city was difficult to conquer. First he captured other coastal cities and took their ships, but even these combined fleets did not enable him to take Tyre. Alexander then decided to build a causeway from the mainland to the island by taking the old city's rubble and throwing it into the sea making a land-bridge. This left the site of the old city flat like a rock due to the scraping of the material to create the causeway out to Tyre. Seven months later, leading an attack of land forces marching in over the causeway reinforced by his fleet, Alexander was able to conquer the city at last. The old city, long deserted, is now a place for fishermen.

Analysis of the prophecy:
- The prophecy depicts the destruction of Tyre, reducing the powerful commercial city to nothing more than bare rock, used only by fisherman.
- It was partly fulfilled by the Babylonians in 572 BC, and completely realized by the Greeks in 332 BC, beyond any control on the part of the Israelites, and recorded by historical sources outside the Bible. Notice how the historical events match all the details of the prophecy.
- The prophecy was written 590-570 BC. The dating and authorship of Ezekiel are beyond any competent dispute.[483]

Mathematician Peter W. Stoner calculated the probability that only random chance enabled Ezekiel to have made this prophecy and be correct in its details. His conservative calculations estimate a chance of one in 75,000,000 (75 million) that Ezekiel at the time of writing could have correctly guessed Tyre's future.[484]

✴ EXHIBIT #12: JESUS' PROPHECY ABOUT JERUSALEM

"As he was leaving the temple, one of his disciples said to him, 'Look, Teacher! What massive stones! What magnificent buildings!' 'Do you see all these great buildings?' replied Jesus. 'Not one stone here will be left on another; every one will be thrown down.'"

MARK 13:1-2

Passages that parallel the above prophecy can be found in Matthew 24:1-4 and Luke 21:5-6.

As discussed earlier, these three gospels likely shared sources; thus they are known as the synoptic gospels. This theory suggests Mark was the first written gospel and used by Matthew and Luke as a source for their gospels. This theory, and the relationship between Luke and the book of Acts, builds a widely accepted case for the Gospel of Mark to have been written well before 70 AD (likely 55-65 AD or earlier).[485]

Jerusalem was destroyed in AD 70 by Roman armies. Following a gruesome 143-day siege, Roman soldiers destroyed the city along with its celebrated temple. Titus ordered his army to preserve all religious buildings, but greedy soldiers promptly disobeyed that order. The heat of the burning city melted the gold overlay of the temple, and much of the previous metal seeped into the joints of the building's massive stones. The soldiers, paid largely by plunder, literally took apart the temple stone by stone to recover the gold.[486] Thus, Jesus' prophecy that "not one stone here will be left on another" was literally fulfilled.

Analysis of the prophecy:

This prophecy meets all the criteria for an unambiguous, unintentional and historical fulfilled prophecy verifiably written well before the event occurred.

FULFILLED MESSIANIC PROPHECIES

Old Testament Scripture contains hundreds of prophecies and allusions to the future Messiah.[487] The Hebrew "Messiah" is translated into Greek as "Christ" and means "the Anointed One." Thus Christ was first a title and later a name for Jesus of Nazareth. Some prophecies were not immediately recognized as such, are a bit vague, and seem to make sense only in hindsight. Many others were recognized by the Jews (Pharisees, Sadducees, and "Teachers of the Law") before the birth of Jesus as foretelling about the Messiah. These prophecies were so intrinsically obvious that the contemporaries of Jesus were expecting the Messiah at any moment. Their downfall was interpreting the prophecies to fit their worldly desire for a mighty leader to end the Roman occupation, whereas Jesus focused on a spiritual kingdom and a heavenly reign.

Earlier[488] we extensively discussed a number of prophecies in detail, identifying Jesus as the promised Messiah. In this section we will probe what many claim is the most explicit and remarkable prophecy about the Christ: Daniel 9:24-27, also known as Daniel's *"Seventy Sevens."* Written toward the end of the Babylonian exile, it foretells the year (even the day) that the Messiah will be presented to the people of Israel.

☼ EXHIBIT #13: DANIEL'S "SEVENTY SEVENS"

> *"Seventy 'sevens' are decreed for your people and your holy city to finish transgression, to put an end to sin, to atone for wickedness, to bring in everlasting righteousness, to seal up vision and prophecy and to anoint the most holy."*

(break between not yet fulfilled and fulfilled part of the prophecy)

> *"Know and understand this: From the issuing of the decree to restore and rebuild Jerusalem until the Anointed One, the ruler, comes, there will be seven 'sevens,' and sixty-two 'sevens.' It will be rebuilt with streets and a trench, but in times of trouble. After the sixty-two 'sevens,' the Anointed One will be cut off and will have nothing."*

(break between fulfilled and not yet fulfilled part of the prophecy)

> *"The people of the ruler who will come will destroy the city and the sanctuary. The end will come like a flood: War will continue until the end, and desolations have been decreed. He will confirm a covenant with many for one 'seven.' In the middle of the 'seven' he will put an end to sacrifice and offering. And on a wing of the temple he will set up an abomination that causes desolation, until the end that is decreed is poured out on him."*
> DANIEL 9:24-27 (EMPHASIS ADDED)

This may well be the most impressive and one of the most complex prophecies about the Messiah in the entire Bible.[489] It is impressive because it predicts almost to the day 550 years in advance, the event we have come to know as Palm Sunday. It is complex, linking as many as ten different books of the Bible in its interpretation and fulfillment. As such, it is not only remarkable evidence for divine inspiration due to fulfilled prophecy, but also shows the unity and integration of books of Scripture written centuries apart. It could well be described as "the most complex story problem in the Bible."

A few observations are necessary before we analyze the prophecy itself:

Three parts to the prophecy: The prophecy consists of three units. The first, a period of "seventy sevens" (Daniel 9:24) has not been completed. The second part deals with "seven sevens" and "sixty-two sevens" (Daniel 9:25-first half of 26), a total of "sixty-nine" out of the earlier mentioned "seventy sevens." This part has been completely fulfilled. The third deals with the remaining "one seven" (Daniel 9: second half of 26-27) and has not yet been fulfilled. As we look for evidences from fulfilled prophecy, we will limit our discussion to the second part of the prophecy.

The "sevens" refer to years: Scholars generally agree each "set of seven" (also translated "week") likely represents a "week of years," or seven years.

The "seventy sevens" are not completed: This span of "seventy sevens" is not completed, as its six notable achievements have not all been realized yet. These are (Daniel 9:24): *"finish transgressions," "put an end to sin," "atone for wickedness," "bring everlasting righteousness," "seal up vision and prophecy,"* and *"anoint the most holy."* Bible scholars universally understand these six achievements to describe Christ's atonement at Calvary and His everlasting reign realized by His second coming.

Jesus Himself referred to this prophecy: On an evening during the Passover week, Jesus refers to this prophecy during one of his last private meetings with His disciples: *"So when you see standing in the holy place 'the abomination that causes desolation,' spoken of through the prophet Daniel – let the reader understand – then let those who are in Judea flee to the mountains"* (Matthew 24:15-16, also alluded to in Mark 13:14).

Daniel received the prophecy from Gabriel in 539-538 BC: Daniel received the prophecy from the angel Gabriel in a vision while praying. We know from Daniel 9:1 this is the first year of the reign of Darius, son of Xerxes, either 539 or 538 BC.

The end of the exile was foretold: It is also intriguing to see the reason why Daniel was praying. In Daniel 9:2 we learn Daniel had read the words of Jeremiah 25:11-12: *"'This whole country will become a desolate wasteland, and these nations will serve the king of Babylon seventy years. But when the seventy years are fulfilled, I will punish the king of Babylon and his nation, the land of the Babylonians, for their guilt,' declares the LORD, 'and will make it desolate forever.'"* (This was written around 627 BC, 21 years before Babylon conquered Jerusalem and exiled Daniel). We also see in 2 Chronicles 36:20-21 a confirmation of the scripture: *"He carried into exile to Babylon the remnant, who* *escaped from the sword, and they became servants to him and his sons until the kingdom of Persia came to power. The land enjoyed its Sabbath rests; all the time of its desolation it rested, until the seventy years were completed in fulfillment of the word of the LORD spoken by Jeremiah."*

As Daniel's exile started at 605 BC, he realized the seventy years were about completed and the end of the exile was at hand. This occurred in 538 BC when the Medo-Persians (Cyrus – see the Isaiah Cyrus prophecy) conquered Babylon.

WHEN DO THE SEVENTY SEVENS BEGIN?

According to the text, the period of seventy sevens starts *"from the issuing of the decree to restore and rebuild Jerusalem"* (Daniel 9:25). What does that mean?

Several decrees are mentioned in the Bible, each of which relates to Jerusalem:

- **The decree of Cyrus, 539/538 BC:** *"…let him go up to Jerusalem in Judah and build the temple of the Lord…"* (Ezra 1:1-4). This is a decree to rebuild the temple.
- **The decree of Darius, 519 BC:** *"…Moreover, I hereby decree what you are to do for these elders of the Jews in the construction of this house of God…"* (Ezra 6:6-12). Here Darius confirmed the decree of Cyrus.
- **The decree of Artaxerxes I to Ezra, 458 BC:** *"…any of the Israelites in my kingdom, including priests and Levites, who wish to go to Jerusalem with you, may go…"* (Ezra 7:11-26). This decree allows any Jew who desires to return to Jerusalem to do so and help rebuild the temple.
- **The "decree" of Artaxerxes I to Nehemiah, 445/444 BC:** *"In the month of Nisan in the twentieth year of King Artaxerxes…so he will give me timber to make beams for the gates of the citadel by the temple and for the city wall…"* (Nehemiah 2:1-8). This text does not specifically mention a decree, but tells how Artaxerxes permitted Nehemiah to return to Jerusalem, even giving him the necessary materials for the rebuilding.

Clearly the decree of Cyrus authorized the rebuilding of the temple, but did he allow the rebuilding of the city? It does not say so. The later decrees in Ezra also only deal with the temple, not the city. The city wall and the city itself were not rebuilt until the time of the last decree as given by Artaxerxes to Nehemiah (445-444 BC). The question remains, whether it was Nisan (the first month of the Jewish year) 445 BC or Nisan 444 BC. Although scholars do not have a conclusive opinion on this matter, we will continue with the 444 BC date as that works out precisely to the fulfillment of the prophecy and coincides with the actual rebuilding of the city.[490]

How Long is the Period of the Sixty-Nine Sevens?

How long is a Biblical year? All ancient calendars were based on a 360-day year, typically 12 full 30-day months (hence 360 degrees in a circle). About 700 BC the solar year was introduced, but the Israelites (King Hezekiah) kept the 30-day month and introduced "leap years" with one extra month (seven in every nineteen years). This seems consistently applied in the Bible, as even the book of Revelation states: "*They will trample on the holy city for 42 months. And I will give power to my two witnesses, and they will prophesy for 1,260 days, clothed in sackcloth*" (Revelation 11:2-3, emphasis added).

So if a Biblical year is 360 days, 69 weeks of years would be: 69 x 7 x 360 days = 173,880 days.

What Happens at the End of the Sixty-Nine Sevens?

According to the passage, at the end of the "seven sevens" and "sixty-two sevens" "*the Anointed One, the ruler*" (Daniel 9:25-26) comes and later on "*the Anointed One will be cut off.*" "*The Anointed One*" is the Messiah, and this clearly refers to Jesus Christ. So, what does it mean that he comes only later to be cut off? To be "*cut off*" is considered to be the death of the Messiah, i.e., the crucifixion. For the "*coming*" three options can be considered:

- Christ's birth.
- Christ's baptism.
- Christ's presentation to Israel on Palm Sunday.

All three are considered possible alternatives. His birth is the most unlikely of the three as the "*coming*" seems associated with an adult. Palm Sunday seems to be the most logical since:

- On earlier occasions in all gospels, Jesus says "*My time has not yet come*" and/or withdraws from the crowds. This includes John 2:4 ("*Jesus replied. 'My time has not yet come.'*"); John 6:15 ("*Jesus, knowing that they intended to come and make him king by force, withdrew again to a mountain by himself.*"); Matthew 16:20 ("*Then he warned his disciples not to tell anyone that he was the Christ.*"); Matthew 17:9 ("*Don't tell anyone what you have seen, until the Son of Man has been raised from the dead.*"); Luke 9:21 ("*Jesus strictly warned them not to tell this to anyone.*"), and so on.
- Jesus Himself arranged the Palm Sunday entry into Jerusalem! This is recorded in all four gospels: Mark 11: 1-11, Matthew 21:1-11, Luke 19:28-41 and John 12:12-19. This is the only time Jesus presented Himself as King, stepping deliberately into the spotlight.
- It is a deliberate fulfillment of Zechariah 9:9: "*Rejoice greatly, O Daughter of Zion! Shout, Daughter of Jerusalem! See, your king comes to you, right-*

eous and having salvation, gentle and riding on a donkey, on a colt, the foal of a donkey."
• *It fulfills the presentation of the Passover* Lamb on the 10th of Nisan, four days before the Passover (on the 14th day of Nisan) as instructed in the Mosaic Law: Exodus 12:1-20: *"... Tell the whole community of Israel that on the tenth day of this month each man is to take a lamb for his family, one for each household... Take care of them until the fourteenth day of the month, when all the people of the community of Israel must slaughter them..."*

SOLVING THE STORY PROBLEM

We've earlier shown that the crucifixion of Jesus was likely at the Passover of 33 AD.[491]

From 444 BC to 33 AD are 444+33 = 477 years. However, the year 0 is not counted (as 1 BC is followed by 1 AD), resulting in 476 years, or a total of 476 x 365 days = 173,740 days. In this period we also have a total of 116 leap years (every 4 years except a century year, but counting a leap year every 400 years) – this comes to a total of 173,856 days. Comparing this to the earlier calculated 173,880 days, only a 24-day discrepancy remains.

These 24 days are easily explained by the difference between the actual day of Palm Sunday on March 30, 33 AD and the start of the prophecy on March 6 (in Nisan as specifically mentioned in Nehemiah 2:1) in 444 BC.[492]

So this prophecy given to Daniel in the sixth century before the birth of Jesus predicts with astounding accuracy the year (even the exact day) that Jesus of Nazareth presented Himself as the Messiah to the Jewish people on Palm Sunday, 33 AD.

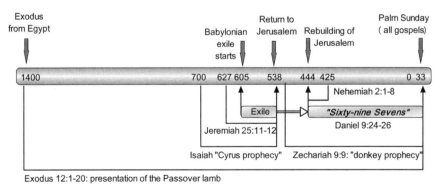

Exodus 12:1-20: presentation of the Passover lamb

Figure 24-3: Daniel's Seventy Sevens: How it All Links Together

A few additional remarks are in place as we ponder this amazing analysis:

- The exact day of the year that instigated the prophecy is unknown. We only know it was in the Jewish month of Nisan. The calculated date of March 6, 444 BC seems to meet that criterion.
- Some scholars place the start of the prophecy in 445 BC and a crucifixion date at 32 AD. However, given the historical evidence for 33 AD, this alternative is not feasible.
- Other scholars assume a 365 day Biblical year, starting at 458 BC. To this they add 483 years (69x7 years) and arrive at 26 AD which they pinpoint as the date of Jesus' baptism. However, this date of 26 AD is not consistent with the 29 AD date for the start of John the Baptist's ministry.[493]

Analysis of the prophecy:

- Even extreme liberal dating of Daniel to the second century BC, combined with the Dead Sea Scroll and Septuagint evidence, demonstrates this prophecy was written centuries before its fulfillment.
- It is explicit and detailed, specifying a starting point, a time period, and the event of the coming of the Messiah.
- It is fulfilled historically and obviously beyond any control of the writer of the prophecy.

Irrespective of the details and the exact dates, one has to stand in awe and amazement at the relationship of the various Scriptures written by different people in different centuries, yet they all perfectly come together at the event which we now call Palm Sunday!

☼ EXHIBIT #14: THE OTHER MESSIANIC PROPHECIES

When we discussed the evidences for Jesus as the Son of God, we analyzed the Messianic prophecies Christ fulfilled from the Old Testament. An overview of the most significant of these prophecies was presented in table 20-1.[494] These prophecies also meet the criteria for divine inspiration of the Bible as introduced at the beginning of this chapter.

Analysis of the prophecies:

- All OT prophecies about the Messiah were written centuries before fulfillment. As proved by the Dead Sea Scrolls and the Septuagint, the OT texts cannot have been written later than 250 BC. Therefore all prophecies in the OT originated centuries before Christ.
- Many of the prophecies are clear and unambiguous. Some have a double interpretation, an immediate and an ultimate fulfillment. Even if we

ignore the vague texts, there are still a substantial number of specific and precise prophecies that point to Christ. This list would at least include Psalm 22, Isaiah chapter 53, Isaiah 7:14, Jeremiah 23:5, Micah 5:2, and Zechariah 12:10.

- Through the texts of the gospels, Paul's epistles, and extra-Biblical sources we have historical confirmation of fulfillment of these prophecies.
- The vast majority of these prophecies lay well beyond the control of Jesus. Apart from a few exceptions, such as Zechariah 9:9 (the donkey on Palm Sunday), Jesus had no control over the events concerning Him that fulfilled the prophecies.

Together with Daniel's "*Seventy Sevens*" the Messianic prophecies strongly support the claim for divine inspiration of the Bible.

CHAPTER 25

Unity of the Bible, the Plan of Redemption

"Do not think that I have come to abolish the Law or the Prophets;
I have not come to abolish them but to fulfill them. I tell you the
truth, until heaven and earth disappear, not the smallest letter, not
the least stroke of a pen, will by any means disappear from the Law
until everything is accomplished."
MATTHEW 5:17-18

MANY BOOKS, ONE STORY

The 1970s blockbuster *Star Wars* trilogy ended in 1983 with the last installment: *The return of the Jedi*. At the end of the 1990s, writer/producer/director George Lucas decided to make a so called "prequel" to Star Wars. This trilogy of three new *Star Wars* films would deal with the events that unfolded before the original 1970s trilogy, explaining how the bad "empire" came to power, how the Jedi's were initially defeated, and how Darth Vader turned to the dark side of "the Force." The original trilogy were renamed episodes IV, V and VI and the new movies were entitled episodes I, II and III for a total of 6 films. Episode I, *The Phantom Menace* was released in 1999, and episode II, *Attack of the Clones* followed in 2002. Before the release of the last movie (2005) of the series, episode III, *Revenge of the Sith*, the expectations were high. Obviously George Lucas had to think of a plot that would link episode II perfectly with the beginning of episode IV. Lucas had to make sure it would be one flow of events, one story, and no open ends nor contradictions.

The above illustration may help us appreciate our Bible even more. Like the *Star Wars* series, the Bible is not one single book, not even a collection of six books, but sixty-six books. And like *Star Wars*, it tells one complete unified story. From Genesis to Revelation, the Bible explains to us how God, before He created us, already had a plan to redeem, or save us through His Son, Jesus Christ (Eph. 3:11, *"This was in accordance with the eternal purpose which He carried out in Christ Jesus our Lord"*). This *plan of redemption* is the consistent and unique theme of the Bible, written over a period of 1,500 years by at least 40 different men from 3 different continents in 3 different languages (Hebrew, Greek, and Aramaic). These men came from various backgrounds, different cultures, lived in various eras and most never met each other. Their writings cover history and prophecies, as well as poetry and proverbs, with each book reflecting a unity of facts, teachings, and purpose. All of history unfolded around God's plan of redemption, and each book of the Bible is a single thread of purpose woven into this incredible tapestry.

Comparing this to our *Star Wars* illustration: it would be as if a total stranger, without knowledge of any of the other *Star Wars* movies would have written the last installment, Episode IV, and it would perfectly bridge the earlier and later episodes. If you think that would be amazing – now consider having the story line written for sixty-six books independently of one another that compliment, and support one another completely – each dovetails with the others. That is the amazing internal evidence of the unity of the Bible!

☼ EXHIBIT #15: THE PLAN OF REDEMPTION[495]

A PROGRESSIVE REVELATION

The Bible is a progressive revelation. If you skip the first half of any good book, you will have a hard time understanding the characters, the plot, and the ending. The New Testament is only completely understood when it is seen as being built upon the foundation of the events, characters, laws, prophecies, covenants, and promises of the Old Testament. It shouldn't surprise us then that the New Testament gives us pointers that indicate the important role of the Old Testament. Passages such as Galatians 3:24 states, "*The old law was given to us as a teacher to bring us to Christ so that we may be justified by faith*" (see also Romans 15:4; 1 Corinthians 10:11; 2 Timothy 3:15). The New Testament points us to the Old Testament. In this manner all of Old Testament history was a teaching or training period to prepare mankind for the arrival of Jesus Christ and His role in the plan of redemption. Consequently, a proper grasp of the Old Testament has a very important purpose in understanding the overall theme of the Bible. It was a teaching or learning period for all of mankind.

What are some of the things we need to learn from that Old Testament period that covers the creation of the universe, mankind, and early earth history?

THE ETERNAL PLAN

The Bible begins with the God of the Bible, who existed before the creation of our physical universe.

We are told in the Bible that God had this plan of redemption before He ever created mankind (Ephesians 3:11; 1:4). Why would this be so? It has to do with the concept of "free will." Free will simply means the ability to choose one's own moral actions without any interference or compulsion. It makes logical sense that if God was going to create a being with free moral agency, a being that could choose to do right or wrong from its own volition, that God would have a plan in place as to how He would react or handle the result of mankind's choices. The plan of redemption is God's plan or reaction to the free moral choice of mankind to sin (break God's) laws.

So why did God create man to start with or even bother with the creation of a physical universe? We can not get inside the mind of God, but are restricted to what little He has revealed about Himself to His creation. What God has revealed is that He has purposed to have spirit beings in heaven that choose to love and worship Him out of their own choice. Before God created our physical universe, we see that He had created spirit beings (called angels) in another dimension (called heaven) that had chosen (free moral agents) at some point to sin against God. He subsequently cast them out of heaven (2 Peter 2:4, *"...God did not spare angels when they sinned, but cast them into hell and committed them to pits of darkness, reserved for judgment"*). It was after this, that He created this dimension (a physical universe) and spirit beings (us), and placed us inside physical containers (our bodies). Just as many computers are labeled with the famous "Intel Inside," all of us should be labeled "Spirit Inside!" It is this spirit, created in the image of God, that separates and distinguishes mankind from the animal world (Genesis 1:27, *"God created man in His own image, in the image of God He created him; male and female He created them."*). We are placed in these temporary *physical* containers in order to train our spiritual bodies to love, serve, and worship Him for His glory.

Our mortal containers restrict or limit our free moral actions completely to this dimension, the physical realm. God desires to see if we will choose to love Him, to worship and serve Him while we are in our physical containers in our time on earth (Deuteronomy 8:2; 13:3, *"...the Lord your God is testing you to find out if you love the LORD your God with all your heart and with all your soul."*). When our containers eventually die, the inevitable fate of all humans, our spirit will return to God and await His final judgment (Ecclesiastes 12:7, *"then the dust will return to the earth as it was, and the spirit will return to God who gave it."*; Revelation 20:13, *"...and the dead were judged...according to their deeds."*). This will determine the eternal fate of you and me, whether we join God in His dimension (heaven) or are cast away from His presence (hell). It all depends on whether we live the kind of life here on earth that demonstrates our willingness to recognize Him as our Creator and love and serve Him while here on earth (1 Peter 1:17, *"If you address as Father the One who impartially judges according to each one's work, conduct yourselves in reverent fear during the time of your stay on earth"*; Acts 17:27, *"so that they would search for God and perhaps grope for him and find him – though indeed he is not far from each one of us.").*

We additionally see that God uses the analogy of a parent to describe our relationship with Him, He is our Father, and we are His children (1 John 3:1, *"How great is the love the Father has lavished on us, that we should be called children of God! And that is what we are! The reason the world does not know us is that it did not know him.").* What do parents desire? – that their children demonstrate their love to them because they actually want to (out of their own choice) – not out of compulsion (because they are made to). God has made us in His image, and this is effectively demonstrated in the love of a parent to a child. It is God's will and desire to have a loving *spirit*-ual relationship with every spirit being that He has created (2 Peter 3:9, *"...He is patient with you, not wanting anyone to perish, but everyone to come to repentance.")*, but that relationship must be defined in accordance with His character and nature.

Two Gods?

Some people have drawn the mistaken conclusion that there must be two Gods in the Bible. There is the God of the New Testament that is all love, joy, forgiveness, peace and happiness, while the God of the Old Testament is a harsh God of justice, punishment, and wrath.[496]

Clearly, on the surface, we see that God seems to *behave* differently towards His creation in the Old Testament than He does in the New Testament, but is He really a different God? No. Consider a parent who lovingly disciplines a small child so that it will learn the things needed to be a productive adult. When my children were little, I, as their father, disciplined them as often as I thought they needed it. They rarely enjoyed it, and, on occasion, would remark, "Daddy, you are mean!" At that point in their lives I might have resembled that God of the Old Testament who appeared harsh toward His creation. But now that my children are grown up, they have a completely different attitude toward "mean dad." We have great relationship with our grown-up children on a completely different level than that of the growing-up training period. That is what the New Testament is trying to tell us about the Old Testament period. As pointed out earlier, the Old Testament was a teaching and training period to prepare us for Christ. That included many disciplinary actions toward people and nations that often appear unnecessarily strident or harsh by later standards and behavior. God behaves differently in the New Testament, and today, toward His creation on the basis of spiritual maturity learned from the training of the Old Testament period. The God of the Old Testament and New Testament is the same God. *"I the Lord do not change."* (Malachi 3:6).

THE NATURE OF GOD

The character or nature of God is defined by the characteristic of holiness – the pure absence of any evil – "*You are not a God who takes pleasure in evil; with you the wicked cannot dwell*" (Psalms 5:4). John says, "*God is light; in Him there is no darkness at all*" (1 John 1:5). John is telling us that God is completely free from any moral evil – He is the essence of moral purity and goodness. The holiness of God is the foundation for His plan of redemption.

It is God's holiness that perfects His attributes of *omnipotence* (infinite power), *omniscience* (perfect knowledge), and *omnipresence* (presence everywhere). Imagine that you or someone you know had the attributes of omnipotence, omniscience, and omnipresence. Would you love or worship that person? Not necessarily. What if that person was evil, a Hitler or a Darth Vader? It is precisely God's nature of holiness that makes all of His attributes perfectly good. It is His holiness that makes Him worthy of our praise, love, and devotion. I know this about God by observing His holiness in His interaction with His creation. Consequently, it creates within me a love for God and a desire to serve Him and to be with Him as my spiritual Father.

"*For the word of the Lord is right and true,...He loves righteousness and <u>justice</u>; The earth is full of his unfailing <u>love</u>*" (Psalm 33:4-5, emphasis added). We also discover that God's holiness is demonstrated to us in one of two aspects, His justice and His love. Again, "*Righteousness and <u>justice</u> are the foundation of Your throne; <u>Love</u> and faithfulness go before You*" (Psalm 89:14, emphasis added). All of our dealings with God are governed by these two aspects of God's holiness.

God's *justice* means that God will never treat mankind unfairly. We can trust His promises, and we can trust His judgments and pronunciations (Deuteronomy 32:4; Job 8:3). We can count on the fact that what He says He will do, <u>He will do</u> (Isaiah 46:8-11). Likewise, if God pronounces a penalty or judgment, not only will it be fair and in the best interests of mankind, but we can be sure that He will follow up on His pronouncement. For example, sin is defined as the breaking of God's laws (1 John 3:4) and God's justice will not allow sin to just go unpunished.

A complimentary element of God's holiness is His *love* for His creation. While His justice is fair and sure, it is administered in the context of His love. His love for His creation seeks to repair what mankind's carelessness has destroyed by committing sin.

God repeatedly states that we are to be holy because He is holy. "*Thus <u>you are to be holy to Me</u>, for <u>I the LORD am holy</u>; and I have <u>set you apart</u> from the peoples to be Mine*" (Leviticus 20:25, emphasis added). God created us as spiritual beings (Genesis 1:26, "*Then God said, "Let us make man* *in our image, in our likeness...*") and wants to have a *spiritual* relationship with His creation. If we are holy, we can then have the spiritual union that a holy God desires.

This forms the basis for the plan of redemption, God's incredible plan of justice and mercy first demonstrated in the Old Testament. So, why was a plan to redeem mankind needed in the first place?

THE PROBLEM OF SIN

Sin is bad. Nothing defines God's character and His relationship to man as much as His absolute abhorrence of sin. God is God. God is holy. God is king. Any breaking of His law results in His absolute revulsion in response to rejection of His will. This rejection of His will is called sin (*"sin is lawlessness"* – 1 John 3:4).

SIN SEPARATES US FROM A HOLY GOD

Sin has dire consequences for God's creation. The first and most significant consequence is that it immediately severs the spiritual relationship that God has with a person. *"Your iniquities have separated you from your God; and your sins have hidden his face from you"* (Isaiah 59:2; Habakkuk 1:13, emphasis added). When one sins, God, because He is holy, must, as it were, turn His face away. To be separated from God, the essence of spiritual life, is so dreadful it is referred to in the worst possible term, *spiritual death* (Ephesians 2:5, *"even when we were dead through our trespasses, made us alive together with Christ – by grace you have been saved;"* see also Colossians 2:13; Romans 6:23; 1 Timothy 5:6). *Because* God is holy, *any* sin, regardless of its motivation, magnitude, or consequences, *must* result in separation from a holy God. To have our *spirit*-ual relationship with God severed, is as if the spirit inside our "container" has died.

Spiritual death is not the only result of sin. We all experience consequences of the *first* sin of humanity. Before sin, man existed in a perfect state of spiritual fellowship with God. As a result of Adam and Eve's first sin in the Garden of Eden (referred to as "the fall") we will all die a mortal death (Genesis 3:19). Our "containers" will not live forever. Mortal death will befall us all and is a reminder of the seriousness of sin. Other consequences of the first sin were pronounced upon mankind as well. Man has to work, and women will have pain in childbirth. The earth is no longer a perfect place but now produces natural disasters which affect all creation (see Genesis 3:14-24). All of this occurred because of the first sin.

While spiritual and mortal death are consequences suffered by each individual, nothing has been done that would deal with sin, that is, remove sin or restore man's *spiritual* relationship with God. All of this changed when man and woman first broke God's law in the Garden of Eden (Genesis 2-3).

GOD'S JUSTICE DEMANDS LIFE AS PAYMENT FOR SIN

There are prices to be paid when we break the judicial laws of our country. For example, when we are caught speeding, we may be required to pay a fine as restitution. If we murder someone, we may be required to spend life in prison or even be executed. These are penalties imposed by our judicial system, penalties imposed for the breaking of judicial laws. Likewise, there is a price that God requires as a judicial penalty or price for breaking His laws (sin). The price God requires for sin is as serious as its consequences.

The first command of God issued in the Garden of Eden clearly elaborated the judicial price for sin, *"from the tree of the knowledge of good and evil you shall not eat, for in the day that you eat from it you will surely die"* (Genesis 2:16-17, emphasis added). Put in the plainest of words, the payment of death is pronounced as the price for sin. This is a judicial price for breaking God's law. Life is the price! God pronounced death as the price for sin, and His justice must be served. Adam and Eve surely suffered the consequences of sin – they died spiritually the instant they sinned, and they were destined to eventually die a mortal death (removed from the garden and the Tree of Life), but that did nothing to remove their sin, or pay the price for their sin – death. The New Testament flatly states that *"...without the shedding of blood there is no forgiveness"* (Hebrews 9:22, emphasis added).

Adam and Eve initially only had one possible choice that would allow them to commit sin. But it was a choice they had control over. When tempted by Satan, they succumbed. Genesis 3:6 describes it this way, *"When the woman saw that the tree was good for food, and that it was a delight to the eyes, and that the tree was desirable to make one wise, she took from its fruit and ate; and she gave also to her husband with her, and he ate."* This is the process that we all follow at some point, well described by James (James 1:14-15) *"But each one is tempted when he is carried away and enticed by his own lust. Then when lust has conceived, it gives birth to sin; and when sin is accomplished, it brings forth death."*

God demonstrated repeatedly throughout the Old Testament the penalty for sin – the death of the sinner (Ezekiel 18:20, *"The person who sins will die."*). God's mercy is already demonstrated, to some extent, in that we are not all immediately struck dead (what we deserve) the instant we sin. God took no pleasure in the death of the sinners, He did not have a blood lust, nor was His justice administered capriciously (Ezekiel 33:11, *"I take no pleasure in the death of the wicked, but rather that the wicked turn from his way and live."*).

What we learn from the examples of the Old Testament is that sin is extremely bad. Sin is an affront to a holy God. It is so bad that God has pronounced the penalty of death on the head of the sinner. This price of death is on the head of every sinner.

We are all pronounced guilty because we each have sinned. Looking over the scope of history, the New Testament writers reflected this chilling and disturbing characteristic of man by observing that *"all have sinned and fall short of the glory of God"* (Romans 3:23, emphasis added).

Man is in a very desperate situation: He has broken the laws of the God of the universe, this has separated him from a holy God, and the price of blood (death) is required by a just God! If one dies a mortal death in this condition he will be eternally separated from God (yet another consequence of sin)! Yet he is unable to pay the price for sin himself.

GOD'S LOVE ALLOWS THE PRICE TO BE PAID BY A SUBSTITUTE

Fortunately, God loves His creation and decided to help pay this price even though it was undeserved. This help is called *grace* (God gives us what we don't deserve – life). He showed His *mercy* (God doesn't give us what we do deserve – death). We deserved God's justice but we received God's mercy. How was His mercy shown? – by blood.

The Bible could be said to drip blood if you squeezed it. The Bible is bloody due to the problem and price of sin. God, in His love and His mercy, allowed the price of life to be paid through an innocent stand-in. This was the purpose of animal sacrifice instituted in the Old Testament. God showed His mercy by allowing the animal to pay the price of death owed by the sinner.

God made provision (or atonement) for the judicial price of sin to be paid by an animal. This is described in Leviticus 17:11 (emphasis added): *"For the life of the flesh is in the blood, and I have given it to you on the altar to make atonement for your souls; for it is the blood by reason of the life that makes atonement."* The life of the animal atones for (literally "covers") or cleanses the sins of the sinner. In this manner the sinner "died" representatively or through the animal as a substitute. What was the result? The removal of sin. For example, in Leviticus 16:30 this result was described as taking place on the Day of Atonement (the yearly sacrifice of animals): *"for it is on this day that atonement shall be made for you to cleanse you; you will be clean from all your sins before the LORD"* (emphasis added).

Why an animal? The animal was innocent of sin, thereby qualifying it to be a substitute for the guilty sinner. An animal was innocent of sin; however, because it was amoral, it couldn't sin. If an animal could have sinned, it would have been liable for its own sin! Sinlessness was required for it to provide a representative or substitute death for the sinner.

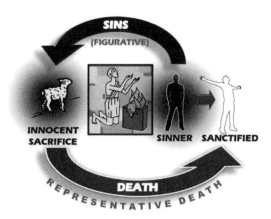

Figure 25-1: Animal Sacrifice in the Old Testament

As illustrated in figure 25-1 it was as if the sins from the sinner were somehow transported over to the innocent lamb. We say figuratively because the lamb did not have a spirit that could sin and consequently could not actually or literally bear sin. This figure of an animal bearing sin is given in the instructions about the scapegoat (see Leviticus 16:21). The lamb was then sacrificed on the altar. When the lamb died, it died representatively, or as a substitute for the sinner. In this manner the sinner is actually viewed as having died. And as a result, the sins of the sinner are removed. This results in sanctification (being made holy – "clean from sins"). And as a result of being made holy, the relationship with a holy God can now be restored (reconciliation).

After Adam and Eve commit the first sin in Genesis 3:1-8, their *"eyes were opened."* They were now aware of their sin, realized they were naked, and made clothes from fig leaves. Then they hid from God. They knew they had broken His law and what the penalty was! Then in Genesis 3:21 we read a curious statement: *"The LORD God made garments of skin for Adam and his wife and clothed them."* Apparently one or more animals were killed to make their garments. The actual death of some animals occur, and Adam and Eve continue to live! Although this account was not written to explain the plan of redemption, it is consistent with taking life to pay for sin through the substitutionary death of the animal(s). The foundational elements of the plan of redemption are present on the occasion of the first sin in the Garden of Eden.

This is the great objective of God's incredible plan of redemption – the removal of sin so that the relationship with a holy God can be restored. By removing sin, the sinner is made holy (*sanctified*). As a result of being made holy, the penalty or price of death is paid and removed (*justification*), we are declared *righteous*, and our spiritual relationship with a holy God is restored (*reconciliation*).

NOT A WORK OR SUPERSTITION

God is not a God of anger and blood lust. He does not need blood to appease a superstitious appetite. Rather, blood atonement demonstrates to mankind the importance of His holiness and the seriousness of sin. Blood (which represents life) is the only thing that will pay the price for, take care of, or atone for sin (Hebrews 9:22) – not good works, good beliefs, good morals, or good intentions!

One of the more important observations we can make about animal sacrifice is that it derived its power from the faith of the believers. The animal had to be killed – one could not just believe in animal sacrifice or treat it superstitiously (Hebrews 9:22). When the animal was sacrificed nothing had been done to actually deserve the removal of sin. Killing the animal was the means of accepting the gift of the removal of sin by the promise of God that sin would be removed by this act of faith. Killing the animal was the means of accepting God's gift of reconciliation by faith.

ANIMAL SACRIFICE IN THE OLD TESTAMENT

Once the importance of the role of animal sacrifice (blood atonement) is properly understood then we readily see it reflected throughout all of the Old Testament era – from the Garden of Eden through the period of the patriarchs to the Mosaic law.

Shortly after the sin of Adam and Eve in the Garden and the subsequent deaths of the animals, we move immediately to the story of Cain and Abel. The entire story of Cain and Abel revolves around sacrificial practice. In Genesis 4:1-5 we read how both Abel and Cain made a sacrifice to the Lord, but Cain's sacrifice was rejected. Ever wondered why that was? Hebrews 11:4 tells us why: "*By faith Abel offered to God a better sacrifice than Cain.*" Simply put, Abel did what God had instructed him to do and Cain did not. To do something "*by faith*" means to do it by the instruction of God (Romans 10:17, "*Faith comes by hearing and hearing by the word of God.*") Cain did not sacrifice an animal (like Abel) but fruits from the soil. That is not what the Lord had instructed. That again is consistent with the plan of redemption that only sacrifice from life = blood can suffice.

Notice that there is not one word in Genesis specifically describing the installation or requirements of the sacrificial system. The early books of the Old Testament are mainly history books. They deal with animal sacrifice from the point of view of a sacrificial system that is understood and reflected as historical fact. In other words, these books present the practice of animal sacrifice as something that the reader already completely understood. They weren't written to explain the sacrificial system.

During the patriarchal period we see Job offering animal sacrifices for the sins of his family (see Job 1:5). Later we see the famous testing of Abraham where God asks Abraham to offer his son of promise, Isaac (see Genesis 22:1-13). When Abraham has passed the test, God rescues Isaac and replaces him with a ram.[497]

However, the Mosaic Law provides us with a detailed description of the requirements for animal sacrifice, explicitly mentioning the requirements for a perfect, spotless, and unblemished animal (Leviticus 22:21-27). Only male animals would be acceptable (Leviticus 22:19). Notice also that the Lord claimed the firstborn of every womb. Exodus 34:19-20: *"The first offspring of every womb belongs to me, including all the firstborn males of your livestock, whether from herd or flock...Redeem all your firstborn sons."* In Numbers 3:40-51 we even see a description of how God allowed the Levites to redeem the other firstborn sons of Israel.

THE LAMB OF GOD

Over a thousand years went by under the system of animal sacrifice. All of the Old Testament events, genealogies, and prophecies have occurred to prepare mankind for the coming of Christ. Then a climactic moment in history arrives. Jesus has arrived on earth and is about to be announced publicly for the first time. John the Baptist is preaching, preparing the *"way of the Lord."* As he sees Jesus approaching, John makes an astounding pronouncement that reverberates throughout history:

"Behold, the <u>lamb of God</u>, who takes away the sin of the world!"
(John 1:29, emphasis added)

There it is! – the entire plan of redemption in one sentence. This declaration of John the Baptist summarizes the entire Old Testament in one sentence. All of the events of the Old Testament had occurred to drive humanity to this destination – the arrival of the Son of God and His announcement as *"the Lamb of God."*

Notice four important observations from this announcement: First, Jesus' death was no accident or a failed mission to set up an earthly kingdom. It was His very purpose in coming to earth. Some people take the position that Jesus' real purpose was to become a political leader and build a kingdom on earth that would rival the Roman Empire. By announcing Him to the Jewish public as the Lamb of God, shows that His very purpose was to die, because that is precisely what the role of a lamb was – to be a sacrifice – and a sacrifice must die. *"For you know that it was not with perishable things such as silver or gold that you were <u>redeemed</u> from the empty way of life handed down to you from your forefathers, but with the <u>precious blood of Christ, a lamb without blemish or defect</u>"* (1 Peter 1:18-19, emphasis added).

Second, this explains the emphasis in the New Testament on the sinlessness of Jesus (1 John 3:5, *"You know that He appeared in order to take away sins; and in Him there is no sin."*). If Jesus had ever sinned, even once, then He could not have been the innocent Lamb of God. If Jesus had sinned, even once, then He would have been liable for His own sins and had the price of death on His head. Suppose I was on death row for murder and you offered to take my place and die for my crime. This would not even be a plausible offer if you were in the next cell awaiting death for your own crime! The requirement for a substitute is that it is not liable for the same judicial sentence. Jesus had never sinned, which qualified Him to step in and pay the price for all sinners.

Third, notice the result of being the Lamb of God. Remember the purpose of animal sacrifice in the Old Testament? It was to remove or cleanse sin. And the result of being the *"lamb of God"* was that it would *"take away the sin of the world."* By the willing sacrifice of himself, Jesus would remove the sins of the world.

Fourth, referring to Jesus as the lamb of God illustrates that Jesus was a fulfillment of Old Testament history. Christ is referred to as our *"Passover lamb"* in 1 Corinthians 5:7: *"Get rid of the old yeast that you may be a new batch without yeast – as you really are. For Christ, our Passover lamb, has been sacrificed."* This is a reference to the lambs that were sacrificed and their blood, which was used to protect the Israelites from the angel of death in Egypt (Exodus 12:3-49). Christ removed the *"old yeast"* (sin) from us by His sacrifice. He fulfilled the Old Testament (Matthew 5:17, *"Do not think that I came to abolish the Law or the Prophets; I did not come to abolish but to fulfill."*).

THE SACRIFICE OF CHRIST IN THE NEW TESTAMENT

Mel Gibson's famous movie *The Passion of the Christ* very graphically depicts the arrest, scourging, and crucifixion of Christ. What the movie does not explain is why Jesus went through the horrific scourging and subsequent ordeal of the cross. Why did Jesus have to have nails driven through His hands and a spear thrust through His side? Why did He have to die in the first place? The answer is now clear. Jesus suffered this punishment and death on behalf of the sinner. *"To whom the stroke was due"* (Isaiah 53:8) and Jesus took our place. He paid the price of suffering and death that was

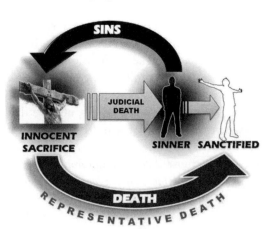

Figure 25-2: Jesus, the Perfect Sacrifice

316

owed by each individual sinner. He did this by choice, out of love for His Father and His desire to do His will (Matthew 26:42: "...*Your will be done*").

Jesus came to die, to take the place of animal sacrifice! Jesus came *"to give His life a ransom for many"* (Matthew 20:28). *"For this is My blood of the covenant, which is poured out for many for forgiveness of sins"* (Matthew 26:28). *"You were bought with a price"* (1 Corinthians 7:23). A price of death that Jesus paid. A payment that humanity did not deserve – such is grace.

By living a sinless life, Jesus qualified Himself as an innocent stand-in to die in the place of the truly guilty – you and me. When Jesus died on the cross, He took our sins upon Him and then paid the price owed of the guilty – death. Christ's death represents in the death of the believer. 1 Peter 2:24 spells this out very plainly, *"He Himself bore our sins in His body on the cross, so that we might die to sin and live to righteousness."* Christ took our sins in His body on the cross, and then died, thus paying the judicial price for sin so that sinner might be viewed as having died to sin (paying the judicial price). This role of Christ is summed up in 2 Corinthians 5:21, *"He made Him who knew no sin to be sin on our behalf, so that we might become the righteousness of God in Him."* Again in Hebrews 9:26-28, *"He has been manifested to put away sin by the sacrifice of Himself...having been offered once to bear the sins of many..."*

SUMMARY

Can you imagine that John the Baptist and Jesus decided to conspire to portray Jesus as the Lamb of God? To what purpose? Were John and Jesus absolute delusional lunatics that schemed up the ability to try to pass Jesus off as a sacrifice and thought that would somehow be beneficial or desirable? John was later beheaded and Jesus was killed on a cross! Jesus and John could never have orchestrated the events and fulfilled prophecies to pull off such a hoax, even if they wanted to!

All of history unfolds to present God's amazing plan of redemption in Jesus Christ. All of the Old Testament was to teach us, or train us, so that we could understand: God's holiness; His justice and love; the terribleness of sin – its consequences and its price; God's mercy demonstrated through animal sacrifice; God's love for mankind in providing an innocent substitute to pay the price for sin; and the coming of the Lamb of God – Jesus Christ; the fulfillment of prophecy in Jesus' life, death, burial, and resurrection; the good news of God's grace. All of this so that those that hear the gospel story, and believe it, can repent of their sins and be united with Christ in His death. When we are baptized into Christ we are baptized *into His* death (see Romans 6:3-23), we die with Christ and our sins are removed, we are given a new life (other places in the New Testament refer to this a new birth, new creation, renewal, or regeneration – see John 3:5; Titus 3:5; 2 Corinthians 5:17), we are freed from sin, we are crucified with Christ, we are sanctified by our faith in the work of Christ (Col. 2:10-12). This is a gift from God (Romans 6:23).

Conclusion

No man could have ever written these books of the Bible to invent this story or produce this savior. While the patriarchs and the priests of the Mosaic Law were offering those perfect, spotless, unblemished animals, little did they know that the real purpose was training and preparing people for the eventual coming of the Lamb of God.

Jesus Christ, the Son of God, came to this earth as a man, so that, as God and man, he could offer the perfect sacrifice, paying the price for our sins, reconciling man to God (Ephesians 2:13-16; 1 Corinthians 6:20). By dying with Christ, we can share His victory over death and have hope of life eternal.

I can die with Christ. You can die with Christ and have a spiritual relationship restored with a holy God. This is the theme of the Bible, as great evidence for divine inspiration. In the words of C.J. Sharp:

> *"If a fragment of stone were found in Italy, another in Asia Minor, another in Greece, another in Egypt, and on and on until sixty-six fragments had been found, and if when put together they fitted perfectly together, making a perfect statue of Venus de Milo, there is not an artist or scientist but would arrive immediately at the conclusion that there was originally a sculptor who conceived and carved the statue. The very lines and perfections would probably determine which of the great ancient artists carved the statue. Not only the unity of the Scriptures, but their lines of perfection, suggest One far above any human as the real author. That could be no one but God."*

CHAPTER 26

Other Evidences for Divine Inspiration

"Jesus answered, 'I did tell you, but you do not believe. The miracles
I do in my Father's name speak for me, but you do not believe because
you are not my sheep. My sheep listen to my voice; I know them, and
they follow me. I give them eternal life, and they shall never perish;
no one can snatch them out of my hand.'"
JOHN 10:25-28

This chapter will address two more exhibits that show the Bible is far more than an ordinary book. We will examine how the Bible, through the power of God's Word has the proven ability to change lives dramatically for the better. And we'll examine the testimony of Jesus Christ, the Son of God, about the divine inspiration of the Scriptures.

☼ EXHIBIT #16: THE EVIDENCE OF THE CHANGED LIVES

"To my own mind," wrote J. Sidlow Baxter, *"the most satisfying proofs that the Bible is divinely inspired are not those which one 'reads up' in volumes of religious evidences or Christian apologetics, but those which we discover for ourselves in our own study of the Book. To the prayerful explorer the Bible has its own way of revealing its internal credentials."*[498]

No doubt that believing and following the Bible has changed many, many lives. Thousands and thousands (how many millions?) of testimonies prove this. The words of the Bible create an impact that can last a lifetime. Biblical principles have the power to change the quality of life beyond cultural norms and expectations. Not making you "wealthy and healthy," but by giving you contentment and peace unknown elsewhere. In the words of the apostle Paul: *"Do not be anxious about anything, but in everything by prayer and supplication with thanksgiving let your requests be made known to God. And the peace of God, which surpasses all understanding, will guard your hearts and your minds in Christ Jesus"* (Philippians 4:6-7).

People get out of debt and shed addictions, marriages are saved and restored, parents become better parents, families grow closer, hate turns to love, forgiveness replaces resentment, and genuine joy replaces material happiness. Following the teachings of Scripture lays a solid foundation for a better and happier life. Some are changed overnight, some are transformed over time. Either way, change for the better occurs. God's Word is the dynamic, transforming power of God. In the New Testament, a Christian is often portrayed as being *"born again"* (John 3:5, 1 Corinthians 5:17, Romans 6:4). Each convert has a new life and begins it as a new creation.

This book would explode in size with even the beginning of a list of such testimonies. My own testimony and those of my family would take many pages. Because this book is about evidences and facts, we will limit this discussion to some observations about the evidence of life-changing power in the Word of God:

- **It happened in the past, and it still happens.** For individual testimonies, refer to the many books written by others.[499] The following quote summarizes them all: *"No other religion, no other philosophy, gives a man so much to live for as Christianity. For this reason Christianity has a record of martyrology absolutely without comparison in the history of religions. Every religion has produced a Socrates here and there willing to drink poison hemlock, or a Buddha willing to forsake wealth and fortune for religious ideals. But where is the stream of martyrs like unto Christianity? What other devotees have been burned, tortured, torn asunder, and in many other diabolical ways have had their flesh baptized by excruciating pain, and yet have suffered it with words of forgiveness on their lips, with hymns of glory sung up to the last minute, with faces beaming and glowing amid smoke and torture, amid bleeding flesh and scorched limbs? And why do they so die? Because Christ has given them so much to live for that they choose to live for Christ and die, rather than deny Christ and live."* [500]

- **The experience is subjective.** A critical observation on the changed life is that it is a subjective experience. For a non-believer this evidence is intriguing because of the vast number of testimonies, but also hard to grasp as it is hard to relate to. Skeptics can easily dismiss this evidence as *"it might work for you, but not for me."*

- **How about other religions?** Other religions also point to changed lives as evidence for the divine inspiration of their "holy book." For instance, many Muslim apologists point to the transformation of lives and culture by the Qur'an as a proof of its divine origin. One has to realize that religion touches and changes the values and beliefs of a person. That person will therefore also live by what he or she believes to be true. The huge difference, however, between Christianity and Islam (and the other religions) is the total freedom of choice that is part of the process of reading and accepting the Bible and the resulting change of life. In Islam it is more of an enforced regime by surrounding culture, family, and country and less of a choice because of reading an inspired book. We will discuss Islam and the other world religions in later chapters, but at this point be aware that the power of the Bible to transform lives is based on the truth of the Word. Genuine faith, when based upon truth, will have this transforming effect.

"Contentment is realizing that God has already provided everything that we need for our current happiness." [501]

☼ EXHIBIT #17: THE TESTIMONY OF JESUS CHRIST

During the transfiguration of Jesus (Luke 9:28-36, Mark 9:2-13, Matthew 17:1-13) Peter, John and James heard God's voice proclaim: *"This is my Son, whom I have chosen; <u>listen to him</u>"* (emphasis added).

So, what does Jesus, the Son of God, say about the divine inspiration of the Bible? Did He teach that the Scriptures are God's Word? Clearly and beyond any doubt, yes! He taught precisely that. Obviously, during Jesus' life, only the Old Testament was available, but on many occasions He referred to these Scriptures, confirming their accuracy and affirming their inspiration:

- *"Do not think that I have come to abolish the Law or the Prophets; I have not come to abolish them but to fulfill them. I tell you the truth, until heaven and earth disappear, not the smallest letter, not the least stroke of a pen, will by any means disappear from the Law until everything is accomplished"* (Matthew 5:17-18).
- *"Jesus replied, 'You are in error because you do not know the Scriptures or the power of God'"* (Matthew 22:29).
- *"Whoever believes in me, as the Scripture has said, streams of living water will flow from within him" (John 7:28).*
- *"It is written in the Prophets: 'They will all be taught by God.' Everyone who listens to the Father and learns from him comes to me" (John 6:45).*

Clearly Jesus taught the Scriptures are inspired. To reject His claim, one must reject the authority of Jesus. The evidence we have discussed in the earlier chapters about the truth of the Bible and the identity of Jesus as the Son of God shows conclusively that Jesus has God's full authority (see Matthew 28:18-20). The argument then becomes:[502]

- If what Jesus taught is true,
- And Jesus taught that the Bible is inspired,
- Then it follows that it is true that the Bible is inspired by God.

CHAPTER 27

Some Intriguing
Observations in the Bible

*"It is the glory of God to conceal a matter;
to search out a matter is the glory of kings."*
PROVERBS 25:1

DESIGN OR COINCIDENCE?

In the 1997 movie *Contact* the main character, Dr. Eleanor Arroway (played by Jody Foster), receives a signal from space on a SETI radio telescope. This signal turns out to be no random noise, but a string of prime numbers. This is interpreted as a sign of design, composed by intelligent beings, because the chance of such sequence of primes by mere chance is remote.[503]

Likewise, we ask, what if we find similar structures or messages in the Bible? Would that not also show these texts were designed and coordinated, not just written independently of one another over the centuries? Would the presence of such *"codes"* not make it more likely that the Bible is inspired and even orchestrated by God?

This chapter will survey structures and messages that appear more than mere coincidence. We will discover remarkable surprises. However, here's a disclaimer on this topic. Yes, we will find these types of messages, and I personally think they are intriguing and surprising. However, I do not consider them objective, undisputable evidence that God inspired the Bible. I believe that, in connection with the previously presented evidences, they corroborate the Bible as God's Word. Solely on their own merits, they are likely subject to much skeptical analysis and rejection. Many will claim they were edited intentionally into the texts by scribes and/or are in fact only coincidence. Thus they are included in this book to be thought provoking illustrations, not as exhibits of evidence. As they are presented, we will evaluate each on a case-by-case basis, using the following criteria:

- **Significant:** Is the message, pattern, or structure significant or "just coincidence?"
- **Unique:** Is the phenomenon unique to the Bible or is it also observed in other (ancient) books?
- **Not intentional:** Is it abundantly clear the feature was not intentionally inserted in the Scripture by a later imposter?

ILLUSTRATION #1: THE "BIBLE CODES"

In 1997 the world was shocked by claims of American journalist Michael Drosnin[504] that he had found coded messages in the Hebrew text of the Torah. These alleged codes correctly described events that have happened in the past, and also predicted events yet in the future. He claimed that in 1994 he had discovered a code predicting the assassination of Israel's prime minister, Yitzak Rabin that took place in 1995.

The principle of this *Bible code*, called by some the *Torah code* is to take the original Hebrew texts and form words with letters that are a certain fixed distance apart. Taken together, these "*Equidistant Letter Sequences*" (ELS) spell out events from the past or the future. Using computer programs, Drosnin (as others before him) searched Hebrew texts with various "skips" (distances between letters) for meaningful words and/or sentences. The skips could be well over multiple hundreds (or even thousands) of letters and in a forward or backward direction. If something meaningful was discovered, the same text would be searched for words that would relate to the topic. For instance, a famous discovery are the so called the *Holocaust codes*.[505] These are a cluster of words in ELS, spelling names and events from WWII and the Jewish Holocaust, mostly in the book of Deuteronomy. Of course, these are "western" words, but spelled phonetically in Hebrew.

Some Words in the Holocaust Code Cluster		
Encoded name	**ELS interval**	**Beginning of ELS**
Hitler	skip 22, reading right to left	Deuteronomy 10:17
Auschwitz	skip 13, reading left to right	Deuteronomy 10:21
Holocaust	skip 50, reading right to left	Deuteronomy 31:16
Crematorium for my sons	skip 134, reading right to left	Deuteronomy 31:28
The Fuhrer	skip 5, reading right to left	Deuteronomy 32:50
King of the Nazis	skip 246, reading left to right	Deuteronomy 33:16
Eichmann	skip 9670, reading right to left	Deuteronomy 32:52
Mein Kampf	skip 9832, reading right to left	Numbers 19:13
Genocide	skip 22, reading left to right	Deuteronomy 33:21

Table 27-1: The "Bible Codes" in the Holocaust Cluster

Ever since the initial publication of Drosnin's book, a wave of followers has embraced the concept, and a flood of critics has disputed the conclusion. This discussion is still on-going.

Analysis of the phenomena:
- Bible codes are possibly significant. They show and claim clear messages that seem beyond simple coincidence, as confirmed by various mathematicians.[506] However, it should also be noted that after initial support for

the codes by renowned mathematicians, enthusiasm seems to have subsided. Some now claim the codes are merely coincidence and that they can also be found in other books such as *Moby Dick* and *War and Peace*. If this were so, it would not make the code unique to the Bible. This claim continues to be disputed by numerous supporters of the ELS codes.

An interesting observation: another Torah code[507]

There is a simple but intriguing ELS code found in the opening versus of all five books of the Torah. The name for Torah in Hebrew is spelled with four letters: תּוֹרָה (Hebrew is written with only consonants and is read from right to left). The name for God in Hebrew is Jehovah or Yahweh, spelled YHWH (יְהוָה)

In both Genesis and Exodus, beginning with the first ת (Hebrew "tau," like our English "t") in each book and skipping 49 letters, the Hebrew word for Torah is formed.

In the third book in the Bible, Leviticus, beginning with the first י (Hebrew "yod," similar to our English "j") and skipping 7 (the square root of 49), the Hebrew word for Yahweh is formed.

In the fourth book, Numbers, the word Torah is spelled, again, starting in verse 1, at a skip of 49, but this time backwards. In the last book, Deuteronomy, Torah is found again at every 49th letter (so this time a skip of 48), spelled backwards, and starting in verse five.[508]

This leads to the following patterns:

Genesis   Exodus   Leviticus   Numbers   Deuteronomy
TORH ➜ *TORH* ➜ *YHWH* ⬅ *HROT* ⬅ *HROT*

Or in the words of Chuck Missler: "*It appears that the Torah always point toward the ineffable name of God!*"[509]

- The Bible codes are clearly not added intentionally.
- Apart from chance versus design, a serious objection concerns the preservation of the original text. Yes, the texts have been accurately preserved over the last 3,500 years or so since the Torah was written. Although these are the first written books of the Bible, they are also likely the closest to any original text of any book in the Bible. Yet they are not identical to the original text. We know – from the Dead Sea Scrolls – that some textual variations have slipped in over the centuries. We can have

very high confidence that the content of the message is still as it was first intended, but there are variations in the spellings of words. Likely other words were added to or deleted from the original text written by Moses and others. This creates a serious problem for the claim that the ELS codes in our current text were put there by God Himself.

- A final consideration is that the original texts of the Torah were written in ancient Hebrew. This did not incorporate vowels, as only consonants were used in a twenty-two letter alphabet. Vowels were added later, around 900 AD by the Masorete scribes. Original pronunciations of most names and even many regular Hebrew words in the Torah have likely been lost and were reintroduced by the Masoretes at the inclusion of their vowel system during their copying of the Scriptures.

ILLUSTRATION #2: THE HEPTADIC STRUCTURE OF THE BIBLE

Throughout the Bible, numbers are used consistently and repetitively with strong emphasis on the number seven. The frequent use of seven is obvious even to an occasional reader of the Scriptures. This phenomena is technically referred to as the *Heptadic Structure of the Bible* (*hepta* is the Greek word for seven) or *Biblical numerology*. The number seven in the Bible is associated with "completeness." Other numbers seem to have symbolic meanings as well (table 27-2).

1	*The number for God, unity*
3	*Trinity / redemption*
6	*"Incomplete," the number of "man"*
7	*"Complete," "full," "perfect"*
12	*The 12 tribes – Israel*
40	*A generation*

Table 27-2: Biblical Numerology

As early as the nineteenth century, scholars[510] have researched the number seven. The word "seven" is used 394 times in the OT (the Hebrew word שֶׁבַע ["sheba"] = seven, seventh, seven times, sevens, etc.) and 87 times in the NT (the Greek word επτα ["hepta"] = seven or seventh).[511] This makes a total of 481 occurrences of "seven" in the entire Bible.

The presence of the number seven (or any multiple of it) is no evidence that the text is divinely inspired. Obviously any author can chose that number at any time. In ancient times the number seven seems to have had a strong symbolic recognition associated with "complete" and "perfect." We find frequent use of seven in most ancient religious texts.

What makes the use of seven in the Bible especially intriguing is the many times the concept of seven is beneath the structure of the text. Below (table 27-3) is an overview, but by far not a complete list:[512]

Sevens in the Bible	
Seven days of creation	*Genesis 1*
Seven days of rain after Noah enters the Ark	*Genesis 7:4-10*
Seven years Jacob serves for each wife	*Genesis 28:18-20; 29:27-30*
Seven good and seven famine years in Egypt	*Genesis 41*
Seven days the waters turn to blood	*Exodus 7:25*
Seven lamps of the Menorah	*Exodus 25:37*
Seven feasts of Israel	*Leviticus 23*
Seven years of the sabbatical year	*Leviticus 25:4*
Seven times seven to the jubilee year	*Leviticus 25:8*
Seven priests with seven trumpets circle Jericho seven times	*Joshua 6*
Seven years Solomon spent building the temple	*1 Kings 6:38*
Daniel's seventy sevens prophecy	*Daniel 9:24-27*
Seventy years in Babylonian exile	*Jeremiah 25:11-12*
Seven loaves fed the 4,000, seven baskets are leftover	*Matthew 15:32-39*
Seven deacons in the early church	*Acts 6:5*
Seven miracles in the gospel of John	*John*
Seven discourses in the gospel of John	*John*
Seven "I am" statements in the gospel of John	*John*
Seven different churches Paul sent letters to	*Paul's epistles*
Seven churches in Revelation	*Revelation 2,3*
Seven promises, seals, trumpets, angels, plagues, etc.	*Revelation*
Seven promises to Abraham, Isaac, and Jacob	*Genesis*
Seven miracles on the Sabbath	*Gospels*
Seven sayings of Jesus from the cross	*Gospels*
Seven appearances of angels	*Gospels and Acts*
Seven elements of the armor of God	*Ephesians 6:14-18*

Table 27-3: Illustration of the Use of Sevens in the Bible

Should we consider the heptadic structure in the Bible as convincing evidence for divine design of the texts? Let's look at the criteria:

Analysis of the phenomena:
- The occurrence of the sevens in the text and the structures is clearly significant.
- It is not necessarily unique to the Bible. Throughout ancient history people have been intrigued by the number seven as a symbol for "completeness" and "perfection." Many ancient (mostly religious) texts contain a preference for the use of seven (though perhaps to a lesser degree than the Bible).
- Are the sevens put in the text intentionally? Sevens that are used in stories or illustrations can be intentionally used by any author. There are a number of events and fulfilled prophecies that also use sevens which can be claimed beyond the control of any writer. And many counts of seven

involve more than one Bible book, making it not possible for the authors to have control of the total number of sevens. However, proving beyond competent dispute that there are a significant amount of sevens in the texts and structures of the Bible will remain a serious challenge.

ILLUSTRATION #3: ISAAC, A SYMBOLIC PROPHECY ABOUT JESUS

"Then God said, 'Take your son, your only son, Isaac, whom you love,
and go to the region of Moriah. Sacrifice him there as a burnt offering
on one of the mountains I will tell you about.'"
GENESIS 22:2

Here is the story of when God tested Abraham's faith. He told Abraham to take his only son Isaac to a mountaintop and sacrifice him. Fortunately this was only a test, so when Abraham was ready to kill Isaac, God intervened and provided a ram as a substitute for Isaac.

Compare the story of Isaac to Jesus and the gospels. There are astonishing parallels:[513]

- Like Jesus, Isaac was miraculously conceived. Sarah, Isaac's mother, was 90 years old when she bore Isaac and had been barren all her life; Abraham was 100 years old (Genesis 17:17).
- Like Jesus, Isaac was his father's beloved son (Genesis 22:2).
- As Jesus carried the cross, Isaac carried the wood for his own sacrifice (Genesis 22:6).
- Like Jesus spending three days in the tomb before the resurrection, the journey to Moriah took three days (Genesis 22:4).

Although these similarities are not expressly delineated in the New Testament, the story of Abraham's offering of Isaac became the "old covenant" counterpart of and paradigm for God's sacrifice of his own son on Calvary very early in post-New Testament Christian literature. The earliest reference is in the Epistle of Barnabas:[514] *"because He also Himself was to offer in sacrifice for our sins the vessel of the Spirit, in order that the type established in Isaac when he was offered upon the altar might be fully accomplished."* [515] Irenaeus, Tertullian, Clement, and Origen also cited the Isaac-Christ parallels. Tertullian saw the firewood Isaac carried as a figure of the cross and emphasized Christ's self-sacrifice: *"Accordingly, to begin with, Isaac, when led by his father as a victim, and himself bearing his own 'wood,' was even at that early period pointing to Christ's death; conceded, as He was, as a victim by the Father; carrying, as He did, the 'wood' of His own passion."* [516]

That is not all! The region of *Mount Moriah* is once again mentioned as the location where Solomon built the temple: *"Then Solomon began to build the temple of the Lord in Jerusalem on Mount Moriah, where the Lord had appeared to his father David. It was on the threshing floor of Araunah the Jebusite, the place provided by David"* (2 Chronicles 3:1). That is interesting. So the location of the temple is in the same mountain range as where centuries earlier Abraham was commanded to go to sacrifice Isaac. The threshing floor of Araunah is described in 2 Samuel 24:15-25 and is the site currently known as the Temple Mount in Jerusalem.

It is not on the top of the mountain, but at a saddle point about 1,500 feet southeast of the actual peak. The mountain peak itself is just outside the walls of Jerusalem as it was in the time of Jesus. That mountaintop, likely the actual location where Abraham was commanded to offer Isaac, was known in the time of Jesus as Golgotha; we now know it better as Calvary! [517]

In the words of Genesis 22:14: *"So Abraham called that place The Lord Will Provide. And to this day it is said, 'On the mountain of the Lord it will be provided.'"*

Analysis of this symbolic prophecy:
- Is it significant? I believe so. Not only are the parallels between Isaac and Jesus striking, but it is also compelling that Abraham is commanded to travel to the same area where we now know Jerusalem to be. Possibly this is even the same mountaintop where two thousand years later Jesus was suspended on the cross as a sacrifice for all people.
- The account is unique to the Bible. No other books claim a similar prophecy and fulfillment.
- There is no way Moses, when he wrote Genesis, could have known the future location of Jerusalem. The site for the temple was revealed to David about five hundred years later, and the location of the crucifixion was chosen by the Romans (who preferred a prominent spot just outside the city walls for the maximum effect) fifteen hundred years after the Abraham – Isaac incident was recorded.

Therefore, I personally believe that the symbolic sacrifice of Isaac, the location of Jerusalem, and possible, even the site of Calvary are impressive illustrations for God's design of the text of Genesis. It shows how irrelevant detail might provide provocative information.

ILLUSTRATION #4: A MESSAGE FROM THE TRIBAL CAMPS

"The Lord said to Moses and Aaron: 'The Israelites are to camp around the Tent of Meeting some distance from it, each man under his standard with the banners of his family.'"
NUMBERS 2:1-2

"Their faces looked like this: Each of the four had the face of a man, and on the right side each had the face of a lion, and on the left the face of an ox; each also had the face of an eagle."
EZEKIEL 1:10

"In the center, around the throne, were four living creatures, and they were covered with eyes, in front and in back. The first living creature was like a lion, the second was like an ox, the third had a face like a man, the fourth was like a flying eagle."
REVELATION 4:6-7

In Numbers 2 are detailed instructions about how the Israelites had to camp by tribe while in the desert: The Levites were to camp around the Tent of Meeting.[518] The tribes of Judah, Issachar, and Zebulun were placed to the east of the tabernacle. That Judah is mentioned first must have raised some eyebrows since Judah was not the oldest son of Jacob (Reuben was the oldest, then Simeon and Gad with Judah as the fourth oldest son – see also Numbers 1). Judah's preferred position (which continues through the history of Israel) can now be understood because that is the tribe of Jesse, David, and ultimately Jesus – the Messianic tribe. So here also we see a symbolic Messianic prophecy.

The second set of tribes – Reuben, Simeon, and Gad – camped on the south side. The tribe of Reuben, descendants of Jacob's eldest son, enjoyed primacy in this group. The third group consisted of the tribes of Ephraim, Manasseh, and

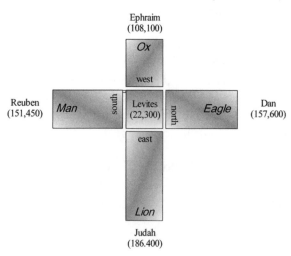

Figure 27-1: The Layout of the Jewish Tribal Camps

Benjamin under the leadership of Ephraim. Ephraim and Manasseh were sons of Joseph, who was a son of Jacob's favorite wife, Rachel. Benjamin was Rachel's only other son, so that tribe's association with Ephraim and Manasseh is readily understandable. The remaining tribes of Dan, Asher, and Naphtali settled on the north side under the leadership of Dan.

Numbers 1 describes a tribal census of all the Israelites, therefore we have the total number of men (woman and children were not counted) per camp (Numbers 1,2): Judah's camp had a total of 186,400 men, Reuben 151,450 men, Ephraim 108,100, and finally Dan's camp numbered 157,600 men. The Levites, camped in the center around the Tent of Meeting, had 22,300 men.

Through Genesis 49:9 (*"You are a lion's cub, O Judah"*) we know that Judah was represented by a lion. Both Jewish and Christian tradition claim that Reuben's ensign was a man, Ephraim's an ox, and Dan's an eagle.[519] These are the same symbols that we find around the throne of God in the vision of Ezekiel 1:10 and John's vision in Revelation 4:6-7.

Imagine the aerial view of the camp if the Israelites followed their tribal camp instruction to the letter.[520] It would look like a giant cross and in the center of the cross, the Tent of Meeting – the place where God would dwell. Around the Tent of Meeting we find the same four symbols as in both Ezekiel's as well as John's vision, both the Old Testament and the New Testament: a lion with a man on one side, an eagle on the other and an ox on the opposite site.

Analysis of this message:
- Is it significant? The image of the tribal camps forming a giant cross and confirming an Old Testament and New Testament vision of God's throne surrounded by the symbols of a lion, a man, an ox and an eagle is quite significant, provided our analysis is correct. However, it obviously rests on some speculative interpretation.
- This is a message unique to the Bible.
- Is this intentionally put into the text by the authors? The link between the symbols of the man, ox, and eagle with the respective tribes of Reuben, Ephraim, and Dan can be disputed, as there is no expressed textual evidence for it. The link between Judah and a lion is supported by Scripture. Also the out-of-the-blue dominant role for Judah is impressive. These last two observations compensate perhaps for the somewhat weaker case for symbols of the other tribes.

Therefore, it is my belief, that the image of the tribal encampment is a compelling illustration that God Himself designed and inspired the books of the Torah, Ezekiel, and Revelation.

SUMMARY

The Bible is the Inspired Word from God

We have seen how recent scientific discoveries and observations shed a new light on the texts of the Bible, especially the Pentateuch. These accounts written about 3,500 years ago contain astounding statements, revealing scientific and medical insights not known to mankind until the last few centuries or even recent decades. The following exhibits were presented:

1. The Genesis creation account is remarkably consistent with our current knowledge about the sequence of the development of life on earth and shows knowledge about natural science not known to mankind until recently.

2. Studies based on specific male and female DNA show that the common male ancestor is much younger than the common ancestor for females. No scientific observation or theory can account for this well-observed phenomenon other than the Biblical flood.

3. DNA in living cells can only be copied a limited time. This scientific observation is remarkably consistent with the 120 year maximum lifespan decreed by God in Genesis.

4. The dimension and specification of Noah's Ark resemble those of a modern day container ship, displaying shipbuilding knowledge only recognized in the last century.

5. The instructed circumcision of male babies on the eighth day coincides with the peaking of blood-clotting proteins.

6. The explicit instructions in the Mosaic Law about hygiene and contagious diseases have been confirmed by medical science only in the last 150 years.

7. The dietary rules outlined in the Mosaic Law are confirmed by modern medical science as an excellent way to reduce risk of cancerous diseases, heart disease, and stroke.

8. Adam and Eve were instructed to multiply, but as they were the only people, their children would have to marry family members. During the time of Moses, God explicitly outlawed sexual relationships with family members. Through genetics we now understand the increased risks of birth defects through in-breeding as the number of small errors in human DNA increases over generations.

Next, we have studied how the Scriptures contain hundreds of prophecies, foretelling events in secular history as well as the birth, life, ministry, death and resurrection of Jesus Christ. The prophecies were written centuries or even millennia before the predicted events took place. Selecting the most explicit prophecies, written well before their historical fulfillment, the following exhibits were presented:

9. Isaiah's prophecy of the return of exiled Jews from Babylon to Jerusalem by decree of Cyrus, King of Persia (Isaiah 44:28-45:1).

10. The multiple prophecies in the book of Daniel about the Babylonian, Medo-Persian, Greek, and Roman empires (Daniel chapters 2, 7 and 8).

11. Ezekiel's detailed prophecy about the destruction of Tyre, ultimately fulfilled by Alexander the Great (Ezekiel 26:3-14).

12. Jesus' prophecy about the *"not one stone left on another"* destruction of Jerusalem by the Romans in 70 AD (Mark 13:1-2).

13. The "Seventy Sevens" prophecy in Daniel that predicts almost 600 years in advance the day of the triumphal entry of Jesus into Jerusalem on Palm Sunday (Daniel 9:24-27).

14. The hundreds of prophecies from the Old Testament, written centuries BC about the Messiah, all fulfilled by Jesus through His birth, ministry, death, and resurrection.

The Bible is not a single book, but a collection of 66 books written by 40 authors over a period of 1,500 years. Still it has one theme, one story: God's plan of redemption for mankind:

15. From cover to cover the Bible outlines how, thanks to God's love and mercy, our sins can be forgiven through the blood of the perfect lamb, Jesus Christ.

Two final exhibits were presented to complete the evidence for God's inspiration of the Bible:

16. Believing and applying the teachings of the Bible has changed, and continues to change, lives of believers through history and all over the world.

17. Jesus of Nazareth, the Son of God Himself, teaches that the Bible is the inspired Word of God. If what Jesus taught is true and He teaches that the Bible is inspired, it logically follows that it is true that the Bible is inspired.

Over time, many have claimed discoveries of patterns in the texts of the Bible and/or symbolic prophecies that prove God's inspiration of the Scripture. In this book, these evidences from design (some call them "Bible codes") have – because of their controversial nature – not been considered "hard evidence." Hence they have not been presented as exhibits of evidence. However, these patterns and prophecies reveal intriguing and thought provoking observations and were shared as illustrations in the last chapter of this section.

Section V:
What Do Others Believe

CHAPTER 28

The World Religions

*"I am the Lord your God, who brought you out of Egypt, out of the
land of slavery. You shall have no other gods before Me."*
EXODUS 20:2-3

A POLITICALLY INCORRECT CONCLUSION

Earlier chapters have presented compelling evidence to demonstrate that a Creator God exists, that the Bible is historically reliable and trustworthy, and that Jesus is indeed God in human form. Additionally, the previous section set forth evidence that the Bible also contains numerous evidences that point to a divine source of inspiration and knowledge. Logically, this had led us to the unavoidable conclusion that Biblical Christianity (Christianity based on the Word of God as revealed in the Bible) is founded on fact and truth. Therefore, the Biblical Christian worldview, as far as it is based on the teachings of the Bible, is true.

This leads to a disturbing conclusion: All religions of the world cannot be equally true. Truth does not contradict itself. So, if our evidence for Christianity is based on truth, other worldviews must rest upon error, whatever its source. Quite a bold, somewhat arrogant, and definitively politically incorrect conclusion. In order to test this statement we need to survey the several Christian variants and the other major world religions: Hinduism, Buddhism, and Islam. Because of its recent growth, most attention will be directed to Islam.

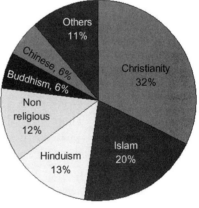

World population: + 2.3% growth per year
Christianity   : + 2.3% growth per year
Islam   : + 2.9% growth per year

Figure 28-1: An Overview of the World Religions

WHAT DO PEOPLE BELIEVE?

Let's start with some numbers:[521] Of the estimated 2006/2007 world population of 6.5 billion people, 2.1 billion people call themselves Christian:

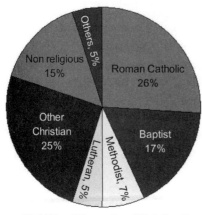

79-80% call themselves "Christians"

Figure 28-2: Religion in America

Roman Catholic, Protestant, Anglican, Eastern Orthodox, and so on; in general *"followers of and believers in Jesus Christ"* (more about this later). That is about 32% of the world population. For the US, according to a 2001 study,[522] this percentage is near 80%. Needless to say, not all denominations are considered fully Christian by others, and not all Christians are equally committed to their faith.

The worldwide number of Christians grows about 2.2% per year, almost equal or slightly less than the estimated annual growth of the world population at 2.3%; so the percentage of Christians of the world's population has been slightly falling during the last few decades.

These numbers indicate Christianity is, by far, the largest religion worldwide. However this is challenged by the growth of Islam, currently with 1.3 billion followers. Islam currently has a following of around 20% of the world population, but is growing at a rate of an estimated 2.9% per year in absolute numbers. Therefore, Islam as a percentage of world population grows about 0.7% per year. If this trend continues, in the lifetime of most readers, Islam will outgrow Christianity as the most "popular" religion. Since Islam is more than just a faith, including also a social and legal system, its continued growth is having and will continue to have even more a major geo-political effect worldwide.

Traditional Eastern religions such as Hinduism and Buddhism have followings of an estimated 950 million people and 375 million people respectively. Both religions are fairly stable in "market share."

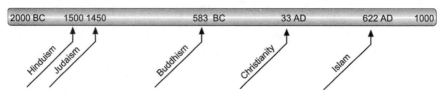

Figure 28-3: Estimated "Birth" of the World Religions

Looking at these numbers, do not forget Muslims, just like Christians and Jews, believe in the existence of God. About 90% of the worldwide population believes in some kind of God. This number is well above 95% in the USA. In history, more than 90% of people have believed in God.

These are quite serious numbers. They indicate a strong conviction in the average human being that "we are not here by accident."

BIBLICAL CHRISTIANITY

Within the 2.1 billion people "labeled" Christians, many different groups have disparate interpretations of the Bible, some embracing other scriptures and revelations. The documentary and historical evidences presented established the reliability and truthfulness of the Bible as the source of God's revelation and Jesus' teachings. I have found no evidence that supports claims of additional gospels and writings or any revelation or inspiration from God to other persons. Therefore, I am compelled to accept the Bible alone as the source for my knowledge about God and His plan of redemption through Jesus Christ. In that respect I call myself a *Biblical Christian*.

Biblical Christians are, in my definition, those who search seriously and carefully for the meaning of the Bible on its own terms, not changing its meaning to fit the times or culture. They are like the ancient Bereans described in Acts 17:11 *"Now the Bereans were of more noble character than the Thessalonians, for they received the message with great eagerness and examined the Scriptures every day to see if what Paul said was true."* The Bereans searched the Scriptures to verify that what was taught was confirmed by the Scriptures. They did not want to believe the gospel because it sounded nice and appealing (like a "health and wealth" gospel or "feel good" message), but they wanted to accept only the truth.

It is likewise with Biblical Christians. They search for the truth and accept it as God's truth even if they do not like it. Additionally, Biblical Christians approach the Bible with reverence and respect and do not believe that other writings are inspired. Neither do Biblical Christians believe in additional revelation outside the Bible through other sources or individuals. The Bible itself teaches: *"the faith ... was once for all delivered"* (Jude 3), there are no later or "latter day" revelations. In other words, *"the Bible alone is all we need for our spiritual authority. All the things we need to know, believe and practice are clearly stated in the Scriptures, which are given by inspiration of God. Anyone with common sense can understand what the Bible says in order to believe in Christ and be saved."* [523]

This definition of Biblical Christianity is not limited to particular denominations, it is more like a canopy that covers a myriad of churches, denominations, and groups, all of whom have beliefs or interpretations of Scripture that they emphasize. What draws these groups together are the fundamental agreements best summarized as these beliefs:

- The Bible alone contains God's Word. There is no revelation outside the Scripture.
- The death of Christ atones.[524] His death (and blood shed) was and is sufficient for all past, present and future sins of mankind.

Obedience versus legalism

Is following the instructions and teachings of the Bible, especially on politically incorrect topics, legalism or obedience? Do we need to read God's Word as a suggestion or a command?

Modern culture clashes at many points with the Bible. Biblical teachings about the submission of a wife to her husband; permitting only men in the roles of elders, deacons, teachers and pastors; marriage between a man and a woman; the sanctity of life versus abortion and euthanasia; head coverings and so on, are all more or less in conflict with our – secular – world and modern way of life. Many will claim these teachings were "from and for a different time" and are no longer applicable. Christians who seek to obey these commands are often called legalists.

However what is legalism? A legalist believes that one can be saved by keeping all God's commands to the letter. Basically, he believes he can live without sin, without breaking God's Law. Therefore, he does not need Christ, as he is without sin. This attitude of "self-righteousness" resulting in a feeling of superiority was what Jesus convicted and condemned in the Pharisees and Teachers of the Law. We know we all sin. Anyone who reads the *Sermon on the Mount* (Matthew 5-7) will realize that it is not humanly possible to keep all commands, and we all fall short of the glory of God (Romans 3:23: *"for all have sinned and fall short of the glory of God"*). Therefore legalism – with the objective to justify oneself by keeping all God's commands – is doomed to fail.

This does not mean we should not be obedient! Jesus Himself teaches to keep His commands. John 14:15: *"If you love me, you will obey what I command"* and John 14:21: *"Whoever has my commands and obeys them, he is the one who loves me."* Being obedient is not the same as being legalistic. If a father ask his son to take the garbage out and the son does as he is told, is he legalistic or obedient? Likewise, we should be obedient to our heavenly Father and do as He asks us to do.

That has nothing to do with being legalistic, but everything with being obedient.

- Salvation cannot be earned through works. Salvation is a gift from God to be accepted through faith. This faith must be active and lead to an obedient response (Romans 10:17: *"So faith comes from hearing, and hearing through the word of Christ."*). Works do not earn salvation, but the lack of an active response and obedience can lead to loss of one's salvation (James 1:14-17, emphasis added: *"What good is it, my brothers, if someone says he has faith but does not have works? Can that faith save him? If a brother or sister is poorly clothed and lacking in daily food, and one of you says to them, Go in peace, be warmed and filled, without giving them the things needed for the body, what good is that? So also <u>faith by itself, if it does not have works, is dead</u>"*).
- Christ will one day return and all will be judged according to one's deeds (Revelation 20:12, emphasis added: *"Then another book was opened, which is the book of life. And the dead were judged by what was written in the books, <u>according to what they had done</u>"*).

Nowadays Biblical Christians are mostly found under the umbrella of *Protestants, Evangelical Protestants,* or *Born-Again Christians.* But be on alert, not all (Evangelical) Protestants or Born-Again Christians meet the above definition of Biblical Christians!

Later,[525] we will look into the history of the Christian faith and survey the main branches of Christianity: The Roman Catholic Church, the Eastern Orthodox Church, and the Protestant churches.

INVESTIGATING THE OTHER WORLD VIEWS

It is not my intention to offend or demean anyone who is not a Biblical Christian. The only reason to research other religions is to investigate their historicity and the evidences for their foundations. Are they based on historical, verifiable evidence? How have their teachings and writings been preserved and passed on over the ages? What did their founder (if applicable) claim as his source of revelation? Are their claims about God, their founder, and his teachings consistent with scientific observations and secular historical sources? To facilitate comparison of various worldviews from an apologetics point of view, we will discuss the following topics about each of the major world religions:

- **Background.** A bird's-eye overview of some current statistics, including origins, history, and demographics.
- **Beliefs about God.** What do they believe about God's existence, nature, and character.
- **Basic teachings.** The core beliefs, values, and teachings especially about life, salvation, and the afterlife.

- **The founder.** Historical setting, background, life, and teachings of the founder.
- **The writings.** What are the sacred writings, how did they come about, how are they preserved, are they historically reliable?
- **Comparing to Christianity.** What are the similarities and differences with Christianity?
- **Conclusions from an apologetics perspective.** Are the claims and teachings consistent with, and supported by, the scientific and historical facts and observations?

In subsequent chapters we will thus investigate Hinduism, Buddhism, and Islam.

What about Judaism?

If we think about Judaism we tend to think about Israel. Surely, many adherents to Judaism live in Israel; however, not all Israelites are believing Jews. In fact, Israel is largely a secular state. Although 80% of its 6.2 million[526] inhabitants claim to Jewish, the country is very different from the Jewish nation described in the Old Testament.

Judaism is significantly small overall; there are perhaps only 15 million Jews worldwide. In the context of this book we cannot discuss Judaism in-depth. Nevertheless Christians should not forget that the first Christians were Jews by descent and that the Christian faith is based on Judaism and they both share the same Old Testament. The difference lies in the person and role of Jesus of Nazareth, the Messiah. For Jews the Messiah still has not come; for Christians the Messiah "completed" Judaism.

Lastly, the state of Israel has been and likely will continue to be the central hotspot in the world. News about the Jewish state will regularly dominate the headlines and news broadcasts.

CHAPTER 29

The Flavors of Christianity

"And I tell you that you are Peter, and on this rock I will build my
church, and the gates of Hades will not overcome it."
MATTHEW 16:18

ONE CHRIST, MANY CHURCHES

The official birthday of Christianity is commonly identified as the coming of the Holy Spirit at the day of Pentecost, fifty days after the Passover on which Jesus was crucified. The event is described in Acts 2:3-4: *"They saw what seemed to be tongues of fire that separated and came to rest on each of them. All of them were filled with the Holy Spirit and began to speak in other tongues as the Spirit enabled them."* Immediately after the apostles were filled with the Holy Spirit, Peter spoke to the crowd, and three thousand people believed the gospel and were baptized (Acts 2:5-41).

Today it is all but impossible to speak of "the Christian Church" because that immediately raises the question: which one? About half of all Christians associate themselves with the Roman Catholic Church, the rest is divided among the Eastern Orthodox Church, numerous Protestant Churches and various other groups including some vocal "Christian" cults.

History itself readily explains why we have these many "flavors of Christianity." Subsequently we will examine the main flavors of Christianity through the lens of Biblical Christianity. Once again I emphasize that it is not my purpose to define the "true church" at the expense of others. We need, however, be prepared to search for a church that meets the principles of Biblical Christianity.

A BRIEF HISTORY OF THE CHRISTIAN CHURCH

Studying Acts and other books in the New Testament, as well as the writings of the earliest Christians along with secular and historical sources, allows us to understand the history and growth of the Christian church to the modern age. History teaches how the Christian church has influenced the world (most times a positive influence, but occasionally negative). It also explains why today there are three main branches of Christianity: Eastern (Greek) Orthodox, Roman Catholic, and Protestant; what the differences are; and how they came about.

The Christian movement, initially known as *"the Way,"* was like a spiritual explosion. Ignited by the resurrection and fueled by the Holy Spirit, the church grew in all directions, geographically as well as socially. It was a unified church with a spiritual vision, a conviction that all Christians should be one body, thought of as *"the Holy Catholic Church."* In the first centuries, the term *catholic* was widely used of the church in the sense that the church was both universal, in contrast to local congregations, and orthodox, in contrast to heretical groups. Jesus sent his disciples into all the world, and Paul had opened the church to the Gentiles. In a sense catholic Christianity was simply a development of Jesus' plans and Paul's efforts.[527]

Up to 313 AD, the church was a non-political movement struggling socially, while expanding in the aftermath of varying degrees of persecution. That year Constantine became the first Christian emperor of Rome, and reigned until his death in 337 AD. Christianity became the favored faith, eventually even the official religion (380 AD) of the Roman Empire. This development had many advantages for the church, as it stopped persecution, facilitated the spread of the gospel, and even made public funds available for ministry and building churches. However, many think the detrimental effects on the church, once it became part of the established regime and a political player, far outweigh any benefits. Generally, this move marked the end of the unified church.

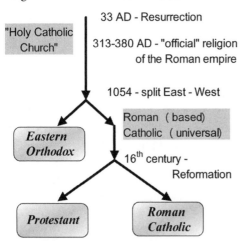

Figure 29-1: The Development of Christianity

During this unified early age of the church, two important statements of faith were agreed upon:

- **The Apostles' creed** (likely dated the second half of the second century); a statement of fundamental Christian beliefs drawn up to oppose gnostic heresies.
- **The Nicene Creed** (formulated 325 AD at the council of Nicea); an expansion of the Apostles' creed, additionally addressed the so called Arian heresy (Arius was a bishop who claimed that Jesus was not God, but only human).

These creeds[528] are still used today by the major branches of Christianity. Often they are seen as the statement of beliefs that unites believers under the banner of Christianity.

Historians recognize by the early Middle Ages (many say even as early as the Council of Nicea) the start of a rift between the Roman and Greek elements of the church. Apart from significant cultural differences between the Greek-speaking East and the Latin-speaking West, political events produced entirely different situations for both. In the West, the demise of the Roman Empire created a vacuum into which the church stepped; the papacy emerged with the Pope wielding political power. In the east, the Byzantine Empire continued another thousand years, and its emperors kept a tight reign on the power of the church. In 1054 AD, the separation of the Eastern Church from the Western church became official because of the papal claim to supreme authority. A lesser issue concerned a clause added to the church's creed stating the Holy Spirit came from the Son of God as well as God.[529]

The next major schism was the Protestant Reformation of the sixteenth century. During those years numerous reformers, of which Martin Luther is the best known, recoiled against Roman Catholic doctrines on salvation, the hierarchical structure, the role of the Pope, the role of saints and statutes, and elevation of church tradition to the same level as that of the Bible. Reformation battle cries such as "*Sola Scriptura*" and "*Salvation by faith alone*" summarize the essential conflict. Once the dust settled, four main groups were identified as Protestantism:[530]

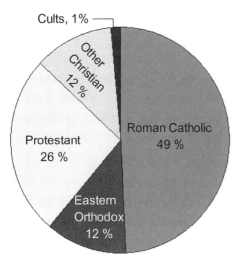

Figure 29-2: Christianity Worldwide

- Lutherans, mainly in Germany and the Nordic countries.
- Reformed and Presbyterian Churches, mainly in Switzerland, Germany, the Netherlands, and Great Britain, where they were known as Presbyterians and Congregationalists.
- Anglicans, originally in Great Britain, but eventually a worldwide communion.
- Anabaptists and spiritualistic groups, mainly in Germany, England, and the Netherlands.

All these groups settled in North America at various times, and further divisions resulted in numerous independent denominations (estimated at more than 900 denominations in the US alone).[531] Mission activities, largely instigated in the nineteenth century, led to establishment of churches in Africa and Asia.

THE ROMAN CATHOLIC CHURCH

The Roman Catholic Church is by far the largest single branch of Christianity, encompassing more than one billion believers, about half of all Christians worldwide.

This book cannot adequately examine the doctrines and teachings of the Roman Catholic Church. As a former Roman Catholic myself, it certainly is not my intent to discredit their beliefs or offend any Roman Catholic reader. We'll limit ourselves to mention some of the main issues that separate Roman Catholicism and other Christian groups:[532]

- **The teaching authority of the church.** Roman Catholicism insists it has the only accurate and authoritative source of interpretation of Scripture. Individual believers are not encouraged to read the Bible and seek its meaning; instead the church will decide that and teach it to the believer. Over the years this has led to numerous doctrines not found in the Bible at all, such as the concepts of purgatory, forgiveness of sins by priests, the role of Mary and the saints, involuntary celibacy of priests, and so on. This has bestowed on the church an authority superior to Scripture; it has also created the concept of papal infallibility.
- **Role of the Pope.** The Roman Catholics believe in the primacy and supreme authority of the Bishop of Rome also known as the Pope. This person is traditionally regarded as Christ's representative on earth and successor to the apostle Peter (thought to have been the first such Bishop of Rome). When defining matters of faith or morals, what the Pope says is considered to be infallible and binding for all Christians.
- **Salvation is by faith plus "works."** Roman Catholics believe the Christian must rely on faith plus "good works." God's grace is mediated through Seven Sacraments. These Sacraments (proclaimed by the authority of the church) are:
  - **Baptism.** For infants or adults to erase original sin.
  - **Confirmation.** To complete baptism and give the Holy Spirit in a fuller outpouring, usually children are confirmed at the age of twelve.
  - **Holy Eucharist.** Also called Holy Communion, the most important sacrament. During Mass, through *transubstantiation*, Christ is presented again and again as a sacrifice for sins.

- **Penance (or Confession).** Through the ministry of intervention by a priest, a believer can be forgiven by God for sins committed after baptism. It involves "acts" or "penances" which a believer must do to be forgiven of his or her sins. The priest assigns a penance that fits the gravity of the sin. Doing penance might involve repeating a certain number of prayers, fasting, or doing "works of love."
- **Anointing the Sick (or Extreme Unction).** The priest anoints the sick (usually dying) believer with oil and prays for this individual.
- **Holy Orders.** The sacrament through which Roman Catholic ministers are ordained to the three levels of bishops, priests, and deacons.
- **Matrimony.** This sacrament joins a man and woman in a lifelong union. Divorce and remarriage cut the believer off from Eucharistic Communion, but not from the church.

For the Roman Catholic, faith in Christ is the beginning of salvation and lays the foundation for justification. Then the believer builds on that with good works, because "*man has to merit God's grace of justification and eternal salvation.*" [533]

- **Purgatory and indulgences.** Catholics believe that even if they do all the works required of them, they are not assured of immediate entrance into heaven, but first must face punishment for their sins in an "in-between" place called *purgatory*. This is a special place of cleansing where believers are made fit for heaven; it is not like a temporary hell, but said to be a state of joy and a place of suffering. Roman Catholics also believe people still alive can shorten time for those in purgatory by prayers, offering Mass for them, and doing good works, which includes acquisition of indulgences. An indulgence can be a partial, or even full pardon for any sin not paid for during life. Therefore, it can reduce or even eliminate time in purgatory. The indulgences are administered by the church and can be given or sold to believers. This last practice was widespread at the end of the Middle Ages and helped spark Martin Luther's initial revolt against the church.
- **Role of Mary and other saints.** Roman Catholics practice *veneration*, which means that they pray to canonized saints, who in turn intercede for them before God in every need. The Gospel of Luke calls Mary highly favored and blessed among women (Luke 1:28), but for Roman Catholics, Mary alone is elevated over all the other saints and given *super-veneration*. Over the centuries, she has gained such a uniquely revered status that the Roman Catholic Church teaches that her virginity continued after the birth of Jesus and she never gave birth to additional children.

Other doctrines include the *Immaculate Conception* (which states that Mary herself was conceived without sin and lived a sinless life, proclaimed dogma in 1854) and the doctrine of the *Assumption* (that she was taken up directly to heaven, proclaimed dogma in 1950).

Roman Catholics point to Matthew 16:18-19 as evidence for their claims of the Pope as the leader of the church: *"And I* [Jesus] *tell you that you are Peter, and on this rock I will build my church, and the gates of Hades will not overcome it. I will give you the keys of the kingdom of heaven; whatever you bind on earth will be bound in heaven, and whatever you loose on earth will be loosed in heaven."* According to the *Catechism of the Catholic Church*, Jesus Himself appointed Peter the "rock" beneath His church, gave him the keys, and made him shepherd of the whole flock. They subsequently claim the Bishop of Rome as Peter's successor, bearing the supreme authority (primacy) over the entire church.

However, careful reading of this passage in the Greek manuscripts shows that the text refers to Peter as "Petros" (meaning a small rock) and to "this rock" as "petra" (meaning a very large rock). Many, if not most, of the Early Church Leaders believed the rock mentioned by Jesus was the faith confessed by Peter and not the man himself. Additionally, the book of Acts shows an important role for Peter in the early years of the church, but clearly he was not the supreme leader. James, the brother of Jesus, shared the leadership of the Jerusalem Church with Peter (Acts 12:17 and 15:13), and Paul clearly did not recognize Peter as "an infallible leader" representing Christ on earth, as he opposed him in Galatia (Galatians 2:11-14). Peter was married (see Matthew 8:14), and Popes are forbidden to marry. If the first Pope could marry, why later deny that privilege to priests and Popes? Lastly there is no verifiable line of succession to link the current Pope to Peter the apostle, there is not even a record of any apostle appointing a successor after Matthias replaced Judas in Acts 1. The concept of apostolic succession is found nowhere in the Bible.[534]

As a concluding invitation to others such as myself who come from a Roman Catholic background: Please read the Bible yourself. The Scriptures are the Word of God. Not only do they not teach the above-mentioned Roman Catholic doctrines, they also teach nothing about special privileges or additional blessings through priests, bishops, cardinals, or the Pope.

THE EASTERN ORTHODOX CHURCH

There are estimated to be 250 million Eastern (or Greek) Orthodox Christians today. The Orthodox Church is centered upon four ancient patriarchates with special positions of honor and authority: Alexandria, Antioch, Jerusalem, and Constantinople. The churches extend across Eastern Europe,

Slavic countries, and the eastern Mediterranean. While each church in each country is self-governing, the churches also communicate with one another in various ways. In the United States the Eastern Orthodox Church has as many as four million members.[535]

In many ways, from the Biblical Christian view, the Eastern Orthodox Church stands close to the Roman Catholic Church, as we can see in the following overview:[536]

- **The Church is in authority of Scripture**. As with the Roman Catholic Church, the Eastern Orthodox Church considers itself to possess sole authority over the Scriptures. Believers are to listen to and obey the church's official interpretation of the Bible. Since there is no single office like the papacy, the Orthodox Church depends upon *Ecumenical Councils*. They believe that the Spirit of God, living in the church, guides the decisions of the bishops and preserves them from error.
- **Apostolic Succession.** Like Roman Catholics, the Orthodox members believe in the apostolic succession of their bishops; however, all bishops share equally in this succession.
- **Salvation and Sacraments.** The Orthodox Church observes the same seven sacraments as Roman Catholics only with differences as to interpretation and emphasis. The Eucharist is central to all Orthodox belief. They believe the actual body and blood of Christ are present in the elements of the bread and the wine. Baptism forgives original sin, with regular confessions required for personal sins. Priests will hear the confession and often give advice or assign penance. They believe salvation is attained through the work of *deification* ("theosis," become like God). Christ's death on the cross and God's grace are the means to enable man to "become God, to obtain theosis."
- **Veneration of saints and icons.** The Orthodox members pray to the saints, particularly Mary, because these people have achieved deification. They stress that saints, including Mary, are not mediators but intercessors, and praying to them is not worship but veneration. An important part of the Orthodox tradition is their use of icons as a symbol of Christ, the apostles, Mary, or a saint.

THE PROTESTANT CHURCHES

We cannot speak of the Protestant Church, because there are perhaps thousands[537] of varieties. Diverse groups such Baptists, Lutherans, Reformed, Presbyterian, Anglican, Anabaptists, and so on all fall under the label of Protestantism. Protestantism is not as much a Church as it is a movement of Churches. Worldwide, 575 million people associate themselves with a Protestant church. About 85% of all Protestants belong to the 12 largest denominations.

The differences between Protestant groups partly center upon the differences between the denominations, but perhaps even more upon the differences between individuals: fundamentalists, conservatives, mainline believers, charismatics, and social activists.

Though Protestants share many core beliefs with Roman Catholics and Eastern Orthodox, two main areas of difference are:

- **Justification by Faith.** The term *justification* refers to the restoration to the right relationship with God. Protestants believe this justification, their salvation, is based on faith alone. One cannot earn salvation by works; it is received as a gift from God. There seems to be little difference among the Protestant groups on this issue. However there are huge differences on the understanding of faith. What does faith mean? Does it mean that merely belief in Jesus and the Bible justifies one, or does faith need to be active and obedient (the Biblical Christian view). If saved, are you saved forever; are future sins always forgiven, or can one lose one's salvation? Answers to these questions shape many of the different Protestant groups.
- **The Protestant Principle.** The Protestant principle[538] is an umbrella term describing the rejection of all forms of idols or idolatry in the church. The Trinity alone is the focus of the church; nothing can be allowed to distract a worshiper from God. Therefore all representations of God such as statues, icons, or paintings are rejected. Also saints (as recognized by the Roman Catholic and Eastern Orthodox Churches) and the Pope are considered idols, and hence these too are rejected.

WHAT ABOUT CHRISTIANS CULTS?

Not because of their size, but because of their active presence especially in the North American society, the identity of some "Christian Cults" should also be discussed briefly.

Cults such as Mormons, Jehovah's Witnesses, Christian Scientists, and so on, are considered varieties of Christianity. Indeed, in their views Jesus plays a more or less important role, but none of these groups acknowledges Christ as God and/or their savior; therefore these groups are not Christian. The confusion between such organizations and Christianity is often a marketing tool used to the advantage of cultists to improve their image and open more doors as they search for proselytes.

Cults are almost always build upon their founder and his (or in some instances, her) claim to a form of latter-day revelation beyond the Scriptures. After a person joins the cult, he is subjected to an effective system of indoctrination, policing, and mind control. In general, cults share most of these characteristics:[539]

- Their founder claims additional, special revelation from God.

- They reject the Trinity. They recognize Jesus as a teacher and prophet, but deny His deity.
- They believe all Christian churches are wrong and only they know the whole truth.
- They claim to believe the Bible, but distort its teachings or make changes to it.
- They deny people can be saved by faith alone, but require good works and strict adherence to their teachings.
- Many times they will use Christian terminology, but assign it a different meaning.

For a brief and very limited overview of two of the largest and most active cults, Mormonism and Jehovah's Witnesses, see the table below (table 29-1).

Mormonism and Jehovah's Witnesses		
	Mormonism, Church of Latter Day Saints (LDS)	Jehovah's Witnesses (JW)
Number of followers	10-11 million worldwide, about 5 million in the USA[540]	6-7 million worldwide, 1 million in the USA[541]
Founder	Joseph Smith, 1823	Charles Russell, 1879
Main Scripture	Book of Mormon	Watchtower books and magazines
Role of the Bible	"The Word of God, as far as it is translated correctly"	The Watchtower translation of the Bible ("the New World Translation of the Holy Scriptures – NWT)
Nature of God	A supreme being who acquired that position by a perfect, righteous life	God – Jehovah – is a single being, there is no Trinity. He is not all-knowing nor all-present
Jesus Christ	One of the sons of God, Mormons can become like him	Michael became man in the form of Jesus. Jesus returned invisibly in 1914 and now rules from heaven
Nature of man	Eternal spirits who can become gods	Sinful, no salvation apart from the teachings of the Watchtower
Salvation	Through works through the LDS church	Through works, especially evangelism
Life after death	Different levels of kingdoms can be attained	Heaven is reserved for only 144,000 JW's

Table 29-1: Mormonism and Jehovah's Witnesses

COMPARISONS AND CONCLUSIONS

As we highlight the differences among Protestants, Roman Catholics, and Eastern Orthodox churches, we should not forget the important beliefs they share in common concerning the Triune God, the Bible, and Jesus of Nazareth. After all, these three "flavors" of Christianity are all based on the divine teachings and sacrifice of Christ: God who became man for our salvation. Though Roman Catholics and Eastern Orthodox believers think Christ's sacrifice needs the addition of sacraments and works, they still agree only His sacrifice makes salvation attainable in the first place.

An Overview of the Main Branches of Christianity				
	Roman Catholic	**Eastern Orthodox**	**Protestant**	**Biblical Christianity**
Number of believers	Over 1 billion	250 million	575 million	Unknown
Geography	Worldwide	Eastern Europe, Slavic countries, Mediterranean	Worldwide	Worldwide
History	Developed from the Apostolic Church	Separated in 1054 AD	Separated in sixteenth century Reformation	Book of Acts, 33 AD
God	Belief in Trinity	Belief in Trinity	Belief in Trinity	Belief in Trinity
Bible	Historical reliable Word of God	Historical reliable Word of God	Historical reliable Word of God	Historical reliable Word of God
Jesus Christ	Messiah and God	Messiah and God	Messiah and God	Messiah and God
Resurrection	Historical fact	Historical fact	Historical fact	Historical fact
Apostles' creed	Completely accepted	Completely accepted	Completely accepted	Completely accepted
Nicene creed	Completely accepted	Completely accepted	Completely accepted	Completely accepted
God's Word	Scripture, Tradition and the Pope	Scripture, Tradition and the bishops	Scripture alone	Scripture alone
Authority	Apostolic succession	Apostolic succession	Varies	The original apostles
Head of the Church	Pope	Council of bishops	Varies	Jesus Christ
Leadership	Pope, cardinal, bishops, and priests	Bishop and priests	"priesthood of all believers"	"priesthood of all believers" and church elders
Salvation	Faith + Sacraments + Works	Faith + Sacraments + Works ➡ Deification	By Faith through Grace through Christ	By obedient Faith through Grace through Christ
Saints and Mary	Veneration and Super-veneration	Veneration to help with deification	-	-
Purgatory	Place of preparation for heaven	-	-	-
Icons	-	Symbols of saints	-	-

Table 29-2: A Comparative Overview of the Branches of Christianity

We tend to define success in terms of numbers and dollars. That, however, is not God's economy. Because a church is considered mainstream does not mean it embraces the true faith. Large numbers do not determine truth. Only the Word of God is an objective standard for truth. Jesus Himself already warned multiple times about how easy it is to make "a wrong turn": "*Enter through the narrow gate. For wide is the gate and broad is the road that leads to destruction, and many enter through it. But small is the gate and narrow the road that leads to life, and only a few find it*" (Matthew 7:13-14).

The table (table 29-2) attempts to compare the shared beliefs and contrasting main differences between the three main Christian views and Biblical Christianity.

Has Christianity failed? Muslims (and others) will contend that the presence of the many different groups proves Christianity has failed. They claim that the true God would never allow His people to be so divided. However, is it not more logical to conclude that Christianity has not failed its followers, but <u>its followers have failed Christianity</u>?

CHAPTER 30
Hinduism

*"The ideal of man is to see God in everything. But if you cannot see
Him in everything, see Him in one thing, in that thing you like best,
and then see Him in another. So on you go. . . . Take your time and
you will achieve your end."*
SWAMI VIVEKANANDA[542]

Hinduism is shorthand for the philosophy, the religious beliefs and practices, and the way of life of many of the people in India. For Hindus in India,
Hinduism is an inseparable part of their existence, a complete approach to life
that involves social class, earning a living, family, politics, diet, etc., in addition
to the items Westerners view as religious.

The origin of Hinduism is generally connected to the Indus River. Others
suggest the term was invented later by Europeans as a common term to capture the complex diversity of religions found among the people of the Indian
sub-continent. Hindus themselves prefer the term *Sanatana Dharma* or *Hindu
Dharma*, which translates into "everlasting law" or "eternal teaching." This
indicates the eternal and revelatory nature of Hindu beliefs.[543]

BACKGROUND

With an estimated 950 million followers and perhaps more, it is the
world's third largest religion after Christianity and Islam. It also contends with
Judaism for the oldest surviving religion, even though it has no known
founder. The vast majority of its adherents (900 million or more) live in India
where more than 80% of the population is Hindu. Other countries with large
Hindu populations include Nepal, Bangladesh, Indonesia, Malaysia, Sri
Lanka, and Pakistan. There thought to be more than one million Hindus in
the USA.[544]

Not traditionally missionary, it has spread through the world as Hindus
have traveled and immigrated. With expanding export of skilled labor from
India to Western countries, Hinduism is a growing phenomenon.

The classical theory of the origins of Hinduism traces the religion's roots back
as far as 3000 BC to an ancient Indus valley civilization. Its development was influenced by the many invasions of this valley. The earliest documented beliefs and
practices of the 1500-500 BC era are often called the Vedic religion. The oldest

surviving textual document of Hinduism is the Rigveda, thought to have originated between 1700-1100 BC, based on linguistic and philological evidence.

During the second half of the Middle Ages, successive waves of Muslim armies invaded and established control over North India. Hinduism declined rapidly, and many Hindus converted to Islam. Some Muslim rulers destroyed Hindu temples and otherwise persecuted non-Muslims, while others were more tolerant.

Today various concepts of Hinduism have become integrated into Western culture. Examples are yoga and transcendental meditation. Alternative spiritualities and New Age lifestyles have also incorporated many aspects of Hindu practices.

BELIEF ABOUT GOD

Most Hindus believe in a One Supreme Cosmic Spirit called *Brahman* that may be worshiped in many forms, represented by individual deities such as *Vishnu, Shiva,* and *Shakti.* Hinduism centers upon a variety of practices meant to help one experience Brahman, who is everywhere and in everything, and to realize the true nature of the self.

This makes Hinduism a pantheistic religion (as "the divine" is considered to reside in ourselves and the world around us). At the same time it is also monotheistic (as there is one supreme being, Brahman) and polytheistic (as Brahman can be represented by multiple deities. Actually there are as many gods as the Hindu would like.

According to the monotheistic and pantheistic theologies of Hinduism, Brahman is, in the highest sense, beyond form, infinite, and eternal. He is changeless and is the very source of consciousness. Brahman is beyond time, space, and causation, and yet he permeates everything and every being. Brahman is beyond gender. Hindu writings declare Brahman to be beyond description, understood only through direct spiritual experience.

The goal of Hinduism is to somehow "wake up" and realize one's own connection to the divine reality. Thus, despite Hinduism's belief in the abstract principle of Brahman, most Hindus worship Brahman on a day-to-day basis in one of Brahman's less abstract personal forms, such as Vishnu, Shiva, or Shakti. Some Hindus worship these personal forms of Brahman for a practical reason: it is easier to cultivate genuine devotion to a personal being than to an abstract principle. Other Hindus consider the personal forms in themselves to be the highest form of truth and worship Brahman as an infinite and yet personal being. It should be noted that superstition plays a major role in the life of a Hindu.

BASIC TEACHINGS

Prominent themes in Hinduism include:

- **Dharma** (individual ethics, duties and obligations). A comprehensive ordering of life according to principles and practices appropriate for one's age and station ("caste") in life. This includes the basics of the Indian caste system, which segments people from birth into certain levels in society, placing each person in the caste where they will live out their life. Although the caste system was abolished by national law in 1949, it remains a significant force throughout India.

- **Samsāra** (rebirth or reincarnation). According to the doctrine of *reincarnation* (Samsāra), the soul is immortal, while the body is subject to birth and death. Many Hindus believe in reincarnation and they believe the action in one's life can determine one's fate in a subsequent reincarnation. Virtuous actions take the soul closer to the supreme divine and lead to a birth with higher consciousness. Evil actions hinder this recognition of the supreme divine, and the soul takes lower forms of worldly life.

- **Karma** (fate or right action). The doctrine of *karma* relates to the law of cause and effect. It states that everything people do (karma) leaves impressions in their mind, which determines what kind of people they will be in the future, and hence their fate.

- **Moksha** (deliverance from the cycle of birth and death). When the cycle of rebirth comes to an end, a person is said to have attained *Moksha*. All schools of thought agree that Moksha implies the cessation of worldly desires and freedom from the cycle of birth and death; the exact definition depends on individual beliefs.

In whatever way a Hindu might define the goal of life – and multiple definitions are allowed – several methods (yogas) have developed over the centuries for people of different tastes and temperaments. Paths one can follow to achieve the spiritual goal of life include: Bhakti Yoga (the path of love and devotion), Karma Yoga (the path of right action), Rāja Yoga (the path of meditation), and Jñāna Yoga (the path of knowledge).

THE FOUNDER

Hinduism is not really a single religion, but many beliefs that interact and blend with one another. Hinduism has no known founder, there are no creedal statements of faith, and no agreed-upon authority.

THE WRITINGS

Hinduism relies on numerous religious texts developed over many centuries, each containing spiritual insights and practical guidance for religious life. Among such texts, the four *Vedas* ("knowledge") are the most ancient, and form the foundation of Hindu philosophy. Other writings include the Brahamanas, Aranyakas, and Upanishads. These are all known as the *Vedic literature* and are considered supernaturally inspired.

Hinduism is said to rest upon "*the accumulated treasury of spiritual laws discovered by different persons in different times.*" The scriptures were transmitted orally, in verse form to aid memorization, for many centuries before they were written down. Through the years, teachings were refined by other sages, and the canon expanded. The great majority of the sacred texts are composed in the Sanskrit language.

While the Vedas are not commonly read by most Hindus, they are yet revered as eternal knowledge with sacred sounds that help bring spiritual and material benefits, and more importantly, for the revelations about Brahman. The Hindu scriptural canon is not closed; even today Hindus believe that, because the spiritual truths of the Vedas are eternal, they may continue to be expressed in new ways throughout the future. New scriptures can continue to be written to express the truths of the Vedas in ways accessible to people of different times and places. Many Hindus even venerate the scriptures of other religions, since it is believed that the "one divinity" can reveal itself in innumerable ways.

COMPARED TO CHRISTIANITY

In Hinduism, Brahman has the power to bring things into appearance. However, the pantheistic component of Hinduism claims God did not create the world: God is the world, along with everything in it. The world was not created, it always was, just like the soul that always has existed and will always exist.

Hindus do not believe in a personal, loving God but in Brahman, a formless, abstract, eternal being without personal attributes.

The Christian Bible contradicts the Hindu concepts of reincarnation, karma, and moskha. Hindus believe the soul is uncreated and eternal. This contradicts the teachings of the Bible that each person is created by God, will die once, and spend eternity in heaven or hell.

Hindus are tolerant of Christianity and any other religion; many even read the Bible as possible additional revelation (as their canon remains open). However, Hindus cannot accept Jesus as the only Son of God. In the words of the great Indian leader Mohandas Gandhi: "*It was more than I could believe that Jesus was the only incarnate son of God. And that only he who believed in him would have everlasting life."* Gandhi also said he could not believe there was any *"mysterious or miraculous virtue"* in Christ's death on the cross.[545]

Comparing Hinduism – Christianity	
Hinduism	**Christianity**
Pantheistic, monotheistic and polytheistic	Monotheistic
Brahman is impersonal	God is personal
Humanity is extended from Brahman	Humanity is separated from the being of God
The soul is eternal	Each of us is created by God
After death, one is reincarnated in a new body	After death, one faces God's judgment
"Salvation" through cycles of reincarnation	Salvation through forgiveness of sins
"Salvation" through self-effort Moksha – merge into oneness with Brahman	Salvation through God's grace by Christ Heaven – eternal fellowship with God

Table 30-1: Comparing Hinduism

CONCLUSIONS FROM AN APOLOGETICS PERSPECTIVE

Hinduism is not a historical religion like Christianity. Its writings and teachings are philosophical and spiritual; they do not allow corroboration from archaeology or other sources. Also Hinduism has evolved with the way of life and culture in India over millennia. It is not clear whether its teachings controlled the development of the culture, or the other way around. Either way, there is no founder or a doctrinal statement of faith to verify historically.

Its most important writings, the Vedas, were written between 1500 and 800 BC. They are not tied to any known person as author, though they were created by an emerging priesthood, the Brahman caste. The Vedas have been preserved orally as well as in writing, but there are virtually no ancient manuscripts. At the same time, since these books do not specify historical events or tie themselves to factual matters, how accurate they are textually makes little difference to its adherents.[546]

As a pantheistic religion, it assumes the "supreme being" Brahman is a non-personal presence in everything around us. It is not completely clear if all Hindus believe in an eternal universe, but the claims of an eternal soul of man seems to indicate such. Science has indisputably proved the universe is not eternal, but began (scientifically known as the Big Bang) and, therefore, will end. For that reason all scientific data conflicts the belief in an eternal universe of man and the pantheistic concept of Brahman.

The Hindu teaching of reincarnation is intriguing and, to many, appealing as a model for eternal life. However, there is no proof that anybody has ever lived and experienced the reincarnation of an earlier life. Also it raises vital questions such as: Where do souls come from, and how are more souls "created" as the human population continues to grow?

Another problem with reincarnation is an apparent built-in self-contradiction. The idea behind reincarnation is that over a number of death-rebirth cycles one's soul gradually improves and becomes wiser and purer, leading to ultimate moksha, the unification with Brahman. In this state of oneness evil is conquered and all is "good." However, Hinduism also teaches that all souls originated from Brahman. How can it be that when the soul left Brahman and started its cycle of improvements that it needed any improvements in the first place? The soul was pure and perfect as part of Brahman, so how could it be imperfect when it left Brahman? This could only be explained if the soul committed some evil while united with Brahman, but that would be a contradiction to Brahman's nature.

In many ways Hinduism baffles the logical mind with its inherent contradictions, and its evident foundation in pagan superstition.

CHAPTER 31

Buddhism

"Buddhism has the characteristics of what would be expected in a cosmic religion for the future: it transcends a personal God, avoids dogmas and theology; it covers both the natural & spiritual, and it is based on a religious sense aspiring from the experience of all things, natural and spiritual, as a meaningful unity."
ALBERT EINSTEIN[547]

Buddhism is not a religion, but more accurately described, it is a philosophy. It encompasses a system to enhance life by "waking up" to the true beauty of reality.

Buddha means "one who has woken up." Most people live asleep, never knowing or seeing life as it really is, and as a consequence they suffer. A Buddha is someone who has awakened to the knowledge of the world as it truly is and in doing so finds release from suffering. A Buddha teaches out of sympathy and compassion for the suffering of others and for the benefit and welfare of all beings.

BACKGROUND

The number of Buddhists worldwide is thought to vary between 250 to 500 million. Data from several countries are uncertain and the lack of formal organization in the Buddhist community makes it hard even to estimate. A "best guess" seems to be 375 million followers.

Buddhism does not actively seek converts, but it thoroughly welcomes anyone who wants to convert. Buddhism can coexist with other faiths.

It was founded in Northern India by the first known Buddha, Siddhartha Gautama. Around 535 BC, he attained enlightenment and took the title *Lord Buddha*. As Buddhism expanded across Asia (following the travels of the Lord Buddha and those of later generations of Buddhist monks), it evolved into three geographically separated forms, each of which has evolved largely independently:

- **Southern Buddhism (Theravada Buddhism).** This form represents the majority (a little over half of the total Buddhist following). It is practiced mainly in Southeast Asia, including Thailand, Burma, Sri Lanka, Cambodia, and Laos.

- **Eastern (or Chinese) Buddhism (Mahayana Buddhism).** Eastern Buddhism (about 35% of all Buddhists) is practiced predominantly in China, Japan, Vietnam, Korea, Tibet, Mongolia, and parts of Russia.
- **Tibetan Buddhism (also called Lamaism).** Lamaism (about 10% of the worldwide Buddhist following) developed in isolation from Theravada and Mahayana Buddhism due to of the remoteness of Tibet.

Modern day Buddhism has emerged as a true international movement. It started as an attempt to produce a single form of Buddhism, without local accretions, that all Buddhists could embrace. In the West it has grown due to its non-dogmatic nature, rationality, possibility of a spiritual guide, and opportunity for personal transformation; all of which have made it attractive to our post-modern, pluralistic society.

BELIEF ABOUT GOD

In its original forms, Buddhism did not teach the existence of a transcendent, imminent, or any other type of god or gods. However, many Buddhists – particularly in Japan – do believe in a variety of deities. Like Hinduism, these gods are arbitrary, chosen by Buddhists.

BASIC TEACHINGS

Buddhism is in part an extension and in part a reformation of Hinduism. In Buddhism, any person awakened from the *"sleep of ignorance"* by directly realizing the true nature of reality is called a Buddha. Siddhartha Gautama, the Buddha, is thus only one among other Buddhas before or after him. Fundamental Buddhist beliefs are:

- **Reincarnation and Rebirth.** Like Hinduism, Buddhism teaches reincarnation; most individuals pass through many cycles of birth, living, death, and rebirth. A practicing Buddhist differentiates between rebirth and reincarnation. In reincarnation, a person can return to life repeatedly. In rebirth, a person does not necessarily return to earth as a human entity again. Buddha compares it to a leaf growing on a tree. When the withering leaf falls off, a new leaf will eventually replace it. It is similar to the old leaf, but it is not identical to the original leaf.
- **Nirvana.** After many such cycles, if a person releases his attachment to desire and the self, he can attain Nirvana, a state of liberation and freedom from suffering. Buddhism teaches humans are trapped in a repetitive cycle of birth, life, death, and rebirth. One's goal is to escape this cycle and reach Nirvana. The mind experiences complete freedom, lib-

eration, and non-attachment. Suffering ends because desire and craving, the causes of suffering, simply end.

- **The Four Noble Truths.** The Buddha's *Four Noble Truths* explore human suffering. They may be described (somewhat simplistically) as:
  - **Dukkha:** Suffering exists, life involves suffering. Suffering is real and almost universal. Suffering has many causes: loss, sickness, pain, failure, the impermanence of pleasure, and so on.
  - **Samudaya:** There is a cause for suffering. Its cause is the desire to have and control things. It can take many forms: craving of sensual pleasures; the desire for fame; the wish to avoid unpleasant sensations such as fear, anger, or jealousy.
  - **Nirodha:** There is an end to suffering. Suffering ceases with the final liberation of Nirvana. The mind experiences complete freedom, liberation, and non-attachment. It lets go of any desire or craving.
  - **Magga:** In order to end suffering, you must follow the *Eightfold Path*.

The form in which one is reborn, animal or human, in heaven or in hell, depends on karma, an impersonal ethical law (like Hinduism). One can escape from this process by attaining Nirvana or enlightenment. Nirvana can be reached by following the *Eightfold Path*.

The Buddha's Eightfold Path
Panna: Discernment, wisdom that purifies the mind: 1) *Samma ditthi:* Right Understanding of the Four Noble Truths. Understanding reality as it is, not as it appears to be.   2) *Samma sankappa:* Right thinking; following the right path in life.
Sila: Virtue, morality: 3) *Samma vaca:* Right speech; truthful, criticism, condemning, gossip, harsh language.   4) *Samma kammanta:* Right conduct; wholesome action, avoiding actions that could do harm.   5) *Samma ajiva:* Right livelihood; supporting yourself without harming others.
Samadhi: Concentration, meditation: 6) *Samma vayama:* Right Effort; Promote good thoughts; conquer evil thoughts, make an effort to improve.   7) *Samma sati:* Right Mindfulness; Become aware of your body, mind and feelings .   8) *Samma Samadhi:* Right Concentration; Meditate to achieve a higher state of consciousness. Be aware of the present reality within yourself.

Table 31-1: The Eightfold Path to Enlightenment

THE FOUNDER

The Buddhist tradition is founded on and inspired by the teachings of Siddhartha Gautama who lived 566-486 BC. Born a Hindu in the foothills of the Himalaya in modern day Nepal (in those days Northern India), Siddhartha Gautama was the son of a local rajan, or chieftain. Siddhartha means *"one who has achieved his aim."* Gautama was his clan name. He was a member of a privileged and wealthy family and grew up comfortably.

After receiving four visions (other traditions claim he made four trips) of suffering and poverty, he was disillusioned with his wealthy life. He left home and adopted the life of a wandering ascetic and embarked on a spiritual quest.

One night in 535 BC, at the age of 30, he sat in meditation underneath a large tree, later known as the Bodhi tree, on the banks of the Nairangana in Northern India. He had a profound experience, and he believed he had gained a deep understanding of the nature of suffering, its cause, and a way to stop it. He assumed the title Lord Buddha (one who has awakened; the one who has attained enlightenment by himself). Lord Buddha then devoted the rest of his life (about 45 years) to traveling and teaching the way to cease suffering. By the time of his death at about the age of 75, he had a considerable following and had established an order of monks and a corresponding order of nuns.

The Buddha did not choose a successor. He believed that the Dharma, his teachings, plus the Vinaya, his code of rules for the monks and nuns, would be a sufficient guide. It took at least one and a half century (some say even 250 years) before a council of Buddhist monks collected his teachings and the oral traditions of the faith into a written form.

THE WRITINGS

During his life Lord Buddha wrote nothing. There is a gap of at least 150 years between his spoken words and the first written records. A gap of that duration (compared to the gospels written within 25-70 years of the resurrection and all by personal witnesses) with multiple generations of oral tradition is likely to raise serious questions about the reliability of the texts.

An additional challenge is that Buddha taught for 45 years, and a staggering amount of material has been attributed to him in one way or another. This raises the obvious question of how to discern what was taught by Buddha and what was added later by his followers.

Buddhist scriptures and other texts exist in great variety. Different schools of Buddhism place different values on them. Some schools venerate certain texts as religious objects in themselves, while others take a more scholastic approach. The Buddhist canon of scripture is known as the *Tripitaka*. This included a large collection of commentaries and traditions; most are called

Sutras (discourses). Tripitaka literally means "three baskets," and refers to the three main divisions of the canon, which are:
- The **Vinaya Pitaka**, containing disciplinary rules for the Buddhist monks and nuns, as well as a range of other texts including explanations of why and how rules were instituted, supporting material, and doctrinal clarification.
- The **Sūtra Pitaka** which contains the actual discourses of the Buddha.
- The **Abhidharma Pitaka** which contains commentaries or systematic expositions of the Buddha's teachings.

Buddhism has no single central text universally referred to by all traditions.

COMPARED TO CHRISTIANITY

Buddhists do not believe in any god, and the philosophy is probably best characterized as a pantheistic worldview. It teaches nothing about creation or a beginning or an end to existence. It embraces concepts such as reincarnation, but with even less detachment than Hinduism, it makes no attempt to understand or explain these concepts. It does not expressly exclude the existence of a god either; therefore, many Buddhist fill in this gap themselves, either with a god or a combination of gods of their choosing (similar to Hinduism).

The Christian Bible contradicts Buddhist teachings of reincarnation and Nirvana. Buddhists believe the soul is uncreated, eternal, and its boundaries will ultimately be extinguished in the state of Nirvana. This contradicts the teachings of the Bible that each person is created by God, will die once, and spend eternity in heaven or hell.

The Buddha gave an eight-fold path to live a better life, without cravings and desires that cause suffering. Jesus gave us a similar set of instructions to improve life in the Sermon on the Mount, but Jesus adds to that God's power (by the Holy Spirit) and authority, and ultimately God's grace in the plan of redemption.

Comparing Buddhism – Christianity	
Buddhism	**Christianity**
Pantheistic	Monotheistic
There is no God or God is Nirvana	God is personal
The soul is "uncreated"	Each of us is created by God
After death, one is reincarnated in a new body or reborn into another life form	After death, one faces God's judgment
We suffer because we crave and desire	We suffer because we sin
"Salvation" through self-effort	Salvation through God's grace by Christ
Enter Nirvana, where the ego is extinguished	Heaven – eternal fellowship with God

Table 31-2: Comparing Buddhism

CONCLUSIONS FROM AN APOLOGETICS PERSPECTIVE

Buddhism, like Hinduism, is not a historical religion like Christianity. Its writings and teachings are philosophical and spiritual; neither requires, nor allows, any corroboration from archaeology or other historical sources. There is no doctrinal statement of faith to verify historically.

According to tradition, some of Buddha's teaching material was assembled by his own disciples at the first Buddhist council in the early fifth century BC. Thus, it would likely be somewhat faithful to what Buddha himself taught. Over the centuries, the Tripitaka has welled by constant addition of new material. Some of it is merely rewrites of popular traditions into Buddhist thought forms. The complete canon stems from no earlier than the first century BC. The overarching problem is not textual accuracy – a lost cause – but simply identifying texts that might have been part of the original. Wooden print blocks in Chinese and Korean exist from roughly the thirteenth century, so from that point on translations into those languages are stable. Nevertheless, there is a sizeable gap between the thirteenth century and the time of the Buddha.[548]

As for its teachings, as a pantheistic religion, it makes no statement about origins or even God. The claims of reincarnation and rebirth suggest that Buddhists believe in an eternal universe. Scientific evidence has shown, beyond dispute, that the universe had a beginning and will also have an end. Therefore, the scientific observations conflict with the Buddhist beliefs.

As with Hinduism, the Buddhist teachings concerning reincarnation and rebirth are interesting and, to many, appealing. However, there is no evidence for reincarnation; the principle goes against logic as there are more people alive today than have lived in the entire history of mankind.[549]

The documentary evidences for the Buddhist scriptures show that they were first written down 150-250 years after the teachings of Buddha. Without even analyzing the accuracy of these texts copied again and again through the subsequent years, the multi-generational gap between the original teaching and the written record raises many questions about what was actually taught by Buddha as opposed to what was added later by his followers.

CHAPTER 32

Islam

*"And in their footsteps we sent Jesus the son of Mary,
confirming the Torah that had come before him:
We sent him the Gospel: therein was guidance and light."*
THE QUR'AN, SURAH 5:46

Islam is an Arabic word that means "submission," said to be the surrender of oneself to the will of *Allah* (God), achieving peace and security by doing so. A person surrenders to the will of Allah by living and thinking in the way Allah has instructed. A *Muslim* is a follower of Islam. Muslim is an Arabic word that refers to one who submits to the will of Allah. Islam is more than a system of beliefs. The faith provides a social and legal system to govern all aspects of life, such as family, law and order, ethics, dress, and cleanliness as well as religious ritual and observance. The *Qur'an* is the holy book of Islam and considered to contain the unaltered word of Allah.

BACKGROUND

Islam is the world's second most followed religion and, at present, the fastest growing. It began in its present form more than 1,400 years ago (founded in 622 AD) in what is now Saudi Arabia. It swiftly became a world faith, and now has as many as 1.3 billion believers.[550] That is about 20-22% of the world population, or otherwise said, one in every five people today is a Muslim. In the USA, estimates reach two million with a increase of more than 100% in the last ten years.[551] Islam actively seeks converts while it aggressively avoids exposure of believers to other faiths.

Although Islam is a purely Arabic religion, fewer than 20% of Muslims live in the Arab world. An estimated 20% live in Sub-Saharan Africa; about 30% in the South Asian region of Pakistan (155 million Muslims), India (130 million), and Bangladesh (125 million).[552] Somewhat surprisingly, the world's largest single country Muslim population is found in Indonesia (about 210 million Muslims).[553] There are also significant Muslim populations in China, Europe (fast growing, especially France and Great Britain), Central Asia, and Russia.

Islam's three holiest places, the cities of Mecca, Medina, and Jerusalem are all in the Middle East. That Mecca and Medina are so revered is obvious from the role these cities – especially Mecca – played in the life of Mohammed. The importance of Jerusalem is somewhat unexpected. There is no indication that Mohammed ever visited Jerusalem. So why is it so important? Jerusalem's special position is partly explained by the important role it plays in the "rewritten" accounts in the Qur'an of Old Testament stories about Abraham and David as well as the life of Jesus. More important is the belief that the site of the Dome of the Rock in Jerusalem is the place where the prophet Mohammad was carried into heaven.

As we have seen, Christianity is currently the largest religion in the world. About 32% of the world population is Christian, a percentage that has remained relatively stable with only a slight decline for decades. However Islam adherence grows at a rate of an estimated 2.9% per year, that is 0.6% more per year than the growth of the world population. If this current trend continues, Islam will become the largest world religion sometime in the mid twenty-first century.

Why is Islam growing so fast on a worldwide basis? It is likely a combination of geopolitics and demographics. Countries with a large majority of Muslims declare themselves an Islamic state and adapt Islamic laws, making Islam the only allowed state religion. Usually this is combined with a non or limited democratic regime. Examples are Saudi Arabia, Iran, Syria, Pakistan, and so on. In these countries freedom of religion is not allowed, or at best severely restricted, thus forcing Islam on all its citizens. On the other hand, some traditionally Christian European countries have ex-colonial ties to many of the countries now predominantly Islamic. These historical ties allow easy entry for citizens from these former colonies into Europe, and the European Union facilitates easy travel within its borders. Many Muslims make these moves for economic reasons. Through this migration, increasing numbers of Muslims relocate to these mostly Christian countries and take their faith with them. The effects of this population shift are multiplied significantly as birthrates decline and family size decreases among the "native" Europeans as opposed to the large Muslim families.

BELIEF ABOUT GOD

There is only one God, called *Allah* ("Al Lah" is the Arabic for the divinity, meaning "the One True God." Allah was also the name of one of the gods worshiped by local pagan religions).[554] Allah's last prophet was Mohammad (pbuh).[555] Mohammad was not a god or divine in any sense, but he was a man, the final prophet, the messenger through whom Allah revealed his will. Muslims revere Mohammad, but they do not worship him. Everything and everyone depends on Allah. All Muslims, whatever their race, belong to one community: the *Ummah*.

Allah is described in the Qu'ran (Surah 112:1-4) as: *"...God, the One and Only; God, the Eternal, Absolute; He begetteth not, nor is He begotten; And there is none like unto Him."* Is Allah the same as the Christian God (Jehovah) as described in the Bible? There are similarities because both religions are monotheistic and also because (as we will discuss later in this chapter) Islam is, in many ways, an outgrowth of Judaism and Christianity. Apart from the fact that both Allah and Jehovah are the only God recognized by each religion, both Islam and Christianity also recognize God as the Creator of the universe; He is sovereign, omniscient, omnipresent, and omnipotent; He has revealed His will and character through prophets, angels, and the written word; He knows the thoughts and deeds of men; and He will judge the wicked. However, there can be no doubt to even the occasional reader of the teachings of Islam and Christianity that both refer to a very different God.[556]

Allah and Jehovah are Not the Same God	
Jehovah (God as described in the Bible)	Allah
Trinity	Singular unity
Heavenly Father	Distant, not a father, no children
Loves the lost	*"Loves not the prodigals"* (Surah 6:142,7:31)
Loves the sinners (not the sin)	*"Loves not those that do wrong"* (Surah 3:140)
"takes no pleasure in the death of the wicked" (Ezekiel 33:11)	*"Allah desires to afflict them for some of their sins"* (Surahs 5:49, 4:168-169, 7:179, 9:2)
Holy, demands complete perfection	Good deeds must outweigh one's bad deeds
He provided a sinless Savior, who took our sins upon Himself	Sent a messenger Mohammed, who warned of Allah's impending judgment

Table 32-1: Comparing Allah and Jehovah

The above table (table 32-1) points out significant differences between Jehovah and Allah, but by far the most important contrast is the view of sin. God as depicted in the Bible loves the sinner, but hates sin (as He cannot tolerate it because of His holiness); the Qur'an teaches that Allah hates the sinners. This fact alone explains why militant Islam approves the killing of anyone not a Muslim (any infidel). Anyone who is not a Muslim is a sinner. As Allah hates the sinners, killing an infidel is doing the will of Allah.

> **Death to the infidel**
>
> A recent illustration of the belief that it is the will of Allah to kill the infidel, is the controversy that arose on September 12, 2006, when Pope Benedict XVI quoted the following passage:[557] *"Show me just what Mohammad brought that was new and there you will find things only evil and inhuman, such as his command to spread by the sword the faith he preached."*
>
> As a result the whole Islamic world was in uproar as the Pope had offended Islam and the prophet Mohammad. Thousands and thousands of people participated in protests around the world with many demanding the Pope's execution. After a few weeks and some vague apologies from the Pope, the protests faded, but this incident shows once again how death is the obvious penalty for any unbeliever.

BASIC TEACHINGS

Islam considers the following six doctrines as the foundation of their faith:

- **Allah.** There is only one true God, and His name is Allah. He is omniscient, omnipresent, and omnipotent.
- **Angels.** Angels are messengers from God. The angel Gabriel brought Mohammed the revelations now recorded in the Qur'an.
- **Scripture.** The divine scriptures include the Torah, the Psalms, the rest of the Bible (as originally revealed, before Jews and Christians corrupted them) and the Qur'an.
- **Prophets.** Islam recognizes a total of 28 prophets, all well known from the Bible (including Adam, Noah, Abraham, Moses, David, and Jesus). The last prophet for all time is Mohammed, the greatest of all prophets.
- **Day of Judgment.** On the last day, Allah will judge all persons based on their good and bad deeds. Allah will decide who goes to heaven or hell.
- **Predestination.** The supremacy of the will of Allah.

There are five duties that every Muslim is obliged to perform, the *Five Pillars of Islam*:

- **Shahadah.** This is the Muslim profession of faith: *"I witness that there is no god but Allah, and that Mohammed is the prophet of Allah."* Muslims must repeat the shahadah in prayer, and non-Muslims must use the creed to formally convert to Islam.
- **Salat.** A prayer ritual performed five times daily by all Muslims. Each salat is done facing to (the Kaaba in) Mecca. However, in the early days of

Islam, when it was based primarily in Mecca, Muslims offered salat facing Jerusalem. Salat is very different from praying on the inspiration of the moment. A precise ritual is followed at separate times of the day set aside for devotion. While an individual can pray by himself, Muslims prefer to perform Salat with others, as this demonstrates the unity of all Muslims.

The Kaaba

The Kaaba is a large cubical building in Mecca. In the days of Mohammed, the Kaaba was considered a shrine, a stone used for various offerings to pagan deities, including a ritual of an annual pilgrimage to honor these pagan gods. Mohammad was born to a tribe whose duty it was to keep the Kaaba.[558]

After Mohammad and his army conquered Mecca, he went straight to the Kaaba, removed 360 idols and declared this to be focal point of the Islamic faith, including the demand for all Muslim to at least make one pilgrimage to the Kaaba during their lifetime.[559]

- **Sawm (the holy month of Ramadan).** During Ramadan, the ninth Muslim month, Muslims abstain from all bodily pleasures between dawn and sunset. Not only is food forbidden, but also smoking and any sexual activity. Muslims must also make sure that they do not do or even think anything evil.
- **Zakat.** Giving alms to the poor. This is a compulsory gift of 2.5 % of one's wealth, given as charity to the poor and needy each year in addition to any charitable gifts a Muslim makes. Giving in this way frees Muslims from the love of money. It reminds them that all they have belongs to Allah.
- **Hajj:** The pilgrimage to the Kaaba in Mecca. All physically able Muslims should make this trip at least once in their life. Mecca is the most holy place. It is the place where Muhammad lived and gained his prophet status. The government of Saudi Arabia issues special visas to foreigners for the purpose of the pilgrimage. Entrance to Mecca itself is forbidden to non-Muslims, and the entire city is considered a holy site in Islam.

The often used term *jihad* means to "strive" or "struggle" in the way of Allah and sometimes is said to be the sixth pillar of Islam, although it has no official status. Jihad has a wider meaning in Islamic literature. It can be striving to live a good Muslim life, praying and fasting regularly, being an attentive spouse and parent, or working hard to spread the message of Islam. Jihad is also used to mean the struggle to spread or defend Islam through holy war. Islam teaches that Muslims martyred during a jihad go directly to heaven and receive special rewards.[560]

The *Sharia* is the Islamic law, determined by traditional Islamic scholarship. It covers all aspects of life, from government and foreign relations to issues of daily living.

THE FOUNDER

Muslims believe Islam is based on the ministry of a man named Mohammad, and on the words that Allah gave to the world through him. They believe that Mohammad did not found Islam. Islam was created by Allah at the beginning of time; in fact, Muslims regard Adam as the first Muslim. Mohammad was the final messenger through whom Allah revealed the faith to the world. Earlier messengers included Adam, Noah, Abraham, Moses, and, of course, Jesus.

Mohammad was not only a religious leader, but a political leader as well. This established the close relationship between religion and politics that ensured the rapid spread of the faith, and its influence on the complete way of life in many countries.

Mohammad was born in 570 AD in Mecca, in Arabia, to a family of the Quraysh tribe. His father died before his birth, and his mother died when he was only six, so Mohammad was raised first by his grandfather, and later by his uncle. The family was not rich, so Mohammad spent much of his childhood tending animals for others in order to earn his livelihood. He later managed caravans on behalf of merchants. He met people of different religious beliefs on his travels and was able to observe and learn about Judaism and Christianity. This explains why Mohammad based Islam on many of the teachings of Judaism and Christianity, its Bible, and its prophets.

When he was 25, Mohammad married Khadija, a wealthy 40-year-old widow. Mohammad soon developed an interest in spiritual matters and would spend time on retreat in the cave of Hira on "the Mountain of Light" (near Mecca). In the year 610, Mohammad claimed to have his first revelation – a vision of the Archangel Gabriel, who told him that he was to be a prophet. Khadija confirmed Mohammad's belief in his mission and declared herself as his first disciple.

Mohammad was mocked at first by people who claimed that God had forsaken him, but the revelations resumed, and over many years Mohammad received the text of the Qur'an in a series of revelations. He proclaimed that the Qur'an was the last book of God, and that he himself was the last prophet.

With a small group of people who believed what he said, Mohammad began to spread the message. He publicly condemned local idolatrous beliefs and religious customs, which did not make him universally popular. In the year 613, Mohammad intensified his public preaching and won more converts. He and his followers were persecuted, and some of them escaped to Abyssinia. A long period of difficulty followed, but Mohammad and his followers remained true to the faith and he continued to preach and convert.

In 622 AD, Mohammad fled to Yathrib (later called Medina) with 70 followers; this is known as the *Hegira* (which means "emigration" or "flight"). This event also marks the beginning of the Islamic calendar. Mohammad formed a tribe from those who accepted him as the Prophet, and gradually Islam grew in strength and acceptance. He defeated his opposition in battle, conquered Mecca, and established a strong political and religious base. In the year 632, Mohammad made a final pilgrimage to Mecca with over 100,000 of his followers, and gave his last sermon. He died a few months later (July 6, 632) in Medina.

HISTORY

The present form of Islam began in Saudi Arabia in 622 AD (the year zero of the Islamic calendar). However, many if not most, of the followers of Islam believe that:

- Islam existed before Mohammed was born.
- The origins of Islam date back to the creation of the world.
- Mohammed was the last, and by far, the greatest of a series of prophets.

Muslims hold that the message of Islam – submission to the will of the one God, Allah – is the same as the message preached by all the messengers sent by God to humanity since Adam. From an Islamic point of view, Islam is the oldest of the monotheistic religions because it represents both the original, and the final revelation of God to Abraham, Moses, Jesus, and Mohammed.

Islamic texts depict Judaism and Christianity as prophetic successor traditions to the teachings of Abraham. The Qur'an calls Jews and Christians "people of the Book," and distinguishes them from polytheists. In order to reconcile discrepancies between the earlier prophets and the Qur'an, Muslims claim that Jews and Christians forgot or distorted the word of God after it was revealed to them. Most early Muslim scholars, and some modern ones, believe it was just distortion in interpretation of the Bible. However, others believe that there was also textual distortion, that Jews changed the Old Testament (Torah) and the Christians the *Injil* (gospels) by altering the meaning, form, and placement of words in their respective holy texts.

By the year 750, Islam had expanded to China, India, along the Southern shore of the Mediterranean, and into Spain. By 1550 they had reached Vienna in Austria! Wars resulted, expelling Muslims from Spain and Europe. Since their trade routes were mostly over land, they did not develop extensive sea trade (like the English, the Dutch, and the Spaniards). As a result, the old world occupation of North America was left to Christians.

Mohammed died in 632 without appointing a successor or creating a system to choose one. As a result, the caliphate was established. *Caliph* is the title for the leader of the *Ummah*, or community of Islam. Early caliphs believed themselves to be both the spiritual and temporal leaders of Islam and insisted that obedience to the caliph in all things was the hallmark of the good Muslim. Arguments over whether the caliphs should be elected or of Mohammed's bloodline started the rift between what is now known as its two main branches of *Sunni* and *Shi'a* Muslims. Besides these two main groups, other sects include *Sufis* (mysticism, self-denial), *Wahhabis* (radical Sunnism, mostly in Saudi Arabia), the *Druze* (a secretive sect in Lebanon and northern Israel), *Alawites* (Shi'a sect, mostly Syria), *Ahmadiyyas* (orthodox cult, Pakistan), and *Sikhism* (a mixture of Islam and Hinduism, India).[561]

Sunnis and Shia	
Sunni	**Shi'ite**
About 80% of Muslims	About 10-15% of Muslims
Mohammed's successor should be elected	Should be from Mohammed's bloodline
Authority of written tradition (the Sunna and Hadith) and guidance from elders	Authority from the Imam ("pope"). Are waiting the return of the 12th Imam (Mahdi)
Separation between civil and religious authorities	Combine religious and political power
Central Iraq, most other Islamic nations	Iran/South Iraq

Table 32-2: Sunnis and Shia

THE WRITINGS

Muslims believe that they have one life, after which they are judged. Muslims are guided to follow Allah's will by:

• The holy book, the *Qur'an*, which Muslims regard as the unaltered word of Allah.

• The example set by Mohammad's life (recorded in the *Sunnah* and *Hadith*).

The Qur'an ("recitation") contains the words of Allah. Muslims believe that it was revealed to Muhammad by the archangel Gabriel. This was originally in oral and written form; they were later assembled together into a single book, the Qur'an (often spelled "Koran" in English). Muslims believe that, because of its divine origin, the Qur'an has not been altered in any way since it was first compiled. Copies of the Qur'an are always treated with the greatest respect.

The only authoritative text of the Qur'an is the original Arabic text. Muslims regard translations of the Qur'an into other languages as paraphrases or inadequate versions of the original. The Qur'an consists of 114 chapters (called *Surahs*) and 6616 verses (called *ayas*), which have names as well as numbers. Its size is about two thirds of the New Testament.

Muslims believe the text of the Qur'an, at the time Mohammed received it from Gabriel, was written on pieces of paper, stones, palm-leaves, shoulder-blades, ribs, and bits of leather; basically anything on hand, and it was memorized.[562] Most scholars estimate the initial group of believers with Mohammed was in the order of 75 to no more than 150 people. These people memorized the texts. However, history also records that during the flight to Medina and the subsequent battles, many of this group's original believers were killed. So the valid question arises, even if part of the text was written down, how much of the memorized text was correctly retained by this small group of surviving Muslims? Records even indicate that until the year 25-30 AH (around 650 AD, that is about 40 years after Mohammed received the majority of the texts), the transmission of the Qur'an was almost completely oral, until the first official version was composed under Uthman (or Othman), the third Muslim caliph.[563] Since there were wide divergences between the *Qur'ans* of Medina, Mecca, Basra, Kufa, and Damascus, *"Othman's solution was to canonize the Medinan Codex and order all others to be destroyed."* Therefore, *"there can be little doubt that the text canonized by Othman was only one among several types of text in existence at the time."*[564] It is this version that has remained uniform and intact, not the original version that came directly from Muhammad.

As Winfried Corduan summarizes about the texts of the Qur'an: *"There is good reason to believe that the Qur'an as it exists today is for the most part what Muhammad taught. Unfortunately, there is little opportunity to evaluate the textual integrity of the Qur'an any further since Caliph Uthman, third in line as successor to Muhammad, destroyed all manuscripts he did not consider correct. Muslims generally claim that the present Qur'an is pure, but even with Uthman's heavy-handed treatment, there are a few known variants."*[565]

The Bible has had an important influence on Islam (or actually Mohammed). For instance, the Muslim proudly traces his ancestry to Ishmael

Comparing Christianity and Islam

	(Protestant) Christianity	Islam
	General comparison	
Meaning of the name	Believer in Christ	Submission to Allah
Name of a believer	Christian	Muslim
Date of founding	33 AD (Resurrection)	622 AD (Hegira)
Name of founder	Jesus of Nazareth (Christ)	Mohammed
Country of founding	Israel (Palestine)	Saudi Arabia
Concept of God	Trinity	Allah is one and indivisible
	Comparing the Bible and the Qur'an	
Sacred writings	Bible	Qur'an
Original languages	Hebrew, Greek, Aramaic	Arabic
Status of the writings	Historical reliable and inspired Word of God	Allah's word as dictated to Mohammed by Gabriel
Additional guidance	Early church writings	Sunnah, Hadith
	The status and role of Jesus	
Status of Jesus	Son of God, worshiped as God, part of the Trinity	Highly respected prophet, less than Mohammed
Birth of Jesus	Virgin birth	Virgin birth
Death and resurrection of Jesus	Crucified by the Romans in 33 AD, resurrected the 3rd day	Neither killed nor crucified.[566] Ascended alive into heaven
	Comparing Jesus and Mohammed	
Role in the faith	Jesus is God and part of the Trinity	Mohammed was the last prophet of Allah
Life on earth	No earthly possessions or power. Executed as a criminal	Arabic warlord. Wealthy leader of an army
Related to the Bible	Fulfilled all OT prophecies	Changed the Bible
Marital status	Not married	Thirteen wives
Communication with God	Prayer	Revelations by Gabriel
Composition of the word	Others wrote about Jesus	Mohammed spoke the Qur'an
Teachings about war	*"Love your enemy"*	*"Kill your enemy"*
	Judgment and salvation	
Status at birth	We are born with a sin nature	Born in submission to Allah
Life after death	Heaven or hell	Heaven or hell
Salvation	By the blood of Christ	Judged by Allah: Good has to outweigh bad deeds
Confessing sins	To Christ/God	To Allah
	Organization	
Believers community	The Church	The Ummah
Day of worship	Sunday	Friday
Church and state	Separated, most Christian countries are democracies	Integrated, most Muslim counties are dictatorships
Legislation	Prerogative of the people	Prerogative of Allah
Religious freedom	No restrictions	Usually only Islam allowed
Basis of calendar	Gregorian solar calendar. 1 AD (4/7 BC?) birth of Jesus	Islamic lunar calendar, 1 AH is the Hegira, 622 AD
Different branches	Catholic, Orthodox, Protestant	Sunni, Shi'ite, Sufi

Table 32-3: Comparing Islam to Christianity

(the son of Abraham with Hagar, Sarah's maid). Muslim beliefs about the nature of God and the resurrection of the body and judgment bear a similarity to what is taught in the Bible. The Qur'an even describes the virgin birth of Jesus, but denies the resurrection (they claim that He did not die on the cross, but somebody else was crucified on his behalf). For Muslims, Jesus is a prophet superior to Abraham and Moses, but far below Mohammed.

Secondary to the Qur'an, the Sunnah and the Hadith are additional instruction to the Muslim. The Sunnah records events of the life of Mohammed and offers examples for ethics and living. As such, it is the basis of the legal code and authoritative in ruling among Islamic states. The Hadith are collections of the sayings of Mohammed. Each Hadith is a narration of the life of the prophet and what he said, as opposed to a biographical sketch.

COMPARED TO CHRISTIANITY

Both Christianity and Islam accept the existence of a personal Creator God. Both also accept many of the same accounts and prophets mentioned in the Bible; however, much caution is required, as Islam claims that the Bible was corrupted and only their somewhat different account is correct. A simplified comparison between Christianity and Islam is shown in table 32-3.

CONCLUSIONS FROM AN APOLOGETICS PERSPECTIVE

The evidence for truth of Islam is very limited. Clearly Mohammed was a historical person who lived in Arabia and founded a religion there. However, all claims for the revelations of Allah to Mohammed are based on Mohammed's personal experiences, subsequently recorded in the Qur'an. No one else witnessed or received these revelations.

Muslims often claim Christians corrupted the Bible, but as we have seen the historical, archaeological, and manuscript evidences for preservation of the original texts in our modern-day Bibles are very strong and compelling.

For the Qur'an, however, this situation is very different. Where are the original manuscripts? What ancient writings have been preserved? How certain can anyone be that the first followers of Mohammed memorized and later recalled all texts perfectly? And compare the process of canonization of the Qur'an to the Bible. The Qur'an was canonized instantly by caliph Uthman through destroying all other manuscripts. Granted, the canonization of the New Testament endured some major struggles, but its criteria were based on apostolic authority and God's inspiration, not the personal preference of one man.

Additionally, there are no claims in Islam for miracles or fulfilled prophecies or any other facts or events that can support or prove divine inspiration or revelation.

Lastly, I find it personally intriguing to read about the characteristics usually associated with Christian cults,[567] like Mormonism and Jehovah Witnesses, and then apply those to Islam. The similarities are striking, like the cults, Islam claims additional revelation, rejects the Trinty, believes only they know the whole truth, distorts the teachings of the Bible, requires works for salvation and has a system that protects their followers from non-Muslim influences.

Comparing the Evidences for Christianity and Islam		
	Christianity	**Islam**
Scripture	The Bible:	The Qur'an:
	• Manuscript evidence	• Revealed to Mohammed only
	• Written by 40 people	• Claims exact words of Gabriel
	• Historically reliable	• No written records for 40 years
	• Fulfilled prophecies	• No historical evidences
	• Consistent accounts	• No logical structure
Founder	Jesus:	Mohammed:
	• Neither worldly nor military	• Spiritual but also military leader
	• Proved His deity with miracles, prophecies, and resurrection	• No evidences for his status as a prophet from Allah
	• Came with a purpose: to complete Plan of Redemption	
Theology	God has a complete plan for people to choose Him by free will and be redeemed through Christ's blood.	Allah demands worship and submission, but there is no clear plan for salvation. Allah will judge good versus bad.
Worldview	Choose to be a Christian by free will. No demands on social or political structures.	Submission is enforced. Islam can be an enforced dictatorship.

Table 32-4: Comparing the Evidences for Islam to Christianity

Chapter 33

Christianity and the Other Religions

"Therefore go and make disciples of all nations, baptizing them
in the name of the Father, and of the Son and of the Holy Spirit,
and teaching them to obey everything I have commanded you."
"The Great Commission" – Matthew 28:19-20

So far, we have examined the differences between the three main branches of Christianity and the basics of the other three great world religions, Islam, Hinduism, and Buddhism. Obviously, our survey was brief and far from complete, but still even this limited analysis identified a number of areas where Christianity is unique among other worldviews. These unique areas make – in my personal opinion – Christianity not just another option, but the only choice.

EXHIBIT #1: CHRISTIANITY IS GROUNDED IN HISTORY

Studying the Christian Bible is like studying history. It extends from the beginning of the universe and through the ancient ages described in Genesis. The birth, rise, and glory days of the Jewish people, all the way to the fall of the kingdoms of Israel and Judah, are detailed in other books of the Old Testament. The New Testament gospels describe the birth and ministry of Jesus of Nazareth and His death and resurrection. The Christian faith grew from the birth of the church into a world religion by reaching across and beyond the mighty Roman Empire as seen in the book of Acts. If we skip Genesis and begin counting with Moses, the Bible covers a period of 1,500 years that can be verified by and compared to non-Biblical historical records. This was also the period during which the authors of the Bible books lived. They were writing their own history, as it happened. Only the Christian faith can claim such an extensive historical foundation.

Hinduism makes no historical claims. It seems to have developed while riding the waves of various cultures of the people of India, influenced regularly by invasions from other peoples. Siddhartha Gautama (Lord Buddha) was no doubt a historical individual. However, neither he nor his followers, seem to care about their world. Buddha's teachings of suffering and its remedies are in a sense timeless, but also reveal a complete disconnection from the world.

Mohammed lived from 570 to 632 AD. His life had major historical impact. However, the Qur'an records only his revelations; it tells little of his life. These revelations do not resemble the narratives found in the Bible. The Qur'an texts are more spiritual and philosophical than historical. On occasion the historical background is clear, especially when it refers to characters known from the Bible, but it does not mention places, dates, names of rulers, customs, trade routes, and so on, as the Bible does. Additionally, Mohammed's revelations started in 610 AD. Before the Hegira of 622 AD he received the majority of the text of the Qur'an. Mohammed died 10 years later, so at best the Qur'an covers only 22 years, compared to the 1,500 years covered by the authors of the Bible.

EXHIBIT #2: JESUS' KINGDOM WAS NOT OF THIS WORLD

When asked by Pilate if He was the king of the Jews, Jesus answered: "*My kingdom is not of this world. If it were, my servants would fight to prevent my arrest by the Jews. But now my kingdom is from another place*" (John 18:36). All through the gospel we read that Jesus turned the world upside down by what He did and taught. The beatitudes (Matthew 5:3-10) tell who His people are: the poor in spirit, those who mourn, the meek, those who hunger and thirst for righteousness, the merciful, the pure in heart, the peacemakers, and those persecuted. They are blessed in the kingdom of Christ, the kingdom of God. Not in our world. In our world these people may well be considered the losers. They end up with the short end of the stick. They get the bad deals. In the eyes of Jesus, in the economy of God, these are the winners, these are the people whom Jesus reaches out to.

Because of this, the Jews missed the Messiah. As we have seen, the Jews were waiting for the Messiah. They were ready. They knew the Old Testament prophecies and were expecting their Savior, but they were putting their stock in the world. They wanted to be liberated from the Roman occupation, reinstating Israel and Judah as independent, powerful kingdoms. So they did not like Jesus' teaching nor His kingdom, and they rejected Him.

In the Eastern religions we see similar teachings by the Buddha and, for instance, by the best known Hindu, Mohandas K. Gandhi. Like Jesus, they were also uninterested in what the world had to offer in terms of power and wealth. They did not preach of the kingdom of God; actually they did not believe in God, but searched for deeper meanings in the spiritual rather than the materialistic world.

Islam's prophet Mohammed taught about spiritual and moral values, as he addressed and attempted to correct the immoral behavior of his contemporaries. Above all, he was a successful businessman and a ruthless warlord. His economic wealth and position (through his marriage to a wealthy widow) helped him gain followers. His army was at first almost destroyed, but ultimately he gained the upper hand and defeated the armies of Mecca to take control of the city. He then expanded his military control to most of Arabia. Completely unlike Jesus, his worldly success enabled Mohammed to establish his religion. If it were not for Mohammed's success as a military leader, we likely would not be discussing Islam!

EXHIBIT #3: ONLY JESUS CLAIMS TO BE GOD

Jesus was not confused about His own identity; He unabashedly claimed to be God.[568] But He also supported it by facts. Jesus performed many miracles; 35 are recorded in the gospels, including various nature miracles. One of the most impressive, the feeding of the five thousand, is attested to in all four gospels.[569] And Jesus fulfilled each of the hundreds of prophecies about the Messiah from the Old Testament with remarkable accuracy, all but a few outside his own control, and well beyond any statistical probability of chance.[570]

When it seemed that Jesus was defeated, that evil had won by crucifying and killing the Messiah, God revealed His greatest miracle of all: The resurrection of Christ.[571] The greatest moment of victory for the Evil One turned out to be the moment of his complete defeat. By the crucifixion, with His blood, Jesus purchased salvation for man. By His resurrection He proclaimed in the most glorious way possible that He was the Son of God beyond the grip of death.

Hinduism had no founder, so there are no claims of deity. Gandhi was a humble man of integrity and had great care for other people. Yet he never claimed to be God. Siddhartha Gautama (Lord Buddha) did not claim to be God, nor are there serious claims that he performed miracles during his lifetime or that there was a resurrection. *"The original accounts of Buddha never ascribe to him any such thing as a resurrection; in fact, in the earliest accounts of his death, namely, the Mahaparinibbana Sutta, we read that when Buddha died it was 'with that utter passing away in which nothing whatever remains behind.'"*[572]

The prophet Mohammed expressly claimed merely to be the prophet of Allah. Mohammed, also, fulfilled no prophecies, nor is there even a single credible account of a miracle he performed. Many Muslims protest that the writing of the Qur'an is the greatest miracle of all. Others argue for some miraculous accounts about Mohammed deeply rooted in tradition, but these are not supported by history or reliable scriptures. But even if this was evidence for Mohammed's divine inspiration, these claims look pale next to the miracles and prophecies fulfilled by Jesus. Mohammed died June 8, 632 AD at the age of 61 in Medina, where his tomb is annually visited by thousands of devout Muslims.[573] Later legends claim that he did not die but ascended to heaven in

Jerusalem (at the location of the modern day Dome of the Rock). However, no credible evidence for this claim has been presented. Whatever Mohammed's destiny, nobody has ever claimed he rose from the dead.

Christ alone claimed to be God. Christ alone provided evidence to support His claims!

EXHIBIT #4: THE BIBLE IS A HISTORICALLY RELIABLE DOCUMENT

We have seen that Christianity is grounded in history, but also that the Bible is a historically reliable book. The accounts in the Bible are not generic stories. They are richly detailed in time, place, and people. They name cities and nations, mountains and oceans, rivers and valleys, customs and idols, rulers and families. We can trace the historical record. Numerous confirmations come through archaeological discoveries of buildings, artifacts, and inscriptions.[574] Questions raised by skeptics and non-believers are not about the historical background of Christianity and its ancient roots in Judaism. These questions always seem to point to details such as a name or a date. They attempt to verify or disprove a particular aspect of the account. As we have seen, although we will never be able to prove through archaeology and history that everything exactly happened as described, no one has been able to disprove even one Bible account.

Compare this to the sacred books of the other religions. The Vedas and Tripitaka are collections of teachings and wisdom, wholly generic of nature and neither allowing nor requiring historical confirmations. The Qur'an covers some historical ground, but is not even presented as a historical document by Muslim apologetic scholars.

EXHIBIT #5: THE BIBLE WAS WRITTEN BY WITNESSES, NOT THE FOUNDER

Trick trivia question: How many books did Jesus write? The answer is *none*. Jesus did not write even one book or letter in the Bible. Of all the 66 books in the Old and New Testament, Jesus penned none. He is the indirect subject of the entire Old Testament, as the prophecies prepare for His coming, and the main character in the New Testament, as the gospels record about His life and teachings. The remainder urges readers to follow His example and to obey His teachings. Yet He did not write any of these books. Is it not amazing that the New Testament is written by nine different writers? These nine men, all but a few eyewitnesses to the resurrection, did not write their books while sharing a large room where they could coordinate their stories. Some might have had access to material of others, but most wrote their accounts independently of one another. They wrote at different locations and at various times, but they told a solitary story, they gave one consistent testimony to the deity of Christ, and they preached one plan of redemption.

Islam claims that the Qur'an is not only God's Word, but also the final revelation to man. It comes from the "mother of all books" (Surah 43:2-4). Muslims maintain that the Qur'an is an exact word-for-word copy of God's final revelation, founded on original tablets that have always existed in heaven. They believe that the Qur'an is an identical copy of the eternal heavenly book, even so far as the punctuation, titles, and divisions of chapters are concerned. They claim that the prophet Mohammed "spoke" the Qur'an. He was the sole author (or the medium through which Allah communicated). These claims can neither be proved nor disproved, and their authority is derived solely from the Qur'an itself.

It is not known who the authors of the Hindu Vedas were. The Buddhist Tripitaka is claimed to have been written by the Buddha (and/or later added to by Buddhist monks).

EXHIBIT #6: THE BIBLE IS THE ONLY DIVINELY INSPIRED BOOK

The Bible claims time and again to be the "Word of God." This is not necessarily a unique claim; other books claim that as well. Only the Bible supports these claims with factual and objective evidences. We have extensively discussed these proofs,[575] including scientific revelations, fulfilled prophecies, unity, transformed lives, and so on throughout the previous chapters.

Neither Hinduism nor Buddhism claim their writings are divinely inspired.

What about the Qur'an? It also expressly claims to be the "Word of God." The Qur'an asserts this in even more clear terms than the Bible, as it is supposed to be the actual words of Allah given by Gabriel to Mohammed. Can it support this claim? Muslims believe that the self-authenticating miracle is the unity and literal style of the Qur'an itself. Iranian Islamic scholar Sayyid Hossein Nasr wrote: *"Many people, especially non-Muslims, who read the Qur'an for the first time, are struck by what appears to be a kind of incoherence... It is neither like a high mystical text nor a manual of Aristotelian logic, though it contains both mysticism and logic...The Qur'an contains a quality which is difficult to express in modern language. One might call it divine magic."*[576]

Some Muslims also claim that the Qur'an is a miracle because Mohammed himself was illiterate. For someone unschooled and illiterate to "speak" the Qur'an can only be mastered by divine powers. However, it is unlikely that Mohammed indeed was illiterate. In his days, writing skills were not difficult to acquire, and given his economic position and experience, it is more than likely that he could both read and write. Even if he was illiterate, he would have had access to scribes to assist him.

Therefore the evidence of the divine inspiration of the Qur'an is limited to the "miracle of the Qur'an" itself, not convincing, and a pale comparison to the evidences for the authority of the Bible.

EXHIBIT #7: CHRISTIANITY OFFERS A COMPLETE PLAN OF REDEMPTION

Christianity does not leave loose ends. The plan of redemption[577] goes full circle. God is holy, and our sin separates us from Him. God's justice demands a price to be paid, the price of death by the shedding of blood. God's grace allows a substitute to pay the price for us. God's love dispatched Jesus, His Son, to earth to pay that price with His blood. By accepting Jesus' payment for our sins, we can be reconciled to God during this lifetime as well as after our deaths, when this reconciliation is fully realized.

This plan of redemption is what the Bible is all about. It is unveiled and unfolded throughout the early history of man. It leaves no open ending. If we accept the gift of Jesus by faith, we can be assured of our salvation. If not, we can be assured of our damnation. It's as simple as that.

Other religions do not offer a similarly complete plan.

Hinduism claims that one needs only "improve" through numerous cycles of reincarnation. Yet the believer will never know with any certainty how successful he or she is in achieving that objective. One never knows upon death if the soul will have reached Moksha, or if another cycle of rebirth, life, and death is required.

The situation with Buddhism is similar. When is one truly free of suffering? How do you measure that, and how do you know? You die, and then what? Do you disappear into Nirvana or are you reborn as a human being or as some other organism. Like Hinduism, it seems to leave many questions unanswered.

The Muslim believes that after death he or she will face the judgment of Allah. And the believer will be judged on the account of his life as an obedient and submissive Muslim and the balance of his good and bad deeds. "*Then those whose balance* [of good deeds] *is heavy, – they will be successful. But those whose balance is light, will be those who have lost their souls, in Hell will they abide*" (Surah 23:102-3). However, when are there enough good deeds to outweigh the bad deeds? How does this economy or scale work? When will you reach a point in life that you can die with the certainty that you will enter heaven? Muslims will always face that question with uncertainty. The Qur'an hints that the believer can be confident of his or her eternal destiny, but there is no guarantee. Even Mohammed himself was uncertain of his own salvation. So Muslims strive mightily to reach paradise, but they continually live with the fear that Allah will judge their arrogance and send them to hell.[578] Only Muslims martyred in a jihad have certainty of heaven.[579]

EXHIBIT #8: DIVINE ACCOMPLISHMENT VERSUS HUMAN ACHIEVEMENT

What does a Christian need to do in order to pay for his or her sins and earn salvation? The answer is that we do not need to do anything. Salvation is a gift from God. In John 3:16-18 Jesus taught: *"For God so loved the world that he gave his one and only Son, that whoever believes in him shall not perish but have eternal life. For God did not send his Son into the world to condemn the world, but to save the world through him. Whoever believes in him is not condemned, but whoever does not believe stands condemned already because he has not believed in the name of God's one and only Son."* Our salvation is not based in the least on our merit, but entirely on the grace of God. *"For in the gospel a righteousness from God is revealed, a righteousness that is by faith from first to last, just as it is written: 'The righteous will live by faith'"* (Romans 1:17). The penalty for sin; death by the shedding of blood, has already been paid by Christ for all sins in the past, the present, and the future. That's why His last words on the cross were: *"It is finished"* (John 19:30), meaning the debt has been paid, paid in full, there is no outstanding balance. The only action left for us to do is accept this gift of salvation.

The Christian view on salvation seems too good to be true. It seems illogical. How can we get the most important thing in life, a ticket to heaven, for free? Nothing in life is free, and when something is offered for free, there is usually a catch. So what is the catch? There is no catch, it is free for us, but it came at a dear price for God. He Himself had to pay the price for our sin by sacrificing His Son for us. We can not even imagine how much of a sacrifice this was. Perhaps a parent can imagine how it would feel to have to sacrifice one of their children. So, salvation was secured, not by human achievement, but by divine accomplishment.

All world religions promise some kind of path to liberation or salvation. Interestingly all these plans are based on something the believer has to do to earn it. In Hinduism you earn liberation by living according to certain principles plus meditation. You can improve your next life and ultimately reach total liberation by achieving Moksha. Buddhists work hard to implement the eight-fold path to reach Nirvana. Muslims believe that by working hard to do good deeds and adhere to the letter of the five pillars, they have a chance to tilt the balance in their favor and be judged by Allah worthy of heaven. But notice, they all have to do the work and are never sure whether they have done enough.

Even Christians struggle with the gift. Therefore, we see pseudo-Christian cults such as Mormonism and Jehovah's Witnesses adding additional instructions and qualifications one has to meet in order to earn salvation. We see the same in the Roman Catholic and Eastern Orthodox churches who accept the sacrifice of Christ as a first step, but then demand the addition of works and sacraments to fully earn and achieve heaven (and limit one's time in purgatory).

God did it all for you! He already did the work; we only need to have faith in His grace. God already loves you; you just need to start loving Him.

SUMMARY

Biblical Christianity
is Unique

As Christianity (ca. 32% of the world population) is built on objective fact and truth, the other world religions cannot have that same foundation. Therefore as a verification of our earlier conclusions, we have discussed the basis for the three other main world religions:

- Hinduism (ca. 13% of the world population) is more a way of life than a religion. Its pantheistic worldview is in contradiction with scientific observations. Its scriptures lack historical verification for authenticity and completeness. Its teachings of reincarnation are and cannot be proved.

- Buddhism (ca. 6% of the world population) is in many ways an extension of Hinduism, revised by the revelations of Siddhartha Gautama (the Buddha). Like Hinduism, its belief in an eternally existing universe defies scientific data. The preservation of its scriptures as the actual teachings of Buddha cannot be reliably verified. Its claims of reincarnation and Nirvana cannot be proved and defy logic.

- Islam (ca. 20-22% of the world population) is the fastest growing world religion. It was founded by Mohammed in the seventh century AD based on alleged revelations from God. The faith includes a complete social and legal system that governs all aspects of life. Like Christianity, the Muslim believes in the Creator, but Allah is very different from God as He reveals Himself in the Bible. The Qur'an lacks the historical, archaeological, and manuscript evidences like the Bible. Unlike Jesus, Mohammed does not make any claims to deity, nor does he provide evidences for the truth and divine inspiration of his revelations.

All three world religions lack a foundation of scientific and historical facts. The development of each of them seems to be more guided by human culture and the success of individuals or peoples than God or the divine.

In comparing the world religions, a number of exhibits were identified that show why Christianity as taught in the Bible is unique and true:

1. Christianity is grounded in history. It starts at the creation of the world. From Moses to the apostles, its development and history cover a period of

1,500 years. Hinduism and Buddhism do not make historical claims. The writings of Islam are spiritual and philosophical and cover at best a period of 22 years.

2. Jesus' kingdom was not of this world, He was not interested in anything tangible this world had to offer. By the world standards of power and wealth He was an absolute failure. The great men of Hinduism and Buddha had a similar view of the world, but Mohammed was besides a spiritual leader, also a powerful warlord. The establishment of Islam was only possible because of his military success.

3. Only Jesus claims to be God. None of the founders or leaders of the other world religions ever made that claim.

4. The Bible is a historically reliable book, not just a collection of generic stories. The detailed accounts can be verified in time, place and people and are confirmed by secular history and archaeology. The writings of Hinduism and Buddhism do not make any historical claims. The Qur'an covers very limited historical ground and is not even presented as a historical document by Muslim scholars.

5. Jesus did not write any part of the Bible. All 66 books were written by others, not by the central figure of the Christian faith. It is not known who wrote the Hindu Vedas, and the Buddhist Tripitaka are claimed to have been written by Buddha. The Qur'an is claimed to have been "spoken" by Mohammed.

6. The Bible is a divinely inspired book, as we have discussed extensively in the preceding section. Neither Hinduism nor Buddhism claim divine inspiration. Islam claims the Qur'an is inspired by Allah but does not provide any evidence to support that claim.

7. The Bible teaches God's complete plan of salvation for mankind. It does not leave open ends nor uncertainty. Hinduism and Buddhism claim "improvement" through cycles of incarnation and rebirth but no certainty of when the objective of Moksha or Nirvana will be achieved. The Muslim thinks he will be judged on the balance of his good and evil deeds, but has no certainty whether he has achieved heaven or not.

8. The Bible teaches that one is saved by faith alone. We cannot do anything to earn salvation; only because God paid the price we can receive the gift of His kingdom. All other religions believe that by one's own deeds and actions salvation can be earned.

Our study of "what others believe" within the scope of this book obviously does not claim to be in-depth or complete. Still it is evident that the other religions look pale in comparison to the avalanche of data and facts that support the Bible and the claims and teachings of Jesus of Nazareth. Additionally, the beliefs and teachings of Biblical Christianity are unique, and only God Himself can have put it together. The following quote from Philip Yancey makes this point once more:[580]

> *"During a British conference on comparative religions, experts from around the world debated what, if any, belief was unique to the Christian faith. They began eliminating possibilities. Incarnation? Other religions had different versions of gods' appearing in human form. Resurrection? Again, other religions had accounts of return from death. The debate went on for some time until C. S. Lewis wandered into the room. "What's the rumpus about?" he asked, and heard in reply that his colleagues were discussing Christianity's unique contribution among world religions. Lewis responded, "Oh, that's easy. It's grace."*
> *After some discussion, the conferees had to agree. The notion of God's love coming to us free of charge, no strings attached, seems to go against every instinct of humanity. The Buddhist eight-fold path, the Hindu doctrine of karma, the Jewish covenant, and the Muslim code of law – each of these offers a way to earn approval. Only Christianity dares to make God's love unconditional."*

Personal Afterword

My personal quest for evidence and truth started in the early Summer of 1999.

I had planned to read a few books and move on, but as I began to read I also started to make astounding discoveries. I remember that as I went through the different books and subjects, one by one the foundations of my comfortable life began to change. Earth appeared to be a unique planet; life could not have started by chance; we did not evolve from apes, nor are we evolving today; the Genesis creation account is not as silly as it had seemed after all; the texts of the Bible had not been changed over the centuries; the gospels bear the marks of honest eye-witness testimony; Jesus did perform miracles; those millennia-old prophecies about the Messiah did fit Jesus' profile very well; the resurrection cannot be explained away, and so on. My reading and research continued. There was so much to learn and discover. It soon became a full-time activity.

After about six months I had reached a point that I felt I had researched and studied all the major questions I had when I started and even many of the additional questions I encountered during my reading. I had expected that at this point I would be sitting in front of pages of notes split into two piles. One pile with all the evidence *in support of Christianity* and one *arguing against it.* Well, indeed I had lots of notes and piles of paper. But the *against* pile was missing. I honestly had not found any solid fact that would go against the Christian claims. Well, perhaps one, the one of "I am not sure whether I want to be a Christian" was still bugging me. Intellectually I had reached a point that I was confronted with the truth and could not logically deny it. Spiritually and emotionally I was not ready to accept Christ. I did not want to become the next guy "who found religion." I did not want to become a Jesus freak. I did not really want to change my life. I did not want to have a new boss. I had worked all my life to be without any bosses. Frankly, that was one of the reasons we moved to the United States. Working for a company that was headquartered 9 time zones and 6,000+ miles away gave me a lot of freedom. And in my mind, being retired was even the best thing possible. So, I was happy where I was and had (I thought) no need for Jesus.

Have you ever noticed that you can fool everyone around you, but yourself? That is where I was. I could not fool myself. I knew Christianity was the truth, so reluctantly I accepted this truth, was baptized, and asked Jesus to forgive my sins and to show me where to go from here.

Well, He did. Not immediately, no major landslides overnight, but gradually. He showed me step by step how to change myself, my life, and even my family, and how to walk His path. It was (and still is) not always easy, but I know now, talking from having been "on the other side," that following Him is ultimately the only thing that matters.

Thank you, Jesus, for saving a wretch like me.

Appendices

Literature for Further Reference

Following is an overview of the sources used as references and input for this book, sorted alphabetically by author, including a cross-reference to the main subjects. Also I have listed some books recommended for further research.

RECOMMENDED FURTHER READING

Some books recommended for further study on the evidence for the existence of God are:
- ***The Creator and the Cosmos*** (2001) by Dr. Hugh Ross. Hugh Ross is an astronomer who became a Christian because of the evidence for the Creator revealed through his study of the universe. In this book he describes the unique characteristics of planet earth in order for life to exist. He also calculates the probabilities for earth to support life "just by chance," how unlikely it is to expect to find other planets like earth in the entire universe, and evidence for design in the fine tuning of our universe and the laws of nature.
- ***The Privileged Planet*** (2004) by Dr. Guillermo Gonzalez and Dr. Jay Richards. Based on cutting-edge evidence and observations from astronomy, cosmology, and astrobiology, the authors conclude that earth's characteristics are unique, making it a truly "privileged planet." Like Ross, they recognize the hand of our Lord, the almighty Creator.
- ***The Case for a Creator*** (2004) by Lee Strobel. Through conducting a series of interviews, Strobel discusses with various scientists the evidence for the existence of a Creator and the lack of real evidence for the evolution model.
- ***Icons of Evolution*** (2000) by Dr. Jonathan Wells. Dr. Wells demonstrates with stunning clarity that the textbook examples so often used to prove evolution are mostly false and misleading.

Some suggested books for further study on the reliability of the Bible, and especially the gospels, are:
- ***Is the Bible True?*** (1999) by Jeffery L. Sheler. Sheler, a journalist by profession, describes in clear language that he believes that the Bible must be critically assessed but that it has considerable historical substance and

Author: Title (year)	God exists?	Bible true?	Jesus = God?	Bible inspired?	World religions
Ankerberg John and Weldon, John: The facts on Islam (1991)					X
Archer, Gleason; Encyclopedia of Bible difficulties		X			
Armstrong, Karen: Islam, a short history (2002)					X
Ashton, John: On the seventh day (2002)	X				
Ashton, John: In six days (2001)	X				
Barna, George: The state of the church (2005)	X	X	X		
Barnett, Paul: Is the New Testament reliable? (1986)		X			
Barnett, Paul: The birth of Christianity: the first twenty years (2005)		X	X		
Barnstone, Willis: The other Bible (1984)		X	X		
Bauckham, Richard: Jesus and the eyewitnesses. The gospels as eyewitness testimony (2006)		X	X		
Behe, Michael: Darwin's black box (1996)	X				
Behe, Michael; Dembski, Willam;Meyer, Stephen: Science and evidence for design in the universe (2002)	X				
Bercot, David: Will the real heretics please stand up (1989)					X
Bercot, David: A dictionary to early Christian beliefs (2003)		X	X		X
Binnings Ewen, Pamela: Faith on trial (1999)		X	X		
Blomberg, Craig: The historical reliability of the gospels (1987)		X	X		
Blomberg, Craig: The historical reliability of John's gospel (2001)		X	X		
Boa, Kenneth; Bowman; Robert:20 compelling evidences that God exists (2002)	X	X			
Bock, Darrell: The missing gospels (2006)		X	X		
Boyd, Gregory; Boyd, Edward: Letters from a skeptic (1994)		X	X		
Bruce, F.F.: The New Testament documents – are they reliable? (1943)		X			
Bullinger, E.W.: Number in Scripture (1967)				X	
Campbell, Jack; McGrath, Gavin: New dictionary of Christian apologetics (2006)	X	X	X		X
Campbell, William: The Qur'an and the Bible (2002)		X			X
Collins, Francis: The language of God (2006)	X				
Comninellis, Nicolas: Creative defense (2001)	X				
Comninellis, Nicolas; White, Joe: Darwin's demise (2002)	X				
Cooper, Bill: After the flood (1995)		X			
Copan, Paul, Tacelli, Ronald, Craig, William Lane, Ludeman, Gert: Jesus' resurrection (2000)			X		
Craig, Ken: The plan of redemption (article, 2007)				X	
Caner, Ergun and Caner, Emir: Unveiling Islam (2002)					X
Darwin, Charles: The origin of species (1859)	X				
Dembski, William: Intelligent design (1999)	X				
Dembski, William; Wilson, John: Uncommon dissent: Intellectuals who find Darwinism unconvincing (2004)	X				
Dembski, William: The design inference (2006)	X				
Denton, Michael: Nature's destiny (1998)	X				
Denton, Michael: Evolution, a theory in crisis	X				
Elwell, Walter: Baker encyclopedia of the Bible (1998)	X	X	X	X	X
Fahlbusch, Erwin and others: The encyclopedia of Christianity (2003)	X	X	X		X
Fernandes, Phil: No other Gods (2002)	X	X	X		

Fernandes, Phil: The God who sits enthroned (2002)	X				
Fernandes, Phil; Martin, Michael: Theism vs atheism (1997)	X				
Foreman, Dale: Crucify him (1987)			X		
Geisler, Norman: Christian apologetics (1976)	X	X	X	X	X
Gesiler, Norman; Nix, William: A general introduction to the Bible (1996)	X				
Geisler, Norman: Baker encyclopedia of Christian apologetics (1999)	X	X	X	X	X
Geisler, Norman; Hoffman, Paul: Why I am a Christian (2001)	X	X	X	X	X
Geisler, Norman; Bocchino, Peter: Unshakable foundations (2001)	X		X		
Gesiler, Norman; Saleeb, Abdul: Answering Islam (2002)					X
Glynn, Patrick: God, the evidence (1999)	X				
Greenleaf, Simon: The testimony of the evangelists (1995)		X			
Griffith-Jones, Robin: The four witnesses (2001)		X	X		
Gonzalez, Justo: The story of Christianity (1984)		X			X
Gonzalez, Guillermo and Richards, Jay: The privileged planet (2004)	X				
Hahn, Scott: The Gospel of Matthew (1999, tape series)		X	X		
Habermas, Gary: The historical Jesus (1996)		X	X	X	
Habermas, Gary; Licona, Michael: The case for the resurrection of Jesus (2004)		X	X		
Halverson, Dean; The compact guide to world religions (1996)					X
Hanegraaf, Hank: Christianity in crisis (1993)	X	X	X		
Hanegraaf, Hank: The third day (2003)		X			
Hanegraaf, Hank; Maier, Paul: The DaVince code, fact or fiction? (2004)		X	X		
Jacobi, Douglas: Genesis, science & history (2004)	X	X	X	X	
Jeffrey. Grant: The signature of God (1996)		X	X	X	
Jeffrey, Grant: The handwriting of God (1997)		X	X	X	
Jeffrey, Grant: Creation (2003)	X				
Jenkins, Ferrell: The early church (1999)					X
Johnson, Philip: Darwin on Trial (1993)	X				
Johnson, Philip: Defeating Darwinism (1997)	X				
Kang, C.H.; Nelson, Ethel: The discovery of Genesis (1979)		X			
Keller, Werner: The Bible as history (1980)		X			
Kelly, J.N.D.: Early Christian doctrines (2003)		X			X
Kitchen, K.A.: On the reliability of the Old Testament (2003)		X			
LaHaye, Tim: How to study the Bible for yourself (1998)		X			
LaHaye, Tim: Why believe in Jesus? (2004)			X		
Lewis, C.S.: Mere Christianity (1952)			X		
Little, Paul: Know what you believe (1970)			X		
Little, Paul: Know why you believe (1967)	X	X	X		X
Ludemann, Gert: What really happened to Jesus (1996)			X		
Lutzer, Erwin: The DaVinci deception (2004)		X	X		
Martin, Walter: The kingdom of the cults (2003)					X
McBirnie, William Steuart: The search for the twelve apostles (1973)			X		
McCormack, R.: Heptadic structure of Scripture with a chapter on seven and four in nature (1923)				X	
McDowell, Josh; Stewart, Don: Answers to tough questions (1993)	X	X	X		
McDowell, Josh: The new evidence that demands a verdict (1999)	X	X	X	X	X
McDowell. Josh: More than a carpenter (1971)			X		
McDowell, Josh; Hostetler, Bob: Beyond belief to convictions (2002)			X		
McDowell, Josh: The DaVinci code		X	X		
McMillen, S.I. and Stern, David: None of these diseases (2005)		X		X	
Missler, Chuck: Cosmic codes (1999)				X	
Missler, Chuck: Hidden treasures in the Biblical text (2000)				X	
Morgan, Robert: Evidence and truth (2003)		X	X		

Morison, Frank: Who moved the stone (1930)		X	X		
Morris, Henry; Parker, Gary: What is creation science (1999)	X				
Morris, Henry; Morris, John: Science, Scripture and the young earth (1989)	X				
Morris, John: The young earth (2003)	X				
Morris, Inch: 12 who changed the world (2003)			X		
Mounce, William: Basics of Biblical Greek (2003)		X			
Muncaster, Ralph: 101 reasons you can believe (2004)	X	X			
Muncaster, Ralph: Evidence for Jesus (2004)	X	X			
Muncaster, Ralph: How is Jesus different from other religious leaders?			X		X
Negev, Avraham: The archaeological encyclopedia of the Holy Land	X				
Nichols, Robert: Bible stories in Kanji (1984)	X				
Olson, Carl; Miesel, Sandra: The DaVinci hoax (2004)	X	X			
Packer, James: Nelson's illustrated manners and customs of the Bible (1995)	X	X			
Rana, Fazale; Ross, Hugh: Origins of life (2004)	X				
Petersen, Dennis: Unlocking the mysteries of creation (1986)	X				
Richards, Larry: Baffling Bible questions answered (1993)	X				
Rineour, Fritz: So, what is the difference? (2001)					X
Ross, Hugh: The Creator and the cosmos (2001)	X				
Ross, Hugh: Beyond the cosmos (1999)	X				
Ross, Hugh: The Genesis question (2001)	X				
Ross, Hugh: A matter of days (2004)	X				
Sagan, Carl: Cosmos (1980)	X				
Sagan, Carl: Pale blue dot (1994)	X				
Sarfati, Jonathan: Refuting evolution (1999)	X				
Schaff, Philip: History of the Christian Church (1910)		X			X
Schepps, Solomon: The lost books of the Bible (1979)		X			
Sheler, Jeffery: Is the Bible true? (1999)	X	X			
Shelley, Bruce: Church history in plain language (1982)					X
Sherman, Edwin: Bible code bombshell (2004)		X		X	
Smith, Huston: The world religions (1991)					X
Sproul, R.C.: Defending your faith (2003)	X	X	X		
Starkey, Walter: The Cambrian Explosion (1999)	X				
Story Dan: Christianity on the offense (1998)	X	X			
Strobel, Lee; Poole, Garry: Exploring the DaVinci code (2006)		X	X		
Strobel, Lee: The case for Christ (1998)	X	X	X		
Strobel, Lee: The case for faith (2000)	X	X			
Strobel, Lee: The case for a Creator (2004)	X				
Torrey, R.A.: Difficulties in the Bible	X				
Walvoort, John: The prophecy knowledge handbook (1990)			X	X	
Ward, Peter and Brownlee, Donald: Rare earth (2000)	X				
Washburn, Del: The original code in the Bible (1998)				X	
Wenham, John: Easter enigma: are the resurrection accounts in conflict? (1992)		X	X		
Wells, Jonathan: Icons of evolution (2000)	X				
Wells, Jonathan: The politically incorrect guide to Darwinism and Intelligent Design (2006)	X				
Williams, Alex; Harnett, John: Dismantling the Big Bang (2005)	X				
Williams, Jimmy: Are the Biblical documents reliable? (www.leaderu.com)		X			
Wilkins, Michael and Moreland, J.P: Jesus under fire (1995)		X	X		
Witherington III, Ben: What have they done with Jesus?		X	X		

makes various historical claims that are credible when checked against other historical and archaeological data.

- **On the Reliability of the Old Testament** (2003) by Dr. K.A. Kitchen. Dr. Kitchen, a historian, describes and analyzes the historical and archaeological evidence, with an emphasis on recent discoveries, for the reliability of the Old Testament.
- **Is the New Testament Reliable?** (1986) by Dr. Paul Barnett. A straightforward and easy-to-read analysis of the evidence for the accuracy and reliability of the New Testament books.
- **The Historical Reliability of the Gospels** (1987) by Dr. Craig Blomberg. Dr. Blomberg, an acclaimed evangelical scholar, describes and analyzes the four gospels, their similarities and differences, authorship and dating, and evidence from non-Biblical sources.
- **The New Testament Documents** (1943) by Dr. F.F. Bruce. A classic, but still accurate and actual presentation of the evidence for the historical reliability of the New Testament.

The following books are recommended for further study on the evidence for the resurrection:

- **The Historical Jesus** (1996) by Dr. Gary Habermas. Dr. Habermas, a philosopher, New Testament historian and renowned scholar, offers a balanced and Biblical argument for the historicity of the New Testament and the evidence for the life, ministry, and resurrection of Jesus of Nazareth. The book extensively discusses Biblical and non-Biblical sources as evidence for the reliability of the New Testament claims.
- **The Case for Christ** (1998) by Lee Strobel. Journalist Strobel interviews in a fact-filled and fast-paced manner fourteen experts to analyze and (dis)prove the truth about the claims for Jesus being the Son of God.
- **The Third Day** (2003) by Hank Hanegraaf. An easy to read, fairly brief summary and overview of the major evidence for the resurrection of Jesus on "the third day."
- **Who Moved the Stone** (1930) by Frank Morrison. A classic, but still a brilliant logical analysis by English journalist Frank Morrison, who by tracing all the details as recorded in the gospels, reconstructs the events around the betrayal, crucifixion, and resurrection of Jesus as they were experienced by all the main characters and witnesses

Recommended further reading on the evidences for divine inspiration of the Bible:

- **Genesis, Science & History** (2004) by Douglas Jacoby. Historian and New Testament scholar Douglas Jacoby addresses the scientific and his-

torical background to the texts of the Bible. You do not have to agree
with all his conclusions and exhibits to still feel enriched by his fresh and
inspiring ideas and convictions.
- *Number in Scripture* (1967, original text about one century ago) by
E.W. Bullinger. A classic, monumental study into Biblical numerology.
E.W. Bullinger (1837-1913) extensively explains the use and meaning of
numbers, most importantly the numbers six (representing "man" and
"incomplete") and seven (for "God" and "complete"). He presents evi-
dence not just from the text of the Bible, but especially and most fasci-
nating from the structures hidden under the texts and stories.
- *The Prophecy Knowledge Handbook* (1990) by John F Valvoort.
Following the structure of the Bible, the author identifies and explains
every prophecy, fulfilled and yet to be fulfilled, found in the Scriptures.
- *Cosmic Codes: Hidden Messages from the Edge of Eternity* (2004) by
Chuck Missler. In this, sometimes perhaps somewhat controversial book,
Dr Missler describes the results of over 50 years of discovery of design and
symbolic prophecies that show the hand of the Creator in the Bible. Not
all presented conclusions will be agreed upon by all readers, but this powerful overview will change the way you read the Bible in the future.

For further study on the world religions in relationship to Christianity you
might find the following books a valuable source of information:
- *So What's the Difference?* (2001) by Fritz Ridenour. A to-the-point,
brief, and factual comparative overview between Christianity and the
major other world religions.
- *The Compact Guide to the World Religions* (1996) edited by Dean
Halverson. An easy-to use handbook on the origins, basic beliefs, and
evangelistic challenges and opportunities of the world's major religions
in comparison to Christianity written by different expert contributors.
- *Unveiling Islam* (2002) by the brothers Ergun Mehmet Caner and Emir Fethi
Caner. A highly recommended book written by two raised Muslim but converted to Christianity college professors. Their background allows the authors to
describe their inside views on the youngest and fastest growing world religion.

Lastly, as we all search and sometimes struggle with understanding how to
apply the Biblical teachings to our day-to-day life, I would like to recommended:
- *Will the Real Heretics Please Stand Up* (1989) by David W Bercot. Based on
a thorough investigation and study of the Bible and the writings of the Early
Church Leaders before the Council of Nicea, Bercot describes how the first
Christians at the close of the age of the apostles lived and stood up for their faith.

APPENDIX B

Dating Rocks, Fossils, and Bones

Geologists claim the earth to be 4.6 billion years old and first life to have appeared about 3.7 billion years ago. But where do these numbers come from? How can scientists claim rocks, fossils, or a bone or tooth to be of a certain age? What methods are used for this dating, and are they reliable? In this appendix we will discuss a brief overview of the most common dating techniques. It will show that under certain conditions, scientifically reliable dating is possible; however, the vast majority of rocks and fossils cannot be accurately dated. Accurate dating of organic material is only possible if these remains are relatively young.

RADIOMETRIC DATING

The best-known ways to assign age to an object is through several techniques jointly known as *radiometric* dating, also called *radioisotope* dating.

Radiometric dating is based on the fact that some radioactive elements undergo decay to produce new elements. For instance, in the case of uranium-lead dating, uranium-238 ("the parent element") will eventually decompose to lead-206 ("the daughter"). Or for radiocarbon dating, the carbon-14 isotope will decay to regular carbon in carbon dioxide. By measuring the quantities of the radioactive elements in the object and knowing the rate (speed) by which the decay occurs, one can estimate the age of the object.

Despite of the fact that scientists in general consider these dating methods to be very reliable, there are several critical factors that must be known to be true:[581]

1. The quantity of radioactive elements that were present when the object was formed/buried must be known. This is particularly important for the amount of daughter material. If some of the daughter material would already be present when the rock was formed, radiometric dating would suggest a much-too-old age.

2. The rate of radioactive decay must have been constant over time. It seems scientifically reasonable to assume that this rate has not changed over the ages, but as mankind has only been measuring radioactive decay for a few decades, there is no certainty that this rate of decay is not changing and/or has not changed over time.

3. The object must have been isolated from outside/external influences. Radioisotope dating assumes a closed system. If either the parent or especially daughter concentrations would have been altered through processes like surface water erosion or ground water leaking, the object could appear much older than its real age.

The above assumptions can be (and are) challenged by various argumentations, and there are examples known of objects for which the exact age is known and they were dated completely wrong by radiometric dating.[582]

All in all, radiometric dating is one of the tools available in the scientific toolkit to help us date objects from the past. However, knowing its limitations can be a valid basis to question its application, and it should not be assumed to be more accurate and absolute than it is often made to be.

DATING OF ROCKS AND FOSSILS

Another significant limitation of radiometric dating is that only rocks can be dated that are igneous, rocks that were "formed" on the site. This includes rocks like basalt, which is a type of solidified lava. Generally speaking, dating is limited to rocks resulting from lava flows. Fossils found in these kind of rocks can therefore be dated using radioisotope techniques.

Sedimentary rocks, such as shale, sandstone, and limestone, cannot be dated through radiometric dating, because these rocks were formed from pieces of rocks or other material which existed somewhere else. Subsequently these rocks were eroded and deposited by glaciers, rivers or streams at other locations. As these rocks contain previously existing sources, accurate dating is not possible.

Therefore, fossils found in sedimentary rocks cannot be dated with radiometric techniques. Dating of these fossils is usually done through the so called *index* method. The fossils are compared to other earlier dated reference fossils which are considered unique for certain time periods. By finding an index fossil that is similar to the fossil on the sedimentary rock, the sedimentary rock is dated at the age of the index fossil.

Unless the original index fossil itself was dated using radiometric dating, the index fossil technique has inherent dangers of circular reasoning. Many critics argue the unreliability of the index tables, and therefore they question any rocks dated by index fossils.

DATING OF ORGANIC MATERIAL

The only available method to date organic material, like once-living plants and animals, and material such as wood, charcoal, bone, shell and fossils, is carbon-14 dating.[583]

The half-life of the carbon-14 isotope is 5,730 years (that means after 5,730 years, half of the original carbon-14 material has disappeared), therefore this method is best used for organic material less than 10,000 years old and is only reasonably reliable for about 5 times the half-life, so for dating objects to maximum 25,000-30,000 years old.

How does it work? In our atmosphere under the influence of cosmic rays, a small amount of carbon is transformed from C-12 to the C-14 isotope. This C-14, together with oxygen, forms carbon-dioxide, which is breathed by living plants. And as some of these plants are eaten by animals, the isotope enters living organisms, but when these plants/animals die, they stop breathing/eating, and therefore no more isotope material is added. By measuring the amount of C-14 still left in the remains of these once living organisms, a fairly accurate estimate can be made for how long ago these remains where formed.

Because radiometric dating methods do not work for organic materials, there are no accurate techniques available to reliably estimate ages for fossils and other organic remains older than approximately 30,000 years.

This identifies an area of great caution. In attempts to estimate the age of modern man and his claimed predecessors, the actual recovered bone fragments or teeth cannot be accurately dated. Therefore the paleontologists scan the area for rocks and date those through radiometric dating or index fossils. The resulting dates are then associated with the recovered remains. Obviously this technique involves the very questionable assumption whether the remains were deposited at the same time as the surrounding rocks were formed and subsequently were never moved. Many would argue this to be more an educated guess than real science, and this explains why the estimated ages of ancient organic fossils seem to change over time.

Fifty Questions to Ask an Evolutionist

1. Who/what made the Big Bang happen?
2. Where did matter come from?
3. Where did the space for the universe come from?
4. Where did the natural laws and constants come from?
5. Where is E.T., where are the aliens?
6. How can we explain the vast amounts of information in animal/human DNA?
7. Where did the first DNA come from?
8. How did molecular machines evolve?
9. How did the first cell form?
10. How did the first cell live in its hostile environment long enough to reproduce?
11. How did life learn to reproduce itself?
12. Why can we not create life in a laboratory?
13. How did male and female sexual organs evolve?
14. With what did the first cell capable of sexual reproduction reproduce?
15. How did single-celled plants become multi-celled?
16. Where is the abundance of transitional species?
17. Why are mutations rare?
18. Why are most mutations harmful?
19. How long would it take for a beneficial mutation to change an entire population?
20. How can mutations (recombining of genetic code) create any new genetic material?
21. What/who was the ancestor for modern humans?
22. Where is the human fossil record?
23. How can humans only have been around for 50,000 or fewer years?
24. Why are there not more than 6.5 billion people?
25. Why are there stone-age cultures in very recent history?
26. How did invertebrates evolve into vertebrates?
27. How was the eye formed?
28. How could wings have evolved?
29. Why can we not make anything from a fruit fly but a fruit fly?
30. Why did some animals – according to the fossil record – not evolve further?

31. How can trees be fossilized (all over the world) standing upright?
32. How were mammoths frozen alive?
33. Why does almost every mountain range have fossils of sea animals?
34. Why does one commonly find ancient rocks on top of new rocks?
35. How can the Cambrian Explosion be explained?
36. How can evolution be contradictory to the Law of Entropy?
37. Why do many claim evolution is a fact but do not want to discuss the evidence?
38. Why are textbooks still using the evolution evidences from the 1960s?
39. If evolution is true, why is it morally wrong to consider other races inferior?
40. Why have we never seen evolution as work?
41. Why are there still monkeys?
42. Wouldn't creatures produced by chance have random thoughts?
43. How does one explain symbiosis?
44. Where are the X-men?
45. Why do we have moral values?
46. How did man evolve feelings and emotions?
47. Why does man seem to have a need for religion?
48. Why is there order in all organisms compared to chaos in the world around it?
49. How do you explain the many Near-Death Experiences?
50. How does the evolutionist know that there is no God?

Do you honestly believe that evolution is a fact?

Early Christian Creeds

Parallel to the canonization of the New Testament, the early church developed statements or confessions of faith, now also known as the Old Roman Creed, the Apostles' creed and the Nicene creed. As actual manuscripts of New Testament writings were only very scarcely available, these creeds were memorized and recited at the moment of baptism by a new believer and shared among Christians during meetings and times of fellowship and prayer.

They were also worded and composed to address heretic influences in the young church by explicitly mentioning certain attributes of God and Jesus and/or certain teachings to differentiate the true Christianity from these heresies.[584]

These creeds are today still recognized as a core definition of our faith and used and recited during Christian services.

THE OLD ROMAN CREED

The oldest creed is now known as the *Old Roman creed* or the *Ramanun*. It occurs first in writings of the mid fourth century. Exact dating of the creed is difficult, but likely the form that has been preserved was developed at the end of the second century – early third century.[585] Notice the very explicit statements about Christ's human nature which address the gnostic heresy that Christ was only a spirit, not a human man.

> *"I believe in God the Father Almighty. And in Jesus Christ his only Son our Lord, who was born of the Holy Spirit and the Virgin Mary; crucified under Pontius Pilate and buried; the third day he rose from the dead; he ascended into heaven, and sits at the right hand of the Father, from thence he shall come to judge the living and the dead. And in the Holy Spirit; the holy church; the forgiveness of sins; the resurrection of the flesh."*

It likely was already used – perhaps in a somewhat different form – in earlier times. An earlier fragment of this creed – probably from early to mid second century or perhaps even the end of the first century simply states:

> *"I believe in God the Father Almighty, and in Jesus Christ his only Son, our Lord. And in the Holy Spirit, the holy church, the resurrection of the flesh."*

THE APOSTLES' CREED

The successor to the Old Roman creed was the *Apostles' creed*. It is first mentioned in writings from 390 AD, but was probably used much earlier, likely already in the second half of the third century. According to ancient tradition, it was composed and used by the original apostles, with each apostle contributing a statement. This is obviously a legend, but it does illustrate how highly esteemed the text was considered to be.[586] The text clearly builds on the Old Roman creed, and like its predecessor, it explicitly addresses the false teachings of Gnosticism about the human nature of Christ. Compared to the Old Roman creed, the Apostles' creed adds statements of belief about the creation, the descent of Christ into hell to defeat Satan, the unity of the church (catholic in this context means united church, there is no relationship to what we now know as the Roman Catholic Church) and the ever-lasting life.

"I believe in God the Father, Almighty, Maker of heaven and earth
And in Jesus Christ, his only begotten Son, our Lord
Who was conceived by the Holy Ghost, born of the Virgin Mary
Suffered under Pontius Pilate; was crucified, dead and buried; He descended into hell
The third day he rose again from the dead
He ascended into heaven, and sits at the right hand of God the Father Almighty
From thence he shall come to judge the quick and the dead
I believe in the Holy Ghost
I believe in a holy catholic church; the communion of saints
The forgiveness of sins
The resurrection of the body
And the life everlasting. Amen."

The doctrinal statements in the above text are clear and concise and although written many centuries ago, this creed still very effectively and correctly describes the core Christians beliefs.

In the words of Philip Schaff:[587]

"As the Lord's Prayer is the Prayer of prayers, the Decalogue is the Law of laws, so the Apostles' Creed is the Creed of creeds. It contains all the fundamental articles of the Christian faith necessary to salvation, in the form of facts, in simple Scripture language, and in the most natural order – the order of revelation – from God and the creation down to the resurrection and life everlasting."

THE NICENE CREED

The Nicene creed was agreed upon as the result of the Council of Nicea in 325 AD. It further expands the Apostles' creed to address the new heresies of those days popularized by Arius (ca. 250-336 AD), a pastor from Alexandria in Egypt. Arius and his followers (called Arianism) claimed that Christ was merely man and not God (so the complete opposite of Gnosticism that claimed that Christ was only spirit/God, not man). Therefore we find more explicit statements about the divinity of Christ, and it also expands the concept of the Trinity, the unity between God the Father, Christ the Son and the Holy Spirit:

"I believe in one God, the Father Almighty, Maker of heaven and earth, and of all things visible and invisible.

And in one Lord Jesus Christ, the only-begotten Son of God, begotten of the Father before all worlds; God of God, Light of Light, very God of very God; begotten, not made, being of one substance with the Father, by whom all things were made.

Who, for us men for our salvation, came down from heaven, and was incarnate by the Holy Spirit of the virgin Mary, and was made man; and was crucified also for us under Pontius Pilate; He suffered and was buried; and the third day He rose again, according to the Scriptures; and ascended into heaven, and sits on the right hand of the Father; and He shall come again, with glory, to judge the quick and the dead; whose kingdom shall have no end.

And I believe in the Holy Ghost, the Lord and Giver of Life; who proceeds from the Father and the Son; who with the Father and the Son together is worshiped and glorified; who spoke by the prophets.

And I believe one holy catholic and apostolic Church. I acknowledge one baptism for the remission of sins; and I look for the resurrection of the dead, and the life of the world to come. Amen."

Footnotes

[1] From Josh McDowell, *The New Evidence that Demands a Verdict* (1999), page 157.

[2] For a detailed discussion on this topic, see chapter 7, Exhibit 8: *The Age of the Human Race.*

[3] G.K. Chesterton, *Heretics* (1950), pages 53-54.

[4] C.S. Lewis, *The Screwtape Letters* (1942).

[5] We will discuss the world religions in more details in Section V: *What Do Others Believe?*

[6] Charles Darwin, *On the Origin of Species by Means of Natural Selection, or the Preservation of Favored Races in the Struggle for Life* (1859).

[7] Institute for Creation Research in Santee, CA. Website *www.ICR.org.*

[8] Answers in Genesis, Petersburg, KY. Website *www.AnswersInGenesis.org.*

[9] The Creation Research Society, St. Joseph, MO. Website *www.CreationResearch.org.*

[10] Discovery Institute, Seattle, WA. Website *www.Discovery.org.*

[11] Reasons To Believe, Pasadena, CA. Website *www.Reasons.org.*

[12] From the Tennessee Anti-evolution Statue, State of Tennessee passed by the sixty-fourth General Assembly March 13, 1925.

[13] Among many sources: Dr Hugh Ross, *The Creator and the Cosmos*

[14] All ages and dates mentioned are current estimates supported by a majority of scientists. However these dates are derived using techniques subject to various criticisms. Please see appendix B: *Dating Rocks, Fossils and Bones* for a more detailed discussion.

[15] See (among other references) *Case for a Creator* (2004), chapter 5, Lee Strobel's interview with Dr. William Lane Craig.

[16] Guillermo Gonzales and Jay W. Richards, *The Privileged Planet* (2004), chapter 10.

[17] See *The Case for a Creator* (2004), chapter 6 for an excellent discussion on this topic with Robin Collins who wrote *The Argument from Design and the Many Worlds Hypothesis* (2002).

[18] Hugh Ross, especially *The Creator and the Cosmos,* chapter 14.

[19] Michael J. Denton, *Nature's Destiny: How the Laws of Biology Reveal Purpose in the Universe* (1998).

[20] Ibid, 45, 108-109. Emphasis added.

[21] Paul Davies, *God and the New Physics* (1983), page 189.

[22] Stephen Hawking, *A Brief History of Time* (1988), page 127.

[23] Carl Sagan, *Pale Blue Dot* (1994), page 7.

[24] Lee Strobel, *Case for a Creator* (2004), page 153.

[25] Among other references, see Hugh Ross, The Creator and the Cosmos (2001), pages 184-185.

[26] The SETI institute, founded in 1984 – *www.SETI.org.*

[27] SETI is no longer funded by federal money.

[28] Peter D. Ward and Donald Brownlee, *Rare Earth* (2000), chapter 12: Assessing the Odds.

[29] Guillermo Gonzales and Jay W. Richards, The Privileged Planet (2004), Appendix A: The Revised Drake Equation.

[30] Guillermo Gonzales and Jay W. Richards, The Privileged Planet (2004), pages 276-278.

[31] Hugh Ross, The Creator and the Cosmos (2001 revised edition), chapter 16: Earth: a Place for Life. See also Hugh Ross in Why I am a Christian, edited by Norman L. Geisler and Paul K Hoffman (2001).

[32] The following examples are all taken from Guillermo Gonzales and Jay W. Richards, *The Privileged Planet* (2004) and Lee Strobel's interview with Gonzales and Richards in *Case for a Creator* (2004), chapter 7.

[33] Ibid, page 66.

[34] *The Genesis of the Copernican Revolution* (1975, translated to English in 1987) by Hans Blumenberg, emphasis added.

[35] *Rare Earth* (2000), chapter 2.

[36] Barred Spiral Milky Way Illustration Credit: R. Hurt (SSC), JPL-Caltech, NASA. From *http://apod.gsfc.nasa.gov/apod/ap050825.html.*

[37] This image of our galaxy, the Milky Way, was taken with NASA's Cosmic Background Explorer (COBE)'s Diffuse Infrared Background Experiment (DIRBE) on 21 November 2001.

[38] Recipe for life – according to BBC website: *www.bbc.co.uk/science/space/life/beginnings/recipe.shtml.*

[39] *The Case for Faith* (2000), page 98, Lee Strobel's interview with Walter L Bradley.

[40] Among other sources, see Lee Strobel, *The Case for a Creator* (2004), pages 229-230.

[41] For an extensive analysis of the Miller-Urey experiment see Jonathan Wells, *Icons of Evolution* (2000), chapter 2 as well as Lee Strobel, *The Case for a Creator* (2004), chapter 3.

[42] Science magazine in 1995 as quoted by Lee Strobel, *The Case for a Creator* (2004), page 37.

[43] Illustration credit: the *U. S. Department of Energy Genome Programs*, http://genomics.energy.gov.

[44] As per a publication by International Human Genome Sequencing Consortium, Finishing the Euchromatic Sequence of the Human Genome. In Nature 431 pages 931-945 (2004). A 2007 publication in Science 316, page 1113 by Michele Clamp counts the number of genes in the 20,500 range.

[45] *www.ornl.gov/techresources/Human_Genome*, the main homepage for Human Genome Project information.

[46] Illustration credit: the *U.S. Department of Energy Genome Programs*, http://genomics.energy.gov.

[47] Hugh Ross, *The Creator and the Cosmos* (2001), chapter 17.

[48] Michael Behe, *Darwin's Black Box* (1996), page 5.

[49] This paragraph contains material from *Origins of Life* (2004) by Fazale Rana and Hugh Ross.

[50] Fred Hoyle, *The Big Bang in Astronomy* in the *New Scientist* of 19 November 1981, page 527, emphasis Hoyle's.

[51] *The Case for Faith* (2000), Lee Strobel's interview with Walter L Bradley, chapter 3.

[52] Panspermia attracts a lot of popular attention, many magazines and public media have addressed this "theory." Some searching on the internet will provide many hits to articles and websites like *www.Panspermia.org.*

[53] Gabriel Dover (Professor of Genetics, University of Leicester), *Looping the Evolutionary Loop* in *Nature* 399, 20 May 1999, pages 217-218.

[54] For the complete interview, see: *http://www.pbs.org/wgbh/nova/origins/knoll.html* (emphasis added). This interview was part of the PBS series *Origins* (2004).

[55] Klaus Dose, *The Origin of Life: More Questions than Answers, Interdisciplinary Science Review 13* (1990), page 348, (emphasis added).

[56] Francis Darwin (editor), *Life and Letters of Charles Darwin*, Volume II, 202. Marc W. Kirschner and John C. Gerhart, *The Plausibility of Life* (2005), page 46-50.

[57] Jonathan Wells, *Icons of Evolution* (2000), chapter 8.

[58] Elmer Noble, Ph.D. Zoology, Glenn Nobel, Ph.D. Biology, Gerhard Schad, Ph.D. Biology, Austin MacInnes, Ph.D. Biology, *Parasitology: The Biology of Animal Parasites*, 1989, p. 516.

[59] Lee Spetner (Ph.D. physics – MIT), *Not By Chance*, 1997, pages 131, 138.

[60] James Perloff, *Tornado in a Junkyard*, 1999, page 25.

[61] Maxim D. Frank-Kamenetski, *Unraveling DNA*, 1997, page 72. (Professor at Brown University Center for Advanced Biotechnology and Biomedical Engineering).

[62] Hugh Ross, *A Matter of Days* (2004), page 127.

[63] E.J. Ambrose, *The Nature and Origin of the Biological World* (1982), page 120.

[64] Among others: Biologist Michael Dougherty in an article on ScientificAmerican.com: *http://www.sciam.com.* Also, see the "human height" in the Wikipedia encyclopedia: *http://en.wikipedia.org/wiki/Human_height.*

[65] See Jonathan Wells, *Icons of Evolution* (2000) for numerous illustrations of how these examples and other "icons of evolution" are used in modern day textbooks as misleading evidences for the evolutionary model.

[66] The term "X-men" comes from the comic book series and movie franchise (2000-2006) describing people ("mutants") who through evolutionary processes have developed special skills and abilities.

[67] Cover article *How We Became Human* in Time Magazine's October 9, 2006 publication.

[68] Jonathan Wells describes Homology as one of the Icons of Evolution. *Icons of Evolution* (2000), chapter 4.

[69] Adapted from Norman Geisler & Peter Bocchino – *Unshakable Foundations* (2001).

[70] See chapter 23: Exhibit #3: *Telomeres – We Cannot Live Forever.*

[71] Cover article 'How We Became Human' in Time, October 9, 2006, page 48.

[72] Jonathan Wells, The Politically Incorrect Guide to Darwinism and Intelligent Design (2006), chapter 2.

[73] Tim Berra, Evolution and the Myth of Creationism (1990), pages 117-119.

[74] Philip E. Johnson, Defeating Darwinism by Opening Minds (1997), pages 62-63.

[75] Charles Darwin, Origin of species, 6th edition, 1872, page 413 (emphasis added).

[76] Michael Denton, (Ph.D. Molecular Biology), Evolution, a Theory in Crisis, page 190.

[77] John D. Morris, The Young Earth (2003), page 70.

[78] Biology, Miller and Levine, 2000, page 680.

[79] Icons of Evolution, Jonathan Wells (2000), Case for a Creator (2004), chapter 3 and other sources.

[80] J.W. Valentine, et al., The Biological Explosion at the Precambrian-Cambrian Boundary, as published in Evolutionary Biology, volume 25 (1991), pages 281,318.

[81] Ibid, page 294 (1985).

[82] See Appendix B: Dating Rocks, Fossils and Bones.

[83] Dr. Hugh Ross, The Genesis Question (2001), chapter 14.

[84] These changes would be small mutations, as discussed in the previous chapter. The effect of these mutations on the human species would be negligible as they would be neutralized through DNA repair and/or would be neutral mutations.

[85] Mitochondria are the "cellular power plants." They convert food molecules into energy. Mitochondria contain DNA that is independent of the DNA in the chromosomes that is stored in the cell nucleus.

[86] Cann, Stoneking, and Wilson, Mitochondrial DNA and Human Evolution (1987) and a number of other studies.

[87] Stoneking, Sherry, Redd, and Vigilant, New Approaches to Dating Suggest a Recent Age for the Human mtDNA Ancestor (1992).

[88] Whitfiled, Suston, and Goodfellow, Sequence Variation of the Human Y Chromosome, published in Nature 378 (1995), pages 379-380.

[89] A. Gibbons, The Mystery of Humanity's Missing Mutations (1995). Published in Science 267:35-36.

[90] R.G. Klein, Evolutionary Anthropology (1992) 1:5-14.

[91] C. Simon, Stone-age Sanctuary, Oldest Known Shrine, Discovered in Spain (1981), Science News 120:357.

[92] Interpretations very, depending on how many generations might have been skipped in the genealogies.

[93] Average number of children is calculated as 2 times $(1+\text{growth rate})^{25}$ (years).

[94] Recovery of the European population following the plagues of 1347 was only two hundred years, chart based on research published in Ian T. Taylor, Darwin and the New World Order (1992), chapter 12.

[95] Behe, Michael: Darwin's Black Box (1996) and Case for a Creator (2004) by Lee Strobel, chapter 8.

[96] Behe, Michael: Darwin's Black Box (1996), page 70-71.

[97] Image from www.ResearchID.org, used on the terms of the GNU Free Documentation License.

[98] Behe, Michael: Darwin's Black Box (1996), page 72.

[99] Norman L. Geisler: Baker Encyclopedia of Christian Apologetics. 1999. page 714-715.

[100] Numerous publications, including the issue of science journal Nature 444 of 30 November 2006, pages 587-591.

[101] C.S. Lewis, Mere Christianity (1952), pages 15-39.

[102] Norman L. Geisler, Baker Encyclopedia of Christian Apologetics (1999), page 278.

[103] Jonathan Wells, Icons of Evolution (2000).

[104] Hugh Ross, Beyond the Cosmos (1999).

[105] van Lommel P, van Wees R, Meyers V, Elfferich I. (2001) Near-Death Experience in Survivors of Cardiac Arrest: A Prospective Study in the Netherlands. Lancet, Dec 15:358(9298):2039-45.

[106] Dr. Raymond Moody, Life After Life (1975). See also P.M.H. Atwater, Coming Back to Life (1988).

[107] Adapted from Peter Kreeft, Questions of Faith, the Philosophy of Religion (2006), pages 54-55.

[108] Sir Arthur Keith (1866-1955), Scottish anatomist and anthropologist. Sir Arthur was an evolutionary scientist and a leading figure in the study of human fossils. Quoted from W.A. Criswell, Did Man Just Happen? (1972), page 73.

[109] Malcolm Muggeridge (1903-1990), British journalist, author and satirist. Muggeridge was a professed agnostic most of his life, but converted to Christianity in his sixties. Quoted from his Pascal Lectures, University of Waterloo, Ontario, Canada.

[110] Dr. T. N. Tahmisian, Physiologist, Atomic Energy Commission. As quoted in: *Evolution and the Emperor's New Clothes* (1983), title page.

[111] Since 1984 Barna Research Group, located in Ventura, California, has been providing information and analysis regarding cultural trends and the Christian church. Website *www.Barna.org*.

[112] The Geneva Bible was one of the earlier English language translations by a team of Protestant scholars who had fled to Geneva, Switzerland to avoid persecution during the Reformation.

[113] Except for 2 Peter 3:15 that refers to Paul's letters in the New Testament.

[114] William D. Mounce, *Basics of Biblical Greek*, (1999), chapter 9.

[115] William L. Craig, *Jesus under Fire* (1995) chapter 1; Gary R. Habermas, *The Historical Jesus* (1996), chapter 1.

[116] *The Five Gospels: What did Jesus Really Say? The Search for the Authentic Words of Jesus* (1993), Robert Funk and the Jesus Seminar.

[117] See chapter 13, Exhibit #14: *The Lost Books Were Never Lost*.

[118] Michael Wilkins, J.P. Moreland (general editors): *Jesus Under Fire, Modern Scholarship Reinvents the Historical Jesus* (1995).

[119] Including: Carl Olson, Sandra Miesel: *The DaVinci Hoax* (2004); Erwin Lutzer, *The DaVinci Deception* (2004).

[120] Among others: Dr. Darrel L Bock, *The Missing Gospels* (2006).

[121] Chapter 13, Exhibit #14: *The Lost Books Were Never Lost*.

[122] For a comprehensive overview see Josh McDowell, *The New Evidence that Demands a Verdict* (1999), chapter 2.

[123] Merrill F. Unger, *Famous Archaeological Discoveries* (1957), page 72.

[124] Millar Burrows, *The Dead Sea Scrolls* (1960), page 304.

[125] Josh McDowell, The New Evidence that Demands a Verdict (1999), page 79 and Gleason Archer, A Survey of Old Testament Introduction (1964), page 19.

[126] R. Laird Harris, Can I Trust My Bible? (1963), page 124.

[127] Jeffery L Sheler, Is the Bible True? (1999), page 151.

[128] Josh McDowell, *The New Evidence that Demands a Verdict* (1999), page 83.

[129] Norman Geisler and William Nix, *A General Introduction to the Bible*. (1986), page 504.

[130] These prophecies are extensively discussed in chapter 20: *Fulfillment of Messianic Prophecies* and chapter 24: *Fulfilled Prophecies – Foretelling the Future*.

[131] Norman Geisler and William Nix, *A General Introduction to the Bible*. (1986), page 205, and Josh McDowell, *The New Evidence that Demands a Verdict* (1999), page 26.

[132] Some claim this happened at the *Council of Jamnia* around 100 AD. Most scholars now believe that there was never a council, but that the Rabbinic school at Jamnia became the substitute for the Sanhedrin after the destruction of Jerusalem in 70 AD and through the teachings of the school, the canon was fixed in the 70-135 AD period.

[133] The theory of the Documentary Hypothesis is described in most books that discuss the reliability of the Old Testament. A comprehensive description can be found in Josh McDowell's, *The New Evidence that Demands a Verdict* (1999), chapters 12 through 26.

[134] G.L. Archer: *A Survey of Old Testament Introduction* (1998), pages 116-124.

[135] We will examine these discoveries in chapter 14, Exhibit #15: *The Old Testament is Historically Reliable*.

[136] Ibid.

[137] Jeffery L Sheler, *Is the Bible True?* (1999), chapter 3; David J Clines, *"Pentateuch,"* page 580.

[138] A comprehensive discussion of this theory and its refutation can be found in G.L. Archer, *A Survey of Old Testament Introduction* (1998), pages 366-390. A nice summary can be found in Dr. Phil Fernandes, *No Other Gods* (1998), chapter 6.

[139] This "Cyrus prophecy" is discussed in detail later, in chapter 24, Exhibit #9: *Isaiah's Prophecy about Cyrus, King of Persia*.

[140] Drane, John William: *Introducing the Old Testament*. (2000), page 200.

[141] McDowell, Josh; Stewart, Don Douglas: *Answers to Tough Questions*. (1993).

[142] Walvoord, John F.: *The Prophecy Knowledge Handbook*. Wheaton (1990), page 94.

[143] Chapter 20, Exhibit #3: *Jesus Fulfilled All Messianic Prophecies*.

[144] These are discussed in detail in chapter 24, Exhibit #10: *Daniel's Prophecies of the World Empires.*

[145] See G.L. Archer, *A Survey of Old Testament Introduction* (1998), pages 423-445. A brief summary can be found in Dr. Phil Fernandes, *No Other Gods* (1998), chapter 6.

[146] For a very complete overview and strong argument for early dating of Daniel, see Stephen R Miller, *The New American Commentary: Daniel,* (1994), page 25-43.

[147] Ibid page 37-38.

[148] See chapter 24, Exhibit #13: *Daniel's "Seventy Sevens.".*

[149] *The Ante-Nicene Fathers Volume I through X: Translations of the Writings of the Fathers Down to AD 325* (1997). Volume 4, page 349. Origen (ca. 185-254 AD) was one of the first apologists in the early Christian church.

[150] Josh McDowell, *The New Evidence That Demands a Verdict* (1999), chapter 3.

[151] Normal L. Geisler, William E. Nix.: *A General Introduction to the Bible* (1986), page 383.

[152] Josh McDowell, *The New Evidence that Demands a Verdict* (1999), page 35.

[153] Summary derived from Normal L. Geisler, William E. Nix.: *A General Introduction to the Bible.* (1986), chapter 22.

[154] Data from different sources, most are mentioned throughout this chapter.

[155] New Testament manuscripts are fragmentary. Earliest complete manuscript is ca. 350; lapse of event to complete manuscript is about 325 years.

[156] Norman L. Geisler, *Baker Encyclopedia of Christian Apologetics.* (1999), page 532.

[157] Philip Schaff, *Companion to the Greek Testament and English Version,* page 177.

[158] Norman L. Geisler, *Baker Encyclopedia of Christian Apologetics.* (1999), page 532.

[159] Chuck Missler.

[160] David Dockery, Kenneth Mathews and Robert Sloan: *Foundations for Biblical Interpretation,* (1994), page 176.

[161] Ibid page 182.

[162] F.F. Bruce, *The New Testament Documents – Are They Reliable?* (rev 1981), page 14-15.

[163] These Early Church Leaders are also often referred to as the Early Church Fathers.

[164] McDowell, Josh; Stewart, Don Douglas: *Answers to Tough Questions.* Nashville: 1993.

[165] Harold J Greenlee, *Introduction to New Testament Textual Criticism* (1977), page 54.

[166] From J.D. Douglas, Philip Wesley Comfort, Donald Mitchell: *Who's Who in Christian History* (1992), Norman L. Geisler, William E. Nix, *A General Introduction to the Bible.* (1986) pages 421-430, *The Ante-Nicene Fathers Volume I through X: Translations of the Writings of the Fathers Down to AD 325* (1997) and other earlier mentioned sources.

[167] Norman L. Geisler, William E. Nix: *A General Introduction to the Bible* (1986), page 421.

[168] Fahlbusch, Erwin; Bromiley, Geoffrey William: *The Encyclopedia of Christianity* (2003), Vol 1, page 112.

[169] Richard Bauckman, *Jesus and the Eyewitnesses* (2006), pages 12-15.

[170] Josh McDowell in *New Evidence that Demands a Verdict,* (1999), page 44-45.

[171] Gary R. Habermas, *The Historical Jesus* (1996), chapter 7 and other sources.

[172] F.F. Bruce in *The New Testament Documents* (1943), page 36.

[173] See chapter 21, Exhibit #8: *The Resurrection Appearances.*

[174] Sir Frederic Kenyon, *The Bible and Archaeology,* page 288.

[175] *Homilies on Joshua,* just before Origen's death.

[176] J.J. Griesbach was probably the first scholar – in 1774 – to have called them the "synoptic gospels."

[177] Richard Bauckman, *Jesus and the Eyewitnesses* (2006), pages 12-15.

[178] Papias as quoted by Eusebius in *The Ante-Nicene Fathers Volume I through X: Translations of the Writings of the Fathers Down to AD 325* (1997), Volume 1, page 155.

[179] Ibid, Volume 1, page 414.

[180] And see also chapter 16: *Can We Trust the Witnesses?*

[181] Blomberg, Craig: *The New American Commentary: Matthew.* (2001), page 44.

[182] Richard Bauckman, *Jesus and the Eyewitnesses* (2006), pages 12-15.

[183] Papias as quoted by Eusebius in *The Ante-Nicene Fathers Volume I through X: Translations of the Writings of the Fathers Down to AD 325* (1997), Volume 1, page 155.

[184] Irenaeus, *Against Heresies, The Ante-Nicene Fathers Volume I through X: Translations of the Writings of the Fathers Down to AD 325* (1997), Volume 1, page 425, see also quote on page 414.

[185] *The Ante-Nicene Fathers Volume I through X: Translations of the Writings of the Fathers Down to AD 325* (1997), Volume 2, page 573.

[186] Brooks, James A.: *The New American Commentary: Matthew.* (2001), page 26.

[187] Bailey, Mark; Constable, Tom; Swindoll, Charles R.; Zuck, Roy B.: *Nelson's New Testament Survey: Discover the Background, Theology and Meaning of Every Book in the New Testament.* (1999), page 65.

[188] *The Ante-Nicene Fathers Volume I through X: Translations of the Writings of the Fathers Down to AD 325* (1997), Volume 1, page 414.

[189] Ibid, Volume 2, page 573.

[190] Ibid, Volume 3, page 347.

[191] Ibid, Volume 5, page 603.

[192] Douglas, Comfort, Mitchell, *Who's Who in Christian History.* (1992).

[193] For more information on the dating of Acts, see among others Polhill, John B.: The New American Commentary: *Acts.* (2001), page 27-32. This topic is discussed in various degrees and detail in most commentaries and books.

[194] Irenaeus, *Against Heresies* 8.1.1. *The Ante-Nicene Fathers Volume I through X: Translations of the Writings of the Fathers Down to AD 325* (1997), Volume 1, page 414: Irenaeus refers to Peter's "departure," likely a euphemism for his death.

[195] Irenaeus, *Against Heresies, The Ante-Nicene Fathers Volume I through X: Translations of the Writings of the Fathers Down to AD 325* (1997), Volume 1, page 414.

[196] Ibid, Volume 5, page 603.

[197] Ibid, Volume 3, page 347.

[198] This reasoning is discussed in detail in Craig L Blomberg: *The Historical Reliability of John's Gospel* (2001), page 27-31.

[199] Borchert, Gerald L.: *The New American* Commentary *John 1-11.* (1996), page 90.

[200] This conclusion can be found in many sources. For an overview: Jeffery L. Sheler, *Is the Bible True?* (1999), page 36-37.

[201] *The Ante-Nicene Fathers Volume I through X: Translations of the Writings of the Fathers Down to AD 325* (1997), Volume 1, page 6.

[202] Ibid, Volume 1, page 75.

[203] Ibid, Volume 1, page 33.

[204] Bailey, Mark; Constable, Tom; Swindoll, Charles R.; Zuck, Roy B.: *Nelson's New Testament Survey: Discover the Background, Theology and Meaning of Every Book in the New Testament.* Nashville (1999), page 569.

[205] Martin, D. Michael: *The New American Commentary: 1, 2 Thessalonians.* (2001), page 33.

[206] George, Timothy: *The New American Commentary: Galatians.* (2001), page 48.

[207] Thiselton, Anthony C.: *The First Epistle to the Corinthians: A Commentary on the Greek Text.* (2000), page 31.

[208] Mounce, Robert H.: *The New American Commentary: Romans.* (2001), page 25.

[209] For the texts of these apocryphal accounts see for instance Willis Barnstone, *The Other Bible* (1984).

[210] From Dr. Darell L Bock, *The Missing Gospels* (2006), page 18-21. Bock uses material from Dr. Kurt Rudolph's *work Gnosis, the Nature and History of Gnosticism* (1983), page 57-59.

[211] See also Appendix D: *Early Christian Creeds.*

[212] Ignatius' Epistle to the Trallians (Volume 1, page 70), and his letter to the church in Smyrna (Volume 1, pages 88-89).

[213] Darell L. Bock, *The Missing Gospels* (2006), pages 'xx' – 'xxiii'.

[214] This paragraph is a summary from Robinson, James McConkey; Smith, Richard; Coptic Gnostic Library Project: *The Nag Hammadi Library in English.* (1996), pages 1-27.

[215] Elwell, Walter A.; Beitzel, Barry J.: *Baker Encyclopedia of the Bible.* (1988), page 874.

[216] Norman L. Geisler, William E. Nix: *A General Introduction to the Bible.* (1986), page 301.

[217] Norman L. Geisler, William E. Nix: *A General Introduction to the Bible.* (1986), page 307.

[218] Darell L. Bock, *The Missing Gospels* (2006), pages 215-217.

[219] Darell L. Bock, *The Missing Gospels* (2006), pages 67-68; Wesley W. Isenberg; *The Nag Hammadi Library in English*. (1996), page 141.

[220] Carl E. Olson, Sandra Miesel, *The Da Vinci Hoax* (2004), page 93.

[221] Harold W. Attridge and George W. MacRae; *The Nag Hammadi Library in English*. (1996), page 38.

[222] George W. MacRae and R. McL.Wilson; *The Nag Hammadi Library in English*. (1996), page 523.

[223] Carl E Olson, Sandra Miesel, The Da Vinci Hoax (2004), page 58,63,75.

[224] Fahlbusch, Erwin; Bromiley, Geoffrey William: *The Encyclopedia of Christianity*. (1999), Volume 1, page 100.

[225] Robinson, James McConkey; Smith, Richard; *The Nag Hammadi Library in English*. (1996), page 124.

[226] Darell L. Bock, *The Missing Gospels* (2006), pages 61.

[227] *The Five Gospels: What did Jesus Really Say? The Search for the Authentic Words of Jesus* (1993), Robert Funk and the Jesus Seminar.

[228] From Michael J Bumbulis, *Is the Gospel of Thomas Reliable? (1995)*.

[229] For a more detailed analysis, see also: Darell L. Bock, *The Missing Gospels* (2006), pages 59-65 and Gary R. Habermas, *The Historical Jesus* (1996) page 211-213.

[230] Norman L. Geisler, William E. Nix: *A General Introduction to the Bible*. (1986), page 303.

[231] See also Darell L. Bock, *The Missing Gospels* (2006), pages 78-79.

[232] Reformed Jewish scholar Nelson Glueck, *Rivers in the Desert: History of Negev* (1959), page 31.

[233] Hallo, William W.; Younger, K. Lawson: *Context of Scripture*. (2000), page 221.

[234] See Exhibit #4: *Authorship of the Pentateuch*, chapter 10.

[235] Willmington, H. L.: *Willmington's Bible Handbook*. (1997), page 889.

[236] Editor, Hershel Shanks: *BAR 06:05 (Sep/Oct 1980)*. Biblical Archaeology Society, (2002).

[237] Willmington, H. L.: *Willmington's Bible Handbook* (1997), page 888.

[238] Including Normal L. Geisler: *Baker Encyclopedia of Christian Apologetics* (1999), page 50.

[239] The *Bible and Spade* Summer 1999 (Vol. 12, No. 3) from the Associates for Biblical Research.

[240] From G.L. Archer, *A Survey of Old Testament Introduction* (1998), page 179.

[241] Robert J. Morgan, *Evidence and Truth* (2003), page 93.

[242] See C. H. Gordon in *The Biblical Archaeologist 3* (1940), page 5.

[243] Cf. Gordon in *Revue Biblique* 44 (1935), page 35.

[244] Rowley, in *Bulletin of the John Rylands Library*, 32 (Sept. 1949), page 76.

[245] J.A. Thompson in *Archaeology & the Old Testament*, page 31.

[246] K.A. Kitchen, *On the Reliability of the Old Testament* (2001), pages 344-345.

[247] K.A. Kitchen, *BAR 21:02 (March/April 1995)*. Biblical Archaeology Society, (2002).

[248] Figure based on research by K.A. Kitchen,, BAR 21:02 (March/April 1995). Biblical Archaeology Society, (2002).

[249] See 'Documentary Hypothesis' discussed in Exhibit #4: Authorship o110f the Pentateuch. chapter 10.

[250] Hershel Shanks, *The Rise of Ancient Israel* (1992), pages 15-16.

[251] Kathleen Kenyon, *Jericho 3*, page 370, as quoted by Bryant G. Wood, *BAR 16:02 (March/April 1990)*.

[252] Bryant G. Wood, *BAR 16:02 (March/April 1990)*. Biblical Archaeology Society, (2002).

[253] Ibid.

[254] Negev, Avraham: *The Archaeological Encyclopedia of the Holy Land*. (1996).

[255] Willmington, H. L.: *Willmington's Bible Handbook*. (1997), page. 890.

[256] Editor, Hershel Shanks *BAR 20:02 (March/April 1994)*. Biblical Archaeology Society, (2002).

[257] André Lemaire Editor, Hershel Shanks: *BAR 20:03 (May/June 1994)*. Biblical Archaeology Society, (2002).

[258] Tammi Schneider, Editor, Hershel Shanks: *BAR 21:01 (Jan/Feb 1995)*. Biblical Archaeology Society, (2002).

[259] James B. Pritchard, *Ancient Near Eastern Texts Relating to the Old Testament*, (1969), page. 280.

[260] Willmington, H. L.: *Willmington's Bible Handbook*. (1997), page 892.

[261] Willmington, H. L.: *Willmington's Bible Handbook*. (1997), pages 892-893.

[262] Lisbeth S. Fried, Editor, Hershel Shanks: *BR 19:05*. Biblical Archaeology Society (2004).

[263] Willmington, H. L.: *Willmington's Bible Handbook*. (1997), page 894.

[264] Josephus, Flavius; Whiston, William: *The Works of Josephus* (1987), The Life of Flavius Josephus, page 403.

[265] Negev, Avraham: *The Archaeological Encyclopedia of the Holy Land.* 3rd ed. (1996).

[266] James F. Strange, Hershel Shanks: BAR 08:06 (Nov/Dec 1982). Biblical Archaeology Society, (2002).

[267] Ibid.

[268] Ibid, also Jeffery L. Sheler, Is the Bible True (1999), page 118; Morgan, Robert J.: Evidence and Truth: Foundations for Christian Truth. (2003), page 96 and Willmington, H. L.: Willmington's Bible Handbook. (1997), pages 894-895.

[269] Ronny Reich, Editor, Hershel Shanks: *BAR 18:05 (Sep/Oct 1992).* Biblical Archaeology Society (2002).

[270] Josephus, Flavius; Whiston, William: *The Works of Josephus* (1987), Antiquities of the Jews 18.95 (emphasis added).

[271] Robert J. Bull, Editor, Hershel Shanks: *BAR 08:03 (May/June 1982).* Biblical Archaeology Society (2002); also L. Sheler, *Is the Bible True* (1999), page 112 (emphasis added).

[272] Josephus, Flavius; Whiston, William: *The Works of Josephus* (1987), Antiquities of the Jews 18.89 and Philo of Alexandria ; Yonge, Charles Duke: *The Works of Philo: Complete and Unabridged.* Peabody (1993) page 784.

[273] Josephus, Flavius; Whiston, William: *The Works of Josephus* (1987), *The Wars of the Jews,* 5.449.

[274] Multiple sources: Normal L. Geisler: *Baker Encyclopedia of Christian Apologetics.* (1999); page 48, Vassilios Tzaferis, *BAR 11:01 (Jan/Feb 1985).* Biblical Archaeology Society (2002); Jeffery L. Sheler, *Is the Bible True?* (1999), pages 110-111.

[275] Gary R Habermas, *The Historical Jesus* (1996), pages 173-175, referring to Hebrew University pathologist Dr. N. Haas.

[276] Such as Jesus Seminar scholar John Dominic Crossan in his books: *Jesus, A Revolutionary Biography,* pages 152-158 and *The Historical Jesus,* pages 391-394.

[277] Paul Barnett, *Is the New Testament Reliable?* (1986), pages 62-63.

[278] Some Bibles translate this as "the city treasurer" (like NASB, NKJV), the King James translates as "the chamberlain of the city."

[279] See John Harvey Kent, *Corinth: Results of Excavations Conducted by the American School of Classical Studies at Athens,* 8/3: *The Inscriptions 1926-1950* (1966) pages 99-100.

[280] Victor Paul Furnish, BAR 14:03 *(May/June 1988),* 2002; see also Josh McDowell, *The New Evidence that Demands a Verdict* (1999), pages 67-68; F.F. Bruce, *The New Testament Documents* (1981), page 96.

[281] A. N. Sherwin-White, *Roman Society and Roman Law in the New Testament,* page 189.

[282] W.F. Albright, *The Archaeology of Palestine* (1960), pages 127-128.

[283] Examples taken from C.H. Kang and Ethel Nelson: *The Discovery of Genesis* (1979) and Timothy Boyle, *Bible Stories Hidden in Chinese Characters (1990).*

[284] See chapter 25, Exhibit #15: *The Plan of Redemption.*

[285] Adapted from C.W.Hensley in *Who's Who in Christian History* (1997).

[286] Josephus, Flavius; Whiston, William: *The Works of Josephus* (1987), *The Wars of the Jews,* 2.94.

[287] Ibid, *The Antiquities of the Jews,* 17.334.

[288] Ibid, *The Wars of the Jews,* 2.118.

[289] Ibid, *The Wars of the Jews,* 2.169.

[290] Ibid, *The Antiquities of the Jews,* 18.113-117.

[291] Ibid, *The Antiquities of the Jews,* 18.63-64. This text is widely thought to have been edited by early Christian influences, the shown quotation is generally accepted as the original text of Josephus.

[292] Ibid, *The Antiquities of the Jews,* 18.95. That Caiaphas was also called Joseph is not mentioned in the NT.

[293] Ibid, *The Antiquities of the Jews,* 18.109.

[294] Ibid, *The Antiquities of the Jews,* 19.344-349.

[295] Ibid, *The Antiquities of the Jews,* 20.103.

[296] Ibid, *The Antiquities of the Jews,* 20.200. The stoning of James, brother of Jesus is not mentioned in the NT.

[297] Tacitus, *Annals* 15:14, emphasis added, quoted from Gary R. Habermas, *The Historical Jesus* (1996), page 188.

[298] Suetonius, *Claudius,* remarks added, quoted from Gary R. Habermas, *The Historical Jesus* (1996), page 191.

[299] Suetonius, *Nero,* 16, quoted from Gary R. Habermas, *The Historical Jesus* (1996), page 191.

[300] Julius Africanus, Extant Writings, XVIII, *The Ante-Nicene Fathers Volume I through X: Translations of the Writings of the Fathers Down to AD 325* (1997), Volume VI, page 136.

[301] Pliny, *Letters*, translated by William Melmoth, revised by W.M.L. Hutchinson (1935), vol. II, X:96.

[302] Ibid.

[303] Remarks added. From the reading in *The Babylonian Talmud*, translated by I. Epstein (1935), vol. III, *Sanhedrin* 43a, page 281, as quoted by Gary R. Habermas, *The Historical Jesus* (1996), page 203.

[304] Lucian, *The Death of Peregrine*, 11-13, in *The Works of Lucian of Samosata*, translated by H.W. Fowler and F.G. Fowler (1949) volume 4 as quoted by Gary R. Habermas, *The Historical Jesus* (1996), page 206.

[305] Dr. Gary Habermas in *Why I Am a Christian: Leading Thinkers Explain Why They Believe* (2001), page 150.

[306] See discussions on authorship and dating in chapter 12

[307] See discussions on authorship and dating in chapter 12.

[308] See discussions on authorship and dating in chapter 12.

[309] See discussions on authorship and dating in chapter 12.

[310] The presented timeline is derived from the events mentioned in Scripture and a detailed analyses by Paul Barnett in his book *The Birth of Christianity: The First Twenty Years* (2005), chapter 4.

[311] *The Ante-Nicene Fathers Volume I through X: Translations of the Writings of the Fathers Down to AD 325* (1997), Volume 1, page 6.

[312] See Exhibit #12: *Authorship and Dating of Paul's Letters* in chapter 12.

[313] F.F. Bruce, *The New Testament Documents* (1981), chapter 6 and Paul Barnett, *Is the New Testament Reliable?* (1986), page 131.

[314] Dr. Gregory A Boyd and Edward K. Boyd, *Letters from a Skeptic* (1994), pages 80-81.

[315] See chapter 12, Exhibit #13: *Authorship and Dating of Paul's Letters.*

[316] Adapted from Gregory A Boyd and Edward K. Boyd, *Letters from a Skeptic* (1994), pages 82-83.

[317] Paul Barnett, *The Birth of Christianity, The First Twenty Years* (2005), page 13.

[318] Adapted from Malina, Bruce; Joubert, Stephan: *A Time Travel to the World of Jesus* (1997), chapter 1.

[319] Ibid.

[320] Paul Barnett, *Is the New Testament Reliable?* (1986), pages 117-120.

[321] For instance Bart Ehrman's book *Misquoting Jesus* (2005).

[322] Just search for *"contradictions in the Bible"* on the internet.

[323] The following summary is derived from Richard Bauckham, *Jesus and the Eyewitnesses, The Gospels as Eyewitness Testimony* (2006), chapter 13.

[324] For possible explanations of many of the alleged contradictions see for instance Hank Hanegraaff, *The Bible Answer Book* (2004), Larry Richards, *Baffling Bible Questions Answered* (1993) or Gleason L. Archer, Jr., *Encyclopedia of Bible Difficulties* (1982).

[325] Two excellent references are John Wenham, *Easter Enigma: Do the Resurrection Stories Contradict One Another?* (1984) and Morison, Frank: *Who Moved the Stone?* (1930).

[326] Ibid. See also Craig Blomberg, *The Historical Reliability of the Gospels* (1987), pages 100-102.

[327] For a detailed analysis of John see: Blomberg, Craig: *The Historical Reliability of John's Gospel* (2001).

[328] Ibid, page 53.

[329] See among others, Craig Blomberg: *The Historical Reliability of the Gospels* (1987), chapter 5.

[330] See also Exhibit #14: *'The Lost Books Were Never Lost'* in chapter 13.

[331] *The Infancy Gospel of Thomas*, text from Willis Barnstone, editor, *The Other Bible* (1984), page 399.

[332] Ibid, page 401.

[333] *The Acts of Paul*, text from Willis Barnstone, editor, *The Other Bible* (1984), page 457.

[334] Ibid.

[335] Dr. William Steuart McBirnie, *The Search for the Twelve Apostles* (1973) pages 251-258, quoting from Aziz S. Atiya, *A History of Eastern Christianity* (1968), pages 25-28.

[336] Ibid, see references and quotations on pages 27-28.

[337] Ibid, pages 176-177. Also Morris A Inch, *12 Who Changed the World: The Lives and Legends of the Disciples.* (2003), page 84.

[338] Various sources in Dr. William Steuart McBirnie, The *Search for the Twelve Apostles* (1973) pages 270-271.

[339] Ibid pages 110-121, see also Morris A Inch, *12 Who Changed the World: The Lives and Legends of the Disciples.* (2003), pages 48-58.

[340] Dr. William Steuart McBirnie, *The Search for the Twelve Apostles* (1973) pages 280-281.

[341] See chapter 15, Exhibit #16: *Confirmations from Non-Christian Sources.*

[342] Josephus, Flavius; Whiston, William: *The Works of Josephus* (1987), The Antiquities of the Jews, 18.63-64.

[343] Chapter 14, Exhibit #15: *The New Testament is Historically Reliable.*

[344] Quoted from Josh McDowell, *The New Evidence that Demands a Verdict* (1999), page 61.

[345] Ibid page 61 as quoted from W.F. Albright, *The Archaeology of Palestine* (1960), page 248.

[346] Ibid page 61-62, as quoted from Millar Burrows, *What Mean These Stones?* (1957) page 291.

[347] Ibid page 62 as quoted from F.F. Bruce, *Archaeological Confirmation of the New Testament, in Revelation and the Bible* (1969), edited by Carl Henry, page 331.

[348] See chapter 12, *Authorship and Dating of the New Testament.*

[349] See chapter 11, Exhibit #8: *Early Church Leader's Letters.*

[350] Paul Barnett, *Is the New Testament Reliable?* (1986), page 121.

[351] Norman L. Geisler: *Baker Encyclopedia of Christian Apologetics* (1999), page 47.

[352] Josh McDowell, *The New Evidence that Demands a Verdict* (1999), page 63, also John Elder, *Prophets, Idols and Diggers* (1960), page 160.

[353] Norman L. Geisler, Thomas A. Howe: *When Critics Ask: A Popular Handbook on Bible Difficulties.*(1992), page 384.

[354] H. Hoehner, *Chronological Aspects of the Life of Christ* (1977), pages 33-37.

[355] Paul Barnett, *The Birth of Christianity, The First Twenty Years* (2005), pages 24-25.

[356] C.S. Lewis, *Mere Christianity* (1952), pages 40-41.

[357] Philip Schaff, *The Person of Christ* (1913), pages 94-95, as quoted by Josh McDowell in *The New Evidence That Demands a Verdict* (1999), page 160.

[358] Dan Story, *Defending Your Faith* (1997), page 85.

[359] Philip Schaff, *The Person of Christ* (1913), pages 97-98, as quoted by Josh McDowell in *The New Evidence That Demands a Verdict* (1999), page 162.

[360] Adapted from Peter Kreeft, *Why I Am a Christian: Leading Thinkers Explain Why They Believe* (2001), page 231.

[361] Norman L. Geisler, *Miracles and the Modern Mind: A Defense of Biblical Miracles* (1992) page 15.

[362] F.F. Bruce: *The New Testament Documents- Are They Reliable?* (1943), page 61.

[363] See Exhibit #18: *The Witnesses are Honest and Trustworthy* in chapter 16.

[364] G.K. Chesterton, *The Father Brown Omnibus* (1951), page 6.

[365] A. T. Pierson, *Many Infallible Proofs*, Volume 2, page 15 as quoted by Morgan, Robert J.: *Evidence and Truth : Foundations for Christian Truth* (2003), page 51

[366] John F. Walvoord in *The Prophecy Knowledge Handbook* (1990) identifies 98 locations in the OT where one or more Messianic prophecies can be found.

[367] Barton Payne lists 191 prophecies in *Encyclopedia of Biblical Prophecy,* (1973), pages 665-670.

[368] Josh McDowell in *The New Evidence That Demands a Verdic,t* (1999), page 164.

[369] Alfred Edersheim: *The Life and Times of Jesus the Messiah* (1896, 2003 edition), volume 2, page 710.

[370] John F. Walvoord in *The Prophecy Knowledge Handbook* (1990), page 94.

[371] John F. A Sawyer, *Isaiah: Volume 1* (2001), page 83.

[372] The fulfillment of many of these prophecies is found in throughout the New Testament. In this overview, we will mention only the first occurrence in the texts.

[373] Alfred Edersheim, *The Life and Times of Jesus the Messiah* (1896, edition 2003), Volume 2, page 731.

[374] Barry R. Leventhal in *Why I Am a Christian: Leading Thinkers Explain Why They Believe* (2001), page 209.

[375] Alfred Edersheim, *The Life and Times of Jesus the Messiah* (1896, edition 2003), Volume 2, page 726 and J.F. Stenning, *The Targum of Isaiah* (1949), page 130.

[376] More about the importance of this event in when we discuss *Daniel's 'Weeks of Sevens'* in chapter 24.

[377] Alfred Edersheim, *The Life and Times of Jesus the Messiah* (1896, edition 2003), Volume 2, page 736.

[378] Ibid.

[379] See the discussion on *The Plan of Redemption* in chapter 25.

[380] Barry R. Leventhal in *Why I Am a Christian: Leading Thinkers Explain Why They Believe,* (2001), page 209-210.

[381] Ibid, page 211.

[382] Adapted from Edersheim, Alfred: *The Life and Times of Jesus the Messiah*, (1896, edited 2003), Volume 1, pages 164-165.

[383] The following is not an attempt to accurately calculate chances, but an illustration to show how fast and dramatic the statistical improbability grows when combining just a few prophecies.

[384] Peter W. Stoner, *Science Speaks* (1963), pages 100-110.

[385] See sidebar on *How Big is Small?*, chapter 4.

[386] William Lane Craig, *Knowing the Truth about the Resurrection*, (1988), pages 116-117.

[387] See Exhibit #15: *Extra Dimensionality* in chapter 7.

[388] *The Ante-Nicene Fathers: Translations of the Writings of the Fathers Down to AD 325.* (1997), Vol 1, page 69.

[389] Ibid, Volume 1, page 166.

[390] Ibid, Volume 1, page 495.

[391] For a detailed overview of these sources, see chapter 15.

[392] Josephus, Flavius; Whiston, William: *The Works of Josephus* (1987), The Antiquities of the Jews, 18.63-64.

[393] Tacitus, Annals 15:14, quoted from Gary R. Habermas, *The Historical Jesus* (1996), page 188.

[394] Remarks added. From the reading in *The Babylonian Talmud*, translated by I. Epstein (1935), Vol. III, *Sanhedrin* 43a, p. 281 as quoted by Gary R. Habermas, *The Historical Jesus* (1996), page 203.

[395] See the discussion on *Scholars and Scriptures* in chapter 8.

[396] John Dominic Crossan, *Jesus: A Revolutionary Biography* (1994), pages 145

[397] Mel Gibson's 2004 movie *The Passion of the Christ* is generally regarded as a reasonably accurate depiction of the Roman practice of scourging and crucifixion.

[398] See also the archaeological evidence of *The Crucified Man of Giva'at ha-Mitvar* in chapter 14.

[399] Adapted from multiple sources, including www.frugalsites.net/jesus.htm, R Lumpkin, *The Physical Suffering of Christ* (1978), CD Johnson, *Medical and Cardiological Aspects of the Passion and Crucifixion of Christ* (1978) and CT Davis, *The Crucifixion of Jesus: The Passion of Christ from a Medical Point of View* (1965).

[400] W.J. Sparrow-Simpson, quoted by Josh McDowell in *The New Evidence That Demands a Verdict* (1999), page 225-226.

[401] See for instance Kevin Bowen's intriguing fictional thriller *Wil's Bones* (2000).

[402] Adapted from Gary R. Habermas, Michael R. Licona, *The Case for the Resurrection of Jesus* (2004), pages 69-74.

[403] The appearances mentioned in Mark 16:9-20 are not listed here because these verses are not included in the oldest extant manuscripts, see also Exhibit #7: *The Manuscript Evidence* in chapter 11.

[404] See the discussions on dating the gospels in chapter 12.

[405] John Wenham, *Easter Enigma: Are the Resurrection Accounts in Conflict?* (1992).

[406] For more information see Exhibit #8: *Early Church Leaders' Letters* in chapter 11.

[407] *The Ante-Nicene Fathers Volume I through X: Translations of the Writings of the Fathers Down to AD 325* (1997), Volume 1, page 11.

[408] Ibid, page 16.

[409] Ibid, page 35.

[410] See also the discussion in Exhibit #13: *Authorship and Dating of Paul's Letters* in chapter 12.

[411] See also Exhibit #9: *Creeds in the New Testament* in chapter 11.

[412] Numerous sources support this dating. For an extensive discussion, see Paul Barnett, *The Birth of Christianity, The First Twenty Years* (2005), appendix B: *Dating Galatians*.

[413] Be aware that in the New Testament days a part of a year was counted like a full year. So if Paul writes *"three years"* in our count it could be only little more than two actual years.

[414] See, among other sources, Gary R. Habermas, *The Historical Jesus* (1996), pages 152-157, Craig L. Blomberg, *The Historical Reliability of the Gospel* (1987), pages 108-110 and *Jesus Resurrection Fact or Figment, A Debate Between William Lane Craig and Gerd Ludeman* (2000) about the evidences for the resurrection. This last source is particularly of interest as in the debate professed non-Christian Gerd Ludemann confirms the authenticity and very early dating of the 1 Corinthian 15 creed.

[415] Clement's letter to the Corinthians in ca. 95 AD. *The Ante-Nicene Fathers Volume I through X: Translations of the Writings of the Fathers Down to AD 325* (1997), Volume 1, page 6.

[416] Various sources in Dr. William Steuart McBirnie, *The Search for the Twelve Apostles* (1973) pages 110-121 and Morris A. Inch, *12 Who Changed the World: The Lives and Legends of the Disciples.* (2003), pages 48-58.

[417] Sources in Dr. William Steuart McBirnie, *The Search for the Twelve Apostles* (1973) pages 80-86.

[418] Ibid pages 124-129.

[419] Ibid pages 131-138. Also *12 Who Changed the World* (2003), pages 77-81.

[420] Ibid, pages 176-177. Also Morris A. Inch, *12 Who Changed the World* (2003), page 84.

[421] Ibid, pages 142-173. Also Morris A. Inch, *12 Who Changed the World* (2003), page 104.

[422] Ibid, pages 192-194.

[423] Ibid, pages 210-231. Also Morris A. Inch, *12 Who Changed the World* (2003), pages 122-126.

[424] Atheist scholar Gerd Ludemann in *What Really Happened to Jesus?* (1995), page 81.

[425] For a more detailed overview of Paul's travels, ministry and epistles, see chapter 16.

[426] Gary R. Habermas, Michael R. Licona, *The Case for the Resurrection of Jesus* (2004), pages 64-65.

[427] Sometimes James, the brother of Jesus, is also referred to as *"James the Just."*

[428] Ibid, The Antiquities of the Jews, 20.200. The stoning of James, brother of Jesus is not mentioned in the NT.

[429] Picture used by permission. The James ossuary (shown on the picture) was on display at the Royal Ontario Museum from November 15, 2002 to January 5, 2003.

[430] Steven Feldman in *Archaeology Odyssey 06:05* (September/October 2003). See also Jerome Murphy-O'Connor in *BR 19:03*. Biblical Archaeology Society (June 2003) and Edward J. Keall in BAR 29:04 (July/August 2003).

[431] See our discussion on *The Integrity of the Manuscript Texts* in chapter 11.

[432] Numerous sources, see for instance Lee Strobel's interview with Bible scholar Craig L. Blomberg in *Case For Christ* (1998) pages 42-44 and Gary R. Habermas, Michael R. Licona, *The Case for the Resurrection of Jesus* (2004), pages 84-92.

[433] See chapter 16: *Can We Trust the Eyewitnesses.*

[434] Gary R. Habermas, Michael R. Licona, *The Case for the Resurrection of Jesus* (2004), pages 93.

[435] For more information on Breakpoint Prison Fellowship, visit www.Breakpoint.org.

[436] Chuck Colson, *An Unholy Hoax*, (March 29, 2002) as published on www.Breakpoint.org.

[437] Gary R. Habermas, Michael R. Licona, *The Case for the Resurrection of Jesus* (2004), pages 95.

[438] Hugh Schonfield, *The Passover Plot* (1965) , see Gary R. Habermas, *The Historical Jesus* (1996), page 70-71.

[439] Donovan Joyce, *The Jesus Scroll* as described by Gary R. Habermas, *The Historical Jesus* (1996), pages 90-91.

[440] Michael Baigent, Richard Leigh and Henry Lincoln, *Holy Blood, Holy Grail* (1982), pages 301-332.

[441] Gerd Ludemann in *What Really Happened to Jesus?* (1995), page 129.

[442] Michael Martin, *The Case Against Christianity* (1991), page 75.

[443] Gary R. Habermas, *The Historical Jesus* (1996), page 130.

[444] John Dominic Crossan in *BAS The Search for Jesus*. Biblical Archaeology Society (2002).

[445] See Exhibit #7: *The Evidence of the Missing Body*, earlier in this chapter.

[446] Gary R. Habermas, *The Historical Jesus* (1996), page 127.

[447] John Dominic Crossan in *BAS The Search for Jesus*. Biblical Archaeology Society (2002).

[448] Norman L. Geisler, Abdul Saleeb, Abdul: *Answering Islam: The Crescent in Light of the Cross* (2002), page 63.

[449] Ergun Mehmet Caner and Emir Fethi Caner, *Unveiling Islam* (2002), pages 220-221.

[450] *Time Magazine*, November 13, 2006, pages 48-55.

[451] Richard Dawkins, *The God Delusion* (2006).

[452] Francis S. Collins: *The Language of God: A Scientist Presents Evidence for Belief* (2006).

[453] See Exhibit #2: *Structure and Order* in chapter 3.

[454] Strong, James: *The Exhaustive Concordance of the Bible: Showing Every Word of the Test of the Common English Version of the Canonical Books, and Every Occurrence of Each Word in Regular Order* (1996), S. H3117.

[455] But cannot explain life, see Exhibit #5: *Life Cannot Have Started by Chance* in chapter 5.

456 I always find it interesting that evolutionists never seem to wonder how it would be possible for 'Mother Eve' to have any children without a male partner, and even more intriguing is that nobody ever questions how it would be possible for both a man and a women to evolve at the same time!

457 Douglas Jacoby, *Genesis, Science & History* (2003), page 41.

458 See chapter 7, Exhibit #8: *The Age of the Human Race.*

459 See the studies mentioned in the footnotes with chapter 7.

460 From www.nature.com – *Nature Genetics* (2000), pp 358-361 and 253-254.

461 See figure 6-1 in chapter 6.

462 Information from the Dover Museum: www.dovermuseum.co.uk.

463 Lindsay, Dennis Gordon: *The Genesis Flood: Continents in Collision.* (1992), chapter 3.

464 John Whitcomb, Henry Morris, *The Genesis Flood* (1960) and Dennis Gordon Lindsay, *The Genesis Flood, Continents in Collision* (1992), chapter 4.

465 Published in Public Library of Science, October 25, 2005: http://medicine.plosjournals.org/perlserv/?request=get-document&doi=10.1371%2Fjournal.pmed.0020391.

466 *Circumcision Found to Lower HIV Risk*, article in the *Los Angeles Times*, December 14, 2006.

467 Douglas Jacoby, *Genesis, Science & History* (2003), page 43.

468 Douglas Jacoby, *Genesis, Science & History* (2003), page 42 ; Holt, L.E. and R. McIntosh (1953), *Holt Pediatrics*; S.I. McMillen MD, David E Stern MD, *None of These Diseases* (2005), chapter 8.

469 S.I. McMillen MD, David E Stern MD, *None of These Diseases* (2005), chapter 3.

470 Numerous historical sources, including Norman Cantor, *In the Wake of the Plague* (2001) and Frederick F Cartwright, *Disease and History* (1991), page 42.

471 Douglas Jacoby, *Genesis, Science & History* (2003), pages 44-45.

472 Ibid page 43-44, also S.I. McMillen & David Stern, *None of These Diseases* (2005).

473 See also Exhibit #6: *No Mechanism for Evolving Species* and the discussion on DNA repair in chapter 6.

474 Among many publications: John Hogue, Michel Nostradamus: *Nostradamus: the Complete Prophecies* (1997).

475 Grant R. Jeffrey, *The Signature of God* (1996), page 162; Henry C. Roberts, The *Complete Prophecies of Nostradamus* (1976), introduction.

476 In his book *The Prophecy Knowledge Handbook* (1990), John F. Valvoort lists more than 1000 prophecies by name and Bible reference!

477 As discussed and refuted in Exhibits #4, #5 and #6 (chapter 10).

478 For corroboration from extra-Biblical sources of these events see: K.A. Kitchen, *On the Reliability of the Old Testament* (2003), pages 70-78.

479 For more details see *The Cyrus Cylinder* in Exhibit #15: *The Old Testament is Historically Reliable* in chapter 14.

480 For a detailed discussion, see chapter 10, Exhibit #5: *The Authorship of the Book of Isaiah.*

481 A more detailed analysis of these prophecies can be found in numerous commentaries and Walvoord, John F.: *The Prophecy Knowledge Handbook* (1990), chapter 7.

482 See chapter 10, Exhibit #6: *The Authorship of the Book of Daniel.*

483 Lamar Eugene Cooper, *The New American Commentary: Ezekiel,* (1994), pages 28-37.

484 Peter W. Stoner, *Science Speaks* (1963).

485 See chapter 12, Exhibit #11 *Authorship and Dating of the Synoptic Gospels.*

486 Many sources, including: Tan, Paul Lee: *Encyclopedia of 7700 Illustrations* (1979); see also the description of the destruction of Jerusalem by the Jewish historian and contemporary Flavius Josephus: Josephus, Flavius; Whiston, William: *The Works of Josephus: Complete and Unabridged, the War of the Jews,* book 6.

487 J. Barton Payne lists 191 prophecies in *Encyclopedia of Biblical Prophecy.* (1973), pages 665-670; John F. Walvoord in *The Prophecy Knowledge Handbook* (1990) lists 98 prophecies. Josh McDowell mentions "nearly 300" in *The New Evidence That Demands a Verdict* (1999), page 164.

488 See chapter 20: *Fulfillment of Messianic Prophecies.*

489 The presented analysis of the 'seventy sevens' prophecy is a majority opinion derived from a large number of sources, including but not limited to: Willmington, H. L.: *Willmington's Bible Handbook.* (1997), page 437-438; Walvoord, John F.: *The Prophecy Knowledge Handbook* (1990), page 248-259; Miller, Stephen R., *The New American Commentary: Daniel.* (1994), page 252-275; Chuck Missler, *Cosmic Codes* (1999), chapter 17 and Josh McDowell in *New Evidence That Demands a Verdict,* (1999), page 197-201.

[490] Some such as Stephen Miller in *The New American Commentary: Daniel.* (1994), page 263 conclude that the first decree of Artaxerxes I to Ezra should be the starting date, because the second 'decree' was not explicit. However, the fact that the OT passage does not use the word 'decree' does not mean it was not precisely that!

[491] See calculation in chapter 17 for dating the crucifixion in 33 AD.

[492] According to John F. Walvoord, *The Prophecy Knowledge Handbook* (1990), page 254.

[493] See calculation in chapter 17 for dating the start of John the Baptist's ministry in 29 AD.

[494] See chapter 20: *Fulfillment of Messianic Prophecies.*

[495] This exhibit is written by Kenneth W. Craig and is a summary of his work on *The Plan of Redemption* (2007).

[496] It is interesting to notice that this was also the believe of the gnostic heresy that was fought by the early church – see the discussion on *The Gnostic Movement* in chapter 13.

[497] See also Illustration #3: *Isaac, A Symbolic Prophecy about Jesus* in chapter 27.

[498] J. Sidlow Baxter, *The Master Theme of the Bible – Part 1: The Doctrine of the Lamb* (1985), page 19.

[499] Like: DC Talk, *Jesus Freaks* (1997) and DC Talk and the Voice of the Martyrs: *Jesus Freaks – Stories of Those Who Stood for Jesus* (2005).

[500] Bernard Ramm, *Varieties of Christian Apologetics* (1961), page 216.

[501] Bill Gothard, founder and president of the *Institute for Basic Life Principles.*

[502] Norman L. Geisler, William E. Nix: *A General Introduction to the Bible,* (1996), page 196.

[503] It is ironic to note that the movie *Contact* was based on a script of Carl Sagan. As an atheist, Sagan considered a simple sequence of prime numbers an evidence for intelligent design, but at the same time rejected the occurrence of vastly more complex strings of DNA letters as evidence for a Creator.

[504] Michael Drosnin, *The Bible Code* (1997).

[505] Chuck Missler, *Cosmic Codes* (1999), chapter 11; Grant R. Jeffrey, *The Handwriting of God* (1997) chapter 7.

[506] Jeffery L. Sheler, *Is the Bible True?* (1999), pages 235-236.

[507] Chuck Missler, *Cosmic Codes* (1999), chapter 10.

[508] As per a note in Missler's book: some claim that Deuteronomy actually starts from the fifth verse.

[509] Ibid, page 128.

[510] Etherbert W. Bullinger (1837-1913), *Number in Scripture* (2006, reproduction from 1894).

[511] According to Strong, James: *The Exhaustive Concordance of the Bible: Showing Every Word of the Text of the Common English Version of the Canonical Books, and Every Occurrence of Each Word in Regular Order* (1996).

[512] E.W. Bullinger, *Number in Scripture* (2006, reproduction from 1894), R. McCormack, *Heptadic Structure of Scripture with a Chapter on Seven and Four in Nature* (1923) and Chuck Missler, *Cosmic Codes* (1999), appendix D. The list in this book is only a limited subset of all the heptadic structures and references identified.

[513] Robin M. Jensen, *Bible Review,* Volume 9, Number 5 (1993).

[514] Ca 100 AD, see chapter 11.

[515] *The Ante-Nicene Fathers Volume I through X: Translations of the Writings of the Fathers Down to AD 325* (1997), Volume 1, page 141.

[516] Ibid, Volume 3, page 165.

[517] Chuck Missler, *Cosmic Codes* (1999), pages 192-193.

[518] Dyer, Charles; Merrill, Eugene; Swindoll, Charles R.; Zuck, Roy B.: *Nelson's Old Testament Survey (2001), page 102.*

[519] These last three associations are on somewhat shaky ground. It seems this (2nd century) tradition is mostly based on Ezekiel 1:10 and Revelation 4:6-7, but not on actual historical evidence. W. Riggens, *The Daily Study Bible Series: Numbers* (1983), page 22 and Chuck Missler, *Cosmic Codes* (1999), page 210.

[520] Chuck Missler, *Cosmic Codes* (1999), page 208-213.

[521] Data for the world religions is from *www.adherents.com/Religions_By_Adherents.html* and *www.religioustolerance.org/worldrel.htm*, data is based on surveys in the 2001-2005 period.

[522] Data for the United States is from surveys as posted on *www.wikipedia.com*, based on 2001 American Religious Identification Survey (ARIS).

[523] Fritz Ridenour, *So What's the Difference* (2001), pages 35-36. This principle is often also referred to as *"Sola Scriptura,"* a Latin phrase coined during the Protestant Reformation, literally meaning "Only Scripture" or "Scripture Alone."

[524] See chapter 25, Exhibit #15: *The Plan of Redemption.*

[525] Chapter 29: *The Flavors of Christianity.*

[526] Data from *The World Factbook 2004*, published by the CIA.

[527] Bruce L. Shelley, *Church History in Plain Language.* (1995), page 28.

[528] For the texts of these creeds, see Appendix D: *Early Christian Creeds.*

[529] Justo L. Gonzalez, *The Story of Christianity* (1984, edition 2004), pages 251-252.

[530] Erwin Fahlbusch, Geoffrey William Bromiley, *The Encyclopedia of Christianity* (2003), Volume 2, page 50.

[531] Huston Smits, The World Religions (1991), page 347.

[532] The following overview is adapted from Fritz Ridenour, *So What's the Difference* (2001), pages 34-50, and some other sources, like Huston Smits, *The World Religions* (1991), pages 346-352.

[533] Mario Colacci, *The Doctrinal Conflict Between Roman Catholic and Protestant Christianity* (1962), pages 140-142 as quoted by Fritz Ridenour, *So What's the Difference* (2001), page 43.

[534] Norman Geisler, Thomas How, *When Critics Ask: A Popular Handbook on Bible Difficulties* (1992) pages 347-348 and Fritz Ridenour, *So What's the Difference* (2001), pages 37-39.

[535] As reported to the United States Census Bureau by the Orthodox churches.

[536] The following overview is adapted from Fritz Ridenour, *So What's the Difference* (2001), pages 52-63, and some other sources, such as Huston Smith, *The World Religions* (1991), pages 352-356.

[537] *The International Bulletin of Missionary Research*, January 2007, estimates as many as 39,000 denominations worldwide. Of course, the great majority of these are 'one-building' sects.

[538] Huston Smith, *The World Religions* (1991), pages 359-362.

[539] Based on Fritz Ridenour, *So What's the Difference?* (2001), pages 111-112.

[540] Various sources, including *www.adherents.com.*

[541] Various sources, including *Yearbooks of Jehovah's Witnesses*, 1996-2007.

[542] Swami Vivekananda, *Vedanta: Voice of Freedom*, Editor Swami Chetanananda (1990).

[543] R.A.C. Bradby in *New Dictionary of Christian Apologetics* (2006), page 308.

[544] According to the 1999 edition of the *Yearbook of American & Canadian Churches.*

[545] *Mahatma Gandhi Autobiography* (1948), page 170.

[546] Dr. Winfried Corduan in *Why I Am a Christian: Leading Thinkers Explain Why They Believe* (2001), page 194.

[547] Quotation often attributed to Albert Einstein. Helen Dukas, Banesh Hoffman editors, *Albert Einstein: The Human Side* (1954).

[548] Dr. Winfried Corduan in *Why I Am a Christian: Leading Thinkers Explain Why They Believe* (2001), page 197.

[549] Also see the other remarks about reincarnation in the previous chapter.

[550] According to the numbers quoted by the Muslim delegation to the United Nations (September 2005). See also estimates *on www.adherents.com.* Adding up all estimates of Muslim population per country by the US State Department gives a total of close to 1.5 billion.

[551] Source *www.wikipedia.org* in article *Religion in the United States.*

[552] Data for Pakistan, India and Bangladesh from the *World Factbook 2004* as published by the CIA.

[553] Ibid.

[554] Huston Smits, *The World Religions* (1991), page 225.

[555] Mohammad is so esteemed by Muslims that it is usual to utter the blessing *peace be upon him* after his name. This is often abbreviated to *pbuh.*

[556] Dean C. Halverson, *The Compact Guide to World Religions* (1996), pages 110-111.

[557] The passage originally appeared in 1391 in *Dialogue Held with a Certain Persian, the Worthy Mouterizes, in Anakara of Galatia*, by Byzantine emperor Manuel II Palaiologos, as an expression on such issues as holy war and forced conversions.

[558] Ergun Mehmet Caner, Emir Fethi Caner, *Unveiling Islam* (2002), page 40.

[559] Ibid, page 60.

[560] Ergun Mehmet Caner, Emir Fethi Caner, *Unveiling Islam* (2002), pages 190-192.

[561] Ergun Mehmet Caner, Emir Fethi Caner, *Unveiling Islam* (2002), chapter 11.

[562] Normal L. Geisler, *Baker Encyclopedia of Christian Apologetics* (1999), page 623 and Dr. William Campbell, *The Qur'an and the Bible in the Light of History and Science* (2002), page 96.

[563] Dr. William Campbell, *The Qur'an and the Bible in the Light of History and Science* (2002), page 99, 110-111.

[564] European Archaeologist Arthur Jeffry as quoted by Normal L. Geisler, *Baker Encyclopedia of Christian Apologetics* (1999), page 623.

[565] Dr. Winfried Corduan in *Why I Am a Christian: Leading Thinkers Explain Why They Believe* (2001), page 192.

[566] See Alternative #6: *The Teachings of the Qur'an*, in chapter 21.

[567] See the brief discussion on Christian Cults in chapter 29.

[568] See chapter 18, *Lord, Liar or Lunatic*.

[569] See chapter 19, *Miracles or Magic?*

[570] Chapter 20, *Fulfillment of Messianic Prophecies*.

[571] For an overview of all the evidences, see chapter 21, *Did the Resurrection Really Happen?*

[572] Wilbur M. Smith, *Therefore Stand* (1945) page 385 as quoted by Josh McDowell, *The New Evidence That Demands a Verdict* (1999) page 205.

[573] Josh McDowell, *The New Evidence That Demands a Verdict* (1999) page 205.

[574] See chapter 14, *The Historical Reliability of the Bible*.

[575] See Section IV, *Is the Bible Inspired by God?*

[576] Sayyid Hossein Nasr, *Ideals and Realities of Islam* (1966), page 47.

[577] See chapter 26: *Unity of the Bible, the Plan of Redemption*.

[578] Ergun Mehmet Caner and Emir Fethi Caner, *Unveiling Islam* (2002), pages 142-151.

[579] Ibid, pages 190-192.

[580] Philip Yancey, *What's So Amazing About Grace* (1997), page 45.

[581] Joe White, Nicholas Comninellis, *Darwin's Demise* (2001), chapter 3 and numerous other sources.

[582] Examples include Sunset Crater in Arizona, Mount Rangitoto in New Zealand and the Grand Canyon, see (among other sources), John D. Morris, *The Young Earth* (2003), pages 54-55.

[583] For a comprehensive overview of carbon dating and other dating techniques and their strengths and weaknesses, see Dr Don DeYoung and John Baumgardner, *Thousands not Millions* (2005) chapter 2 and 3.

[584] See also chapter 13, *The Lost Books of the New Testament* describing the reaction to the gnostic movement.

[585] Fahlbush, Bromiley, William: *The Encyclopedia of Christianity* (2003).

[586] Ibid.

[587] Philip Schaff, *The Creeds of Christendom, Volume 1: The History of Creeds*, (1983), pages 14-15.

Index

Acknowledgements

This book was only made possible thanks to the hard work and encouragement of many people. It would not be practical to mention everybody by name who contributed information, articles, questions, remarks, and suggestions and the ones who spent hours reading and reviewing. Thank you so much!

There are two people I would like to thank in particular, because their contribution was more than crucial. First of all I'd like to express a huge thank-you-and-I-love-you to my wife, Jacoba, who spent days and days reading, correcting and more reading and correcting. Without her support and inspiration I am not sure I would have finished this project. And I would like to especially thank my ex-customer, ex-colleague, spiritual mentor, brother in Christ and friend Ken Craig. Ken's always available listening ear, advice and input were invaluable. Ken is also the author of chapter 25 in this book: *The Plan of Redemption*. This material represents the core of his on-going speaking ministry of sharing and explaining the gospel message.

About the Author

Rob VandeWeghe earned a masters degree in electrical engineering and computer science from the Technical University of Delft, the Netherlands (1982, with honors) and studied business economics at the Erasmus University in Rotterdam, the Netherlands (1985, comparable to a bachelor degree).

He worked more than 15 years for a multi-national information technology consulting organization, which he helped grow from a local company with 300 employees (1983) to an international organization with offices in 30 countries and more than 20,000 employees (1999). He was responsible for various multinational projects and businesses in Europe, North and South America and Australia. He retired from his position as vice-president for the North American Consulting Division in 1999.

Since, he has felt compelled to research and study the evidences for the Christian faith. Finding these truths convicted him to commit his life to Christ. The drive to share these evidences with others triggered the founding of Windmill Ministries. In this ministry, Rob and his wife Jacoba want to encourage and equip Christians by building and re-enforcing the foundation of truth on which one's beliefs are grounded.

Rob, Jacoba, and their family have lived on the beautiful Olympic Peninsula in the northwest corner of Washington State since 1997.